# ACADEMIC FREEDOM IN CONFLICT

Feb 2015
Edmonton

## CAUT Series titles

*Universities at Risk: How Politics, Special Interests and Corporatization Threaten Academic Integrity*, ed. James L. Turk (2008)

*Free Speech in Fearful Times: After 9/11 in Canada, the U.S., Australia, & Europe*, eds. James L. Turk and Allan Manson (2006)

*Time's Up! Mandatory Retirement in Canada*, eds. C.T. (Terry) Fillin, David MacGregor, and Thomas R. Klassen (2005)

*Disciplining Dissent*, eds. William Bruneau and James L. Turk (2004)

*Let Them Eat Prozac* by David Healy (2003)

*Counting out the Scholars: How Performance Indicators Undermine Colleges and Universities* by William Bruneau and Donald C. Savage (2002)

*The Oliviery Report: The Complete Text of the Report of the Independent Inquiry Commissioned by the Canadian Association of University Teachers* by Jon Thompson, Patricia Baird, and Jocelyn Downie (2001)

*The Corporate Campus: Commercialization and the Dangers to Canada's Colleges and Universities*, ed. James L. Turk (2000)

*Universities for Sale: Resisting Corporate Control over Canadian Higher Education* by Neil Tudiver (1999)

# ACADEMIC FREEDOM IN CONFLICT

## THE STRUGGLE OVER FREE SPEECH RIGHTS IN THE UNIVERSITY

EDITED BY JAMES L. TURK

JAMES LORIMER & COMPANY LTD., PUBLISHERS
TORONTO

James Lorimer & Company Ltd., Publishers acknowledges the support of the Ontario Arts Council. We acknowledge the financial support of the Government of Canada through the Canada Book Fund for our publishing activities. We acknowledge the support of the Canada Council for the Arts, which last year invested $24.3 million in writing and publishing throughout Canada. We acknowledge the Government of Ontario through the Ontario Media Development Corporation's Ontario Book Initiative.

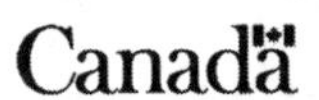

Cover design: Meghan Collins
Cover image: iStock

**Library and Archives Canada Cataloguing in Publication**

Academic freedom in conflict : the struggle over free speech rights in the university / edited by James L. Turk.

Includes bibliographical references and index.
Issued in print and electronic formats.
ISBN 978-1-4594-0629-2 (pbk.).--ISBN 978-1-4594-0630-8 (epub)

1. Academic freedom--Canada. 2. Academic freedom--United States. 3. Freedom of speech--Canada. 4. Freedom of speech--United States. 5. Teaching, Freedom of--Canada. 6. Teaching, Freedom of--United States. 7. College teachers--Civil rights--Canada. 8. College teachers--Civil rights--United States. I. Turk, James, 1943-, editor of compilation

LC72.5.C3A23 2014 378.1'2130971 C2013-907869-X
C2013-907870-3

James Lorimer & Company Ltd., Publishers
317 Adelaide Street West, Suite 1002
Toronto, ON, Canada
M5V 1P9
www.lorimer.ca

Printed and bound in Canada.

# CONTENTS

## IV. ACADEMIC FREEDOM AND EQUITY



## V. ACADEMIC FREEDOM AND THE GROWTH OF UNIVERSITY-INDUSTRY COLLABORATIONS



## VI. ACADEMIC FREEDOM AND FREEDOM OF EXPRESSION

# PREFACE

Academic freedom is a central, arguably the central value, of university life. Anything which interferes with it has to be justified by reference to prior or higher values. I can think of very few, other than perhaps the protection of human life: certainly not institutional solidarity; certainly not institutional reputation.[1]

*–Harry W. Arthurs, 1995*

The issue of limits may be as old as the concept of academic freedom. It was discussed at Oxford in 1380, at Trinity College and Columbia University during World War I, and at universities across the United States and Canada during the early Cold War period. In 1996 the American Association of University Professors (AAUP) organized publication of a series of essays on limits by Henry Louis Gates, Ronald Dworkin, Joan W. Scott, Edward W. Said, and others, prompted in part by "political correctness" controversies.

Today academic freedom is under stronger attack than at any time in the past half century. The academy and much of the world are in the grip of neo-liberalism — the fundamental principle of which is that all aspects of human activity should be maintained in a state of "pure competition." The result, as Michel Foucault foresaw in his 1979 lectures at le Collège de France, is a dramatic increase in the insecurity and exploitability of all but very wealthy individuals and organizations. Unsurprisingly, the greater concentrations of wealth and power enabled by neo-liberal government policies are accompanied by erosion of effective democracy and civil liberties in general and of academic freedom and academic integrity in particular.

Over the past century, a comprehensive concept of academic freedom developed and became widely accepted in North America. The key elements as we understand them in Canada are freedom of research and publication; freedom of teaching; freedom of extramural expression; freedom of intramural expression. Academic freedom is an individual right, as well as a right of academic staff collectively. There are no clear and explicit limits to academic freedom as it intersects with the law, institutional autonomy, or professional norms.

This does not mean that there are no limits to academic freedom. One is implied: members of the academic staff do not have the right to limit the academic freedom of other members of the academic staff. Collective agreements and similar documents set out duties and responsibilities of academic staff, in articles separate from the article on academic freedom. Also, there are professional codes of ethical conduct in disciplines ranging from medicine to mathematics.

The 1958 dismissal of Harry Crowe by United College in Winnipeg — an institution with religious aims — polarized the city of Winnipeg and galvanized academics across Canada, including their relatively new federation, the Canadian Association of University Teachers (CAUT). In some respects, the aftermath of the Harry Crowe dismissal parallels what happened as a result of the dismissal of Edward A. Ross by Stanford University in 1900, which occasioned the first committee of inquiry into such an event (an investigation established by the American Economic Association) and helped lead to the formation of the American Association of University Professors (AAUP) and its formative 1915 declaration on academic freedom.

Crowe's private letter to a colleague that reached the eyes of the college principal criticized the college administration and organized religion, and on this basis he was dismissed. The report on the case by the CAUT investigatory committee of Saskatchewan economist Vernon

C. Fowke and Toronto law professor Bora Laskin (later Chief Justice of the Supreme Court of Canada) was central to the establishment of modern academic freedom in Canada.

But that individual right of academic freedom has been, and continues to be, jeopardized by reference to law, assertions of institutional autonomy, and restrictive views of professional norms.

Trinity College, Cambridge, dismissed Bertrand Russell in 1916 after he was convicted and fined for public criticism of the government's harsh treatment of a conscientious objector. Two years later he was convicted and sentenced to six months in prison for public criticism of the government's war policy. Despite the two convictions Russell was reinstated in 1919.

Columbia University dismissed James McKeen Cattell in 1917 after he sent a petition to three Congressmen urging them not to support legislation that would authorize use of conscripts in the European war. Despite no charges or convictions, Cattell was not reinstated even after the war ended.

During the early Cold War period a number of professors were dismissed by universities across the United States for exercising their rights as citizens and blacklisted from university employment. Several of these were later hired by universities in Canada and the UK.

There are, of course, cases of professors properly dismissed for illegal acts, as in the case of Valery Fabrikant, who murdered four colleagues at Concordia University in Montreal in 1992 and was sentenced to life in prison.

Institutional autonomy has been invoked to limit academic freedom, as in the Harry Crowe case. In 2010, the Association of Universities and Colleges of Canada (AUCC), the association of Canadian university presidents, released a new statement on academic freedom explicitly claiming that "academic freedom must be based on institutional integrity . . . and institutional autonomy."[2] It was encouraging that David Naylor, the president of Canada's largest university, publicly distanced himself from the new policy issued by his AUCC colleagues, and declared his support for his university's more comprehensive policy, which is similar to CAUT's.

Perhaps the most contentious discussion of limits comes in relation to professional norms. While academic freedom is a professional right necessary for academics to fulfill their roles as scholars and educators, the narrow assertion of professional norms has served to undermine academic freedom. In medicine and economics, in particular, professional norms are often used to suppress critical voices, especially those challenging dominant paradigms and powerful corporate interests.

We need to remember Thomas L. Haskell's observation that "trustworthiness" of knowledge and training is assured by "perpetual exposure to criticism" in academic communities of scholarly experts, criticism "more severe" than in other types of community.[3] Thus ongoing severe criticism provides the foundation for professional norms — a foundation undermined when such criticism is suppressed.

I would like to conclude this preface with a remark by historian Frank H. Underhill, one of Canada's leading public intellectuals during the 1930s and 1940s. A social activist who engaged in partisan politics, Underhill was denounced by premiers of Ontario and threatened with dismissal several times by the University of Toronto because he practised what he preached: "The best way to defend academic freedom is to exercise it."[4]

–Jon Thompson
President, Harry Crowe Foundation

# INTRODUCTION

*James L. Turk*

Post-secondary educational institutions serve the common good of society through searching for, and disseminating, knowledge and understanding, and through fostering independent thinking and expression in academic staff and students. Robust democracies require no less. These ends cannot be achieved without academic freedom.[1]

Academic freedom is often understood as the name for freedom of expression in academic settings. That is not the case. Freedom of expression is a *general* right protected in the United States by the *First Amendment* and in Canada by the *Canadian Charter of Rights and Freedoms*. Academic freedom, on the other hand, is a *special* right of academics — a right to freedom from prescribed orthodoxy in their teaching, research, and lives as academics; a right necessary so that teaching and scholarly research are not corrupted by the will of politicians, special interest groups, religious authorities, the media, corporations, donors, or board members. It is not a privilege or a luxury but the foundation that makes possible the work of academics to fulfill their societal obligation to advance knowledge and educate students.

In this sense, academic freedom is a professional right — a right necessary to fulfill one's professional obligations as a teacher and scholar. But as a professional right, it has professional constraints.

Matthew Finkin and Robert Post nicely illustrate the difference between freedom of expression and academic freedom, "Although the *First Amendment* may prohibit the state from penalizing the *New York Times* for misunderstanding the distinction between astronomy and astrology, no astronomy professor can insulate himself or herself from the adverse consequences of such a conflation."[2]

No freedom is without limits, and the limits to all freedoms are always contested. The reason is simple. Just as any freedom protects and permits certain activities, it restricts those who want to curtail the very same activities. The boundary with respect to what is protected is never fixed, but the result of the push and pull between conflicting forces, as any even cursory look at the American *First Amendment* or the Canadian *Charter* jurisprudence will illustrate. It is in that sense that any freedom is a social construction that is always under construction. This is no less true for academic freedom.

Academic freedom as it exists in North America can trace its origins to developments in German and Swiss universities in the late eighteenth century.[3] Its particular contemporary formulations have been developed by academic staff organizations in response to inappropriate efforts to limit, curtail, redirect, or halt faculty work as teachers and scholars. The first, and arguably most important, articulation of academic freedom in the United States was the newly formed American Association of University Professors' "1915 Declaration of Principles on Academic Freedom and Academic Tenure."[4]

The creation of the AAUP, led by Arthur O. Lovejoy and John Dewey, and the subsequent drafting of the "1915 Declaration," were animated by the inappropriate attack on scholars in the late nineteenth and early twentieth centuries. No case played a bigger role than the firing of Edward A. Ross, a prominent economist at Stanford University. Ross's public condemnation of the use of cheap immigrant labour by American industry deeply offended Mrs. Leland Stanford, wife of the university's founder and chair of Stanford's Board of Governors. The Stanford fortune had been built on the basis of cheap immigrant labour. Mrs. Stanford ordered the university president to fire Ross, which he did.[5]

Lovejoy and Edwin R. A. Seligman, the two principal drafters of the "1915 Declaration," had been witnesses to Ross's firing. But the Ross case was by no means unique. The AAUP history of that period notes: "The committee of fifteen [chosen to draft what became the "1915 Declaration"] had scarcely been constituted when a number of cases of alleged infringement of academic freedom were brought to its attention. These cases were not only numerous, but also diverse in character . . ."[6]

While the formation of the Canadian Association of University Teachers thirty-six years later emerged from a desire of faculty to better co-ordinate their terms and conditions of work, the decisive event in CAUT's history, several years after it was formed, was the firing of historian Harry Crowe by the president of United College [now the University of Winnipeg] over a personal letter Crowe wrote to a colleague criticizing those who had been fundraising for the church-related college (a responsibility he saw belonging to the administration) and expressing concern about the possibility of a Conservative victory in the upcoming federal election.[7]

The Crowe case became a national *cause celebre,* galvanizing the relatively new CAUT to set up its first investigatory committee and publishing its first report on a violation of academic freedom.[8] Since then, the articulation and defence of academic freedom has been a centrepiece of CAUT's work, much like the AAUP.

The path to reasonable consensus on academic freedom has been difficult. While few oppose the concept itself, many seek to limit its breadth and restrict its application. None of the four key aspects of academic freedom — freedom of teaching, freedom of research and publication, freedom to express one's views of the educational institution in which one works ("intramural academic freedom"), and freedom to exercise one's rights as a citizen without sanction by the university or college ("extramural academic freedom")[9] — has been free from threat — either historically or today. Special interest groups have wanted to be able to shape what and how subjects are taught,[10] politicians have tried to use the public funding of research to dictate what can be studied,[11] university administrators have attempted to restrict criticism of their institutions,[12,] and many have pressed universities to sanction academics for unwanted public utterances.[13]

The present volume examines what should and should not be the limits to academic freedom — to what extent is a claim of academic freedom appropriate or inappropriate; what limits can be placed on what academics do or say without undermining their academic freedom.

The starting point is university autonomy and the extent to which the institution's autonomy can allow it to limit the academic freedom of its staff. Universities have necessarily been accorded relative independence *as institutions* from outside authority. This tradition has been traced back to Bologna in the twelfth century that exempted students and teachers from tolls and taxes, and protected them against injustice, Paris in the thirteenth century where the university had a recognized right as a body corporate to award degrees[14], and to universities appropriating the medieval idea of liberty as that into which the state does not enter.[15] In the modern period, the 1997 UNESCO General Conference adopted a statement that described the university's institutional autonomy as "that degree of self-governance necessary for effective decision making by institutions of higher education regarding their academic work, standards, management and related activities consistent with systems of public accountability, especially in respect of funding provided by the state, and respect for academic freedom and human rights."[16]

Commonly the institutional autonomy of the university has been described as the basis of academic freedom — that which insulates academic staff from the inappropriate intrusion of outside forces. While there is a measure of truth to that — university autonomy helping make possible the academic freedom of its academic staff — it is important not to conflate university autonomy with academic freedom. To the extent that autonomy of the university as an institution is translated into "institutional academic freedom," the stage is set for the institution to assert its institutional right to limit the academic freedom of its academic staff and to deny them any redress outside the institution.

To pretend that building a moat around the university protects the academic freedom of the academic staff ignores the porous boundary between the university and the external world. There is no clearer example than Ross, who was fired at Stanford by the president of the university at the behest of the chair of the Board of Governors. In the commercialized university of today, where vestiges of the self-governing collegium are rapidly being replaced by a corporate management structure, university autonomy and institutional academic freedom are, more often than not, being used to limit, not protect, the academic freedom of the academic staff.

Part One of this book explores institutional autonomy and academic freedom. Constitutional scholar David Rabban[17] examines the increasing prominence of the concept of "institutional academic freedom" in American constitutional law and its implications. He argues it "threatens to overwhelm, and even to eliminate, *First Amendment* academic freedom as an individual right of professors."

Len Findlay[18] then looks broadly at the changing character of the contemporary university, and how university autonomy has become a threat to academic freedom rather than a means to ensure it. As "the university" is transformed from a collegium of its academic staff into a corporation managed by its senior administration, Findlay argues its autonomy becomes a tool for intruding on individual academic staff's academic freedom, not a protection for professional self-regulation by colleagues within the institution.

The arbiter of standards for academic work (and, hence, academic freedom) is not the corporate institution, but the collective academic staff in the institution and in the academic discipline within which the scholar works. While a member of the public has the freedom of expression to claim that the world was created in six days six thousand years ago, and that dinosaurs and humans cohabited the earth, university biologists in their teaching and research do not because such a claim has no recognized scientific or scholarly basis.

The usual debates about what exceeds the boundary of academic freedom are not so clear cut. If academic freedom is based on professional standards and disciplinary norms, to what extent can those standards and norms inappropriately restrict academic freedom by rejecting approaches that challenge conventional scholarly wisdom within the discipline or propose moving beyond the discipline? The double-sided nature of academic disciplines means they simultaneously are helpful as a way to organize knowledge and legitimate inquiry and destructive if standards are applied narrowly or dogmatically to stifle inquiry or restrict questions about the nature of the discipline itself.

Part Two of the book examines the necessary but uneasy relationship between academic freedom and disciplinary norms. Matthew W. Finkin[19] starts from the position, following the "1915 Declaration," that "academic freedom is a professional liberty in the exercise of which the faculty member is required to observe a professional standard of care." He then discusses and responds to criticism of this view and illustrates his position through a careful examination of, and commentary on, the controversial case of Ward Churchill, a tenured professor of American Indian Studies at the University of Colorado. Following a public furor over an essay Churchill wrote in the aftermath of September 11 that referred to the victims of the World Trade Center bombings as "little Eichmanns," the university launched an investigation, in the course of which allegations of research misconduct arose, and for those Churchill was fired.

Mark Gabbert[20] addresses the same issues, starting from a concern that "a too one-sided emphasis on professional norms risks having the effect of producing not critical minds but . . . well, normal academics." He critically examines different perspectives and also ends with a discussion of the Churchill case to highlight the key issues he sees it raising with respect to academic freedom and disciplinary norms.

In the third article in Part Two, Joan Scott[21] discusses the tensions inherent in the theory and practice of the academy as a self-regulating community. She explores those tensions and argues that, while they are unresolvable, they have to be addressed as the ideal of academic freedom must be pursued if we are to preserve what is best about universities and university education.

The issues discussed in Part Two are followed up in Part Three with a specific focus religious universities and the extent to which the requirement for a faith-based homogeneity on campus is antithetical to academic freedom. AAUP and CAUT have taken different positions on this matter. In its still current "1940 Statement of Principles on Academic Freedom and Tenure," the AAUP allowed "limitations of academic freedom because of religious or other aims of the institution" provided these limitations were "clearly stated in writing at the time of the appointment."[26] However, in its "1970 Interpretive Comments" on its "1940 Statement," AAUP reversed its position: "Most church-related institutions no longer need or desire the departure from the principle of academic freedom implied in the 1940 Statement, and we do not now endorse such a departure."[27]

CAUT considers a required commitment to a particular ideology or statement of faith as a condition of employment to be a violation of academic freedom and has established procedures for investigating allegations that a university has such a requirement.[28] To date, CAUT has investigated such allegations in relation to five Canadian universities and has posted the investigatory reports' findings that each does require a faith test.[29]

Although most religiously affiliated universities do not require a faith test as a condition of initial or continuing employment, those that do often deny that this is a violation of academic freedom.[30] The articles in Part Three address the relationship between faith requirements and academic freedom. John Baker[33] offers a philosophical analysis of whether it is plausible to claim that an institution can require compliance with tenets of a religion while being capable of fulfilling the societal roles expected of a university.

William Bruneau[31] examines religious conviction within universities, tracing the history of religious universities in Canada. He identifies major arguments made by defenders of religious requirements within universities as well as the counter-arguments of critics. Noting these two very different ways of viewing university teaching, research, service, administration, and outreach, he argues that the value of academic freedom could and should contain them both.

Gerald Gerbrandt[32] closes Part Three with a personal perspective on these issues as the President Emeritus of Canadian Mennonite University and formerly as a faculty member at the Mennonite Bible College. Affirming his commitment to academic freedom as essential to all universities, he nevertheless considers it appropriate and justifiable for Christian universities to expect their faculty members to be practising Christians — "without making use of the argument that religious freedom gives such institutions a kind of exemption to override academic freedom." His article elaborates the reasons and provides a perspective on academic freedom from within a faith-based Christian institution.

Part Four examines the tensions in relation to academic freedom and marginalized academics and students. Anver Saloojee[22] extends issues raised in Scott's article to look specifically at the tension between academic freedom and freedom from discrimination as universities have become more diverse. Saloojee takes the position that scholarly work felt to be racist should not be defended in the name of academic freedom, citing the controversial case of Western University psychology Professor Philippe Rushton.[23] Saloojee also questions whether teachers should cite racist, homophobic, Islamophobic, or sexist quotes and texts so as to deconstruct them in class, given the impact such texts have on students.

Richard Moon[24] takes up the question of whether there should be more restrictions on freedom of expression in the university in order for it to fulfill its educational mission, noting that the injury of racist and other forms of bigoted speech may be more harmful in the closer environment and tighter community of the campus. He identifies potential problems with greater restriction of expression within the university and explores the issues through an examination of the annual campus Israeli Apartheid Week.

In the final article in Part Four, David Schneiderman[25] addresses respectful workplace policies that universities and colleges have adopted as the diversification of post-secondary educational institutions has given rise to challenges to traditional academic practices. He notes the serious tension between such policies and academic freedom, which is deemed by many to be irresolvable. He proposes reframing the matter using a version of federalism that recognizes pluralism and autonomy as a means of facilitating diversity.

Part Five looks at the implications of the closer working relationships of universities and the corporate sector. All three of the authors start from a premise that there are basic differences in the objectives of universities and corporations — differences that can compromise the independence and public mission of the university and its academic staff. Sheldon Krimsky[34] looks at institutional conflicts of interest and how they should be dealt with to allow a full realization of academic freedom. Risa L. Lieberwitz[35] traces some of the history of the tightening university-industry embrace and explores the actual merger of university and corporate interests in the case of the Cornell University New York City Technology program. In my closing article[36], I point out examples of the corporate undermining of scientific inquiry, review studies on the extent to which universities have compromised their academic integrity in corporate collaborations, and discuss recent initiatives that point the way to protecting academic integrity and academic freedom when universities enter into partnerships with corporate or special interest groups.

In Part Six, Jamie Cameron[37] concludes the book with an examination of the implications for academic freedom of the growing movement for civil discourse. She examines American and Canadian university respectful workplace and civil discourse policies. She argues such policies institutionalize a standard of civility — or courtesy — that threaten the freedoms that anchor the university mission.

Protection of academic freedom requires engagement with questions of its limits. Conceived too restrictively, academic freedom does not permit real inquiry and new ways of thinking necessary for the advancement of society. Conceived too expansively, purporting to permit everything, it will effectively permit nothing — losing credibility if seen as a claim for unrestricted licence by academic staff.

Social recognition of, and scope for, academic freedom depends on public understanding that it is a requirement for the job as an educator and scholar. Academic freedom is not a luxury, not a perk, not a bonus but a necessity to do the work entrusted to educators. It is impossible to advance knowledge unless one has a protected right to question the unquestionable, to explore new territory, to advance new ideas, to subject conventional wisdom — whether scholarly or popular — to rigorous critique, to challenge the status quo in the name of advancing our understanding of the world, and to share one's views with students, colleagues, and the public at large. These are not easy things to do. They make people, often powerful people, uncomfortable. Without academic freedom, they mostly will not be done, and society will be the worse for it.

# I. ACADEMIC FREEDOM AND INSTITUTIONAL AUTONOMY

# 1

# PROFESSORS BEWARE: THE EVOLVING THREAT OF "INSTITUTIONAL" ACADEMIC FREEDOM

*David M. Rabban*

## INTRODUCTION

"Institutional" academic freedom as a concept in American constitutional law has received increasing prominence in recent decades. Particularly troubling for professors, some judicial decisions and academic commentary have maintained that the extension of the general *First Amendment* protection of free speech to academic freedom, which originally safeguarded professors against external interference from the state, should be understood only as a grant of institutional autonomy, a barrier to judicial review of decisions made within the university. This approach threatens to insulate from judicial scrutiny claims by professors that university governing boards and administrators violated their academic freedom.

The United States Supreme Court decisions in the 1950s and 1960s that initially identified the academic freedom of professors as a distinctive *First Amendment* right recognized that the institutional autonomy of universities from the state can contribute to the academic freedom of individual professors. The explicit extension of *First Amendment* academic freedom to universities as institutions began in 1978 with Justice Powell's opinion in the landmark affirmative action case, *Regents of the University of California v. Bakke*. Subsequent Supreme Court decisions observed that the institutional academic freedom of universities could conflict with the individual academic freedom of professors. In deciding cases brought by professors against universities, numerous lower court decisions have addressed the tension between individual and institutional claims of academic freedom. These decisions have yielded varied results, sometimes supporting the professor, sometimes supporting the university, and sometimes reaching an accommodation compromising the competing claims of individual and institutional academic freedom. The majority opinion in a widely noticed decision in 2000 by an angrily divided circuit court of appeals maintained more dramatically that the *First Amendment* right of academic freedom extends only to universities, not to individual professors. Both before and after this decision, some academic commentators similarly argued that the *First Amendment* protection of academic freedom should be limited to universities as institutions. The constitutional status of individual academic freedom was placed in further doubt by a closely divided Supreme Court decision in 2006. In a case involving the *First Amendment* rights of public employees generally, the five-person majority held that speech "pursuant to the official duties" of public employees is not protected by the *First Amendment.* Although the case involved a government lawyer, the majority recognized and the dissent emphasized that the holding could jeopardize the academic freedom of university professors. The majority acknowledged that a different *First Amendment* analysis might apply to the scholarship or teaching of a professor, but left the resolution of this issue to future litigation, which has produced numerous inconclusive decisions in the lower courts. Despite these developments, many cases, supported by significant scholarship, continue to recognize *First Amendment* academic freedom as a right of individual professors.

In this essay, I trace the evolution of "institutional" academic freedom in American constitutional law and examine recent judicial and scholarly analyses that construes it in ways that jeopardize the existing constitutional protection for the individual academic freedom of professors. I also examine judicial and scholarly resistance to the construction of *First Amendment* academic freedom as an exclusively institutional right. I conclude with guarded optimism that the *First*

*Amendment* will continue to protect individual academic freedom, though I recognize that its security ultimately depends on professors themselves.

## THE INCORPORATION OF ACADEMIC FREEDOM INTO THE FIRST AMENDMENT

The United States Supreme Court did not address the constitutional meaning of academic freedom until the 1950s, prompted by government investigations into the loyalty of professors during the Cold War. Previously, American understandings of academic freedom derived from the founding document of the American Association of University Professors (AAUP): the "1915 Declaration of Principles."[1] This declaration focused on the threat college trustees posed to the academic freedom of professors, though it also recognized in passing the danger that legislators might try to use the state's purse strings to manipulate the academic inquiries of professors, particularly when scholarly views might deviate from strong public opinions or from established government policies.

The Supreme Court first incorporated academic freedom into the constitution in a 1957 case involving Paul Sweezy, who refused to answer questions from the attorney general of New Hampshire about his guest lecture at the University of New Hampshire or about the political activities of the Progressive Party in the state. Chief Justice Earl Warren's plurality opinion in *Sweezy v. New Hampshire* maintained that this government inquiry "unquestionably was an invasion" of Sweezy's *First Amendment* "liberties in the areas of academic freedom and political expression — areas in which the government should be extremely reluctant to tread." In this passage, Warren identified academic freedom and political expression as distinctive *First Amendment* liberties and attached them to *Sweezy* as an individual. Elaborating the *First Amendment* right of academic freedom, Warren stressed more generally the importance of preserving what he called "the essentiality of freedom in American universities."[2]

Justice Felix Frankfurter, who had been a professor and an active member of the AAUP at Harvard Law School before his appointment to the Supreme Court, wrote a concurring opinion in *Sweezy* that emphasized the close connection between university autonomy and academic freedom. Government intrusion into the intellectual life of a university, he warned, would jeopardize the essential functions of professors.[3] To support his analysis of academic freedom, Frankfurter quoted at length from a South African statement that defined a university as "characterized by a spirit of free inquiry," whose "business" is "to provide that atmosphere which is most conducive to speculation, experiment and creation." The statement identified "the four essential freedoms of a university — to determine for itself on academic grounds who may teach, what may be taught, how it shall be taught, and who may be admitted to study."[4]

*Keyishian v. Board of Regents*, decided in 1967, was the Supreme Court's next significant discussion of the protection afforded academic freedom under the *First Amendment*. The majority in *Keyishian* relied on *Sweezy* while declaring unconstitutional a complex system of New York statutes and regulations designed "to prevent the appointment or retention of 'subversive' persons in state employment."[5] The majority emphasized that academic freedom is "a special concern of the *First Amendment*"[6] and quoted a lengthy passage from Warren's opinion in *Sweezy*. In *Keyishian*, as in *Sweezy*, the Court focused on the academic freedom of the individual professors who challenged the state action. Although the Court also recognized in both cases that academic freedom requires insulating the intellectual life of the university from state interference, it did not develop a distinctive concept of institutional academic freedom.

Beginning in the late 1970s, however, the Supreme Court and the lower federal courts began to attach the *First Amendment* protection for academic freedom to the university as an institutional entity, often relying on the language of Frankfurter's concurring opinion in *Sweezy*. These cases arose in very different contexts from the earlier litigation, in which professors were litigants who understandably viewed the autonomy of the university from the state as a means to protect their own academic freedom against external attacks. In some of the subsequent cases, by contrast, individual professors were not litigants. Rather, the university defended various institutional decisions from state intrusion. In more troubling recent cases, professors as individuals and universities as institutions have asserted conflicting claims of academic freedom against each other.

The judicial application of academic freedom to the university as an institution began in 1978, when Justice Lewis Powell provided the pivotal fifth vote for the majority in the landmark affirmative action case, *Regents of the University of California v. Bakke*. Powell invoked the academic freedom of the university in defending his position that race can be a constitutionally legitimate factor in selecting a university's student body. "Academic freedom," Powell wrote, "though not a specifically enumerated constitutional right, long has been viewed as a special concern of the *First Amendment*." He maintained that the four essential freedoms of a university, identified in the South African statement quoted by Frankfurter in his concurring opinion in *Sweezy*, "constitute academic freedom."[7] For Powell, the fourth of those freedoms, to determine "who may be admitted to study," provided *First Amendment* grounds for a university to use race as a factor in student admissions.

Twenty-five years later, in *Grutter v. Bollinger*, the Supreme Court majority "endorsed" Justice Powell's analysis in *Bakke* in an opinion by Justice O'Connor that upheld the affirmative action program at the University of Michigan Law School. While citing *Sweezy* and *Keyishian*, Justice O'Connor observed that "Justice Powell invoked our cases recognizing a constitutional dimension, grounded in the *First Amendment*, of educational autonomy."[8] Interestingly, O'Connor referred to "educational autonomy" even though Powell in *Bakke* referred to the "academic freedom" of the university. Did she consciously substitute "educational autonomy" for "academic freedom," seeking to avoid equating the two terms, or did she conceive of educational autonomy and institutional academic freedom as the same thing? Unfortunately, nothing in her opinion helps answer this question, though I think it is possible, especially given the lack of clarity in prior judicial decisions referring to academic freedom, that she made a deliberate choice to use educational autonomy as an alternative.

In his biting dissent in *Grutter*, Justice Thomas included a short section on academic freedom as part of his general attack on affirmative action. Observing that the constitutionalization of academic freedom began with Frankfurter's concurring opinion in *Sweezy*, Thomas emphasized that "much of the rhetoric in Justice Frankfurter's opinion was devoted to the personal right of Sweezy to free speech."[9] "I doubt that when Justice Frankfurter spoke of governmental intrusions into the independence of universities," Thomas added, "he was thinking of the Constitution's ban on racial discrimination."[10]

Supreme Court decisions have cited institutional academic freedom in contexts other than affirmative action. In a 1981 case involving a university's right to regulate the use of campus facilities by student groups, Justice Stevens wrote a concurring opinion asserting that the application of general *First Amendment* principles "may needlessly undermine the academic freedom of public universities." He emphasized that universities, in "performing their learning and teaching missions," routinely and appropriately make decisions based on the content of speech, a suspect category in general *First Amendment* jurisprudence. Selecting the professors to appoint and reward, choosing the books to purchase for the library, developing the curriculum, and allocating scarce university resources and facilities among student groups, he observed, all require evaluation of the content of expressive activities.[11] He rejected the view that a public university has no greater interest in the content of student speech than a local police chief has in the content of speech by a citizen in a public space. "A university," he observed, "legitimately may regard some subjects as more relevant to its educational mission than others."[12] Three years later, Stevens again relied on the academic freedom of the university in rejecting the challenge by a medical student to a faculty decision dismissing the student on academic grounds.[13] More recently, Justice Souter, concurring in a decision that upheld a mandatory student activity fee to fund extracurricular student speech, cited the *First Amendment* protection of academic freedom while deferring to the university's judgment, expressed through the Dean of Students Office, about the academic importance of extracurricular activities as a "second curriculum." The Supreme Court's "understanding of academic freedom," Souter maintained, "has included not merely liberty from restraints on thought, expression, and association in the academy, but also the idea that universities and schools should have the freedom to make decisions about how and what to teach."[14]

## THE TENSION BETWEEN INDIVIDUAL AND INSTITUTIONAL ACADEMIC FREEDOM

It is important to stress that none of the Supreme Court cases recognizing a *First Amendment* right of institutional academic freedom involved conflicts between universities and individual professors who asserted their own rights to academic freedom. Yet Justice Stevens alluded to such possible conflicts in the case involving the medical student. "Academic freedom," he noted, "thrives not only on the independent and uninhibited exchange of ideas among teachers and students . . . but also, and somewhat inconsistently, on autonomous decision-making by the academy itself."[15]

In contrast to the Supreme Court, various lower courts have addressed the tension between institutional and individual academic freedom while adjudicating disputes between faculty members and universities. In a 1979 decision, a federal district judge who ordered the reinstatement of a Marxist professor acknowledged "a fundamental tension between the academic freedom of the individual teacher to be free of restraints from the university administration, and the academic freedom of the university to be free of government, including judicial, interference."[16] The judge found that the university decided not to reappoint the professor because he had publicly declared his membership in the Progressive Labor Party, an affiliation protected by general *First Amendment* principles. The judge did not find that the university had also relied on the professor's insertion of Marxist viewpoints into his history classes. Yet the judge added that if he had found the non-renewal so motivated, he would have relied on various lower court decisions holding that "academic freedom protects a teacher's choice of teaching methodology at least when . . . the school has failed to establish standards or otherwise to notify the teacher that his methods are unacceptable."[17]

Six years later, Judge Richard Posner, formerly a law professor at the University of Chicago, similarly observed the "equivocal" meaning of *First Amendment* academic freedom: "It is used to denote both the freedom of the academy to pursue its ends without interference from the government . . . and the freedom of the individual teacher (or in some versions — indeed in most cases — the student) to pursue his ends without interference from the academy; and these two freedoms are in conflict, as in this case."[18]

Albert Piarowski was the Chair of the Art Department at Prairie State College in Illinois. As part of an exhibit featuring work of the department's faculty, Piarowski contributed eight stained-glass windows. Five were abstract, but three depicted "naked brown women" in various sexually explicit poses. In response to complaints from students, cleaning women, and black clergymen, administrators ordered Piarowski to remove the windows from the exhibit on the main floor of the college's principal building.[19]

Judge Posner acknowledged the administration's concern that the content of some of these windows would offend potential applicants and thus make it harder to recruit students, particularly black and female students. Judicial interference with the administration's attempt to protect the institution's image, he observed, would "limit the freedom of the academy to manage its affairs as it chooses." On the other hand, he assumed that Piarowski's own academic freedom precluded the university from denying him the right to display his windows in a less conspicuous place on campus. Balancing the competing academic freedom claims of the college and the professor, Posner upheld the removal of Piarowski's windows from their original location while indicating that they could be exhibited in another gallery in the same building.[20]

Of greatest concern to professors, a divided decision by the entire Fourth Circuit in 2000, *Urofsky v. Gilmore,* claimed more broadly that the *First Amendment* right of academic freedom extends only to universities. The majority stated that the principles of individual academic freedom in the "1940 Statement of Principles on Academic Freedom and Tenure," issued jointly by the AAUP and the Association of American Colleges, reflect widely shared professional norms within the academic community, but are not part of the academic freedom protected by the *First Amendment*. The professors who were the plaintiffs in the Urofsky case challenged a Virginia statute providing that no state employee could use computers owned or leased by the state to access information "having sexually explicit content" unless "agency heads" gave prior approval in writing.[21] Melvin Urofsky, the lead plaintiff, alleged that this act prevented him from assigning students online research regarding federal indecency law. Other plaintiffs alleged that the statute restricted their scholarship and teaching by prohibiting online research on topics such as sexually explicit themes in Victorian poetry and various aspects of human sexuality.[22]

After rejecting the assertion that the statute infringed the *First Amendment* rights of all affected state employees, the majority opinion also denied the more specific claim that it violated "the *First Amendment* academic freedom right of professors at state colleges and universities, and thus is invalid as to them." The majority concluded that "to the extent the Constitution recognizes any right of 'academic freedom' above and beyond the *First Amendment* rights to which every citizen is entitled, the right inheres in the University, not in individual professors."[23] Following a lengthy (and largely inaccurate) summary of the history of litigation about academic freedom beginning with *Sweezy*, the majority asserted: "the best that can be said for [the professors'] claim that the Constitution protects the academic freedom of an individual professor is that teachers were the first public employees to be afforded the now-universal protection against dismissal for the exercise of *First Amendment* rights." Any asserted right of individual academic freedom, the majority maintained, extends only as far as the general *First Amendment* rights of all public employees. The majority added that since providing *First Amendment* protection to all public employees, the Supreme Court "has focused its discussions of academic freedom solely on issues of institutional autonomy."[24]

Immediately after concluding that a distinctive right of *First Amendment* academic freedom does not extend to individual professors, the majority observed in a footnote that constitutional issues could arise if university administrators used their statutory authority to deny professors access to the Internet. According to the footnote, "while a denial of an application under the Act based upon a refusal to approve a particular research project might raise genuine questions — perhaps even constitutional ones — concerning the extent of the authority of a university to control the work of its faculty, such questions are not presented here."[25] Presumably, such questions were not raised in the Urofsky case because no state university in Virginia had actually denied a professor permission to use computers owned or leased by the state. But by conceding that the denial of a request could raise constitutional questions, the majority seemed to be asserting that professors retain general *First Amendment* rights, if not the specific *First Amendment* right of academic freedom, against universities.

This footnote did not satisfy other judges on the Fourth Circuit. Four of the fourteen judges who decided the case dissented on general *First Amendment* grounds without discussing the constitutional meaning of academic freedom. These four dissenters were not reassured by the discretionary authority of state agencies to allow employees access to the Internet. They observed that such discretion could be withheld illegitimately. They also emphasized that the very existence of unfettered administrative discretion, even if not used, tends to intimidate people into self-censorship. By censoring themselves, all kinds of public employees with professional training — psychologists, social workers, doctors, librarians, and museum workers, as well as professors — would deprive the public of the benefit of their expertise.[26]

In a separate opinion, Chief Judge J. Harvie Wilkinson, formerly a law professor at the University of Virginia, concurred in the majority's judgment while disagreeing with its reasoning. He claimed that the majority's opinion did not protect the *First Amendment* rights of state employees generally.[27] Yet he focused on the academic freedom of the individual professors. Citing *Keyishian*, he explicitly recognized a distinctive *First Amendment* right of academic freedom for individual professors, which benefits society at large.[28] Unlike many other state employees, he emphasized, professors at state universities "are hired for the very purpose of inquiring into, reflecting upon, and speaking out on matters of public concern." These professors, he added, "work in the context of considerable academic independence. The statute limits professors' ability to research and to write. But in their research and writing university professors are not state mouthpieces — they speak mainly for themselves." A professor's right of academic freedom, he asserted, "cannot be divorced from access to one means (the Internet) by which the inquiry is carried out."[29]

Wilkinson nevertheless concurred in upholding the statute. He recognized legitimate state interests in guarding against improper use of the Internet to examine sexually explicit material that bears no relationship to any legitimate academic purpose. Unlike the dissenters, he was reassured by the statutory provisions granting university administrators discretion as "agency heads" to allow access by professors to sexually explicit material that does relate to serious scholarly inquiry. Wilkinson cited the Supreme Court's prior recognition of tension between individual and institutional academic freedom and conceded that decisions by university administrators could abridge the academic freedom of individual professors. Yet he also cited the Supreme Court's frequently stated reluctance to "second guess" the academic judgments made within universities. The record of the case, he observed, revealed that several professors had received waivers from administrators and contained no evidence that such a request had ever been denied. On this basis, Wilkinson expressed confidence that the traditional governance structure in higher education would uphold the academic freedom of individual professors. In contrast to the professors who challenged the statute, he did not believe "that a free academic institution will invade the freedoms of its own constituent members."[30]

## SCHOLARLY SUPPORT FOR AN EXCLUSIVELY INSTITUTIONAL RIGHT OF FIRST AMENDMENT ACADEMIC FREEDOM

Scholars as well as judges have placed increasing emphasis on *First Amendment* academic freedom as an institutional rather than an individual right. Pointing out that judges do not have the expertise to evaluate academic judgments, several scholars have urged limiting *First Amendment* academic freedom to the protection of university autonomy. Recognizing a constitutional right of academic freedom for individual professors, these scholars maintain, jeopardizes the necessary institutional autonomy of universities by inviting adjudication of disputes between faculty and administrators or trustees that are beyond the competence of judges to assess. These scholars acknowledge that judges must reverse decisions by university administrators and trustees that penalize faculty based on ideology or discrimination. But they provide little elaboration about how judges should determine whether an administrative decision is based on academic or impermissible grounds. They sometimes indicate that the very assertion of an academic ground should preclude judicial review. At the same time that they resist recognition of a *First Amendment* right of individual academic freedom, these scholars support the traditional "professional" conception of individual academic freedom from administrative interference, as defined and policed by the AAUP. They point out that professors, unlike judges, have the expertise to assess claimed violations of individual academic freedom. In addition, they often express great confidence that disputes about academic freedom within universities can be effectively resolved through the shared professional norms of the university community and, in the rare instances when they fail, through the investigations and censures of the AAUP.

An article by Peter Byrne in the *Yale Law Journal*, published in 1989, was the first major scholarly argument that the constitutional conception of academic freedom as a *First Amendment* right should primarily insulate the core activities of the university from interference by the state rather than protect faculty against actions by university administrators and trustees. Byrne conceded a "very limited judicial role"[31] in reviewing decisions by universities against faculty, "as when regents at a state university penalize a scholar against his department's recommendation on grounds clearly linked to the political direction of his scholarship." Yet Byrne immediately added that such cases "are extremely rare" because they would "severely damage" a university's reputation.[32] When faculty members file lawsuits claiming that university administrators have violated their individual rights to academic freedom, Byrne concluded, judges should determine whether the administrators acted in good faith on academic grounds. And in making this determination, judges should not assess whether the stated academic grounds are adequate or distinguish between faculty groups or administrators in deferring to good faith judgments. "The Constitution," he reasoned, "cannot impose any ideal structure of authority among the constituents of the university." He also observed that no standards of academic adequacy "have been or could be established by academic custom that are sufficiently accessible to provide a legal standard or test."[33]

While resisting judicial review of disputes within universities, Byrne stressed that it would be entirely appropriate for professors and their organizations, such as the AAUP, to engage "outside the coercive domain of law" in more rigorous scrutiny of the propriety of administrative justifications for allegedly academic decisions against faculty.[34] Universities "so perverse" that they "prohibit or consistently discourage" the academic freedom of professors, he also maintained, should lose the protection of *First Amendment* academic freedom. He was confident that this risk would deter university abuses and "lessen fears" that the institutional academic freedom of universities under the *First Amendment* would permit extensive violations of the individual academic freedom of professors that, under his analysis, would be outside constitutional protection.[35]

Interestingly, immediately after the *Urofsky* decision, Byrne wrote that the majority opinion "sickens me" and that its use of his article to "strip away legal protection for free intellectual inquiry leaves me distraught." Yet this distress did not prompt him to revise his analysis of the protection for academic freedom provided by the *First Amendment.* Indeed, he explicitly disagreed with the plaintiffs in *Urofsky* and the AAUP, who had asked the Supreme Court to reverse the decision based on an individual *First Amendment* right of academic freedom. Rather, he hoped the Supreme Court would reverse *Urofsky* as an inappropriate state intrusion into the intellectual life of universities because the requirements of the Virginia statute were imposed on universities rather than being adopted by any of them.[36] Ultimately, the Supreme Court itself decided not to review Urofsky.

Subsequent important scholarship has reinforced Byrne's emphasis on *First Amendment* academic freedom as an institutional rather than an individual right. Frederick Schauer, a leading scholar of the *First Amendment*, relied on general themes in *First Amendment* analysis in supporting this position. "The strongest argument against creating genuinely distinct individual academic freedom rights," he concluded, "is based on the proposition that granting individual academics enforceable rights against their academic supervisors would inevitably restrict the *academic* authority of the institution itself."[37] In a recent book, *First Amendment Institutions*, Paul Horwitz reiterated many of Byrne's arguments while claiming that Byrne's analysis did not go far enough in protecting the institutional autonomy of universities. An individual *First Amendment* right of academic freedom, Horwitz maintained, would overly protect the speech of professors who might violate disciplinary norms and insufficiently protect "the obligation of university administrators to govern the enterprise according to its academic mission."[38] Byrne, Horwitz protested, had an unconvincingly narrow conception of a university's academic mission. Whereas Byrne worried that any conception of a university's mission beyond the fundamental values of disinterested inquiry and critical discourse would threaten to bring the defence of institutional academic freedom into disrepute, Horwitz maintained that Byrne's approach risked "reifying" the mission of a university as well as the meaning of academic freedom. Instead, Horwitz urged that "the boundaries of what counts as academic judgment ought to be loosely defined."[39]

In a concession he relegated to a footnote, Horwitz acknowledged that a university could claim that it had dismissed a faculty member on wholly academic considerations even though the decision was actually based on improper political grounds. While recognizing a role for judicial review of the evidence in such a case, Horwitz emphasized that "when in doubt, the court should defer rather than intervene."[40] Echoing Byrne's confidence in the commitment to academic freedom within the university community, Horwitz added that even if institutional academic freedom requires judicial deference to institutional autonomy, the "principal stakeholders" of universities — "academics, students, and administrators" — are likely to resist departures from academic values.[41]

## SCHOLARLY RESISTANCE TO AN EXCLUSIVELY INSTITUTIONAL RIGHT OF FIRST AMENDMENT ACADEMIC FREEDOM

Although Byrne, Schauer, and Horwitz provide significant scholarly support for limiting the *First Amendment* protection of academic freedom to universities as institutions while leaving the individual academic freedom of professors to the traditional processes of the academic world, other scholars have resisted this analysis. Even before Byrne's pioneering article, Matthew Finkin warned against equating academic freedom with institutional autonomy, pointing out that they "are related but distinct ideas."[42] Institutional autonomy, he observed, may protect academic freedom within the university, but it may also protect property interests of the university that have nothing to do with academic freedom and that may even interfere with it.[43] He worried that a *First Amendment* concept of "institutional" academic freedom would substitute "a simple act of labeling" for "more exacting assessments" of whether or not an invasion of university autonomy threatens academic freedom.[44] Finkin was particularly concerned that *First Amendment* protection for "institutional" academic freedom would "perversely, in the name of academic freedom," immunize the very administrative prerogatives that had been used to deny academic freedom to professors, abuses that had led to the formation of the AAUP and its formulation of principles of academic freedom in the "1915 Declaration."[45]

Soon after Byrne wrote and partially in response to him, I challenged his elevation of institutional over individual academic freedom in *First Amendment* analysis. I disagreed with his view that in what he called "intra-academic" cases, administrators, and apparently even trustees, should receive the same degree of judicial deference as professors. I pointed out that trustees and many administrators lack the professional expertise Byrne ascribed to them.[46] In *First Amendment* and employment discrimination cases, I also observed, judges had demonstrated the ability to respect academic expertise while assessing if stated academic grounds were pretexts for illegal or unconstitutional university decisions.[47] For example, the judge in the case involving the Marxist professor, discussed earlier in this essay, appropriately refused to defer to the claim by administrators that poor teaching explained the non-reappointment. The judge convincingly concluded that expression protected by the *First Amendment*, not the alleged academic justification of deficient teaching, best accounted for the university's decision. He pointed out that the administrators had never informed the professor about perceived deficiencies in his teaching during his three years on the faculty, that the university had never previously dismissed or failed to renew the contract of a full-time faculty member, that the decision against reappointment occurred almost immediately after the professor created a political furor throughout the state by announcing his belief in communism and his membership in the Progressive Labor Party, and that the meeting between the chancellor and the professor just before the notification of his non-renewal focused almost exclusively on the professor's beliefs. In cases involving employment discrimination, judges similarly were able to cite persuasive evidence to support determinations that discrimination, not the academic considerations cited by administrators, explained the results. For example, evidence that the administration required the publication of two books from a female professor who was denied tenure, but only one book from men who had received tenure, helped convince an appellate court that the vigorous criticism her scholarship by administrators, who overturned the favourable tenure recommendations of various faculty committees, constituted a pretext for discrimination.[48]

In contrast to Byrne's claim that judges should not differentiate between professors and administrators in deferring to assertions of professional expertise, I commended judicial decisions that cited unanimous recommendations of faculty committees as grounds for skepticism about claims by administrators that they had relied on legitimate academic grounds in reversing them.[49] Judicial respect for peer review, I maintained, furthered the deference to professional expertise that Byrne himself so valued.[50] Byrne's assertion that universities should forfeit the protection of institutional academic freedom if they "prohibit or consistently discourage" the academic freedom of professors, I added, did not, as he hoped, "lessen fears" that his elevation of institutional academic freedom in *First Amendment* analysis would permit extensive violations of individual academic freedom. Based on my extensive study of legal cases and reports of AAUP investigating committees, I observed that many violations of individual academic freedom have occurred in universities that ordinarily respect it and, therefore, in Byrne's analysis, would not forfeit their institutional academic freedom.[51]

Two recent and very important scholarly discussions of the *First Amendment* protection for academic freedom also challenged the emphasis on institutional over individual rights. Interestingly, both were written by law professors who also served as deans. Judith Areen, the former Dean of Georgetown Law School, highlighted the primary role of faculty peer review in suggesting the appropriate *First Amendment* analysis when a professor claims that a university has retaliated for speech on academic matters. If the professor can establish that protected academic expression was the basis for the university's action, she asserted, the burden should shift to the university to prove that the action was justified. Proof by the university that an authorized committee of the faculty supported the university decision should prompt the judge to conclude that the decision was made on academic grounds and, therefore, to defer to it unless the professor could demonstrate that the faculty itself departed substantially from academic norms. The burden on the professor to demonstrate such a departure should be "extremely high." On the other hand, if the university, through the administration or the governing board, either did not consult with the faculty or overturned a faculty recommendation, it should have the burden of proving that it acted on legitimate academic grounds. Judges, Areen concluded, "should avoid infringing the academic freedom of academic institutions unless their intervention is necessary to protect the academic freedom of faculty."[52]

In a major theoretical analysis of the relationship between the *First Amendment* and academic freedom that stressed the contribution of scholarship to the general *First Amendment* value of "democratic competence," Robert Post, the current Dean of Yale Law School, maintained that under a proper understanding of *First Amendment* academic freedom judges should defer to professional scholarly standards as determined by "disciplinary experts," but not "to university administrators who possess neither the capacity nor the pretense of exercising professional judgment."[53] Very effectively, he observed that Paul Sweezy should still have won his case if lay administrators rather than the state attorney general had tried to determine the economic truth of his lecture.[54] Post claimed that "the supposed tension between the institutional and individual accounts of academic freedom is based upon a misunderstanding." Stressing that neither institutions nor individual professors, as such, exercise professional standards, Post urged judges "not to confuse the question of when deference is appropriate with the question of whether academic freedom inheres in institutions or in individuals."[55]

## JUDICIAL RESISTANCE TO AN EXCLUSIVELY INSTITUTIONAL RIGHT OF FIRST AMENDMENT ACADEMIC FREEDOM

Judges as well as scholars have resisted arguments that *First Amendment* academic freedom should be an institutional rather than an individual right. The reasoning of the Fourth Circuit in the Urofsky case has not taken hold within the American judiciary. In *First Amendment* cases presenting competing claims between professors and administrators, judges have reached a wide variety of results, sometimes finding for the professors, sometimes for the administrators. Many of these decisions do not even refer to institutional or individual academic freedom, though some do. A significant proportion of them address whether or not classroom speech meets professional standards, finding for the professor if it does and for the administration if it does not. Others involve faculty criticism of administrative decisions and disputes over who has the authority to make academic decisions. In a major and closely divided decision in 2006, *Garcetti v. Ceballos,* the Supreme Court held that public employees are not protected by the *First Amendment* when they speak "pursuant to their official duties."[56]

The case involved a government lawyer, and the Court, in response to concerns raised by Justice Souter in dissent and perhaps also to similar concerns raised by the AAUP amicus brief, recognized that its holding "may have important ramifications for academic freedom." As Souter warned, the "ostensible domain beyond the pale of the *First Amendment* is spacious enough to include even the teaching of a public university professor, and I have to hope that today's majority does not mean to imperil *First Amendment* protection of academic freedom in public colleges and universities, whose teachers necessarily speak and write 'pursuant to official duties.'"[57] Observing that "expression related to academic scholarship or classroom instruction implicates additional constitutional interests that are not fully accounted for by this Court's customary employee-speech jurisprudence," the majority explicitly did not decide whether its analysis "would apply in the same manner to a case involving speech related to scholarship or teaching."[58] Subsequent lower court decisions have considered if speech by professors raised such "additional constitutional interests" and have reached differing results. Moreover, in many areas outside the context of disputes between professors and administrators, recent judicial decisions have protected the free speech and academic freedom of individual professors. Although the increased scholarly and judicial attention to institutional academic freedom at the expense of individual academic freedom is extremely troubling, I review some of these cases to support my prediction, which is less confident than I would prefer, that American courts will not generally rely on the institutional academic freedom of universities as a barrier to judicial review of claims by professors that universities have disciplined them for speech that meets professional standards.

Cases addressing whether or not classroom speech meets professional standards often arise when professors discuss sex or religion. In a 2001 case, the court was sympathetic to a professor's claim that the college had not renewed his appointment in retaliation for classroom expression protected by the *First Amendment*. The court highlighted "the robust tradition of academic freedom" identified in *Keyishian* and rejected the administration's argument that the case was "nothing more than an internal employment dispute." During a lecture on language and social constructivism in a course entitled Introduction to Interpersonal Communication, the professor asked his class to suggest words that have been used to serve the interests of the dominant culture while marginalizing oppressed groups. Students suggested words such as "nigger" and "bitch," which prompted complaints from a black female student. The student contacted a local civil rights leader, a minister, who told the college president that he would discourage students from attending the college unless it took corrective action. The professor was not appointed the following semester.[59] Differentiating this case from an earlier decision the same year that upheld discipline against a professor for the gratuitous use of profanity in class, the court stressed that the professor's "speech was germane to the subject matter of his lecture on the power and effect of language" and "was limited to an academic discussion."[60] The court, therefore, concluded that the college could not refuse to reappoint him for this classroom episode.

In a 2006 case about classroom speech, Judge Diane Wood, formerly a law professor at the University of Chicago, used a similar analysis while rejecting the *First Amendment* claims of an instructor in cosmetology who had introduced religious material into her teaching. Invoking examples from other fields, Judge Wood pointed out that a college is not required to permit a chemistry professor to teach a novel by James Joyce or a math professor to teach the law of torts. On the other hand, she emphasized, the *First Amendment* does preclude the imposition of ideological orthodoxy in the classroom and protects a professor's freedom "to express her views on the assigned course."[61]

Cases involving faculty criticism of administrative decisions have reached different results based on factually specific judicial assessments of the relative weights of the professor's interest in expression and the institution's need for efficiency. Judges have applied the *First Amendment* to protect professors who criticized the president's proposal to build a new arts centre[62] and who, while serving on the dean's advisory committee, objected to his proposed reorganization of an academic department.[63] Yet judges in another case determined that a university's interests in harmony among co-workers outweighed the

*First Amendment* interests of the chair of the department of medicine who objected to moving the location of the medical school.[64] Perhaps the administrative responsibilities of the department chair, which the judges themselves did not highlight, accounted at least in part for this different result.

Courts have been overwhelmingly unsympathetic to claims by professors that they have *First Amendments* rights to make independent decisions about issues such as teaching "fundamentals" in an introductory English course,[65] teaching an upper level Spanish course in English rather than Spanish,[66] providing a detailed syllabus,[67] using standard teacher evaluations,[68] and, perhaps the most heavily litigated context, assigning grades.[69] Many of these cases involved departures by individual professors from university standards, to which the courts deferred whether they were developed by faculty or by the administration. In the case requiring the teaching of "fundamentals," the judge observed that the "*First Amendment* guarantee of academic freedom provides a teacher with right to encourage a vigorous exchange of ideas within the confines of the subject matter being taught, but it does not require a university or school to tolerate any manner of teaching method the teacher may choose to employ." The administration had determined that teaching "fundamentals" was important for its students, who were generally unsophisticated and came from "somewhat restrictive backgrounds,"[70] and the judge upheld the refusal to renew the teaching contract of a professor based on "deviation from the teaching standards thought appropriate by her superiors."[71] Interestingly, a rare decision upholding the *First Amendment* right of a professor to assign a grade also upheld the right of administrators to change that grade. After recognizing that prior cases had afforded *First Amendment* protection to the academic freedom of both universities and individual professors, the judge concluded that the professor's assignment of a grade based on his professional judgment is constitutionally protected speech, which a dean violated by ordering him to change it. Yet the judge added that the dean could change the grade himself without violating the professor's academic freedom.[72]

Lower court decisions construing *Garcetti* have been less generous in protecting academic speech than most professors would understandably prefer. Whereas I have argued that *First Amendment* academic freedom should protect intramural speech on university affairs related to critical inquiry, such as the content of the curriculum and the integrity of the peer review process,[73] and Judith Areen has emphasized that it should protect speech about academic governance,[74] decisions construing *Garcetti* have only recognized an "academic freedom" exception to the "official duties" analysis of *Garcetti* in the contexts of scholarship and teaching. While some decisions construing *Garcetti* have rejected an exception for additional academic speech, none has denied *First Amendment* protection for these core professional activities.

In the case that most directly addressed the academic freedom issue raised but not resolved in *Garcetti*, the judge rejected the claim by the chair of a medical school's department of obstetrics and gynecology that a professor's advocacy of forceps delivery was made within his official duties and was, therefore, unprotected by the *First Amendment*. The judge recognized "an academic freedom exception to the *Garcetti* analysis," at least where "the expressed views are well within the range of accepted medical opinion."[75] Emphasizing that courts should be generous in defining the "accepted" range," the judge noted that the use of leeches, which had been considered the height of medieval superstition when he was an undergraduate, had become acceptable in modern medicine since the advent of microsurgery in the 1980s.[76] The disastrous impact on Soviet agriculture from Stalin's enforcement of the "biological orthodoxy" associated with Lysenko, the judge added, provided "a strong counterexample to those who would discipline university professors for not following the 'party line.'"[77] A subsequent circuit court decision in another case asserted that the lower court had "misread *Garcetti*" by extending its "official duties" analysis to a professor. The same circuit court that had decided the Urofsky case reasoned that "*Garcetti* would not apply in the academic context of a public university"[78] regarding speech by professors "within their respective fields."[79]

On the other hand, many cases since *Garcetti* have refused to recognize an "academic freedom" exception. Some of these cases conceded that an "academic freedom" exception covers professional speech related to scholarship and teaching even as they refused to apply it to additional academic speech; other cases did not even refer to the language in *Garcetti* about academic freedom. In one case, the court refused to protect the speech of the head reference librarian who served on an elected faculty-staff committee to select the book that all incoming freshmen would be assigned to read. Distinguishing this case from the one involving forceps delivery, the judge reasoned that the librarian's discussion of book selection "pursuant to an assignment to a faculty committee" did not concern "scholarship or teaching" and, therefore, was "unprotected, regardless of the existence of an 'academic freedom' exception" to *Garcetti*.[80] Other cases have similarly limited the "academic freedom" exception to scholarship and teaching while refusing to protect faculty speech opposing the selection of a university president,[81] advising a student in a disciplinary proceeding,[82] or claiming misappropriation of federal grant funds.[83] One decision soon after *Garcetti* simply ignored its reference to academic freedom while applying its "official duties" analysis to deny *First Amendment* protection for speech by a professor about various academic matters, including an alleged financial conflict of interest by a colleague, objections to the use of lecturers rather than tenured faculty members, and claims that administrators had violated faculty governance in making academic appointments. In a particularly disappointing passage, the judge observed that "a faculty member's official duties are not limited to classroom instruction and professional research,"[84] thereby indicating his view that teaching and scholarship are also official duties unprotected by *Garcetti*. Yet because the facts of this case did not involve teaching or scholarship, the decision did not actually deny *First Amendment* protection for them. These post-*Garcetti* cases are extremely troubling. It is nevertheless significant that no decision has allowed the punishment of professional speech related to teaching and scholarship, and that the few decisions directly pertaining to teaching and scholarship explicitly recognized the "academic freedom" exception for them left open by *Garcetti* itself.

The continuing vitality of *First Amendment* academic freedom for individual professors, moreover, is manifested in other recent cases that do not construe *Garcetti*. For example, in 2011 a court dismissed a lawsuit brought by the Turkish Coalition of America against a professor who declared that its website was "unreliable" and cautioned students to avoid it. "The ability of the university and its faculty to determine the reliability of sources available to students for use in their research" and to "critique academic views held and expressed by others," the judge concluded, are protected by *First Amendment* academic freedom.[85] In 2012, another court dismissed the claim by a manufacturer seeking damages against a professor who allegedly made false and misleading statements about its product in an article published in a peer-reviewed journal. Conceding that the academic freedom protected by the *First Amendment* does not give professors license to publish falsehoods, the judge stressed that the article contained debatable opinions, not false facts.[86] In the context of a dispute between a professor and a university, a circuit court decision in 2011 reiterated the fundamental proposition that a university's refusal to hire a professor based on political ideology would violate her *First Amendment* right of academic freedom.[87] All three of these cases quoted the Supreme Court's language in *Keyishian* identifying academic freedom as "a special concern of the *First Amendment*."

## CONCLUSION

The evolution of university autonomy into an independent *First Amendment* right of "institutional" academic freedom threatens to overwhelm, and even to eliminate, *First Amendment* academic freedom as an individual right of professors. Uncertainty about the potential application of the "official duties" test of *Garcetti* to university professors exacerbates concern that the *First Amendment* protection of academic freedom, to the extent that it remains viable at all, will be limited to universities as institutions. Yet cases continue to uphold the academic freedom of individual professors, sometimes in the face of competing claims of institutional academic freedom. No case has denied *First Amendment* protection to the core professional duties of teaching and scholarship, and some cases have extended it to speech criticizing decisions by university administrators. Lack of conceptual clarity and a profusion of often inconsistent judicial opinions are the most striking characteristics of the current law of *First Amendment* academic freedom.

The continued judicial recognition of an individual right of academic freedom protected by the *First Amendment* is extremely significant. Limiting *First Amendment* academic freedom to universities, as some scholars and judges have urged, threatens the academic freedom of professors. The confident assertion that the shared professional norms of the university community will protect the individual academic freedom of professors, especially if those norms are policed by the AAUP when deviations occur, is not persuasive. Based on my extensive experience with the AAUP, as staff counsel, general counsel, and Chair of its Committee A on Academic Freedom and Tenure, and on reading hundreds of legal decisions over many decades, I know of too many instances when members of the university community — administrators, trustees, and sometimes professors themselves — violated those professional norms. Although the AAUP has been remarkably successful in policing academic freedom, it has never had the resources to prevent or correct all or probably most violations of it. Even when the AAUP has investigated and censured universities for infringing the academic freedom of professors, the remedies associated with the removal of censure most often involved improvements in the general conditions of academic freedom, including changes in administrative personnel and new institutional policies. In addition, the university generally provided some form of redress, often symbolic, to the professors harmed. These professors rarely received full compensation for their financial losses and often were not reinstated. Judicial decisions finding violations of the academic freedom or free speech of a professor, by contrast, typically ordered reinstatement and full back pay. The internal processes of the academic community are no substitute for what Byrne calls the "coercive domain of law."

On the other hand, members of the university community and the AAUP were not helpless in the many decades between the founding of the AAUP in 1915 and the Supreme Court's 1957 decision in the

Sweezy case, which first brought academic freedom within the protection of the *First Amendment*. The AAUP actively and often effectively promoted and defended the academic freedom of professors during this period, frequently in collaboration with sympathetic people within universities, administrators, and trustee,s as well as faculty. Professors and their organizations should try to shape the law, but they should also work within universities to assert, and hopefully to establish, institutional support for individual academic freedom. It is possible to recognize the additional power of legal enforcement and urge the continued application of the *First Amendment* to protect individual academic freedom, yet also realize, as the founders of the AAUP understood, that professors must ultimately depend on themselves.

# 2

# INSTITUTIONAL AUTONOMY AND ACADEMIC FREEDOM IN THE MANAGED UNIVERSITY

*Len Findlay*

"Universities today are strangely quiet places." [1]

"We've probably never needed universities more." [2]

Institutional autonomy is a necessary but not a sufficient condition for the effective exercise of academic freedom. Such autonomy can create a domain for distinctively academic agency. However, it can as readily prove to be a frail, permeable domain, revealing little enthusiasm for or resolve to protect what the Supreme Court of Canada praised as "free and fearless" academic agency.[3] Formally constituted autonomy and university charters notwithstanding, the independence of post-secondary institutions has been and can still be relinquished or abused, functioning as a consoling illusion of the limits of political interference and economic influence or as a pretext for controlling academic work and the dissemination of its findings. The contingency and vulnerability of institutional autonomy are evident in the recent and regrettable trend in Canadian academe toward the simultaneous shrinking and inflation of this version of independence. Here and now, the independence of post-secondary institutions is reduced by external interests while being increased internally as a form of executive privilege to be wielded as a weapon against the academic freedom of academic staff. Meanwhile, institutional leaders claiming to *be* the university try to conceal the contradictions of their own practice in the conflicted notion of institutional autonomy as something to be apologized for and traded away in the name of accountability or exigent partnership, and also as managerial obligation and entitlement to control intramural and extramural freedoms key to the effective undertaking of academic work and to institutional health and the public interest.

The "managed university"[4] uses autonomy as an alibi for transforming itself from independence and collegial self-governance into bad compliance and uncollegial intimidation, both of which are designed to contain and commercialize the academic activities of academic staff. Indeed, academic capitalism seems in even better shape in Canada today than when Richard Wellen reviewed *The Exchange University* in 2009. New versions of the extramural and intramural are being used by academic managers to simultaneously extend and decrease the limits of their own powers, this with a view to requiring academic staff to adhere to and promote a neo-liberal agenda posing as the public interest. Understanding this process is a necessary but, alas, not a sufficient condition for the mobilization of academic staff against the co-optation of colleges and universities by doctrinaire advocates and enforcers of accountability and austerity, aided and abetted on numerous Canadian campuses by corporate compradors like Robert Dickeson.[5] At a time when fiscal transparency resembles nothing so much as "the fog of war," in academic institutions as well as governments, there is therefore an urgent need to identify, unpack, and replace the managerial contradictions within current administrative appeals to institutional autonomy as the version of academic freedom that must enjoy priority over the rights and responsibilities of individual members of academic staff. What follows here is a brief attempt to clarify and assist this process, using the notion of limitation to identify the limits of managerial legitimacy, to suggest the expansiveness of managerial desire, and to spell out the implications of both for academic freedom.

## AUTONOMY: WHAT, WHOSE, AND HOW MUCH?

Autonomy has a long and complicated history linguistically and politically. However, the linguistic record cannot simply ingest political history in an act of discursive imperialism. Nor can political theory reduce language to a docile instrument of political power. Politics and language need to treat each other as quasi-peers constantly subject to peer review, and perhaps never more so than when it comes to the understanding and practice of autonomy. The term in ancient Greek and in innumerable later borrowings, glosses, and translations expresses the idea of self-legislation. However, the act of defining self-hood (*autos*) and law (*nomos*) occurs always and inescapably inside rather than outside a field of power relations and the play of interests. The situation is well-captured by George Steiner:

> Translation cannot render nor commentary circumscribe the network of discriminations and contiguities which comprises the Greek terms *Θέμις*, *Δίκη*, and νόμος. The rough and ready equation with 'right,' 'justice,' and 'law' not only misses the shifting lives of meaning in each of these fundamental Greek words, but fails altogether to translate the interplay in both *Θέμις* and *Δίκη* of pragmatic or abstractly legalistic connotations on the one hand, and of archaic but active agencies of the supernatural on the other. The stucco or even marble allegories and statuary of our lawcourts give no corresponding sense of a transcendent and, at times, daemonic embodiment. Yet it is within this intensely energized terrain of values and applications covered, bounded by these three terms, that the worlds of Creon and Antigone collide.[6]

Autonomy may offer the promise of disinterestedness, but it can never deliver on that promise beyond dispute and without remainder. Autonomy, therefore, should not be viewed as some kind of palladium, an immutable guardian *audessus de la mêlée,* but as the determinate product of a set of interactions between language and politics in a particular setting. For our purposes, autonomy is a permanent academic work site, even and especially on campuses where the edifice complex — now comprising stucco, marble, plastic, glass, and steel — is most in evidence and a donor-administrator priesthood physically and symbolically omnipresent.

The constructedness, inherent instability, and negotiability of autonomy becomes clearer when one considers who lays claim to it and who determines the fate of that claim. One of autonomy's siblings, sovereignty — and its markedly Canadian cousins, Quebecois "sovereignty association" and Aboriginal self-determination — remind us of the exclusionary tendencies of elites, tendencies captured in the lexical and political singularity denoted by the term *mon*archy: the rule of one. According to this linguistic and logical chain, there is only one exemplar of autonomy, one person truly and fully sovereign in the kingdom. All other claimants to autonomy are premature or treasonous, or both. However, monopolistic power constantly endeavours to have its cake and eat it too; in other words, to appear natural and desirable rather than arbitrary. Absolutists look in the mirror only in private, if at all. In public, they act as though they are the mirror itself in which all subjects are invited or required to see themselves. Sovereign singularity rightly sees naked absolutism as its inalienable right but also as inciting others to resistance and sedition, or even assassination. Such sovereignty therefore pluralizes its appeal, but only at the cost of fracturing its originary self-hood. The doctrine of *The King's Two Bodies*[7], to take a well-known example, entails a pluralizing of sovereign self-hood on the way from absolutism to democracy,[8] or the rule of the people, the many (also known to Edmund Burke and others as "a swinish multitude," precisely in a context where Burke wishes "learning, not debauched by ambition, had been satisfied to continue the instructor, and not aspired to be the master!"[9]). In sum, autonomy may claim to be absolute and unconditioned but it is neither, no matter how it intimidates or conciliates its subjects or deludes itself. And all derivatives or analogues of autonomy as sovereign power, including parliamentary supremacy and university autonomy, are subject to the same conditions and concessions. No matter who claims autonomy, the reality will always be relative and contestable. Autonomy of any sort is therefore best understood as a site of conflict and/or negotiated, conditional agreement about definitional power and its practical outcomes. However, to say so is not to diminish the importance of autonomy but to insist, rather, that it always be approached as a report on consequential power relations and the structures and protocols of legitimacy such relations enable in particular settings.

There is never domination without resistance. Final solutions are never fully that, no matter how appallingly complete they may appear or claim to be. Accordingly, how much power can particular forms of autonomy plausibly claim and effectively exercise? Where is dependency hidden or strategically simulated within any apparently freestanding structure within inescapable fields of interdependence? What chance is there that we can and will heed Ojibwa legal scholar John Borrows's appeal in 2002 for more declarations of *inter*dependence rather than *in*dependence, and do so within a more generous, just, and sustainable knowledge economy?[10]

One might imagine that all derivatives of political autonomy will be lesser than their source, becoming lesser, perhaps, the further away they lie from centres of political power. However, such reasoning is deeply problematic. For instance, it affirms the primacy and directive or deterministic force of the political as such, but only in the guise or disguise of a particular political arrangement in a particular setting and time. It is hence a reductive pseudo-universal, and logically fallacious to boot. If everything is "really" political, then nothing is (a lesson from structuralist demonstrations of how language operates as a system of oppositions and differences). The political as such is relational as well as intrinsic, like the linguistic sign, and hence also composite and arbitrary as in the Saussurean account.[11] In order to be itself, the political must have its Others, a set of alterities usually located in the private sphere and in what came to be known as civil society (Hegel's *bürgerliche Gesellschaft* so thoroughly worked over by Marx in 1843 as part of his own political and intellectual transformation).[12] It is in the interests of autonomy (aspiring to be hegemony) to feign an eagerness to recognize and respect its own proper limits and the existence of other forms of power beyond (if not necessarily opposed to) the dominant version of the political. And so we have the ancient and enduring notion of poetry (and art more generally as a form of creation or making) as one of the Others of politics, and independent in its own right. Such forms of imaginative and aesthetic autonomy can, of course, be forbidden or abolished, as Plato endeavours to do by banishing the poets from his ideal *Republic* (Book Ten).[13] However, the control or abolition of the imagination is as undesirable as it is unachievable, as Plato himself inadvertently reveals, his form of philosophical writing being a frequently poetic testimony to the dialogic imagination with its masterful character portrayals, intellectual drama, and riveting myths. And as with art, so with the academies and self-sequestering intellectual communities that led over sectarian centuries and seas of doctrinal turbulence to the modern university. Where there is no imagination, no art, there is no humanity. When we stop thinking ideographically (humanistically) as well as nomothetically (scientifically), inside and outside universities, we will be extinct or hell-bent on self-extinguishment. Instrumentalist attacks on the humanistic academy in particular imperil the entire system and its multiple beneficiaries (as documented in Findlay 2012).[14]

Much of what I have claimed about autonomy can be explicitly connected to theorizations of the limit as such, many of which associate themselves with politics and legitimacy. One example must suffice here. In *Political Theology: Four Chapters on the Concept of Sovereignty*, Carl Schmitt (1888-1985), then teaching at the University of Bonn, described autonomy/sovereignty (*Souveränität*) as the right to determine the state of exception (*Ausnahmezustand*), that state or set of conditions which entitles the sovereign to suspend or abrogate the laws that normally prevail and to which (arguably) the sovereign also is normally subject. Three features of this claim are especially relevant to discussion of the limits of academic freedom. The first is that the claim is made by a thoroughly credible academic whose "brilliance" is acknowledged by friend and foe alike.[15] Schmitt held important appointments in German universities and government until 1945, and used his skills, status, and academic freedom to undermine the independence of institutions and their resident scholars, all the while practising bad territoriality in insisting that decisionist sovereignty is never a question of "sociology" but the concern of jurisprudence alone.[16] Schmitt, like Stephen Harper, had no desire to "commit sociology."[17] The second relevant point is that this claim is made by a proto-Nazi during the Weimar period, taking his cue from the political right who are looking for a new theory of authority that will make governing more efficient and orderly, an academic alibi for ultraviral process and physical thuggery. Scholarship never happens in a political vacuum or from an external Archimedean point. Scholarly detachment is relative and aspirational rather than fully achieved. Third, this theorization of (sovereignty/autonomy/*autoritas*) exemplifies the menace of exceptionalism in the limitation or circumvention of the normative in the name of restoring normative order. Authoritarianism becomes the new normal by claiming to nourish and restore traditional norms. Not coincidentally, this move ushers in a series of authoritarian appeals to "crisis," which for Schmitt is more interesting than the "rule" because "it confirms not only the rule but also its existence, which derives only from the exception."[18] Appeals to crisis will soon create pretexts for the Nazi purge (with substantial student and faculty support) of German universities and analogous institutions in countries they invaded and sometimes occupied (see, e.g., Steinweis).[19] Schmitt's example, and its political take-up, even by the antipathetic left,[20] remind us of the need for special vigilance whenever notions of limits are invoked, and the need for rigorous critique of the sovereignty assumed and asserted by those who do so. To repeat, autonomy and its analogues constitute a site of permanent process, adjustment, and contestation. Institutional autonomy is not a self-evident good but something to be continuously scrutinized, lest it be squandered or abused precisely in order to corral and cow the individual bearers and defenders of academic freedom and to control their ability to act individually and collectively on the basis of academic processes and values decided on by them.

## NEO-LIBERAL LIMITATIONS AND THE COERCED COLLEGIUM

If the Canadian state, like the Weimar Republic and the Third Reich, can impact the autonomy of its post-secondary institutions, what is that impact likely to be, directly and indirectly? The current government of Canada is in equal measure secretive and punitive in the way it pursues its agenda. It cloaks and advances its policies with unrelenting partisanship, doing its business along the line between political friends and political enemies originally popularized by none other than Carl Schmitt.[21] The Harper government protects and augments its own autonomy by violating that of the public service and a whole range of entities supposed to function free of political direction. The Harper government proudly boasts a communications "war room" where language and politics converge in "attack ads" and numerous other expressions of belligerence, using secrecy, redaction, muzzling, and spin. The Harper government cleaves to a politics of fear, exerting its sovereignty through recurrent appeals to a state of exception. Joseph Goebbels would surely have approved. But Carl Schmitt would have worried about crying "Wolf!" so often as to imperil the very polity such alarmism declares itself committed to defending. It is, as Alan Gregg has eloquently argued, an "Orwellian" scenario in which transparency is opacity, fact fiction, memory amnesia, frugality recklessness, and much else.

Now all this semiotic thuggery and micro-vindictiveness in high places might not matter so much, if other institutions insisted on their independence. Alas, too many provinces adopt this federal tone of exceptional action in extreme circumstances, this despite the seething differences produced by unco-operative federalism in Harperland. Meanwhile, at the level of what used to be collegial administration and is now senior management, post-secondary institutions follow suit, invoking an academic state of exception to coerce the collegium through politically familiar policies of secrecy, redaction, muzzling, and spin. Senior academic managers are now recruited through secret processes and wooed with indefensibly lucrative compensation packages. If academic staff and their collegial processes are largely sidelined while leaders are selected, is it any wonder that they will continue to be spurned, co-opted, or stonewalled once those leaders begin to lead? If academic managers model themselves on federal ministers and corporate executives, is it any wonder they become impatient with the peculiar ways of the collegium and the expectation that they should be facilitators rather than rulers, facilitating the work of colleagues that they may not understand or approve of? Is it any wonder that they reserve their most intense animus for CAUT and its unionized membership? Is it any wonder that, in the traditional home of unencumbered inquiry, academic managers feel the need to create barriers to keep themselves safe from inconvenient probing and the urge to understand rather than simply obey? Is it any wonder that, feeling increasingly inauthentic and under siege from those they consider not peers but employees, academic managers divert resources from core academic activities to brand management, creating a court culture and roster of team players for themselves while seizing the right to decide on the current state of exception and the ultraviral actions, which must flow therefrom in order that their institution emerge, mysteriously leaner but stronger, from this crisis?

There seems to be a very direct line from the *modus operandi* of the Harper government through the federal granting councils and the Association of Universities and Colleges of Canada (AUCC) to academic managers in our publicly funded post-secondary institutions. Market muscularity trumps evidence and rational analysis at every turn, while the internal contradictions of free-market fundamentalism parse out as freedom for the profiteer, restriction for the scholar and researcher; trust for the business community, distrust for academic labour; the quest for market orders producing academic marching orders. Current attempts to pick winners and play favourites within academe from the outside make a mockery of institutional autonomy while threatening to make an equivalent mockery of academic freedom. And this is why recent action, and inaction, from the AUCC is so predictable and so pathetic. AUCC has been culpably uncritical of federal efforts to assert academic sovereignty through budgetary bundling and concealment. Moreover, AUCC has been feeble at best in its attempts to explain the value of academic work as an "economic asset" produced by a system that is "open to change,"[22] an ominously vague and passive formulation.

Nor is the elite group of U15 institutions any better than the AUCC in this regard. The U15's new website is afflicted with fantasies of eminence and uncritical invocation of market-driven notions of competition. Its evidence of "impact" is heavily economistic while terms like "learned" and "critique" are nowhere to be found. The completeness of the buy-in to governmental and corporate instrumentalist agendas is depressingly clear, while the dominant temporalities are the business cycle and the political cycle, not a lifetime of inquiry. When notionally autonomous institutions take to protective coloration and eager abjection in the name of academic excellence, we can be fairly certain that the academic managerial class will not heed the call to mobilize against investor impatience and impulsive picking of winners. No, they will mostly, and eagerly, work against the recovery of autonomy by academic staff and students in any way they can. How, then, will mobilization against the managed university occur?

## INSTITUTIONAL AUTONOMY *FOR* ACADEMIC FREEDOM

One of the most serious flaws in the new AUCC "Statement on Academic Freedom" entails the promotion of institutional autonomy as a proxy for neo-liberalism in its claim to a form — indeed the most invaluable and pertinent form — of academic freedom in the current state of exception. This attempt at pre-emption casts academic administrators as accountability and austerity mongers, institutional brand managers, and eager participants in the First World scramble to recruit international students. This profound and damaging blunder on the part of AUCC has been accepted enthusiastically by most university and college presidents, with the notable exception of the former President of the University of Toronto, David Naylor. Academic managers have sought to stage or consolidate a series of internal coups and external capitulations on the basis of the new AUCC document, their decisions based on the ingestion of academic freedom by institutional autonomy asserted unilaterally *in extremis*. Instead of favouring this power grab, they ought to see themselves as in service to an academic agenda and its guarantors, namely, academic freedom and the collegial governance it prefers and operates. Institutional autonomy is a subordinate piece of the composite sovereignty of universities and colleges expressed in bi- and tri-cameral structures. If funders and academic managers fail to realize and act upon this truth, then excellence and prosperity will be the first casualties, with democracy not far behind. To repeat, how then does mobilization occur?

## INDIGNEZ VOUS! [TIME FOR OUTRAGE!]

I could have chosen for this concluding section the heading "Red Square" or #idlenomore. That choice would have foregrounded the capacity of our students to mobilize, and underscored the pressing need for a new intergenerational academic politics, if not a new intergenerational social contract such as is being explored under the aegis of the Royal Society of Canada in November of 2013.[23] However, such a heading brings with it two related kinds of vulnerability. Who did these young people sporting *le carré rouge* or heeding the socially mediated summon to prayer, song, and round dance really represent? The spoiled brats of contemporary Quebec? Naïve exemplars of the Indian problem? Such claims can be readily refuted,[24] but rather than doing so here, I wish to appeal to another example, one drawn from the oldest living generation who perhaps know better than others what results from failing to resist when fundamental freedoms and rights are diminished or suspended by dominant forces who insist on defining the state of exception.

Stéphane Hessel, the author of *Indignez Vous!*, was born in Berlin in 1917, became a French citizen in 1937, and during the ensuing war functioned as a soldier, an intelligence analyst, underground resistance fighter, and then escapee from Buchenwald and Dora-Mittelbau, before assisting (with Canadian John Humphrey) at the newly formed United Nations with the drafting of the *Universal Declaration of Human Rights*. Late in life, after a visit to the Middle East, this erstwhile resistance fighter, diplomat, and strong supporter of an Israeli state, wrote a pamphlet that has sold in the millions in a remarkable range of languages, and precipitated a remarkable act of silencing at an elite academic institution, L'ÉNS in Paris. Like Carl Schmitt, but in a very different register and to very different ends, Hessel's critique of Israel's actions in Gaza, and willingness to speak and write in favour of a boycott that might revitalise the peace process, brought a torrent of abuse upon his head as well as a swell of admiration and support from inside and outside universities around the world. His talk at the ENS was cancelled because of pressure from outraged Jewish groups. Hessel was outraged in his turn, taking a stand of the sort that academic freedom enables, if it does not require, scholars to take. To their enduring shame, academic managers shut down this much-honoured and deeply honourable man, at least in their notionally autonomous domain. But those who gave in to pressure, because they feared for the future of their institution, put the ENS at enormous risk in the name of protecting it. Audacious decisiveness doubled as despicable cowardice. Critique of Israel by a distinguished former *normalien* with impeccable pro-Semitic credentials was ruled off limits in an action Carl Schmitt would probably have deemed impeccably "commissarial." However, these decision makers could not detach Hessel's comments about Gaza from his comments about economic, social, and environmental justice — in France and across the globe — that had already made him a hero to so many. This man was not for turning or fracking. Hessel incarnated the human, for Schmitt a non-political category tied to the inhuman and "followed in the 19th century by an even deeper division, between the *superhuman* and the *subhuman,*"[25] as an unswerving commitment to human rights that should inspire and outrage us all. Hessel's treatment by the ENS throws into bold, and one hopes lasting, relief the frailty of institutional autonomy as a guarantor of anything, and the recurrent and arguably increasing capacity of the managed university across the Western world to forget its vocation and soundest forms of governance, consequently lose its way, and demonize those it ought most openly and unconditionally to celebrate: exemplars and guardians of academic integrity and the proposition that *nothing* is off limits to academic inquiry and debate within and beyond the frames of disciplinary expertise and professional norms.

Leaving *l'affaire Hessel* (like *l'affaire Dreyfus* ) to activate or intensify your outrage and resolve, and to prod us all into thinking more about ways to build progressive alliances beyond and against the managed university, I conclude with commentary from closer to home by

Rinaldo Walcott of the University of Toronto and an engaged participant in the Harry Crowe Conference from which this volume derives:

> To turn the analytical lens away from languages of domination toward languages of freedom and unfreedom is, for me, an attempt to reanimate what might be at stake in this moment of heightened information technologies and global flows of people, planned and unplanned; unprecedented corporate greed that is called profit, and the collapse of that scheme; the unabating spectacle of the commodity as a new life form; and the pervasiveness of neo-liberal ideologies, alongside the reassertion and display of new and old colonialisms that are symbiotically and incessantly reorganizing all of human social life. It seems to me that our task as scholars, artists, activists, and cultural workers more broadly is to think this moment in a fashion that requires more action and less sentiment.[26]

This is the voice of a scholar activist who will not abandon thinking for action, or naively or brutally separate action from sentiment. Instead, he urges his mostly academic readers to move aspirationally toward a transformative emphasis on action and a discursive emphasis on freedom rather than power. When the commodity goes viral, our managers and minders go ultraviral. That is arguably as true inside the academy as outside it. And the resurgence of freedom talk and freedom action for which Walcott argues must entail the reassertion of academic freedom as characterized in the policy documents of the Canadian Association of University Teachers and not in the managerial script produced by the AUCC. This is indeed a time for outrage, to combat the neo-liberal outrages we have witnessed and endured. May we idle no more!

# II. ACADEMIC FREEDOM AND DISCIPLINARY NORMS

# 3

# ACADEMIC FREEDOM AND PROFESSIONAL STANDARDS: A CASE STUDY

*Matthew W. Finkin*

## I. INTRODUCTION

The concept of academic freedom in the United States was shaped by the historical circumstances attending its birth. The terrain is familiar, but needs to be briefly traversed.

In the antebellum American college, governed by lay or ecclesiastical authority, the faculty stood in the eyes of its governors as little to be distinguished from hired hands; genteel, to be sure, but hired hands nonetheless. Toward the turn of the twentieth century, Americans of scholarly disposition, many having studied abroad, especially in Germany, sought to professionalize the academy. In this they made common cause with those university presidents who sought to shape their institutions more along German lines: to instil the capacity and desire for critical thought in the undergraduate body; to prepare experts for the professions and public service; to nurture future scholars.

The professoriate of the time, imbued with a sense of pride in its expertise, its independence of mind and mission, could not long endure the status of underling bidden to pipe the payers' tunes. The resulting manifesto, the "1915 Declaration of Principles on Academic Freedom and Tenure," captured the mood of the moment: within her sphere of professional competence a professor is not subject to lay disposition; she enjoys a professional liberty to test received wisdom, to propose new ways of thought, even to essay that which may be thoroughly distasteful — indeed, profoundly offensive — to the larger community from which the institution drew support.

At the time, that was rather much to ask. The profession sought to assuage any doubt in the matter, of the usefulness to society in the allowance of such liberty, by joining the claim of academic liberty to a corollary obligation: "the liberty of the scholar within the university to set forth his conclusions, be they what they may, is conditioned by their being conclusions gained by a scholar's method and held in a scholar's spirit" — that is, are the product of the exercise of a professional standard of care the determination of which, however, must lie in the hands of the academic profession, neither the governing board, nor donors, nor an outraged citizenry.

The bargain struck in 1915 — liberty in research, teaching, and publication in return for adherence to professional standards in its exercise — has been challenged by Professor Judith Butler,[1] taking as her target an essay by Robert Post.[2] Post's essay is exegetical of the profession's theory of academic freedom[3]. It is the profession's theory to which Professor Butler's critique is directed.

Professor Butler seems to see an antinomy in the profession's theory. The major premise is that academic freedom includes the liberty to challenge a discipline's fundamental assumptions, for how else does a discipline grow and change over time? The minor premise is that these can be the very standards of professional care, of truth-seeking and truth-expressing (if, that is, there is any truth) that cabin the exercise of that liberty. The conclusion: to sanction such a person, on the ground that her academic work fell afoul of the standards the dissident rejects, would abridge her academic freedom. Yet that, Professor Butler seems to claim, is just what the American conception of academic freedom does, the consequence of which is to abet a stultifying academic conservatism:

> If we assume that professional norms never abrogate academic freedom, and that dissent and debate over what those norms should be undermine academic

> freedom, we end up subscribing to a model of intellectual conservativism . . .[4]

A difficulty in addressing Professor Butler's critique is the conditional form in which much is said: the "if we assume" here, the "perhaps the profession" there,[5] and the "putative profession" later on.[6] On closer inspection, two different stances seem to be taken: one categorical, resting on the claimed antinomy; the other more moderate and which would appear, albeit on pragmatic grounds, to ameliorate the theoretical antinomy.

The following explores the two, then proceeds on to a real case. In it, the faculty member challenged professional norms in just the way that Professor Butler would seem to account to be an exercise of academic freedom, but which claim the relevant academic body rejected. The case gives us a vantage point from which to evaluate the critique and the role of professional norms in qualifying the exercise of academic freedom.

## II. THE APPARENT ANTINOMY

Professor Butler commences by taking up the idea of the academic profession as a "norm-bearing collective," which she accepts, but which she puts this way:

> [P]erhaps the profession is a community that is fundamentally a venue for debate and disputation in which norms are scrutinized, revised, invoked in evaluative judgments, reconsidered, and subjected to innovation. This community is also always debating the terms by which admission to it is decided.[7]

A fair statement. But she then qualifies it by insisting, or suggesting, that under the profession's theory dissent would be allowable only to the extent it conformed to extant norms and which theory would accordingly deter the creation of "'paradigm shifts.'"[8] Of this, she points out, norms change: whole new fields of study have emerged — women's studies, performance studies — out of dissent from prevailing academic norms. Might this not cause us to jettison the notion that any professional norm obtains? Not so. Each of these and their like has its own norms; she does not dispute the existence of any norm whatsoever. Thus, the question actually becomes: "which norms ought to be invoked and for what reasons."[9] "[I]nnovation . . . depends in part on working and elaborating new norms over and against established fields of knowledge."[10] The rub is that the profession's conception requires a set of *common* standards without which "the disciplines will lose the authority they require to make and enforce academic judgments" consisting in the application of accepted norms to academic work.[11] As we shall see, that is quite right. And so to it she offers this riposte:

> If it were always clear in advance which community and which discipline ought to judge a piece of work, and how membership in that community was determined, then one could rely on that putative community to make a judgment, and the matter would be finished. But scholarship often finds a home in one department at one university when it would never find a home in the same department at another university. This is because there are serious and important differences about which norms the discipline should use, whether the norms should take into account interdisciplinary work, and, if so, in what way, and whether modes of judgment need to be revised by virtue of new challenges to the discipline or new ways the discipline has been configured in light of interdisciplinary work.[12]

Professor Butler does not question the authority of those making these judgments — in performance studies or women's studies — to make them. The legitimacy of the decisional process depends on whether the decision makers have "thought critically and well about the norms that are needed to understand the work . . . or are willing to take account of changes and innovations in the field."[13]

At this juncture Professor Butler seizes on Robert Post's use of the phrase "norm application" to distinguish it from "norm interpretation." This attributes to Post a rigidity he explicitly rejected;[14] but it should be pursued nonetheless as it forms one of the pillars of Butler's critique.

Norm application she takes to be an essentially technical, almost mechanical, process of laying a scholar's work aside the presumptively static prevailing professional norm, akin to laying the facts of a case against the chancellor's foot, which process is foreordained virtually by definition to doom scholarship that challenges those norms.[15] Norm "interpretation," in contrast, is the more generous and capacious approach she describes above, one that opens the discipline up to new and creative modes of scholarship, which, apparently, only those engaged in it are equipped to decide.

To buttress her argument Professor Butler catalogues instances not only where a field of study has been reshaped, but also where important discoveries and new discursive practices were stymied, sometimes for considerable periods of time, by entrenched authority that failed the "social negotiation" of norm interpretation. Thus, she circles back to what she was willing to concede earlier, that academic freedom cannot be free of any and all normative judgment; it is, rather, that the decision-maker should have reasons — good reasons — for invoking the academic norms they "choose."[16]

## III. THE CRITIQUE ASSESSED

Professor Butler seems to make two claims. One questions the profession's theory. The other might actually be consonant with it. Let us take each in turn.

### A. THE CATEGORICAL CLAIM

Return to the assumption Professor Butler sets out in the sentence near the close of the introduction: that, according to the profession's theory, professional norms "never abrogate academic freedom."[17] Professor

Butler seems to argue that when these norms thwart or blunt the dissemination of new, arresting, and fecund lines of inquiry or discursive practice ("paradigm-shifting" approaches), adherence to them — but only an apparently mindless "technical' application — does abrogate academic freedom. Whence the antinomy.

Professor Butler is quite correct in that the profession's theory of academic freedom does not account honest professional disagreement about the value of academic work as an abridgement of academic freedom. But it is not clear, by the light of her less categorical version, that she would either, so long, that is, as those making the decision were equipped to make a sound judgment and were sufficiently open-minded.

Analysis is assisted here by use of an example proposed by Judith Jarvis Thomson.[18] Let us suppose a professor of astronomy discovers, as the product of years of deep study, that the medieval university was quite correct in including astrology in the curriculum.[19] Though they could not have known it at the time, our astronomer concludes that when several strands of contemporary string theory are strung together, the interconnectedness of all matter is revealed in such a way as to show how the alignment of the stars does influence human affairs. Let us further suppose that our astronomer insists on teaching this conclusion in his class, not as a possible philosophical consequence of contemporary physical theory, but as a fact of the physical universe which the students must grasp and display as fully as they do the heliocentric theory of the solar system. And let us suppose that his teaching dissents from prevailing astronomical norms, surely a fair assumption. To the profession, the application of those norms to deny him use of the classroom for that purpose would not be an abridgment of academic freedom.

Genuine disputes within a discipline about what work does or does not measure up are just that, intramural disputes about disciplinary standards, not cases of infringement of academic freedom. And Professor Butler would seem to acknowledge as much in that she is apparently prepared to concede that not quite all norms can be dispensed with. Whence her use of the word "never" in the statement of her challenge. But if some norm does apply, then an abridgement of academic freedom would be worked only when the judgment turned out, perhaps decades later, to have been wrong. In other words, if some dissenting views on what is work worth doing can profoundly transform a discipline whilst others are dead ends, and as some judgments that the latter is so would not abridge academic freedom (as some norm has to apply lest we license just everything and anything a professor professionally utters to be an exercise of academic freedom), only those judgments later determined to have been erroneous would abridge academic freedom. Professor Butler attempts to avoid this *reductio ad absurdum* by singling out not retrospective error, but the application of an absolutist notion of professional norms and a mechanical conception of norm application up front, so to speak.

The latter draws sustenance from Professor Butler's manufacture of a distinction between norm "application" and norm "interpretation," that is, from Professor Post's choice of words. Possibly because Professor Butler professes literature she sees significance in the use of one or the other. But Professor Post is a constitutional lawyer, and in constitutional law almost every "application" of the text is or can be an interpretive act. In fact, this is often so in the more mundane legal world of statutory application where even the resort to a dictionary can be contested terrain.[20]

Analysis thus returns to the claim that the profession's conception is one of norm absolutism. Neither theory nor practice supports the claim. Of the former, the profession's theory, Professor Thomson, discussing to our astrologer, returned as well to the "1915 Declaration":

> [N]ew fields, indeed, new ideas generally, have the burden of proof. And it might be worth noting also the connection between this point and that "conservative influence" the "1915 Declaration" said the university is likely to exercise. By its nature, as the declaration says, a university is committed to caution, and to "a reasonable regard for the teachings of experience." We fail to display that reasonable regard

> if we suppose that we are not entitled to act on beliefs based on past experience unless we can prove them true. No doubt some of those beliefs may be mistaken . . . it is fair to say, more strongly, that none of those beliefs is immune to revision later. But in the absence of reason to think revision is called for, responsible decision making does not merely allow, but calls for relying on them.[21]

As she explains, "reasonable regard for the teachings of experience" does not sanction a "willful refusal to be open to new experience." It is only that "that the university should not flutter in the winds of changing current fashion, which is entirely compatible with the prescription that the university should not allow itself to be dominated by the orthodoxy of a past fashion."[22] That an academic judgment turns out to have been mistaken — that we might later learn by convincing experimental evidence that the alignment of the stars really does affect the conduct of human affairs — does not mean that a judgment made today to disallow it being taught as a scientific truth was not responsibly made[23]; even less that it abridged academic freedom.

On the latter, the profession's practice, it is true, as Professors Thomson, Butler, and others have noted, important discoveries have been lost and keen but dissonant insights have been thwarted, sometimes for long periods of time, by the resistance of entrenched academic authority. (When this is the product of prejudice — on religious, gender, or racial grounds — as, at times, it was, academic freedom will have been violated, for no professional judgment was involved.) The dimensions of this phenomenon are unknown[24]; but the reasons are not invariably those of an excessive love of the familiar or a pigheaded closedmindedness, nor can we know the full extent to which genuine rubbish has been quite rightly consigned to the academic trash heap and would-be adherents directed toward more useful careers.[25] Given what Professor Butler takes to be an inherently conservative thrust of the "1915 Declaration," it might be viewed as rather remarkable that schools of thought, whole movements — feminism, deconstructionism, history "from the bottom up," post-colonial studies — scoffed at earlier are now considered not only respectable but *de rigeur* in some institutions, which poses the intriguing question of whether the heirs of these prior heresies will be open in turn to new approaches that challenge *them*.[26]

## B. THE PRAGMATIC TURN

Professor Butler posits a professional community "in which norms are scrutinized, revised, involved in evaluative judgments, reconsidered, and subject to innovation," in which, in other words, they are "chosen." And that is quite right, subject, however, to two caveats, the first of which Professor Butler seems to scoff at, the second of which follows from the first. First, as Thomson argues, the act of choosing is a rational process. One must have a reason, a good reason, to choose as one does. Second, inherent in the process is the ability to choose to reconfirm an extant norm when one has good reason to do so; that is, howsoever open-minded and generously receptive a reconsideration, to fail to be persuaded that a revision or innovation in standards is in order is not a violation of academic freedom.

Overarching is the question Professor Butler earlier put, of who decides, who chooses the applicable norm. Our astrologer would surely argue that his astronomical colleagues have such an excessive commitment to prevailing norms as to be precluded from judging the value of his work, that their closed- mindedness (if not hostility) works a violation of his freedom to midwife the birth of a breakthrough in our understanding of our relationship to the physical universe. He would argue, that is, for the creation of a department of astrology whose incumbents would be sympathetic to disciplinary norms that the hidebound in astronomy reject.[27] To make his case, he would surely point to the fact, as Professor Butler does, that the academic mansion has many houses: for the hard sciences, the social sciences, the humanities, the professions (and semi-professions), even the studio and performing arts — music, sculpture, dance — each with distinctive modes of judgment, different epistemologies, and even values. He might advert to the following from Professor Butler, that "norms have origins other than the well-meaning and well-educated judgments of professionals. Academic norms are wrought not only from cognitive judgments but also from a confluence of historically evolved and changeable institutional and discursive practices."[28] And, so, why not astrology?

Professor Butler's genealogy is a bit foreshortened. As Robert Wuthnow observed, ideas "are shaped by their social situations and yet manage to disengage" from them, to become subject to cognitive means of evaluation that are divorced from the social situations that gave rise to them.[29] Further, David Hollinger reminds us that, "any particular disciplinary community exists within what we might see as a series of concentric circles of accountability in an informal but vitally important structure of authority." That "in order to maintain its standing in the learned world as a whole, a given community must keep the communities nearest to it persuaded that it is behaving responsibly, and it must also, partly through the support of these neighbouring communities, diminish whatever skepticism about its operations might arise in more distant parts of the learned world, and beyond . . ."[30] That, for example, a program in performance studies or Asian-American studies has authentic scholarly content and is not merely fashionable babble or a form of academic clientism parading under a false banner.

In Professor Thomson's example, the institution's faculty — a body of presumably "well-meaning and well-educated professionals" — must make the cognitive judgment of whether astrology meets the academic profession's norms, not astrology's. It is a judgment properly placed before it and which it must decide; the decision cannot be delegated or shirked. Should the faculty judge that astrology fails to meet professional standards, it will not have violated anyone's academic freedom.

In sum, the "1915 Declaration" recognizes that a becoming degree of open-mindedness is necessary to give breathing space for new knowledge to flourish. However, the drafters in 1915 did not dispute the fact that common norms do or should exist or that a body representative of the academic profession — not the claimant group alone — is rightly situated to make that decision.

So let us turn to a case where both issues were presented: where a common norm was challenged as antithetical to, and a different norm demanded in the name of, a distinctive discursive community. The claim was made in a hearing held before a body representative of the institution's faculty as a whole. The faculty hearing committee rejected the claim. Did it have good reason to do so? Or was its decision one of unsympathetic norm application that abridged academic freedom and abetted a stultifying conservatism?

The norms applied in it were ethical. This might be thought to be at a remove from qualitative evaluation. After considering the following, however, it should become apparent that these are not segregable categories; that both involve standards of professional care.

## IV. THE WARD CHURCHILL CASE

Ward Churchill was a tenured professor of American Indian Studies at the University of Colorado. He was also chair of the University's Ethnic Studies Department. The events in question were set out by the Colorado Supreme Court:

> In late January 2005, public furor erupted over an essay that he wrote in the immediate aftermath of the September 11, 2001, terrorist attacks on the World Trade Center in New York City. Among other provocative claims, the essay likened the civilians killed in the World Trade Center to Adolf Eichmann, a Nazi officer and convicted war criminal for his role as the primary planner of the Holocaust. In preparation for a speaking engagement by Churchill at Hamilton College in January 2005, the college's newspaper discovered his essay and published its controversial content. Some students organized to protest Churchill's visit. The story and Churchill's essay were subsequently picked up by national media outlets and quickly mushroomed into a national controversy.

> In response to the public outcry condemning Churchill's essay, the Regents [the university's governing board] held a special meeting on February 3, 2005. Before and after the meeting, several of the Regents and Chancellor Phil DiStefano made statements to various media outlets suggesting that they hoped that Churchill would be dismissed as a result of his essay. At the conclusion of the meeting, the Regents unanimously voted to authorize DiStefano to create an ad hoc panel to investigate Churchill's academic works.
>
> [T]he ac hoc panel reported to DiStefano that the content of Churchill's essay, which it found did not engender imminent violence or unduly interfere with university operations, constituted protected free speech and therefore could not serve as the grounds for a for-cause dismissal of a tenured employee. During this preliminary inquiry, however, the ad hoc panel received several complaints that Churchill had engaged in repeated instances of academic misconduct in his published scholarly writings. In response to those complaints, DiStefano announced that the university would formally investigate Churchill for nine alleged instances of academic misconduct.[31]

A committee of enquiry was empanelled. After reviewing the academic record and Churchill's responses, given orally and by written submission, the committee ruled that seven of the nine allegations before it had merit and should be pursued.

The case was then presented to an Investigative Committee of the University's Standing Committee on Research Misconduct. It found several forms of academic misconduct to have been engaged in, acquitting Churchill of one allegation of plagiarism. The case was then presented for hearing before the Faculty Senate Committee on Privilege at Tenure, a standing committee of the faculty with jurisdiction in the matter. In other words, the Committee on Research Misconduct's report constituted an academic indictment, a set of charges, which the university administration was obligated to prove before the faculty's hearing committee, and, under the rules, by clear and convincing evidence.

A hearing was held. Professor Churchill, represented by counsel, presented evidence on his behalf, cross-examined opposing witnesses, and the like. On May 3, 2007, the hearing committee sustained some, but not all, the charges against Churchill. It was unanimous in concluding that Professor Churchill had fallen below minimum standards of academic integrity and that that warranted sanction. However, the committee was divided on what the sanction should be: two members favoured dismissal; three recommended the sanction of a one-year suspension without pay and a reduction in rank. The university president recommended to the university's governing board that Churchill be dismissed. Churchill appeared before the board and was heard by it. The board then voted to dismiss him. Churchill next sued in state court under a federal civil rights law and, after all the dust had settled, lost.

The interest here centres on only one aspect of the academic misconduct of which he was found guilty, not the lawsuit. But, because rather much has been made of it, a digression on the legal situation, for the purpose of clearing the stage for the academic, not the legal issues, may be helpful.

## A. AT LAW

Professor Churchill sued in state court for monetary damages and injunctive relief, i.e., an order returning him to his academic position. Relief was sought under a federal statute that allows a suit to be brought against persons acting under colour of state law who cause a person to be deprived of any right secured under the constitution. According to the Colorado Supreme Court, however, state law set out another route to legal relief apart from the federal statute. A person can secure judicial review of the action of governmental bodies or officers where, in the exercise of a judicial or quasi-judicial function, they are alleged to have abused their discretion. In such a case, the matter would be heard before a judge on the basis of the record compiled in the judicial (or quasi-judicial) proceeding; but a claim of violation of the *First Amendment* could be heard in such a proceeding inasmuch as action violative of free speech would, by definition, be an abuse of discretion. Although, in contrast to this state law, the federal claim could be heard by a jury, under the federal statute it would be for a judge, not a jury, to decide on the propriety of an injunction. Professor Churchill chose not to make a claim under state law.

On the federal claim, Professor Churchill alleged that the defendants violated his constitutionally protected right to free speech by: (1) initiating an investigation into his academic integrity in retaliation for his controversial but constitutionally protected speech; and (2) terminating his employment because of his controversial but constitutionally protected free speech.[32]

That is, his referring to the victims of the World Trade Center bombing as "little Eichmanns," not the published scholarship which the hearing committee held to have fallen short of professional standards.

At trial, the court granted the university's motion for a directed verdict on the first claim. Federal law has made it all too clear — rightly or wrongly — that the initiation of an investigation alone does not constitute such "adverse action" as to work a constitutional wrong. Even if the administration and governing board instigated the investigation because of Churchill's protected speech, in an effort to see if he had otherwise misconducted himself, the inquiry worked no constitutional harm per se.

The second claim was submitted to the jury. The jury found that Churchill was terminated in retaliation for his free speech. It awarded him one dollar in damages.

The issue of retaliation having been resolved, the trial court devoted a considerable portion of its opinion to whether Churchill should be reinstated. It declined to order that remedy. As the Colorado Supreme Court later explained:

> Just because the university used the discovery of Churchill's academic misconduct as a pretext for its

> violation of his constitutional rights, the trial court reasoned, does not make the findings condemning his lack of academic integrity any less meritorious.[33]

However, on appeal, the Colorado Supreme Court held that the governing board, in hearing and deciding Professor Churchill's case, functioned in a quasi-judicial capacity. As such, it was immune from suit for monetary damages under the federal statute, just as a judge would be. This would seem to leave Professor Churchill without any means of vindicating his right of free speech. Not so, said the Court. Professor Churchill had had available an avenue of review (although perhaps not for money damages) via Colorado law, noted above, but which he chose not to invoke. In the event, Professor Churchill lost the dollar the jury had awarded.

However, it is not obvious that that loss was of critical concern to him in contrast to reinstatement to his academic position. On that, the availability of an injunction posed a vexing technical question because it was unclear under federal law whether the immunity for money damages the court granted the trustees affected a court's power to grant injunctive relief. The Colorado Supreme Court avoided the question. It assumed the power to be available, but sustained the trial court's decision: as Churchill had been found to have engaged in academic misconduct and, as he testified, he "disagreed with the University's standards of scholarship" the trial court was within its discretion to conclude that reinstatement would "risk further instances of academic misconduct."[34]

Some in the academic community have taken strong issue with the Court's decision. The following, for example, appeared in an opinion piece in *The Chronicle of Higher Education*:

> The *First Amendment* right to speak out as a citizen — what the American Association of University Professors [AAUP] calls "extramural speech" — should have protected the University of Colorado professor Ward Churchill, who wrote an essay after September 11, 2001, in which he attacked the stock traders who

> worked at brokerage firms in the World Trade Center as "little Eichmanns." The university understood that right, and so, responding to pressure to get him off the payroll, found instances of "research misconduct." A jury concluded that was a pretext; but the courts decided that Churchill should lose his case anyway, because the university committee that had recommended his firing was "immune" from suit.[35]

Alas, this is not quite right. First, the AAUP's *Statement on Extramural Utterances* does separate political speech from professional speech. It acknowledges the faculty member's right to engage in the robust free play of ideas, and so the use of inflated rhetoric, that all persons enjoy in the political realm whilst nevertheless holding the faculty member to a professional standard of care in disciplinary discourse. The distinction, as Professor Butler has noted, can be fragile; it is sometimes difficult to distinguish the speaker's specific capacity when addressing an issue of public moment.[36] The statement acknowledges the conundrum.[37] Consequently, it would allow for inquiry into professional speech when the speaker's political speech gives reason to wonder whether the speaker's treatment of the facts in addressing a political question, by willful misstatement or wanton neglect, might characterize her professional work as well.[38] From what appears, the administration acted in conformity with AAUP policy, at least facially.

Second, the immunity-bearing body should to be clarified. The Colorado Supreme Court found the members of the university's governing board, the body that ordered Churchill's discharge, to be immune from suit. The university committee that had recommended a sanction was a standing body of the faculty, two of whom did recommend discharge; but Professor Churchill did not sue the members of that committee. However, the governing board did conduct a hearing. It heard an appeal from the faculty's decision. What strikes an observer as discordant is that the board would seem to have been acting as more of an employer than a judge. Consequently, the immunity issue is unsettling, and, perhaps, legally unsettled; but, for Professor Churchill, what was at stake in it was a dollar.

Third, and closely related, the Colorado Supreme Court did not refuse to order Professor Churchill's reinstatement — to cause him to "lose his case" in that sense — because the board of trustees was immune from suit. The Court refused to order reinstatement because it found no abuse of discretion in the trial court's reasoning: that it would be wrong to order on to a faculty a person whom the faculty found to have engaged in grave academic misconduct and who continued to reject the standards the faculty found he had violated.

The fourth and last really is the critical issue, the finding of "pretext." The jury found that but for Professor Churchill's "little Eichmann" speech he would not have been discharged. That much is indisputable. In that sense, his dismissal was caused by his speech: had he never uttered those words the whole train of events would never have been set in motion. But "cause" is not so simple a matter.[39] The administration's *motive* was surely to rid the institution of Churchill. Had the faculty not found misconduct, however, one is hard-pressed to conceive how the matter could possibly have proceeded that far. What gave the board *cause* to dismiss, what allowed it to effect its end, was the hearing committee's unanimous finding of academic misconduct.

By placing that finding within quotation marks the commentator rather scoffs at it. Whether she should or not will be taken up below. As much as can be said on Churchill's side of the legal ledger is that, if the faculty hearing committee was correct, the Board of Trustees railroaded a guilty man.[40]

## B. PROFESSORIAL NORMS AND PSEUDONYMOUS AUTHORSHIP

Professor Churchill was charged with several acts of academic misconduct. In one of these, in which the facts were undisputed, Professor Churchill challenged the applicability of the professional standard that the charge invoked. That is the issue of interest here. Thus the undisputed facts ought be laid upon the page.

In 1992, a volume was published entitled, *The State of Native America: Genocide, Colonization, and Resistance*, edited by M. Annette Jaimes. The book contains fifteen chapters and an epilogue. Three of these are authored or co-authored by Professor Churchill. Among the other twelve is one by Annette Jaimes, "Federal Indian Identification Policy: A Usurpation of Indigenous Sovereignty in North America." Ms. Jaimes is identified as a post-doctoral fellow at Cornell University. One is by Lenore A. Stiffarm and Phil Lane Jr., "The Demography of Native North America: A Question of American Indian Survival." Ms. Stiffarm is identified as an Associate Professor at the University of Lethbridge, Alberta, Canada, and Mr. Lane as a "recognized Indian leader." One is by Annette Jaimes and Theresa Halsey, "American Indian Women: At the Center of Indigenous Resistance in North America." Ms. Halsey is identified as a "long-time community activist." One is by Rebecca Robbins, "Self-Determination and Subordination: The Past, Present, and Future of American Indian Governance." Ms. Robbins is identified as an editor and former assistant professor of education at Arizona State University. And one is by Jorge Noriega, "American Indian Education in the United States: Indoctrination for Subordination to Colonialism." Mr. Noriega is identified as a lecturer in American Indian Studies at the University of Lethbridge. One essay appears under the authorship of an institute which is described as a collective founded by Professor Churchill and Winona La Duke, identified as a "well-known Indian rights and environmental activist."

The following year, Professor Churchill published *Struggle for the Land: Indigenous Resistance to Genocide, Ecocide, and Expropriation in Contemporary North America*. In it, he cites the Stiffarm and Lane chapter,[41] the Robbins's chapter,[42] and the Jaimes's chapter[43] from the previous book as independent authority regarding statements he set out in text. The six authors listed above did not write those chapters. Professor Churchill did. In his submission to the hearing committee Professor Churchill stated that, "from time to time" he publishes written work pseudonymously, sometimes, as here, using the names of actual people who have agreed to the arrangement.

According to the report by the hearing committee[44] and Professor Churchill's published commentary on the report thereafter,[45] he defended the practice on four grounds:

- No written rule of the university or of any professional body explicitly prohibited the "ghostwriting" of academic work.

- Ghostwriting is practised by and so must be an accepted practice in other disciplines, among academic historians and political scientists, for example, and is "apparently 'acceptable [. . .] in some law schools.'"

- In any event, once the person for whom the piece was written takes responsibility for it, by placing her or his name on it, authorship becomes unimportant.

And, especially relevant for purposes here,

- Whatever the norm may be in other disciplines, in American Indian Studies the source of the material is of no importance; what is important is what is said, not who said it.[46]

To a lay audience, this manner of argument might seem discordant, as it did to Sigmund Freud.[47] But the hearing committee was a judicial body and Professor Churchill's argument is a perfectly permissible instance of pleading in the alternative: "(1) there is no norm, no rule prohibiting what I did; (2) there is a norm, but what I did was consistent with it; (3) if there is a norm to the contrary, it should be abandoned because what I did embraced a more reasoned approach; and, (4) what I did is justified by the discursive practice in this discipline even if contrary to the practice considered normative in others."

As did the hearing committee, let us take these in turn.

1. *The absence of a particularized rule prohibiting ghostwriting.* The hearing committee concluded that writing a scholarly work, the authorship of which would be attributed to others, and especially for the purpose of relying on these works as independent scholarly confirmation of the originator's claims, was "inherently deceptive." No rule, no "specific guideline" was necessary. It is simply a matter of academic honesty. A further word on the absence of an explicit prohibition would be in order.

The American academic profession has not seen it as necessary or even useful to specify the many ways in which professional unfitness for office may be manifested, to propound an exacting code of conduct. A university is not a prison. In a prison setting the inmate suffers a loss of liberty and must endure conditions grounded in penal purposes that are quite at odds with the liberties of free individuals. To the extent that is so, the rules circumscribing inmate behaviour must be ascertainable by those governed by them and in reasonable detail, subject to the possible consequence that that which is not forbidden must be allowed.

A university faculty is a professional body subject to norms of professional behaviour, not to codes of conduct. It is enough that academic dishonesty is generally understood within the profession to be wrongful. If Professor Churchill's conduct was dishonest, was wrongfully deceptive, no more need be said of a precise regulatory nature to make it so.

2. *Ghostwriting is an acceptable academic practice as evidenced by its commonality in other disciplines.* Professor Churchill argued that ghostwriting is commonly practised in political science, may be taught in departments of communication or public relations, is not uncommon even among historians who have ghostwritten works — pointing particularly to Arthur Schlesinger Jr.'s ghostwriting John F. Kennedy's inaugural address — and is an accepted practice in schools of law.

The hearing committee drew a sharp distinction between politics, corporate public relations, and scholarship. Politicians may have others, even those in the academy, draft position papers, testimony, speeches, and the like advancing their — the sponsoring politicians' — positions under the sponsors' names. And a department of public relations might well instruct students in "image management," in how to draft corporate testimony, press releases, and the like. But, as the hearing committee opined, these do not purport to be academic scholarship. The committee found no evidence that the ghostwriting of scholarly work for subsequent scholarly attribution was considered an acceptable practice in any discipline, though it made a sidelong reservation about law.

As an aside, one would have to delve into the evidentiary record to glean what generated that caveat. Judges do employ clerks and, depending on the judge, a clerk might draft a judicial opinion. But that is a scribal function.[48] The decision is the judge's, not the clerk's. Law professors may avail themselves of research assistants to compile law, or other bibliographic material, and the professor might use these in producing scholarly work. At some point, it might even be that some of a student's work is taken over in bulk. But incorporating the work of one's apprentice is a far cry from one academic attributing to another academic work which the latter had not written.

Pseudonymity has an ancient lineage. Medieval alchemists deployed it, for example, to give greater legitimacy to what they had to say by saying it under the authorship of revered figures.[49] Professor Churchill deployed it to give greater legitimacy, the appearance of the weight of scholarly judgment, to what he had to say. When Professor Churchill wrote, in effect, that, "Annette Jaimes and Leonore Stiffarm and Phil Lane and Rebecca Robbins agree with me," or I with them, in actuality he was agreeing with himself. This constitutes deception.

3. *Academic ghostwriting is an acceptable practice because the person to whom the work is ascribed accepts responsibility for it.* According to the hearing committee, by the proposition's logic the person to whom authorship is knowingly attributed could well submit the work as part of her or his dossier for academic appointment, promotion, or tenure.[50] Such, however, would be a "fraudulent depiction of scholarly accomplishment."[51] The academy relies on accurate attribution for evaluation of candidates and incumbents; even sources of funding must be disclosed for the purpose of sound evaluation of research results. In the academy, who says it cannot be separated from what is said.

4. *The standard of care in American Indian Studies allows for the attribution of one scholar's work to another.* This brings us to the crux of the matter. As Professor Churchill put it, his practice draws from "the communally-interactive and sharing context of the indigenous societies — markedly different from that of the generally individualist and competitive 'mainstream' . . ."[52] According to one of his witnesses, "In traditional Indian practices, 'authorship has no importance

whatever'"[53]; and according to another of his witnesses, ghostwriting is "'clearly, clearly within the accepted realm of discursive stances of [an] [American] Indian studies scholar.'" "[A]nybody who reads anything in postcolonial theory knows that the idea of pose is absolutely necessary for a minority scholar to say certain things,"[54] referring to "certain themes sketched in" an essay by Homi Bhabha, "How Newness Enters the World."[55]

The two arguments should be disaggregated. The latter would seem to claim that Professor Churchill laboured under a need, perhaps even an "absolute necessity," to pose as someone else in order to say what he did. Let us assume straightaway that a poet or novelist might see the need to speak in another's voice; even that a minority scholar writing in a post-colonial milieu might be constrained to inhabit the colonial power's form of academic discourse.[56] But it does not follow that one who is at once an academic and an American Indian activist labours under the absolute — or any — necessity to pose as another academic and American Indian activist in order to write what he does; nor did Professor Churchill make any offer of proof as to why he had to publish any of these pieces pseydonymously in order to say what these pieces said.

Which turns analysis to the former and, arguably, stronger claim, of the discursive practice in the discipline of American Indian Studies. On it, the hearing committee found no evidence, other than the opinions of Professor Churchill's two witnesses, that the attribution of one scholar's work to another was an accepted practice in ethnic or American Indian Studies. According to the committee's summary of the evidence, neither of the two expert witnesses, professors of American Indian Studies, submitted or made reference to any pseudonymous scholarly work in the discipline, of others or their own.

To pursue the argument a bit further, it does not follow that the authorial practice observed in a communally interactive and sharing indigenous society is one that applies to an academic department engaged in the study of such societies, with respect to its scholarship. The two communities are not the same; nor are their endeavours. To be sure, it might be argued that the one should be transposed into the other: that a department of American Indian Studies should be a non-competitive, non-individualistic body engaged in the production of collective work on a pseudonymous basis.[57] In support of it, Professor Churchill could point to the fact that one chapter in *The State of Native America* was produced by just such a body. But it identified itself as such, in counterpoint to the rest of the book. Were this to have been Professor Churchill's claim, it is not clear why any of the work in the book, or in the field, should bear individual authorship.

## 5. ON REFLECTION

Did the University of Colorado's Faculty Senate Committee on Privilege and Tenure violate Professor Ward Churchill's academic freedom? The argument that it did proceeds from the four elements of Professor Butler's critique.[58] First, the body hearing the matter was not that of the relevant discursive community, it was a putative body and of a transdisciplinary character at that. Second, and closely related, the committee took itself to be bound by a common professional standard, not one geared to the community of discourse in American Indian Studies. Third, it applied a professional standard mechanically; that is, it declined to interpret standards in such a way as to be sympathetic and open to an approach that challenged the prevailing norm. Fourth, it abetted academic conservatism and in so doing signalled a decided lack of open-mindedness to and sympathy with disciplinary dissent.

The argument that academic freedom was not abridged proceeds from the "1915 Declaration" as further explained by Post, Thomson, and Hollinger. Academic freedom is a professional liberty in the exercise of which the faculty member is required to observe a professional standard of care. It falls to the academic profession — or, here, an institution-wide body representative of it — to decide what norms are common to the profession and to see that they are observed. In this case, the standard involved was one of academic honesty all of a piece with the shared understanding that a professor may not falsify evidence or misrepresent the facts. The hearing body heard witnesses and entertained argument from those supporting the proposition that pseudonymous authorship of scholarly work, contemplating future reliance on that work by the actual author without accurate attribution, ought to be allowed in the discursive community of American Indian Studies. It deliberated on the arguments and explained its thinking on them. It was not persuaded. Should it have been?

# 4
# THE RIGHT TO THINK OTHERWISE

*Mark A. Gabbert*

In 1940, reflecting on a professional culture of freedom, academic and otherwise, that had existed at Cornell University when he became a faculty member in 1917, the historian Carl Becker observed that "a professor, as the German saying has it, is a man [*sic*] who thinks otherwise."[1] It appears that he often expressed this opinion: the distinguished historian of US foreign policy, Fred Harvey Harrington, an undergraduate student of Becker in the 1930s, repeated to his graduate students at the University of Wisconsin Becker's saying that "a professor's *purpose* . . . [is] 'to think otherwise."[2] This right to think otherwise implies an individual component to academic freedom that in my view we overlook at our peril.

Not that we have any excuse for missing it. General strictures against institutional censorship and imposition of prescribed doctrine are, after all, designed to protect the individual teacher and scholar. In the most recent statement of the Canadian Association of University Teachers (CAUT), we are told that academic freedom entails for the individual academic:

> the right, without restriction by prescribed doctrine, to freedom to teach and discuss; . . . to carry out research and disseminate and publish the results thereof; . . . to produce and perform creative works; . . . to engage in

> service to the institution and the community; . . . to express one's opinion about the institution, its administration, and the system in which one works; . . . to acquire, preserve, and provide access to documentary material in all formats; and freedom to participate in professional and representative academic bodies. Academic freedom always entails freedom from institutional censorship.

And in the next clause we read that:

> Academic freedom does not require neutrality on the part of the individual. Academic freedom makes intellectual discourse, critique, and commitment possible.

Finally, lest there be any doubt about the relation between university autonomy and the individual nature of academic freedom, CAUT concludes with the following:

> Academic freedom must not be confused with institutional autonomy. Post-secondary institutions are autonomous to the extent that they can set policies independent of outside influence. That very autonomy can protect academic freedom from a hostile external environment, but it can also facilitate an internal assault on academic freedom. Academic freedom is a right of members of the academic staff, not of the institution. The employer shall not abridge academic freedom on any grounds, including claims of institutional autonomy.[3]

These passages are forcible reminders that, at bottom, it is the freedom of the individual academic that must be protected.

Most recently, in a work that certainly pays ample tribute to the normative power of disciplines, American Association of University

Professors' (AAUP) Past-President Cary Nelson reconfirms this emphasis on the individual:

> Although I agree that academic freedom cannot simply be construed as an individual right, it is fundamentally exercised by individuals within professional and institutional traditions . . . Academic freedom means that institutions should be very reluctant to intervene in an individual faculty member's teaching and research.[4]

But of course this emphasis on the individual's right to academic freedom exists in tension with a powerful insistence that academic work must be carried out within a framework of professional or disciplinary norms. Although the nature of such norms is not always specified, they run the gamut from the AAUP's 1915 insistence that academic work must be carried out through "a scholar's method"[5] to a more recent emphasis on the universally accepted disciplinary findings of disciplines which have achieved the status of "dogmatic knowledge"[6], so generally recognized are they in a particular field of inquiry. However defined, on this view, it is by defending a perimeter with the razor wire of norms that we protect what Thomas Haskell, writing about the "1915 Declaration," has called the "community of the competent" whose aim is "to establish authority and cultivate reliable knowledge."[7] From this perspective, such norms, methods, and findings are the basis for the production of expert knowledge, and it is precisely the untrammelled possibility of producing such knowledge that the provision of academic freedom is supposed to make possible.

An impressively lucid and thorough assessment of the place of disciplinary norms in our understanding of academic freedom is found in the work of legal scholars Matthew Finkin and Robert Post.[8] Since their work is chiefly concerned with countering what they take to be the danger of treating academic freedom as a right of individual academics at the expense of the justifiable limits on such freedom imposed by academic norms, their argument is particularly important to take into account here.

Based on the AAUP's "1915 Declaration" on academic freedom, Finkin and Post's position is grounded on the assumption that the university is an institution that exists for the public good as a site where expert knowledge can be produced. Academics, as the experts who create this knowledge through their research or communicate it in the classroom, must be free to carry out their scholarly work without interference from a lay public which does not possess disciplinary competence. Academic freedom is, therefore, best understood as the freedom of the community of scholars to function within a framework of professional norms and findings rather than an individual right akin to the rights to free speech that the public has under such protections for free expression as the *First Amendment* of the US Constitution.[9]

The point is that, while in the general realm of public opinion all views are equally protected, in academic life no such egalitarian reception exists. Instead, the acceptability of any purported academic findings must be warranted through some form of peer review as meeting the scholarly standards for validity in a particular discipline. Failure to meet these standards means that the findings are ruled out as not consistent with what is currently known. In sum, academics are hired, given tenure, and promoted on the basis of their capacity to produce work within a framework of disciplinary norms and findings that they must respect and of standards for truth that they must meet. The university is not a world where, as in the public realm, anything goes. *The New York Times* has a right to promote astrology; but an academic astronomer taking this view would soon find herself outside the discipline and out of a job, academic freedom being no defence against such a blatant violation of what could be considered the dogmatic findings of astronomy.[10]

Finkin and Post's rigorous emphasis on disciplinary expertise as the framework for academic freedom in research and the classroom[11] has to stretch a bit when it is necessary to address the question how academic freedom covers the realm of intramural utterances. While it is easily shown that experts in a discipline have the clearest claims to academic freedom in the realm of research and the classroom, one might think it is less certain how this qualification could establish the right of academics to participate in institutional governance and to criticize the policies of university administrators. But notwithstanding that particular disciplinary expertise does not necessarily apply to specific issues of university governance, Finkin and Post note the AAUP's designation of the faculty member's status as more than a mere "employee"; and they affirm the essential place of collective deliberation as assuring the success of institutions that must operate for the public good. The importance of the faculty member's experience as a scholar and educator therefore justify a level of intramural participation in post-secondary institutions that would not be acceptable in a private business existing for private purposes.[12] Here it must be said that the reach at least of more specialized professional norms has met a limit, especially by comparison with the realm of research where presumably a discipline's standards and findings have the most potent impact. Citizenship in the academy is warrant enough for this participation. In this realm, at least, something like free speech among academics, even when critical of the employer, must exist.

With respect to the problem of the protection for extramural utterances supposedly provided by academic freedom, Post and Finkin lay out the AAUP view that university administrators who proceed to discipline or fire professors whose public statements create adverse public images of post-secondary institutions thereby create an unacceptable chilling effect on individual academics which undercuts academic freedom in the realms of research and teaching. Extramural speech is, nevertheless, subject to considerations of whether the speech in question indicates academic incompetence and this is a matter for experts in the field to determine and not lay people.[13]

A view of the university as a knowledge producer, powerful as it is in capturing much of what post-secondary institutions do, does run up against a problem when it comes to developing justifications for academic freedom that cover the work of academics in the creative arts. Here the difficulty is to determine whether, for example, a novel written by a professor of creative writing is a contribution to knowledge like that made by other disciplines and hence protected by academic freedom in research or whether it is better seen as an extramural matter. The authors survey what they see as the somewhat ambiguous AAUP decisions on this question and conclude that the place of the arts in academic life is unclear.[14]

This analysis appears to pose a choice between a considerable stretching of our usual notion of what constitutes "knowledge," or removing the work of creative artists from the university to the public sphere. Perhaps this difficulty would be partly addressed if it were recognized that the university is not simply a knowledge factory. Rather, it is also a conservatory designed to preserve and further the capacity for a range of self-expressive artistic and cultural practices. Academics teach their students how to deploy the demanding modes of expression these practices require and how to apply them in innovative and sometimes controversial ways. The scholarly work of such academics, embodied in creative works intended to extend the capacity for cultural expression, should be as much protected as academic work against interference as that of any other professor. In the arts, of course, the place of professional norms, dogmatic knowledge, and prevailing practice must often give way in the face of individual creativity.

Finkin and Post are well aware of the problematic tension that prevails between the current methods and findings of any academic discipline and the reality that such methods and findings are inevitably themselves the objects of scholarly criticism and hence subject to revision. On the one hand, there is the discipline with its norms and authority, and on the other hand there are the practitioners in the field who may well call the current accepted norms and findings into question. The problem arises when this tension eventuates in a skeptical approach leading to an antinomianism that threatens to undercut the legitimacy of disciplinary standards as the basis for the progress of knowledge. Since it loses a sense of the limits imposed by academic norms, they see such a view as threatening to undercut the public respect for academic freedom which is based on the assumption that it promotes the production of useful knowledge.[15] They register the validity of some criticisms of peer review, but, citing Thomas Kuhn, they see it as an element of "normal science" involving "the unexceptional application of unexceptional professional norms".[16] On this view, the great threat posed by a definition of academic freedom as an individual right is that, instead of enforcing professional norms, skeptical peer reviewers will authorize individual dissent at the cost of weakening the scholarly standards which alone defend academic freedom against lay interference.[17]

Finkin and Post are not indifferent to the importance of providing protection for dissent from the existing consensus in any given discipline. In this regard, they argue for a "sensible and wise equilibrium between innovation and stability."[18] They cite with approval Joan Scott's eloquent account of how disciplines evolve through an ongoing critical encounter with prevailing norms:

> Disciplinary communities . . . [sic] share a common commitment to the autonomous pursuit of understanding, which they both limit and make possible by articulating, contesting, and revising the rules of such pursuits and the standards by which outcomes will be judged . . . This recognition insists on a place for criticism and critical transformation at the very heart of the conception of a discipline and so guarantees the existence of that scholarly critical function that discipline is meant to legitimate and that academic freedom is designed to protect.[19]

They might also have cited Judith Butler's further perceptive elaborations on the processes of norm transformation, which were specifically a response to a piece by Robert Post.[20] Butler has a lively sense of the way in which individual academics on the ground deal with dissent from their own normative positions, ranging from narcissistically driven refusal to consider innovation to generous admiration for new and original work.[21] What matters to Butler is a capacity "to be open to a clash of norms"; and by her standards "a good faculty member will welcome and reward a well grounded interpretation that defeats his or her own."[22]

It is, however, fair to ask whether either the Finkin/Post plea for "equilibrium" or the Scott/Butler hopeful confidence in the healthy and ethical functioning of disciplines adequately addresses the problems that arise from the commitment to normal science that undergirds these views. Though the Scott/Butler language calls us to meet an admirable ideal, in the end it arguably rests on a highly idealized view of how open the prevailing norms are to revision and of the way in which they are enforced. Certainly in this discourse the right to think otherwise is not robustly front and centre.

In light of the concern with skepticism about disciplinary knowledge that drives the vigorous defence of norms, it is worth considering the barriers against any such skepticism and the weight of practices in favour of prevailing perspectives. A too one-sided emphasis on norms risks having the effect of producing not critical minds but . . . well, normal academics. How could it be otherwise, when one considers the ranks of norm bearers that aspirants to membership in the community of the competent must please: undergraduate teachers, graduate advisors, and dissertation committees; followed by hiring committees and tenure committees; and promotion committees; and peer reviewers of work; and all this in synergistic combination with the norms of granting agencies. Throughout, the norms and their bearers are presumably fully in charge. With all this normative grinding there is little danger of producing too many closet enthusiasts of intelligent design; or astrologers masquerading as astronomers; or historians explaining the recent history of the Middle East as an episode in salvation history. But on the other hand, how likely is this process to turn out many critical thinkers? Is the encouragement to think otherwise at the centre of things? The risk is creating colleagues not much given to critical perspectives on either their discipline or the profession much less on the employer. The result may be the production of anxious careerists who, to paraphrase past AAUP President Cary Nelson's complaint, are too preoccupied with meeting the norms to participate in collegial governance.[23] Under the circumstances, who can blame them?

Once hired, disciplinary pressures hardly abate. Indeed, the technical means for increasing them are available as never before, providing a temptation for the ambitious university administrator. For example, in August 2012 Thomson Reuters Corporation published an ad in which they claimed that their web-based InCites technology for assessing research output and significance had been adopted by Canada's largest fifteen research universities. The technology was promoted this way:

> Built on data from Thomson Reuters Web for Science, the customized data sets in inCites provide analytics on authors, journals and fields, as well as connect to the universities' proprietary research management and profiling systems for full workflow integration . . .
>
> InCites is a customized, web-based evaluation tool that enables universities to analyze their research productivity and compare their output with that of their peers. The solution provides normalized metrics for repeatable analysis of outcomes, cross-regional impacts, discipline comparisons and standardized, accurate reviews for promotion and tenure processes. InCites can also serve as a support solution in ongoing quality assurance activities . . .[24]

Such bibliometrics presumably make it possible to reduce the complexities of considering promotion and tenure cases to applying a numerical score. Indeed, Thomson Reuters's claims to be able to parse the numbers in a way that "normalises citation average for subject field and age of papers Meaning [*sic*] you can now compare the geneticist with the historian."[25] Facing up to this digital big brother hardly inspires an academic to take alternative approaches that might not get published in the highly ranked journals or even at all, or to undertake projects that will take a long time. Who can afford disciplinary skepticism in such an environment?

Strategies of this kind are not limited to research. Consider the perhaps somewhat less insidious turn to the "tuning" of degree programs. "Tuning" is described as "a process of detailing learning outcomes at the program-of-study level — a mostly faculty-driven process to determine what students should know, and be able to do, by the end of their degree." The virtue of "tuning" is allegedly that it establishes outcomes on the basis of a faculty input at a number of institutions internationally not just the faculty deliberations at one university. Originally begun in Europe, it now counts participants in Latin America, Japan, Africa, and China.[26] Will courses now have to be designed to assure they are "in tune" with some set of agreed upon normative outcomes?

A different sort of assessment that points to the invulnerability of prevailing orthodoxies to transformative criticism appears at the end of sociologist Vivek Chibber's recently published study of the subaltern studies tradition in post-colonial theory. After nearly three hundred pages of vigorous critique of the assumptions and findings of this school of historical analysis finishing with claims about post-colonialism's failure to take account of recent historical developments, Chibber asks what the likelihood is that this particular version of normal science will be dethroned. The answer: probably not very high. After all, he notes, a dominant school of thought is not simply a set of ideas. Post-colonial theory is promoted through specialist journals, embodied in academic positions, and supported by specialist professional associations and book publishers. Moreover, any weakening of the theory's status presents a problem for the many academics whose scholarly production and standing are linked to it. Against these more material factors, mere argument and evidence may have no immediate impact.[27] One need not accept Chibber's conclusions about post-colonial theory to register the realism of his view of the difficulties of revising that or any other disciplinary stance. The essential point is that disciplinary norms are often well-defended against the skepticism that so worries Finkel and Post, and immune to the critical transformations promoted by Hunt and Butler.

Needless to say, the emphasis on norms can be highly popular with the employer. We were reminded of this a year ago when the Association of Universities and Colleges of Canada (AUCC) produced its brand-new, state-of-the-art policy on academic freedom apparently designed to serve the purposes of the neo-liberal corporate university. The statement omitted any mention of faculty rights to participate in institutional governance or any guarantee of protection for extramural utterance, and it made problematic claims for institutional constraints on academic freedom. Along with this went strong assertions of the responsibility of faculty members to meet professional norms while exercising their academic freedom. Among these propositions was that "Faculty have an equal responsibility to submit their knowledge and claims to rigorous and public review by peers who are experts in the subject matter under consideration and to ground their arguments in the best available evidence."[28] To this, CAUT responded that "However innocuous the intention [of this statement], the effect can be chilling. Do you mean that if peers view one's work negatively, one no longer has the academic freedom to pursue the idea?"[29]

The CAUT response is perfectly reasonable. And yet how effective can CAUT's objection be in an environment where we actually say so little about the proper limits of peer review to restrain the individual scholar? About the power of norms to shape our work? Should we not be saying more about the right of academics to be wrong, even in the view of their peers who supposedly represent the community of the competent? An overemphasis on professional or disciplinary norms at the expense of the autonomy of the individual academic opens the way for these kinds of employer offensives. And it is arguably a factor that encourages the highly problematic claim that institutions have academic freedom.

At the institutional level, of course, disciplinary knowledge and norms are always in play. Some version of them, for example, regulates who gets hired and who does not. Is this a place where any but an orthodox, neo-classical economist need apply? Will the only acceptable candidate for a position in Soviet history be one who takes a Foucauldian line on Stalinism? Will a paleo-Marxist who thinks he can salvage the social interpretation of the French Revolution get an interview? Then there are the local institutional norms for tenure, promotion, the awarding of grants, and so on. By now, we are in a realm of standards that are sometimes very far from being simply under the jurisdiction of the "community of the competent" alone. For the autonomy of that community is arguably eroded by the participation of administrators with a veto power and goals of their own; granting agencies with their own priorities; and, of course, the government and interested private sector actors. So given the evident potential for disciplines to affirm an orthodoxy that does not meet the standard for provisionality, and given the possible drift of norm setting to regions outside the control of the professoriate, the existence of norms in all their complexity and multiplicity may turn out to be something other than just a benevolent barrier against interference with the work of experts in search of knowledge.

Let us take a somewhat different case of the clash or contestation of norms. A Department of Economics for decades contained members representing a wide range of theoretical approaches. In addition to the usual neo-classical economists, there were Marxists and institutionalists, and some members were demographers or labour historians. For many years, a rough balance between the so-called orthodox and the heterodox others was deliberately maintained by careful hiring. Then there was a stretch of time during which retirements put the neo-classical contingent in the majority. This coincided with the arrival of a new dean who made it a project to assure the dominance of the orthodox side. The dean overturned hiring recommendations that would have benefited the heterodox side. Soon every new hire was a neo-classical economist, leaving the heterodox increasingly marginalized.

Subsequently, an external curriculum review recommended further strengthening the orthodox side. In the aftermath, teaching assignments and proposed revisions to courses threatened to make things more precarious yet for the minority. As a result, the right of the minority to think otherwise is arguably at risk, including the right of each individual to teach according to his or her best professional judgment. Here we have conflicting disciplinary norms, with the administration promoting one faction and leaving the other feeling like an endangered species. The solution to this is not to have recourse to parsing the norms, but rather to affirm that duly hired, tenured, and promoted academics have a right to pursue their own individual best professional judgment about such fundamental matters as what problems to investigate, and how to approach them, and what to teach, and how to teach it.

Departments inevitably change over time. Nothing says an academic unit has to be staffed in the same way now as it was twenty-five years ago. On the other hand, what of the individual rights of those colleagues who do not accept the neo-classical model of economic analysis? Would it be proper for them to be relegated to the remote fringe, potentially having their access to advanced students and to an adequate array of courses cut off? Are we simply to say, "Well, the majority of academics sets the norms" and academic freedom is not in question? Here it seems to me that a recognition of the individual right of such unorthodox colleagues to think differently ought radically to restrain any effort to force their conformity with some disciplinary orthodoxy, even if most economists accept it as gospel. To leave dissenters defenceless undercuts the critical contestation of norms that we claim is fundamental to academic life.

There is a further, very serious problem. It is that the reverence for norms can be played upon in quite insidious ways. As Ellen Schrecker has recently put it:

> Especially during moments of stress, when strong outside pressures demand the sacrifice of an institution's squeakiest wheels, many of its leading professors capitulate. The external trappings of due process ease the operation. Faculty members and administrators go through the motions of an official investigation that cloaks their capitulation in the language of academic freedom and claims that the culprit somehow violated the norms of the scholarly community and is no longer qualified for its membership. Rarely do the victim's colleagues protest. After all, it takes both prescience and courage to recognize how seriously the proposed dismissal threatens academic freedom and then to stand up against it. Such solidarity is as uncommon within the professoriate as it is in the rest of American society.[30]

Schrecker's own work on McCarthyism has provided a major example of how this deployment of professional norms as a fig leaf for political motives can work. American academe failed to protect from dismissal colleagues who were members of the Communist Party or refused to co-operate fully with Congressional investigators of alleged Communists among faculty members. The justification for this was in part the claim that any member of the Communist Party was a person who had entirely given up the intellectual autonomy necessary to the search for truth. Ruthless participants in a secret and amoral conspiracy, slaves of Communist dogma, manipulated by a foreign power, such individuals had no right to membership in the academy. [31] By definition, these creatures had placed themselves outside the "community of the competent," and universities should protect their autonomy and purge themselves of such before external authorities took the matter in hand.[32] Coming to this conclusion supposedly had nothing at all to do with politics; instead, firing the Communists could be presented as a matter of defending the norms of the academic enterprise by excluding those who were unfit for the life of the mind.

This rationale was widely accepted by the academic community, which was apparently happy enough to wrap itself in the norms. Some one hundred academics paid for this with their jobs or suffered other professional setbacks.[33] A more vigorous sense of the rights of the individual academic against the professional views of a majority of colleagues might have made it much more difficult to take this line.

The political deployment of the argument from professional standards is arguably still very much with us. The most recent example of it is the case of Ward Churchill, a well-known scholar of American Indian Studies and tenured full professor and Chair of the Department of Ethnic Studies at the University of Colorado, Boulder.[34] A radical critic of US policy, Churchill's comment in 2001 asserting that the employees of the Twin Towers on 9/11 were "little Eichmanns" created a public furor when it became widely known in 2005. The issue was soon a national *cause célèbre*, with Churchill becoming the *bête noire* of conservatives for whom the academic left, multiculturalism, and the existence of non-traditional departments like Churchill's were a standing offence. Administrators at the University of Colorado at Boulder found themselves under intense political pressure to punish Churchill for his outrageous comment: the governor demanded Churchill's ouster, and a livid state legislature passed a motion insisting that he be sacked. The Governor, Republican Bill Owens, had already chosen his side in the fight against people like Churchill, having earlier helped organize a meeting of the university's regents with representatives of the conservative American Council of Trustees and Alumni (ACTA). When university President Elizabeth Hoffman refused demands of Owens and the regents to dismiss Churchill, she was forced to resign. She was replaced by Hank Brown, who had once represented Colorado in the US Senate and was himself a member of ACTA. In the meantime, the Department of Ethnic Studies was swamped with hostile, often vicious e-mails demanding Churchill's head.[35]

Struggling to maintain some control of the situation while meeting rising political demands for action, in early February the university's Interim Chancellor, Phil Di Stefano, struck an ad hoc committee constituted of himself and two deans to investigate Churchill's scholarship and conduct, and determine whether there was a case for dismissal. What the committee found was that Churchill had merely exercised his constitutional right to free speech and hence could not be fired for his offensive comments. But Chancellor Di Stefano also reported to the regents the committee's discovery of several allegations that Professor Churchill was guilty of academic misconduct. Di Stefano referred these allegations, which were based on claims of Churchill's opponents within the discipline of American Indian Studies, to the university's Standing Committee on Research Misconduct. Though dropping two of the nine charges, the committee found the others serious enough to strike a committee of investigation to look into the matter. In Ellen Schrecker's opinion, by turning the case into one of academic misconduct to be resolved through academic due process, the university hoped to keep control of the case and head off objections from bodies such as the AAUP.[36] In any case, by taking refuge in the norms one could avoid the *First Amendment*.

As most are aware, Churchill was convicted of academic misconduct and dismissed. Though four of the five members of the Investigation Committee (IC) recommended penalties short of dismissal, the university's Standing Committee on Research Misconduct recommended Churchill be fired, and the chancellor concurred. Churchill appealed to the university's committee on Privilege and Tenure, which dropped two of the charges but still upheld the verdict of misconduct. Two of the five members of Privilege and Tenure voted to fire Churchill but the other three recommended lesser penalties. Though all of the committees found serious misconduct, in the end, only one of the three committees involved voted for dismissal; and a majority of the academics (ten of nineteen) involved in the process were in favour of lesser penalties. But, of course, the committees were never anything but advisory, which left the final decision to fire in the hands of President Brown and the popularly elected lay board of regents.[37]

Reasonable people will continue to disagree about the Churchill case. That said, for many, perhaps most, academics who had followed the case the norms had been upheld and that was an end to it.[38] For some, however, the Churchill case raised many questions. There were the problems of fairness: the IC had remained vague throughout on exactly what standards it was using to assess Churchill's scholarship.[39] Churchill was never informed that the committee chair had, prior to her appointment, written an e-mail that assumed his guilt; yet she was appointed, though it was also decided that any of the nearly 200 UC faculty members whose names had appeared on a petition in favour of Churchill were biased and hence disqualified from serving on the IC.[40] The IC's five members included only one person who had expertise related to Churchill's field of American Indian Studies, an interdisciplinary field where, in the opinion of one recognized expert, the questions of identity and genocide at issue in the case were "exceptionally controversial" matters.[41] Churchill was therefore faced with a committee that was arguably importantly unaware of the methods and issues of American Indian Studies. In the aftermath of the IC's report, two separate groups of faculty members and others from CU and elsewhere filed charges of research misconduct against the IC itself;[42] and in 2011 the Colorado Conference of the AAUP wrote a vigorous critique and refutation of the committee's findings.[43] The Colorado Conference report was partly based on advice from American Indian

Studies scholars Professor Eric Cheyfitz of Cornell University and Michael Yellow Quill of the University of Kansas and so reflected the expertise of two specialists in the field.[44]

Finally, there was the undeniable fact, recognized by all those involved, that the whole Churchill affair had been triggered by the public outcry in response to his constitutionally protected extramural comment; and there was the corresponding realization that the initial decision by Di Stefano to investigate was a violation of the university's own stated commitment to protect the academic freedom of its faculty, including protection of extra mural utterance.[45] The right to think otherwise is not easy to exercise if there is a standing threat that those who do so are likely to be subjected to a level of academic review not imposed on those who think the way most everyone else does.[46] Moreover, looked at from another perspective, Churchill's encounter with the investigation might be seen as at least partly about conflicting norms. The norms in question were, of course, politically inflected in the sense that Churchill's stance that US history is a story of genocide shaped both his activist politics and his assessment of scholarly questions and practices while those of colleagues possibly wedded more to notions of American exceptionalism were unlikely to view Churchill's position with much sympathy.[47] The eleven academics who filed one of the complaints of research misconduct against the IC concluded that "the Report turns what is a debate about controversial issues of identity and genocide in Indian studies into an indictment of one position in that debate."[48] Whatever one thinks of the charges against Churchill and his firing, the case is a reminder that in the battle over norms, counsels of ethical practice may have little purchase.

In the end, Churchill had one alternative left, which was the legal system. He sued the university for wrongful dismissal, and a six-person jury agreed that the university had fired Churchill for his *First Amendment* protected speech. It awarded him one dollar in damages — a sum which was the minimum allowable and supposedly took account of Churchill's claim that he only wanted justice not money. At this point, the National Council of the AAUP passed a resolution calling on the university to return Churchill to his position and declaring that the whole matter had been inappropriately treated as a discipline case instead of a scholarly dispute[49]. But this was not to be. The trial judge concluded that the university regents were legally protected against suit. He therefore quashed the jury verdict, remarking later that the courts should be reluctant to interfere in the affairs of the academy.[50] Churchill appealed the decision all the way to the Colorado Supreme Court, but without success.[51]

When Churchill appealed the Colorado decision to the US Supreme Court, the university's opposing brief emphasized the deference owed the institution. Reaching back to Justice Frankfurter's remarks in *Sweezy v. New Hampshire* (1957), the university's lawyers reminded the court of the university's right "to determine for itself on academic grounds who may teach, what may be taught, how it shall be taught, and who may be admitted to study". Thus, "When judges are asked to review the substance of a genuinely academic decision . . . [*sic*] they should show great respect for the faculty's professional judgment." By its refusal to hear the case, the Supreme Court implicitly accepted this position, which the university welcomed as a confirmation of its "right and obligation to ensure high professional standards from its faculty."[52]

Notwithstanding the findings against Ward Churchill, it was stretching the point to claim that this was merely "a genuinely academic decision." The origins of the case in an initial exercise of Churchill's academic freedom to make extramural utterances, and the refusal of a majority of the faculty committees or of faculty members involved in the case to recommend dismissal undercut that simple conclusion. As noted, Churchill's firing was carried out by lay persons, the very same ones who had howled for his dismissal before any academic investigation was in the offing. His right to think otherwise and say so was violated from the beginning.

The Supreme Court's decision not to hear the Churchill case represents an ongoing judicial drift in the US away from any tendency to regard academic freedom as an individual right and toward vesting it in the university. A key case here is *Urofsky v. Gilmore*, which involved a state law in Virginia forbidding state employees from accessing sexually explicit materials on line with the employer's equipment without a supervisor's permission. A group of university professors whose work entailed accessing such materials filed suit against the state on grounds that the laws violated their academic freedom in both research and teaching. Though they won in the lower court, the state appealed, and the professors lost. In its judgment, the Circuit Court observed that, insofar as academic freedom had any constitutional standing at all, it was not as an individual right but as an institutional right of self-governance enjoyed by the university. There was, therefore, no violation of academic freedom in the requirement that professors wishing to access sexually explicit material get permission from a university official such as a dean.[53] According to Sheila Slaughter, the case affirms a neo-liberal emphasis on the importance of untrammelled administrative authority as essential to good management;[54] and as she notes, the Supreme Court's refusal to review *Urofsky* implicitly affirms the attribution of academic freedom to institutions rather than individual academics.[55]

None of this leaves the individual academic's right to think otherwise in very good health. By contrast, the norms seem to be in pretty fine fettle. Certainly academic freedom as an individual right, however restricted by disciplinary norms we may think it to be, is threatened by the drift in US cases to attributing academic freedom to the university itself or by developing notions of university autonomy that have a similar impact. If ever there were a need for a more robust discourse about the rights of individual academics to think otherwise, whether against the prevailing norms of their disciplines, the policy proposals and decisions of university administrators, or on broader public questions, now is certainly that time.

In the end, for all that we must emphasize membership in the "community of the competent" as the basis for the individual's academic freedom, that freedom remains a possession of the individual academic. The individual academic's right to be free of "prescribed doctrine" requires that we defer to her or his right to think differently in any given circumstance. Any normative boundaries must be very broad indeed. As Judith Butler has reminded us, it is important to resist the temptation to "legislate a norm" where in fact the norms are multiple and contested. And it is our ethical obligation to "recognize good work that adheres to modes of inquiry and method that we do not share".[56] Two decades ago in a dispatch from the battle over norms, Joan Scott wrote that "universities . . . are places where separate and contingent, contradictory and heterogeneous spheres of thought have long coexisted; the grounds for that coexistence are acceptance of differences and an aversion to orthodoxy."[57] Protection of the individual academic's freedom to think otherwise is a crucial element in preserving this essential quality of university life. Failing this, we are left with a situation like that which existed at Harvard in the 1950s, where left-wing economists were often denied tenure ostensibly on grounds of incompetence — though the real reason was pressure from the conservative Board of Overseers. According to then Dean McGeorge Bundy, one such controversy over a Liberal candidate prompted John Kenneth Galbraith to observe that in these cases "Competency is always a disguise for something else."[58]

All that said, the balancing of a respect for disciplinary standards with the rights of the individual academic to think otherwise remains a permanent challenge for defenders of academic freedom. These difficulties only increase with the claims to university autonomy pressing against the academic freedom rights of individual faculty. The danger that academic standards will be eroded by epistemological skepticism is much less serious than the threat that the individual academic's freedom to think otherwise will be increasingly crushed.

Finally, on the matter of the limits to the reach of norms, it is salutary to keep in mind the thinking of Ronald Dworkin on academic freedom.[59] From an institutional perspective, Dworkin sees it as inevitable and entirely acceptable that academics should be hired on the basis of how likely it is that they will conform to the prevailing disciplinary norms and findings. At the moment of hiring and granting tenure, the reigning local community of the competent must have full liberty to distinguish among candidates on the basis of contributions to normal science.[60] Once this moment has passed, however, the individual academic's freedom must be increasingly respected.[61] What Dworkin refers to as "conversions" over time to other perhaps radically dissident approaches to professional work must be tolerated,[62] because academics must not be hindered in carrying out their "responsibility to speak, and write and teach truth as they see it."[63] On this view, the norms have the most power at the beginning of careers as they inform the decisions of academic "gatekeepers" who are in charge of hiring.[64] Given the rewards and pressures, no doubt the norms and prevailing disciplinary knowledge will typically continue to dominate most careers, but a space must be kept open for those who come to think otherwise.

With Dworkin there is a shift beyond Finkin and Post's definition of the university solely as a knowledge producer. For him, academic freedom is a critical element in "society's support for a culture of independence and of its defense against a culture of conformity."[65] While the production of knowledge and teaching the disciplines remain fundamental, the university also emerges as a space for ethical development enabling a capacity for individual choices about what is important and true. For Dworkin making this possible is a highly valuable contribution to the creation of a social order in which individual integrity and authenticity can flourish. The health of the university and society as a whole requires that those in it are operating on the basis of what they really think and not on some externally imposed norm.[66] This takes us back to Carl Becker's happy reflections on his life at Cornell, where the right to think otherwise was the fruitful governing principle of academic life.

# 5
# THE LIMITS OF ACADEMIC FREEDOM

*Joan W. Scott*

In its early articulations, at least in the United States, academic freedom was more than an individual faculty member's right. It was, in the words of Matthew Finkin and Robert Post, a compact between society and the university community, "the price the public must pay in return for the social good of advancing knowledge."[2] The title of their 2009 book, *For the Common Good*, conveys that notion: knowledge is a social good, which requires extraordinary protections. Academic freedom thus had a larger aim than *First Amendment* protection of free speech, which was, after all, guaranteed to all citizens of the nation. "Were academic freedom primarily a protection for the value of free and critical inquiry, which is a universal value in a democracy, public control over scholars would seem neither more nor less justifiable than restraints that apply to the public generally."[3]

The compact between society and the university community is premised on the idea that this is a self-regulating community in which disciplinary bodies certify the competence of their members according to strict rules of professional practice. The regulation occurs in at least two ways: first by discipline — individual scholars, in effect, have to pass a series of tests that demonstrate mastery; second by the institution of the university itself — the autonomy it supposedly enjoys from the pressures of politicians, businessmen, and others, rests on the procedures it has established for community membership, responsibility, and deportment.

Finkin and Post insist that without this compact, academic freedom is a weak, if not empty, concept. While that is undoubtedly true, I think they underestimate the tensions inherent in the theory and practice of a self-regulating community. In this essay I look at some of these tensions and I argue that they are unresolvable. This doesn't mean we should do away with the principles on which academic freedom rests; they are the ideals to which our actions aspire. It does mean that we become more aware of the difficulties we necessarily encounter when we attempt to act according to those principles.

***

The first tension is the one between disciplinary orthodoxy and innovative thinking. The idea of a self-regulating community of scholars emerged in the US along with new disciplinary associations at the end of the nineteenth century. Disciplinary associations were depicted as uncorrupted by the play of interests that shaped the world outside the academy, even if the scholars they licensed dealt, as Dewey put it, with "face-to-face problems of life, not with problems of technical theory." Dewey wrote about "an organized society of truth-seekers" by which he meant the newly created disciplinary associations of his day, those inter-collegiate bodies that set standards of inquiry and assessed the validity (the apparent scientific quality or truthfulness) of the ideas offered by their members.[4] In return for fulfilling one's responsibilities to the discipline, one received protection from outside intervention. It was, wrote Arthur Lovejoy in the 1937 edition of the *Encyclopedia of the Social Sciences*, "qualified bodies of his own profession" that protected an individual scholar from interference by "political or ecclesiastical authority, or from the administrative officials of the institution in which he is employed."[5] Glenn Morrow in the 1968 edition of the *International Encyclopedia of the Social Sciences* echoed his forebearers:

> Even after prolonged examination and testing, the claim [to truth] can be accorded only a high degree of probability; and its status is never immune to later

> criticism. These conditions imply a community of scholars and scientists cooperating with one another through mutual criticism and selecting and recruiting new members through disciplined and systematic training. These very requirements tended to produce such a community, animated by a professional spirit and resentful of any attempts by incompetent outside authorities to control its activities or judge its results.[6]

Indeed disciplinary authorization was meant to defend those whose work was unavoidably controversial against charges of partisanship and from political retribution. If their colleagues attested to the soundness of their methods and the plausibility of their interpretations, these faculty could be represented not as interested parties, but as objective seekers after truth.

Yet, as is well-known to all of us, disciplinary communities are hierarchical with a power dynamic of their own. If the community certifies the competence of its members and protects them from external meddling, it also establishes methods of inquiry ("disciplined and systematic training"), standards of judgment ("selecting and recruiting new members"), as well as behavioural norms ("co-operating through mutual criticism"). Those who write the history of disciplines and those of us who have broken new ground in our fields know that discipline and disciple can be synonyms as well as antonyms, and that punishment is not always the alternative to discipline, but often its regulatory tool. The devastating review, the charges of incomplete research, mockery by one's elders can bring an end to a promising academic career, especially one that engages in a critique of disciplinary premises. These are not external interventions by the incompetent into the workings of the academy; they are internal conflicts, involving not public morality or conventional social belief, but disciplinary *politics*. And, of course, even the line drawn between disciplinary politics and those of the "outside world" is not a clear one, since, as Dewey and his colleagues recognized a century ago, research in the human sciences especially is often inspired by contemporary concerns with inevitable political ramifications.

Those of us historians who challenged prevailing views in the name of disciplinary redefinition well remember the kind of opposition we faced when we asked who got to count as a historian, what got to count as history, and how those determinations were made. The critique — and it was a critique in the technical philosophical sense of the term: an interrogation of founding premises, an illumination of methodological and interpretive blind spots — was aimed at the very grounds on which the field was based and at the notion that there could be a single prototype of a disciplinary subject. A woman historian was not just a historian with female genitals, but someone who might bring different perspectives to her work. How did those perspectives affect the idea of an appropriate historical inquiry? Women's history was not just another topic, a minor theme in the exalted stories of nations and their leaders, it was for many of us an inquiry into the founding assumptions of so-called mainstream history. (African-American history, post-colonial history, queer history offered similar interrogations.) The reply was often furious, and it wielded the weapons of the strong in a defence of scholarship against corruption by politics. They were professionals; we were politicizing history by exposing the ways in which standards of inclusion effectively discriminated on the basis of gender or race. They were defending the terrain of disinterested history; we were substituting ideology for scholarly rigour. Reviewing a book on nineteenth-century French women, Norman Hampson dismissed it as "uterine history," and Lawrence Stone, offering his ten commandments to historians of women, warned of the dangers of "distorting evidence" to "support modern feminist ideology" — as if the meaning of evidence were unequivocal and otherwise presented no problems about the position, point of view, and interpretations of historians.[7] Accusations from feminists of male bias were greeted as political and ideological; the men's rejection of women's history was taken as a defence of the integrity of the field.

Post-structuralism met an even more vehement refusal, the intensity of which differed according to discipline. Lawrence Stone (erstwhile champion of history) denounced Foucault as a failed or *faux* historian. Some literary critics (and many others, of course) used Paul De Man's early Nazi writings to call the entire "linguistic turn" into question. The charges of nihilism and moral relativism, of destruction (a play on Derrida's deconstruction), and irrelevance portrayed the struggle in Manichaean terms. The guardians of orthodoxy were defending mastery and excellence against those who, they claimed, were directly or indirectly bringing political considerations into a hitherto purely objective arena. Hence John Searle:

> The biggest single consequence of the rejection of the Western Rationalistic Tradition is that it makes possible an abandonment of traditional standards of objectivity, truth, and rationality, and opens the way for an educational agenda, one of whose primary purposes is to achieve social and political transformation.[8]

In 1985, as these struggles were unfolding, a report of the American Association of University Professors' (AAUP's) Committee A on Academic Freedom and Tenure warned that orthodoxy might endanger academic freedom, in effect acknowledging the existence of power dynamics internal to disciplinary communities. The report came in response to an inquiry from Stanford law school Professor Paul Brest about a comment by Paul Carrington, then Dean of the Duke law school. Carrington had written that those who identified with "critical legal studies" disqualified themselves from any law school faculty appointment. The report rejected Carrington's statement, maintaining that belief in the governing principles of a discipline ought not to be a condition of employment:

> In many instances a show of disrespect for a discipline is, at the very same time, an expression of dissent from the prevailing doctrines of that discipline. There is more than a sonant connection between respectfulness and respectability; there is no wide gap between respectability and ideological conventionalism. Thus, while a litmus test of belief in the worth of a subject

> as a minimum qualification for appointment to a position where one is expected to teach it or teach about it may seem modest in the abstract, on reflection it may prove to be very mistaken; it may end by barring those most likely to have remade the field . . . It is not merely that the long history of academic freedom teaches that charges of irreverence can readily serve as covers to objections to unorthodoxy; rather, it is that it is all but impossible to extenuate the one without abetting the other.[9]

The internal/external, thought/action contrast, which makes power and politics the activity of threatening outsiders has, on the one hand, been taken as the necessary condition for faculty and university autonomy, yet — as the AAUP statement makes clear — it also masks the challenge posed by the legitimating disciplinary authority to the free exercise of critical thought. Disciplinary communities provide the consensus necessary to justify academic freedom as a special freedom for faculty. But the inseparable other side of this regulatory and enabling authority is that it can suppress innovative thinking in the name of defending immutable standards. Paradoxically, the very institutions that are meant to legitimize faculty autonomy can also function to undermine it.

* * *

Another tension has to do with the relationship between the institution of the university (understood as the community of scholars beyond their disciplinary affiliations) and individual faculty members. There are two aspects to this tension I want to explore. The first has to do with what Marjorie Heins calls "academic freedom as an institutional right."[10] She notes that although there were earlier precedents, it was only late in the twentieth century that the US Supreme Court introduced "a tension between claims of university autonomy . . . and teacher autonomy . . ." Heins cites a passing remark by Justice John Paul Stevens in a case involving the right of a university to terminate a medical student. Stevens noted that academic freedom "thrives not only on the independent and uninhibited exchange of ideas among teachers and students . . . but also, and somewhat inconsistently, on autonomous decision making by the academy itself."[11] Universities have refused, on these grounds, to respond to discrimination claims by faculty who were denied tenure. They claim that academic freedom protected them from having to reveal confidential peer-review materials, citing Justice Frankfurter in *Sweezy v. New Hampshire* (1957) that among the four freedoms a university possessed was the right "to determine for itself on academic grounds who may teach." This notion, of course, has its positive side when it is invoked against the outside interference of politicians, lobbyists, and others. Judith Shapiro, former President of Barnard, fended off a group of alumnae who sought the firing of anthropology Professor Nadia Abu el Haj, on the grounds that she was critical of Israel's treatment of the Palestinians, and that this criticism showed she lacked scholarly integrity. Shapiro replied that the university and Abu el Haj's colleagues — the community of scholars — were the best judges of her competence to write and teach. The negative side, though, is evident when a university claims that academic freedom protects its right "to set its own agenda, to police its employees, and to hire and fire free from interference by the state."[12] When it is the state that investigates and adjudicates charges of employment discrimination based on sex or race or other differences, and it is the university that discriminates, this creates a conflict not easily resolved.

* * *

The need for the university to protect itself from outside interference and thus to discipline faculty who are thought to bring disrepute to the institution is another aspect of this tension. This usually comes under the rubric of responsibility (what is expected from faculty in return for the rights they enjoy), especially in the area of extramural speech. To what extent do a professor's words and actions outside the classroom — despite being protected by the *First Amendment* in the United States's guarantee of freedom of speech — violate his or her duties to the community of scholars to which they belong? Finding an appropriate answer has roiled members of Committee A over the years, as they went back and forth between free speech rights on the one hand, and the "peculiar obligation [of professors] to refrain from intemperate or sensational modes of expression," on the other.[13] In the AAUP's 1940 statement, the admonition to "make every effort to indicate that he is not an institutional spokesman" was added to the list of professorial responsibilities when exercising extramural speech.[14]

Despite these warnings, it has been difficult to arrive at a usable definition of professorial responsibility in relation to extramural speech, as any number of cases demonstrate. Here I will cite only three. The first case actually occasioned a debate among AAUP leaders about the value of invoking "academic responsibility" as a test of professorial merit. It concerned an assistant professor of biology at the University of Illinois in 1963 who wrote a letter to the editor of the student newspaper which so outraged public opinion that he was dismissed by the president. Leo Koch's letter was about sex. In response to an article by two students complaining about the ritualized nature of relations between men and women on campus, Koch counselled greater freedom. Arguing that the students treated the issue too narrowly, he diagnosed a "serious social malaise . . . caused . . . by the hypocritical and downright inhumane moral standards engendered by a Christian code of ethics which was already decrepit in the days of Queen Victoria."[15] The cure was to end the psychological inhibition of healthy needs by condoning sexual intercourse "among those sufficiently mature to engage in it without social consequences [i.e., by using modern contraceptives and with good medical advice] and without violating their own codes of morality and ethics." The response, as one can imagine, was explosive. It was led by the Reverend Ira Latimer, a member of the University of Illinois's Dad's Association who (following the double standard of the day) wrote to parents of *women* students. He called Koch's letter "an audacious attempt to subvert the religious and moral foundations of America" and identified it as the "standard operating procedure of the Communist conspiracy."[16] Letters of protest poured in to university administrative offices. Following the recommendations of the executive committee of the College of Liberal Arts and Sciences, the president decided that "Professor Koch's published letter constitutes a breach of academic responsibility so serious as to justify his being relieved of his University duties." He went on "the views expressed are offensive and repugnant, contrary to commonly accepted standards of morality and their public espousal may be interpreted as encouragement of immoral behaviour. It is clear that Mr. Koch's conduct has been prejudicial to the best interests of the university."[17] Here was a statement that called for condemnation if one took critical thinking to be the mission of the university and if the free speech rights of citizens were to be respected. There was never evidence presented either that Koch (a botanist) uttered these views in his classroom or that he was unfit to teach his subject. Indeed, his colleagues on the faculty senate committee on academic freedom concluded that at most his letter deserved a reprimand. The AAUP investigating committee agreed, concluding that there were administrative violations both procedural and principled, and it called upon the board of trustees to resist public pressure, to "take a broader view of the function of the university and the value of academic freedom . . . to recognize [the university's] maturity, its ability to absorb a few gadflies and its need for uninhibited freedom of discussion."[18]

The investigating committee went on at some length about the utility of the notion of academic responsibility, arguing, in effect, that in cases of extramural utterance an individual faculty member's rights as a citizen could not be limited by such a vague and ambiguous term. Citing a passage from John Stuart Mill's "On Liberty," they maintained that "any serious application of the standard would tend to eliminate or discourage any colorful or forceful utterance. More likely . . . the standard would be reserved as a sanction only for the expression of unorthodox opinion."[19] These comments gave rise to heated debate among the members of Committee A (which receives and acts on these investigatory reports) and to the publication, along with the report, of two statements on "Academic Responsibility," one the majority view, the other a dissent. While not disagreeing with the investigators' conclusion that Professor Koch had been denied due process and while conceding that "academic responsibility is admittedly very difficult to define," the majority nonetheless insisted that academic responsibility was a standard worth enforcing because: "we can hardly expect academic freedom to endure unless it is matched by academic responsibility."[20] The notion might, of course, be abused, but this was not grounds for denying its importance. "The remedy is, instead, insistence on proper procedural safeguards, a highly significant role for the faculty. . . and a vigilant oversight by this Association."[21] The dissenters were not convinced. They insisted that the majority had misinterpreted the 1940 statement which, on the question of speech outside the classroom, was unambiguous: "by law, in the expression of his opinions, the teacher is no less free than other citizens."[22] The only legitimate ground for dismissal was — historically and in the present — "demonstrated unfitness to teach."

> To speak of 'academic responsibility' as a standard or test for dismissal because a teacher has expressed an unpopular opinion without anchoring it to unmistakable particulars is to waver on a floating bog of semantics.[23]

The dissenters continued, a special standard of academic responsibility not only treated teachers differently from other citizens, but it also opened

> a Pandora's box of all the coercive and compulsive crusades of sectarian, political, and economic pressure groups together with consequent attempts at dismissal by administrators who are unable to resist the public pressure engendered by such groups whose causes often contain more heat than light.[24]

Oberlin College English Professor Warren Taylor, the author of the dissent, undoubtedly had the previous decade's experience in mind. During the McCarthy period, many faculty were fired, some for having admitted to membership in the Communist Party, some for simply having been accused of such membership, some for having declined to name names, and others for having taken the *Fifth Amendment*.[25] "Academic responsibility" was directly or indirectly used as a justification for these firings. Sometimes the need to protect the university from legislative intervention was the reason, sometimes the refusal of the professor to come clean with his colleagues inside the university was the issue, sometimes it was that communism was by definition antithetical to free thought. Thus the American Committee for Cultural Freedom (the group of Cold War intellectuals founded in 1951) argued that "a member of the Communist Party has transgressed the canons of academic responsibility, has engaged his intellect to servility, and is therefore professionally disqualified from performing his functions as a teacher."[26] This logic substituted for any need to provide concrete evidence of scholarly or pedagogic unfitness. And it ruled out the possibility that, for some faculty at least, communism was more about developing a critical theory of society than it was about offering unquestioned obeisance to the Soviet state.

Most often, as Warren Taylor had predicted, academic responsibility was invoked when administrators or trustees were unable to resist public pressure to punish a professor whose off-campus speech had offended some group's sensibility. In these cases, the responsibility was not to think freely (not to exemplify the function of the university), but to protect the public reputation of the university (by refraining from the expression of critical ideas). AAUP investigators found themselves time and again arguing against administrative judgments "in applying what are necessarily somewhat imprecise standards for the limits of propriety of extramural controversy."[27] In most of these instances, in fact, faculty committees (and AAUP investigators) made a case for a professor whose extramural speech was deemed outrageous based not on the content or style of that speech, but on the fairness (according to AAUP recommendations) of procedures followed in judging the individual and, usually more importantly, on the quality of his or her professional standing as a scholar and teacher. In this they carefully restricted "academic responsibility" to the fulfillment of teaching and disciplinary requirements, thereby reinforcing the distinction between knowledge production and politics as forms of activity, not as personal qualities that separated professors from ordinary people. That they did not usually prevail is an indication, I think, of the difficulty of maintaining the distinction in practice.

The second case is that of Angela Davis, who was not renewed as a lecturer in philosophy at UCLA in 1970 because of her membership in the Communist Party and because in public speeches she attacked police as "pigs" and maintained that academic freedom was an "'empty concept' if divorced from freedom of political action or if 'exploited' to maintain such views as the genetic inferiority of black people."[28] Her colleagues argued that nothing in her lectures or classroom behaviour indicated dereliction of duty.[29] Students talked about her courses as rigorous and open-minded; they were not expected to parrot her conclusions which were, in any case, offered as tentative interpretations. If her off-campus rhetoric was inflated, inaccurate, and even "distasteful and reprehensible," it had not spilled over into her research and teaching. One of the few regents who opposed her firing noted that "in this day and age when the decibel level of political debate . . . has reached the heights it has, it is unrealistic and disingenuous to demand as a condition of employment that the professor address political rallies in the muted cadences of scholarly exchanges. Professors are products of their times even as the rest of us."[30] Absent here was the idea that "academic responsibility" extended beyond one's purely academic responsibilities. Although the style and manner of one's performance counted (Davis was said to be as calm in the classroom as she was outrageous in public), it did so only within the walls of academe. Though this was the dissenting opinion of a regent in the Davis case, it came increasingly to characterize the restriction of the notion of academic responsibility to things academic. There was indeed a separation between knowledge and politics, but an academic could participate in both as long as she distinguished between her roles as a scholar and a citizen. Academic freedom was meant to guarantee this separation in theory, difficult as it might be to maintain in practice.

But what if a professor's political engagement led to revelations about the quality of his or her scholarship? This is what happened in the case of Ward Churchill at the University of Colorado. Churchill's reference to the World Trade Center's September 11, 2001, bombing victims as "little Eichmanns" who deserved their fate, infuriated the regents of the university. In response to demands from the regents and the governor that he be fired immediately, the administration of the university (following AAUP procedures) asked a faculty committee to examine his professional competence. The inquiry into his work produced information about "research misconduct" considered so damning that neither the committee nor the AAUP felt they could come to his rescue. It was certainly true, his colleagues conceded, that there would have been no examination of his scholarly opus if the political charges hadn't been made, yet given the questionable nature of his academic credentials and the extensive criticism that came from within his own field of American Indian studies, it was extremely difficult to make a strong bid for his retention.[31]

Although the Churchill and Davis cases differed on the question of the scholarly integrity and teaching performance of the professor, both were fired and for the same reasons: their extramural speech incurred the wrath of outside groups whose power influenced the decisions of university administrators. These were cases that revealed the weakness of the notion that a full separation was in fact possible between thought and action, scholarship, and politics. Academic freedom was easily compromised by a notion of academic responsibility that could be extended to include the responsibility to protect the university from exactly those forces that Dewey and his colleagues in 1915, and subsequent generations of AAUP spokesmen, warned would compromise its mission of free and critical inquiry.

* * *

The separation between extramural speech and classroom speech posits a separation that is hard to maintain because it doesn't take account of the fact that one's sense of responsibility as a citizen could affect one's scholarship. That was surely the case for the AAUP founders, many of whom were treated punitively for their progressive views on economics and politics.

That has been the case recently for teachers of Middle Eastern studies who are perceived to be too critical of Israel's current policies; for biologists who reject creationism; and for historians who are deemed insufficiently patriotic according to neo-conservative standards. But where is the line between polemical advocacy and critical scholarship in work that is informed by some kind of deeply held political or ethical commitment on the part of the professor? This is especially the case in the humanities and social sciences, where scholarly work necessarily engages social issues. It is here (as John Dewey noted) that the protection of academic freedom is most vital. Social scientific research, he warned, was more likely to come up against "deep-rooted prejudice and intense emotional reaction" because it addressed "habits and modes of life to which the people have accustomed themselves. To attack them is to appear to be hostile to institutions in which the worth of life is bound up."[32]

It is precisely in these cases that the university's institutional interest and the autonomy of individual faculty ought to coincide in defence of academic freedom, but, as Heins has pointed out, the pressures of politics and money have made these increasingly antithetical interests.[33]

In pointing out the ongoing tensions that the principle of academic freedom mediates, I don't mean to call its utility into question. On the contrary, it seems to me that it is precisely because the tensions evident a century ago continue to trouble the relationships among faculty, administrators, and boards of trustees; because the value of critical thinking is regularly under siege in the disciplines, the universities, and the nation; and because the tensions I've been describing are not susceptible to final resolution, that we need this principle in our ongoing struggle to preserve that which is best about universities and university education — the commitment to free and unfettered inquiry as an ideal which we reach for, even as its attainment never seems quite complete. The French historian/philosopher Michel de Certeau put it nicely in a discussion of ethics: "Ethics," he wrote, "is articulated through effective operations, and it defines a distance between what is and what ought to be. The distance designates a space where we have something to do."[34] Academic freedom is the principle that gives us something essential to do on the increasingly fraught terrain of the university.

# III. ACADEMIC FREEDOM AND RELIGIOUS BELIEF

# 6

# ACADEMIC FREEDOM AS A CONSTRAINT ON FREEDOM OF RELIGION

*John Baker*

## FRAMING THE QUESTION

1. My question in this paper is whether plausible sense could be made of an institution's claim that it can (i) require compliance with some or all of the tenets of some religion and yet (ii) be capable of fulfilling the societal roles which any institution deserving to be called a university can reasonably be expected to fulfill.

The question, framed this way, is not a question about a clash between secular and religious beliefs and values, for Anglicans or Muslims exercising their academic freedom in a university that *required* Roman Catholic beliefs or values would face as serious difficulties as those faced by an atheist.

It is reasonably clear that a religious sect could endow and in various ways support a university without *necessarily* generating serious problems for the exercise of academic freedom.

It is much less clear that an institution could with plausibility claim that it respects the academic freedom of its academic staff even though it espouses (perhaps in a mission statement) specific religious tenets and in its various rules and practices requires, as a condition of employment or of continuation of employment, that its academic staff accept and comply with these tenets. Such a requirement might appear (i) in its rules or practices in relation to hiring, promotion, tenure, (ii) in its decisions about what can be taught and how, (iii) in its decisions about what lines of inquiry may be followed in research or scholarship, and (iv) in its rules and practices about the power of academic staff to decide questions of governance.

In this paper I set out to ask what is to be said of such a claim by such an institution.

If the issues here are to be addressed without begging questions and without discussing straw men, then we need to be careful always to bear in mind some fundamental points about academic freedom, about freedom of religion, and about the nature of universities.

2. Firstly, just as universities are institutions that first came into existence at a date (or through a period of time), so academic freedom comes into existence at a date (or, again, through a period of time).[1] Secondly, different accounts can be given of what it is for an institution to deserve being counted a university, of what involved in academic freedom, and of what is to count as freedom of religion, accounts which are not only different in wording but also different in substance. Thirdly, what have been counted as acceptable accounts of academic freedom and of freedom of religion have changed and developed over the years.[2] Fourthly, the questions of what *have* been counted as acceptable accounts of academic freedom and of freedom of religion are different questions from the questions of what *are* acceptable accounts. Fifthly, as far as I know, no plausible arguments exist against the claim that there are limits on what society may reasonably permit its members to do or say in an exercise of their freedom of religion: we clearly should not accept the claim that my religious beliefs permit me to kill my disobedient children.[3] And, finally, the question of whether freedom of religion *has* been viewed as trumping academic freedom or vice versa is different from the question of whether there are reasons to so view it, i.e., whether there are good reasons so to view it.[4]

My questions in this paper are questions about how academic freedom and freedom of religion *ought* to be analyzed and about whether we *ought* to count freedom of religion to trump academic freedom.

3. There are various corollaries of the six points made in the last section.

Firstly, if we are to avoid begging questions and to avoid discussing straw men, then we have to avoid making essentialist assumptions about academic freedom, freedom of religion, and what can count as a university. What institutions count as universities, what counts as academic freedom, and what freedom of religion involves is not something fixed and immutable. Therefore, we cannot answer the questions we are facing about academic freedom, freedom of religion, and the nature of universities simply by citing definitions of their fixed and immutable (i.e., "essential") nature. Moreover, no discussion of what *have* been counted as acceptable accounts of academic freedom and of freedom of religion can decide the questions of what *are* acceptable accounts. There are good reasons to say that to address those questions we need to face the fact that these concepts are what the philosopher Gallie called "essentially contested concepts": they are concepts whose analysis is to be decided on not by ***conceptual analysis***, but by social and political and even moral argument. The question about the relations between academic freedom and freedom of religion in a university can only be settled by bringing to bear such arguments. Correspondingly, the question of whether freedom of religion trumps academic freedom or vice versa can only be settled by means of the same kinds of arguments.

A further corollary of the six points is that the question I am addressing in this paper is, as it stands, not a *legal* question. It is certainly not a question that can be *settled* by examination of the wording of the *Charter of Rights and Freedoms*, by examination of rulings by the Supreme Court of Canada, let alone by review of decisions and ruling by lower courts or by arbitration panels. It is significant that, when, in her very interesting and important 2004 paper "Freedom of Religion and the Rule of Law: A Canadian Perspective,"[5] Chief Justice Beverley McLachlin argues that respect for the rule of law can and *should* be viewed as a constraint of the *Charter* right to freedom of religion and freedom of conscience, the arguments she brings to bear for *this* claim are best construed as being social, political, and moral arguments.

4. A plausible consequence of the above is the suggestion that to address the issues under discussion in this paper we need to use an approach which, in a phrase taken from legal theory, can be called the "living tree" approach. The phrase "living tree" was first introduced into Canadian law in the famous Persons case.[6] In law it names an approach to constitutional questions which eschews appeals to fixed and unchangeable notions and instead espouses the view that the concepts used in stating constitutional claims are to be interpreted in ways sensitive to the *changing* social, medical, technological, and practical realities. In his 2007 book *A Common Law Theory of Judicial Review: The Living Tree*[7] the philosopher of law W. J. Waluchow puts the point very nicely on page 183, thus:

> On this conception . . . constitutions, and hence those Charters that enjoy constitutional status, in no way represent attempts to establish *fixed* points of agreement and *pre-commitment*. By its nature, a Charter is "a living tree capable of growth and expansion within its natural limits". It is an instrument that must, within limits inherent in its constitutional role, be allowed to grow and adapt to new contemporary circumstances and evolving normative beliefs . . . [emphasis added]

Very much the same is true, I suggest, of the kinds of reasoning appropriate to examinations of the interplay between academic freedom, freedom of religion, and the nature of the university. Questions about how to analyze the idea of a university, the idea of academic freedom, and the idea of freedom of religion and about how to frame claims about the value of academic freedom and of freedom of religion and about their role in universities are questions about moral, social, political, and legal structures, structures which have a history. These structures have a dynamic life which can change through time, and in describing and discussing them we cannot but use essentially contested concepts. And, finally, questions about how best to organize these structures have to be seen as being normative questions and, as such, questions which require appeal of social, political, and moral values.

Putting these very familiar ideas together I can say the following: (i) that the question of whether it is possible both to respect academic freedom and to respect freedom of religion is a question *only* directly faceable if we recognize the dynamic, essentially contested, living tree nature of the concepts at work; (ii) that we need to see ourselves as facing a situation where there are no fixed points; and (iii) that hence we need social, political, and moral arguments or at least outlines of such arguments at each step in the investigation of the issues.

In line with this approach I suggest that, without very good argument, we cannot rule out the possibility that more than one kind of academic freedom could not only be imagined but also put in place. Without good argument, we cannot even rule out the possibility of putting in place some new and different kind of academic freedom, a kind of academic freedom that preserves the very values by appeal to which we argue that academic freedom is needed in any institution which can reasonably be counted as having the status of a university (as opposed to a religious seminary).

This being said, in the following I will offer an argument against this possibility.

5. Various different conceptions of academic freedom, of freedom of religion, and indeed of what it is to be a university are then possible. There are moreover various different views that might be adopted as to what we ought to say are limits that should be placed on the exercise of academic freedom and on the exercise of freedom of religion.

Let me therefore begin by outlining the core of the most common versions of statements of academic freedom. Some parts of this core are perhaps contentious,[8] but for my purposes it will do.

I will say that academic staff members have academic freedom if and only if **(a)** they are free (i) to teach, (ii) to carry out research, (iii) to disseminate the results of their research, (iv) to express their opinions about the governance of their university whether those opinions are expressed in intramural or extramural forums, and (v) to express opinions about matters of public interest again whether these opinions are expressed in intra or extramural settings and (b) they can exercise these freedoms without the need for deference to prescribed doctrines or orthodoxies and without fear of penalty for such exercise.[9]

I now turn to the substance of my argument. I begin by describing what I will call the "Newman Ideal" in honour of Cardinal John Henry Newman, the nineteenth-century English churchman and academic.[10] In the Ideal, as I will describe it, the university has a right and perhaps a duty to impose certain religious constraints on its own functioning and specifically it requires that certain substantial religious views be adopted. Newman's thinking on these issues is very complex and subtle, and my co-opting of his name for what I will describe (though not completely unfair) certainly does in some ways involve a distortion of what he in fact says. This said, the name "Newman Ideal" has the virtue of being strongly evocative of a certain tradition, a tradition whose foundations I want to criticize as being fundamentally flawed.

## THE NEWMAN IDEAL

6. Imagine the following structure which some feel is an ideal worth striving for: in this ideal the university would be a community of like-thinking scholars devoting their lives to promoting and protecting certain religious beliefs, ***and*** to studying and publishing ideas, arguments, theories about morality, justice, and other political values, and about certain cosmological and metaphysical ideas ***in ways compatible with*** these religious beliefs. In the ideal, academics would have academic freedom to study and teach whatever they wish in whatever way they wish, so long as the study and the teaching is compatible with the fundamental tenets set out in the mission statement of the university.

Imagine that we added to the Newman Ideal that those espousing this ideal do not believe that *all* universities need to be like this: they are perfectly happy if *others* espouse *different* ideals. Imagine that they *also* say that universities in which the Newman Ideal is realized *are to be* and *can be* respectful of the academic, human, and indeed the *Charter* rights of present and future academic staff members. More specifically, they say that they respect these rights by publicizing unambiguously in advertisements for applicants for academic positions in the university

(i) that they do indeed require academic staff members to comply with certain specific religious rules, (ii) that they do require academic staff members to be believing members of the official religion of the university, (iii) that the decision by academic staff members to abandon their beliefs and/or not to comply with the religious rules will be viewed as a decision which, after due consideration and under procedures set out in a collective agreement, is tantamount to resignation from the academic positions they hold.

The idea of course is that, if an academic staff member knows and consents to the rules, then accepting a position as an academic staff member in a university that espouses the Newman Ideal is her or his free and autonomous choice: he or she does not have to accept a position at this university — she or he can pursue her or his academic career in some other university.

I will now present a critique of this Newman Ideal. The critique is designed to show that for a university to adopt the Newman Ideal would be for that university to adopt a set of rules for its governance that are incompatible with and indeed antagonistic to many of the claims that make it the case that institutions called universities can play the roles we require of them, roles they need to play if they are to be counted a great public good. The basic argument in lots of configurations is familiar enough but like all arguments it will live and breathe in its details.

## A CRITIQUE OF THE NEWMAN IDEAL

7. My critique of the Newman Ideal proceeds by first making a series of what I will call "preliminary ground-setting points." Once these preliminary ground-setting points are presented, my critique of the Newman Ideal and indeed anything like it drops out as a simple and obvious corollary.

8. It is tempting to say that Socrates was the first person in the Western world whose academic investigations brought him into direct conflict with the religious beliefs of his fellow citizens — his conflict was deadly for him. There have been many since his time whose recognizably

*academic* activities have perhaps less dramatically been circumscribed by those exercising what they take to be their religious rights. Galileo is a figure usually mentioned at this point, but I think that the experience of the eighteenth-century Scottish philosopher David Hume is almost as important in human terms: he decided not to publish his groundbreaking essay "On suicide"[11] because he realized that this would bring him into conflict with the religious authorities at the time — if the reasoning of that essay had been more widely known there would have been much less nonsense talked about the right to life that has been and still is being talked.

But though their *work* was recognizably academic, neither Socrates nor Hume held academic positions when doing their work: they were not academics in the modern sense of the word and hence in the modern usage of the phrase "academic freedom" they do not have academic freedom rights to be infringed. This is my first preliminary ground-setting point.

9. Perhaps we should just say that it was Socrates's and Hume's freedom of expression rights that were infringed. But even that is problematic, since it is not clear that these rights were acknowledged at the time and they were certainly not enforced, and some might argue the thesis that the only rights a person can reasonably be said to have are those that are recognized and to some enforced. This thesis has been called the *social recognition thesis of rights*. The thesis states that for someone in a certain society to *have* a right to do or to receive such-and-such in a certain society it is necessary that that right be acknowledged and at least to some extent enforced in that society and that otherwise the right is merely an *aspirational right*, "aspirational" here being (like "imitation") a defeater. It is because of discomfort with the view encapsulated in this thesis that the talk of *natural* rights first appeared, natural rights being rights that people have whatever is the social structure of the society in which they live, rights they have by virtue of their nature (as persons), rights that *ought* to be acknowledged and enforced whether or not they are in fact acknowledged and enforced.[12]

My second preliminary ground-setting point will be the claim that something like the social recognition thesis (though in a form much more sophisticated, certainly, than the version I have just outlined) has to be accepted for academic freedom rights. Academic freedom rights are not natural rights; they exist only if they are to some extent acknowledged and enforced in the institutional structures. People can have academic freedom rights only if there exist institutions in which the rights are to be held and only if in the social structures of those institutions acknowledge and to some extent protect those rights. In the absence of such structures academic freedom rights are, at most, aspirational rights.

10. If Socrates and Hume were not academics, the nineteenth-century philosopher, Henry Sidgwick, was certainly an academic: he was a fellow of Trinity College, Cambridge, and Knightbridge Professor of Moral Philosophy. Tenure of a fellowship at Trinity required signing the "Thirty-nine Articles" which, in one form or another since the sixteenth century, had set out some of the fundamental religious doctrines which defined the Church of England. Early in his career Sidgwick felt comfortable doing so, but by 1869 he had come to realize that he no longer believed the religious theses that the articles stated and correspondingly concluded that on grounds of conscience he must resign his fellowship.[13] I mention Sidgwick's experience for several reasons, but the point I want to draw attention to here is that the infringement of Sidgwick's academic freedom rights was made possible because the college's governing body exercised what nowadays would be called its *institutional autonomy* rights in a certain way. Specifically, Trinity College *in an exercise of its institutional autonomy* made the acceptance of certain religious beliefs a condition of employment as an academic member of that institution. The point here is the familiar one that, although it is essential that it be remembered and acknowledged that universities and institutions of higher learning need the freedom to make autonomous judgments as to how best to fulfill their institutional role as the developers of knowledge and the providers of higher education in the community, it is equally essential to realize that in exercising this role they may infringe those very

rights that those designated as academic staff in the institution need if they are to be able to fulfill *their* roles in the institution. The point is that the needed institutional autonomy of universities must not be allowed to infringe the academic freedom rights of the academic staff in the university. Indeed, if it is argued (as surely it must be) that only academics have the training, education, and experience, and hence the expertise to understand the complexities that attach to university research and teaching and that hence the governance of a university requires granting an essential and central role to its academic staff, then it follows that wise exercise of institutional autonomy is *only possible* if the academic freedom rights of academics is acknowledged and counted fundamental to the governance of the university.[14] Trinity College, Cambridge, was exercising its institutional autonomy rights in requiring subscription to the "Thirty-nine Articles," but in so doing was infringing the academic freedom rights of its academic staff.[15]

Similarly and more recently, several Canadian universities and university colleges have, in their different ways, in exercising their institutional autonomy (for whatever reason and under whatever pressure from outside bodies like churches and religious sects), imposed on their academic staff as a condition of their continued employment the requirement that they teach and do their research and in some cases live their private lives in ways that are subject to certain limits accepted and imposed on religious grounds.[16]

This, then, is my third preliminary ground-setting point: institutional autonomy rights are rights of institutions; academic freedom rights are rights of individual academics; and institutions in exercising their institutional autonomy rights need to avoid infringing the academic freedom rights of academics if the autonomy is to be exercised in ways which do not make it difficult or impossible for the institution to fulfill its role as a university.

But there are further lessons to be learned from the experience of Henry Sidgwick.

11. There are some very important lessons concerning the possibility

of what I will simply call "change of mind." The claims that academic staff members count true or at least worthy of acceptance when they take on academic positions at a university may not, indeed will probably not, be the exactly same claims that they would accept after some years of study, research, and teaching. Of course, one would hope not. For one would hope that any academics engaging in serious study in preparation for teaching or engaging seriously in research would constantly be willing to pay attention to worries that might be raised not only about the substantial claims and theories that they accept and are teaching, but also about the methods that can and should be used in assessing such claims and theories and to revise these claims if need be in the light of those worries, if those worries turn out on investigation to be well-grounded. No doubt at any given time many of the claims and theories they accept are claims and theories they have no reason to revise or replace, but for any self-respecting academic nothing should be viewed immune to revision or abandonment if evidence, argument, or reason is found or offered for such revision or such abandonment. But if an academic does not revise or abandon or seek to modify or correct a substantive view or a view about how to investigate some question when doubt is raised about the basis for the substantive view or the reliability of methodological view, then it is hard to make sense of what the academic is doing in teaching and research. For the alternative to being open to the possible need to revise one's claims and one's methods of inquiry and doing so will involve persisting in beliefs that one acknowledges need revision and in the continued use of methods of inquiry that one acknowledges are unproductive or even counter-productive. That is surely paradigmatically irrational. Indeed, it is very hard to see how a university can fulfill the roles that a university needs to serve in a society if the need for revision is not accepted and indeed embraced. One would ask why one should call such an institution a university rather than, for example, a religious seminary. I will refer to the points I have made in this paragraph as *the theses of the essential desirability of openness to revision*. The statement of these theses is my fifth preliminary ground-setting point. I feel the need to emphasize that my argument for the theses of the essential desirability of openness to revision applies completely generally to all universities — not merely to institutions espousing the Newman Ideal.

It is a plausible corollary of the theses of the essential desirability of openness to revision that teaching and research concerning religious issues in a university need to be viewed as being fraught with academic dangers. It is a more striking corollary that any demand that religious beliefs and practices play any role in decisions about university governance whether in relation to teaching and research or more widely needs to be viewed as being seriously problematic. Notice I say "dangerous" and "problematic": I do not say "inappropriate." The dangers and problems may be avoidable, but for them to be avoided enormous care is needed. To explain my point here I need to make some points drawn from the philosophy of religion: this done I will be able to explain and justify my comments about the dangers and problems here. My claim will be (i) that on one view of the ways in which religious claims can be rendered worthy of acceptance (what I will call the "scientific-theology" view), the problems consequent on the essential desirability of openness to revision can be avoided if care is taken, but (ii) that on another view of the ways in which religious claims can be rendered worthy of acceptance (what I will call the "faith-theology" view), the problems are much more serious: in fact, I think that they are unavoidable·

12. Consider the implications of the theses of essential desirability of openness to revision for claims that are in fact religious claims. Even though academics may, when they accept appointments as academics at some institution, embrace certain religious beliefs, with the passage of time those same academics may after careful reflection come to have doubts about these religious beliefs: they may even be tempted to abandon them.

The implications of this can take two forms. At the risk of opening up an unmanageably complex set of issues, I need to describe the two forms these implications can take. The differences between the two forms of the implications of theses of the essential desirability of openness to revision turn on the epistemological question of how, if at all, religious claims can be established or at least rendered worthy of acceptance or belief ("rendered worthy of acceptance," for short).

One view (actually a family of views) about how religious claims can be rendered worthy of acceptance is that they can be so rendered, if at all, only by investigations which are based upon empirical evidence and constrained by the canons of scientific and philosophical reasoning, canons which themselves must be counted as essentially revisable in the light of evidence and argument. On this view, religious claims are to be viewed as one special subclass of scientific claims and subject to the same canons of assessment as are other scientific claims. I will therefore not unnaturally refer to this view as the scientific-theology view.[17]

On the second view (again it is in fact a family of views), at least some fundamental religious claims can only be rendered worthy of acceptance in ways which, in the end, will depend on claims of faith. As I am construing *faith* here, if one says that one believes such-and-such *on faith,* then one is saying that one does not know how to establish what one believes by well-evidenced or well-reasoning inquiry. In this sense faith functions as an alternative or even a rival to reasoned or scientific investigation or inquiry.[18] Not unnaturally I will refer to this view as the faith-theology view. The crucial feature of the faith-theology view is its acceptance of the thesis that, though there are some fundamental religious claims which cannot be rendered worthy of acceptance by the means countenanced by scientific-theology, these same claims can nevertheless be counted worthy of acceptance as a matter of faith. A common variant of this kind of view involves mention of some experiences of phenomena or entities either of the believer or of some person who reports the experiences, the experiences not being explicable as being classically empirical experiences, and the phenomena and entities not being "natural" phenomena or entities.[19]

13. I turn now to the lessons to be learned from the implications of the theses of the essential desirability of openness to revision.

Consider firstly the situation where the university in an exercise of its institutional autonomy not only demands acceptance of certain religious claims and practices, but also espouses (or at least acquiesces in) the use of a scientific-theology about how religious claims can be rendered worthy of acceptance. Clearly in this case the university's stance is deeply confused: on the one hand it at least acquiesces in the claim that religious claims can only be shown to be worthy of acceptance if the methods of science are brought to bear on those claims, but, on the other hand it, in effect, insists that at least some of the claims should be viewed as being "privileged" or "protected" in the sense that they are held, for some reason, not to be open to review even in the light of actual or possible empirical or other rational disconfirmation. It would be tempting to conclude that such a university was less interested in making possible the acquisition of evidence-based religious knowledge than in forcing its academic staff and students into some rigid uniform mould, a mould adoption of which, apparently, cannot be warranted by the evidence-based reasoning that it elsewhere espouses.

As an aside, it is worth noticing that these kinds of problems can arise not only when, exercising of its institutional autonomy, a university insists on acceptance by its academic employees of some *religious* claims; it can equally well arise if the university insists, as a condition of employment (or continued employment), that its academic employees accept certain non-religious claims, claims, for example, about which scientific theories are to be accepted as a condition of employment, claims about which political or economic or historical theories are to be accepted, claims about what are the most effective ways to bring students to an acceptable level of understanding of materials to be taught, claims about which courses are *worth* teaching. I wish I could say that few universities would be so arrogant and foolish as to claim that, as an exercise of its institutional autonomy, it had the right to set as a requirement of employment as an academic staff member the acceptance of certain substantive scientific, political, economic, or historical claims or claims about pedagogy, but certainly such a claim would be widely viewed as arrogant and foolish if done in too public or direct a way. And yet some universities have indeed done something similar in relation to religious beliefs and, despite some outcry from the community at large, they seem to be able to get away with it.

14. Consider now the situation where in some university there is general acceptance of faith-theology — perhaps the university explicitly or implicitly espouses such a theology. In such a university, the requirement that academic staff accept certain religious claims is not in quite the same obvious way open to the response I outlined above in relation to universities that espouse a scientific-theology: after all, it might be said, on a *faith*-theology view there *is* no space for evidence, reasoning, argumentation in relation to those religious claims that *are* a matter of faith. In universities espousing a faith-theology, the most that citation of evidence and the presentation of reasoning and argumentation can address is the foundational question of whether claims grounded merely in faith should reasonably be allowed to have a role in decisions as to what is to be taught or investigated in an institution with aspirations to be classed as a university.

What are we to say about such a university and, more importantly, what are we to say would be the implications of a university taking such a stance?

I begin with the point I made in paragraph eleven to the effect that the claims that academic staff members count worthy of acceptance when they take on an academic position may not be exactly the same as those that they count worthy of acceptance after they have spent some years in study, research, and teaching. I commented that one would wonder how seriously they have taken their study and research if there was no change in their beliefs.

Now consider the situation such academic staff members find themselves in if among the claims which their study and research suggest do need revision or even abandonment are the very claims acceptance of which their university counts as a condition of employment or of continued employment. What are such academic staff members to do if they finds themselves in such a situation?

There are various possibilities, none of them savoury.

Firstly, if the academic staff members inform the governing body of the university of their doubts or of their change of mind, then the academics may lose their positions with all that that may involve for their careers — the consequences here can be particularly damaging if the loss of faith comes later in life.[20] Also serious is the fact that if the university refuses to bend, then it may have to face the possibility of losing academic staff members that it otherwise may value very highly.

But another and (from the point of view of the capacity of the university to fulfill its role) perhaps more disturbing possibility is that the academics, realizing that their academic careers may be in jeopardy, may, in fear for their careers, decide to soft pedal their change of mind or even conceal it; they may structure their teaching in ways that avoid the issues where now their considered views differ from the officially sanctioned views of the university; they may decide in their research not to pursue lines of inquiry which would reveal their differences from the officially sanctioned views, and if they do pursue them they may decide not to submit to journals papers which might reveal their change of mind. In this scenario the cost to the university is that members of its academic staff are alienated and no longer fully engaged in fulfilling the university's goals.

A third possibility is that the academic staff members, aware that colleagues in secular universities (universities like where, perhaps, they were educated) would have an academic freedom right to voice their reservations, may come to experience the kinds of psychological problems which, in the literature of professional ethics, is referred to as "burnout" and "moral distress"[21]. The presence of such psychological states in professionals can seriously interfere with their capacity to fulfill their professional duties. And this is no less true of academic staff than of other professionals.

A fourth and perhaps yet more serious problem from the point of view of the university is that the psychological problems can lead to the phenomenon referred to in the professional literature as "subversion": subversion occurs when professionals come to believe that the rules under which they work are irrational or counterproductive; they then, instead of trying to secure revision or abandonment of the irrational or counterproductive rules, behave in ways consciously or unconsciously designed to undermine respect for the rules or even to subvert the goals that imposition of the rules was designed to serve.[22]

But by far the most serious problem facing an institution which has aspirations to be classed as a university is in effect the problem that I reviewed in section eleven above. I will very briefly review the main steps of my reasoning there.

In section eleven I pointed out that the claims that academics would count worthy of acceptance at the beginning of their academic careers could, indeed should, not be the exactly same claims that they would accept after some years of study, research and teaching. I pointed out that surely one would hope that any academic engaging seriously in research or engaging in serious study in preparation for teaching would constantly be aware of the need to refine, revise, or abandon any of the views that such study suggests are in need of refinement, revision, or abandonment. I said that for any self-respecting academic nothing should be viewed immune to revision or abandonment if evidence, argument, or reason is found or offered for such revision or such abandonment. But if academics are not willing to refine, revise, or abandon views that in the light of study have become suspect, then it is hard to make sense of what they are doing when preparing their teaching and when doing their research. The alternative to being open to the possible need to revise one's claims and one's methods of inquiry and in fact to doing so is to persist in beliefs that one acknowledges need revision and to continue to use of methods of inquiry that one acknowledges are unproductive or even counter-productive. Such persistence is surely paradigmatically irrational. I said that it is very hard to see how a university *can* fulfill the roles that a *university* needs to serve in a society if the need for revision is not accepted and indeed embraced. And I said that one should ask why one should call such an institution a university rather than, for example, a religious seminary. All of these points I referred to as the theses of the essential desirability of openness to revision.

15. The upshot of my arguments in sections eleven to fourteen is that, if a university requires as a condition of employment or continued employment that academic staff members accept certain substantive religious claims, then whether that university buys into a "scientific-theology" or a "faith-theology," the university faces very serious

problems — problems so serious as to cause the institution to cease to be counted as a university. The upshot of these sections is then (a) that what I have called the Newman Ideal is untenable, at least in the form I have described it; (b) that the answer to the question with which I began this paper has to be that no plausible sense could be made of an institution's claim that it can (i) require compliance with some or all of the tenets of some religion and yet (ii) be capable of fulfilling the societal roles which any institution deserving to be called a university can reasonably be expected to fulfill; and (c) that, if an institution tries to exercise its institutional authority to impose on its academic staff members a requirement that they accept certain religious tenets, then that exercise of institutional autonomy should be viewed as involving an inappropriate and unacceptable infringement of their academic freedom.

# 7

# ACADEMIC FREEDOM AND RELIGIOUS CONVICTION AT CANADA'S FAITH-BASED UNIVERSITIES AND COLLEGES

*William Bruneau*

In a discussion of religious conviction in the university, it is well to have a reliable guide. Etienne Gilson will do. Gilson was a talented French historian of great Catholic universities in the Middle Ages and a shrewd observer of academic politics in Canada as in France.[1] In a public lecture in Toronto in 1969, he offered an intriguing simile for Christian universities: "Why, they are like the climbing rose, *Rosa albertine*. Their blooms are lovely but necessarily protected by ferocious thorns."[2]

Gilson thought confessional universities[3] could and should be committed to reason, all the while recognizing the limitations of reason in matters of faith. That is why they required protective "thorns," meaning they should amass political support to counter narrow-minded demands for rigid doctrinal purity, or to resist politicians wanting to get their hands on the universities. Gilson insisted that a "religiously minded university" should have a prior commitment to academic freedom.

Audience members were divided between those who suspected religious universities of intellectual perfidy and those who loved the idea of a university as Cardinal Newman understood it. In the lengthy discussion following Gilson's talk, participants recalled Canada's long and colourful history of religiously tinted higher education. As colony and nation, it has been home to Catholic, Anglican (or Episcopal),

Baptist, Presbyterian, and United Church universities and colleges.

But in 1968 we thought history had ended, much as Francis Fukuyama later predicted in *The End of History and the Last Man*.[4] Between 1950 and 1970, mid-sized and larger confessional universities had all gone public in Canada. We thought the hold-outs would not last much longer.

But we were wrong. In the 1990s and 2000s, private faith-based and religiously minded higher education institutions, mostly Protestant, have revived or been refounded (some are listed in Appendix II). A significant number provide theological and pastoral education to future pastors or missionaries. Nearly all claim to offer university-level education in the arts and sciences. In a sea of secular public higher education, and although they are tiny by comparison, they are exceptions to many rules. Their way of thinking about the different claims of reason and religion are in many cases distant from those of Etienne Gilson.

These institutions rely in varying degrees on indirect public funding, despite their private legal status and their confessional character. Although organized religion has declined significantly in popularity since 1945, confessional educational institutions nonetheless continue to press for public support and public funding.[5] Forms of public support range from designation as "charitable entities" under Revenue Canada rules, to access to the Canada Student Loans Program, to funding from federal granting councils (Trinity Western University is an example), to preferential tax deals with local municipal authorities, to funding of specialized training programs.[6]

None of this detail should distract from the larger question of academic freedom, the assurance that teachers and professors may teach, do research, and carry out public service — freely commenting on social and administrative practice in the university and in the largely society — and doing all these things without fear of discipline or punishment. Academic freedom has been and remains an unresolved problem of confessional, private higher education in Canada.

The trouble is, of course, that in confessional private higher education there isn't much academic freedom. Instead professors, staff, and students must agree, at appointment or admission to the universities with which I am concerned, to accept the truth of Christian doctrine, to live by certain rules and standards of private and public behaviour, and to say they will not criticize publicly the university or its policies.

In British Columbia, the largest such institution is Trinity Western University [TWU], with over two thousand undergraduate students paying about $21,000 per year in fees. TWU is chartered by the provincial government (all universities in Canada must have a government charter) and recognized by the British Columbia Degree Quality Assessment Board.

Meanwhile, in Caronport, Saskatchewan, there is Briercrest Bible College (604 students). In Moncton, New Brunswick, there is Crandall University (one thousand students). The list goes on: thirty-three on the membership roster of Christian Higher Education Canada, a relatively recent federation of confessional universities and colleges.[7] These institutions do not often figure in academic or journalistic coverage of Canadian post-secondary education. That fact is less important than their official designation as universities in Canada.[8]

One administrative policy at these institutions has attracted particular attention in the past fifteen years. Several of these institutions ask professors, staff, and students to pass a faith test. People unable to subscribe to the test are not to be appointed or admitted.

Not all religiously affiliated or religiously "guided" universities had or have faith tests. Some display only one or two features of a "faith test" in the classic sense. United [Church of Canada] College in Winnipeg[9] was the site of an influential academic freedom case in 1958, during which a professor (Harry Crowe) was fired for criticizing the college principal and announcing his disdain for the Christian religion.[10] United did not have an explicit faith test, but imposed policies amounting to one. Crowe failed that implicit test, experienced the disciplinary consequences, and was made jobless.[11]

A faith test in the fullest sense requires that a candidate for appointment or continuing employment in a university will affirm he or she is a practising Christian. The affirming person will then say that his or her private and public life will be ordered according to Christian doctrine and under policies agreed by the administration and board.

A person committed to academic freedom will of course object to requirements that he or she accept a religious doctrine or dogma without criticism of it. In one of his many articles and speeches on the question of religion and science, Bertrand Russell wrote this in 1929:

> A certain kind of scientific candour is a very important quality, and it is one which can hardly exist in a man who imagines that there are things which it is his duty to believe. We cannot therefore really decide whether religion does good without investigating whether religion is true . . . there is a certain tendency in our practical age to consider that it does not much matter whether religious teaching is true or not, since the important question is whether it is useful. One question cannot, however, well be decided without the other.[12]

One would rightly suppose that professors and researchers would object to policy requiring them to agree to the "inerrant truth" of the *Holy Bible*. But in a confessional university, where academic freedom is absent in theory and/or practice, their objection must be kept quiet. They must accept university policy and practice, or at any rate, must agree not to criticize it in the public square.

The faith test offends in other ways. Teachers may be required to promise not to drink alcohol to excess (or to drink it at all) either on campus or off, not to smoke (any substance, really), and/or not to engage in pre-marital or extramarital sexual flings on campus or off.

At Trinity Western in Langley, the faith test in 2013 included the assertion that marriage is possible only between a man and woman,[13] and that "gay, lesbian or bisexual students may be subject to disciplinary measures including expulsion" if they act on their natural proclivities. But more, a faith test meant that those who for some reason "lose their faith" and could no longer assent to it may be expelled from "the community."

We come now to a crucial feature of the "classical" faith test: that it implies *administrative discipline*.

Whether written or enshrined in common practice, a faith test promises that discipline will follow a breach of doctrinal or political limits. Suppose a university president says Christianity and socialism are necessarily incompatible, or that the *Genesis* creation "story" is entirely true to fact; and suppose a brash, young assistant professor announces to the press that her president is foolish and wrong, and that the writers of *Genesis* were similarly foolish and wrong — but that Marx was a clever and righteous man; then her days on the teaching staff are numbered.

In short, these are places where discrimination is formally possible — at the point of admission for students or appointment for professors — and afterward during students' undergraduate days, or during professors' and staff's periods of contracted employment. Tenured appointments are rare. Tenure, where it exists in some form, means only "an extended contract of employment, with continuation at the pleasure of the board."

One might say that teachers in faith-based universities were consenting adults and knew what they getting themselves into when they were appointed. We might even agree that confessional institutions have every right to exist, as they are private and religious in character, and thus consistent with the Canadian constitution. Even if one grants these things, the imposition of a faith test has fatal consequences for academic freedom, not to mention for our imaginary brash, young assistant professor.

Another consequence deserves attention, and that is the way faith tests work to create ideologically homogeneous communities. That homogeneity explains why the presidents of faith-based institutions can reasonably say that "nobody complains at our place."

Jonathan Raymond, president of Trinity Western University [TWU] in British Columbia, said as much in a recent (2013 January 21) interview with CBC Vancouver radio host Rick Cluff. [14] In that instance, Trinity Western had decided to open a "Christian" law school with the full expectation that every faculty member and every student in that future law school would pass the faith test and sign the TWU "Community Covenant."[15] The Canadian Council of Law Deans considers the TWU policy on gay and lesbian students contravenes principles of social justice widely agreed in Canadian legal education.[16]

As of mid-2013, it was still uncertain if the TWU law school would proceed. But a homogeneously heterosexual Christian law school is possible. There have been energetic complaints from outside TWU.

How and why has religious conviction returned to haunt the halls of Canadian higher education? Two approaches to this question have merit, historical and philosophical-political.

* * *

The short historical answer is that religious conviction never ceased in the halls of Canada's universities and colleges. What *has* changed is the way Canadians deal with conflicts between the claims of institutional religion and the claims of reason, science, social change, and democratic practice.

Most religiously minded Canadian professors and students have long since resolved these conflicts. They work, study, and serve in public universities and agree that academic freedom is crucial to them, as it is to the generality of Canadian academics and students (granting that academic freedom for students is not the same thing that it is for university teachers).

The roots of this liberal and plural arrangement go back at least to the mid-twentieth century. After 1945 Canadians expected broader access than ever to post-secondary education. Access meant more than just increased admission rates. It also implied a different kind of "access" — to academic research and to its benefits. Since Newton, Spinoza, and Leibniz, the sciences — natural, humane, moral, and social — have delivered extraordinary results. They have incidentally shown the value of open-minded inquiry, the value of skepticism about religious and ideological claims of all sorts.

When Canada's vets returned, and afterward during the baby boom of the 1950s and 1960s, Canadians associated the idea of "progress" with the sciences, but connected social and economic progress with access to higher education.

These increasingly popular ideas — healthy skepticism and the possibility of broader access to university education — help explain increasing federal and provincial commitment to the funding of post-secondary education after 1945. Canadians placed increasing faith (in its non-religious sense) in the social and industrial utility of teaching and research, even if it might be years or decades before cultural and economic benefits were realized. Canadians trusted that an educated life was likely to be a happier life.[17]

Meanwhile Canada was taking an increasingly pluralist view of society, law, and morality. Pluralism was given a boost by the cultural "revolutions" of the late 1960s, the rising women's movements of the 1970s and 1980s, and by the onset of official policy on multiculturalism. Canada became an explicitly pluralist society in law and in social practice.[18]

There was and is a paradox in Canada's immigration history. On one hand, immigration gave the nation enough Mennonite, Baptist, Calvinist, Lutheran, Presbyterian, Methodist, and Catholic supporters to assure the creation of confessional universities and colleges in the nineteenth and early twentieth centuries. On the other, those same patterns of immigration, carried into the late twentieth century, helped to encourage a plural and liberal society.[19]

For all these reasons, there was little public reaction when in the 1950s and 1960s well-established Catholic and Protestant universities cut their ties with sponsoring denominations and "went public."[20] For university teachers, the divorce was greeted with relief. This did not mean that faithful Christians, Muslims, Buddhists, and Zoroastrians could not or did not teach or study in Canada's secular public universities. At my own University of British Columbia [UBC], a secular public institution, there are professors and students who held and hold views that would please the Pope or Billy Graham. But none of them have had to pass a faith test. After the 1960s, especially, they have freely debated religious and political matters without having to look over their shoulders.[21]

By 2011, public secular universities and colleges were educating well over a million undergraduate and graduate students in Canada.

The Canadian Association of University Teachers by 2012 represented almost seventy thousand professors, librarians, researchers, and other academic professionals at these institutions.

Meanwhile university governance changed significantly. By 1960 few university presidents had the unilateral authority and power they once enjoyed.[22] Canadian professors were rapidly organizing faculty associations and unions in English and French Canada. Their aims were to bargain collectively for adequate salaries, to develop procedures assuring fair and just treatment of members in these academic communities, to press for shared university governance — and to insist on provisions for academic freedom in their collective agreements with university administrations.[23]

The Harry Crowe affair of 1958, already mentioned, moved the ball down the field. In 1958 the regents of United College, a university in Winnipeg owned and operated by the United Church of Canada, fired history professor Harry Crowe. Crowe had written a private letter to a colleague in Ontario, a document mildly critical of the personality of the principal. When the letter was mysteriously passed to Principal Lockhart it turned out Professor Crowe had not just criticized Lockart, but said Christianity was a "corrosive force."

Lockhart and the board forced Harry Crowe out of United College, never giving reasons, never offering Crowe an opportunity to defend himself, never bothering to excuse their arbitrary decisions. Declaring solidarity with Professor Crowe, and for the sake of academic freedom, seven colleagues resigned from United College in 1958—59. In the CAUT Report on the case, the writers — Professors Fowke and Laskin (later of Canada's Supreme Court) — observed that:

> the administration of United College, judged by its conduct, seems to hold the view that religious belief is so fragile that it may be shattered by a breath of criticism.[24]

From that moment the Canadian Association of University Teachers [CAUT] and its Academic Freedom and Tenure Committee were vitalized. They proceeded to take a prominent role in Canadian academic life.

The Academic Freedom and Tenure Committee and the larger governing CAUT Council after 1958 developed a statement on academic freedom, since revised. The statement emphasizes strongly the question of "doctrine":

> *Academic freedom includes the right, without restriction by prescribed doctrine, to freedom to teach and discuss; . . . freedom to express one's opinion about the institution, its administration, and the system in which one works[.] Academic freedom does not require neutrality on the part of the individual. Academic freedom makes intellectual discourse, critique, and commitment possible. All academic staff must have the right to fulfil their functions without reprisal or repression by the institution, the state, or any other source.*[25]

Sometimes working with local associations and sometimes on its own, the CAUT and the committee worked to make the statement widely known and used in promotion, tenure, dismissal, and professorial discipline cases.

Since the CAUT openly opposed university policies requiring adherence to doctrine, it was only a matter of time before the organization decided to make a list of institutions with such policy. In 2006 it adopted "Procedures in Academic Freedom Cases Involving Allegations of Requirement of an Ideological or Faith Test as a Condition of Employment."[26] After CAUT studies of their policies and practices, five universities have been listed as faith-based institutions since 2009: Trinity Western University (Langley, British Columbia), Redeemer University College (Ancaster, Ontario), Providence University College (Otterburne, Manitoba), Crandall University (Moncton, New Brunswick), and Canadian Mennonite University (Winnipeg, Manitoba). Three of these institutions chose to write responses to CAUT's reports concerning them. All reports and responses were published and made available on the Internet.[27] Some Canadian academics have taken to calling this the "Grey List," but the CAUT has so far insisted that the purpose of the list is precisely the one given in the "procedures" mentioned a moment ago.

In all five CAUT reports, the main themes concern doctrine, agreement not to criticize the institution in public or to undermine it in private (a requirement variously interpreted and understood), and discipline in cases where teachers can no longer meet or pass the faith test. Publication of these reports produced energetic responses in the daily and religious press (a summary list of responses appears in Appendix III).

In the noisy debates of the early 2000s, history was certainly on the minds of participants — as a way of explaining the survival of confessional private religious universities and colleges in Canada, or as a way of thinking about moral and psychological questions those institutions like to ask. One of the very biggest questions is whether religious claims and conviction can coexist in a university with a thorough commitment to academic freedom.

* * *

To see how some confessional universities may be thought to threaten academic freedom, I turn to the last four years of popular and academic debate on confessional higher education.

A review of arguments against (and for) the reports and publications of the CAUT on "faith tests" in confessional universities suggests several lines of moral and epistemological discussion. Arguments for and against confessionalism have raged for decades (if not centuries) in academic journals, in obscure denominational newspapers, and in the popular media. If it wasn't Darwin, it was the higher criticism of the *Bible* in the 1920s; if it wasn't the holy writ of liberal capitalism it was the Social Gospel. The argument goes back a very long way in Canada as elsewhere in the world.

This recent Canadian discussion of academic freedom and religious conviction embodies old, longstanding claims for and against confessional and non-confessional university education. The concepts and the logic deployed in Canada's religious and secular daily press tell us much about the "resilience" mentioned earlier, whether it be the resilience of pluralist and skeptical views in Canadian society, or the reliance of Canada's religious minorities.[28]

I now offer a snapshot of confessional and non-confessional positions mentioned in the relevant debate since 2010. A representative list of sources, most of them journalistic, appears in Appendix III.

I begin in each instance with the views of supporters of confessional higher education, then describe arguments that have been made in opposition to (or alternation to) each one. Where possible, I advance two or more sides of the case. The whole point is to show the tension between so-called "confessionalists" and liberally minded skeptics and pluralists. It may be that none of this will change the minds of determined and faithful Christians on the one hand, or stubborn supporters of academic freedom and moderate skepticism on the other.

1. *If faith-based or "confessional" universities are autonomous, that autonomy gives "freedom" to require employees to adhere to a particular doctrine.*

This is the position of Canadian Mennonite University [CMU] in Manitoba but also of Trinity Western University. It begins with a widely agreed view that university autonomy is universally agreed to be a good thing.

In its *report* on CMU, the CAUT committee had this to say:

> [This statement] confuses institutional autonomy with institutional academic freedom. Universities may be said to have autonomy but not academic freedom . . . academic freedom always and exclusively resides in the individual faculty member and . . . academic institutions do not have and should not be said to have academic freedom. (p. 13)

An example helps to show what is at stake. Suppose an "autonomous" confessional university, the University of XYZ, insisted that moral prescriptions in the *New Testament* are ethically superior to prescriptions written after the year AD 450 , and required the Department of Religious Studies to hold this view in its teaching, research, and service. The claim of ethical superiority does not rely on principle so much as it does on the religious conviction of everyone ever hired at the University of XYZ. At XYZ there might be some discussion of utility, consequentialism, logical "transcendence," and so on. But any successful argument at XYZ would have to begin and end with religious conviction of one kind or another.

But its autonomy does not ensure that the University of XYZ thinks better, teaches better, negotiates better, or serves better than the public university down the road. Both may be autonomous, but that is only the beginning of the argument about their moral or educational superiority.

The University of XYZ is legally entitled to its views, and free to impose such policies on staff and students, but XYZ is a university in name only. Academic freedom does not exist in any reliable sense at XYZ, partly because the autonomy of the University of XYZ has become a licence to impose ideological uniformity on everyone who studies or teaches there.

Teachers and students at confessional universities will say, with justification, that there is real variety in the thinking and the behaviour of people at the University of XYZ. However true that may be, a difficulty remains: it is the overarching power of the institution, an arbitrary power to require uniformity of religious opinion and social behaviour — sexual behaviour especially — of everyone at XYZ.

2. *We proponents of confessional, faith-based higher education have studied in public secular universities. We found them full of people living under a rigid ideology, an ideology of secularism, reinforced by political correctness. Our faith convictions were excluded from the public square.*

A non-religious observer might say that the pot is calling the kettle black. Since confessional universities freely announce their commitment to an ideology and a doctrine, they are not well-placed to criticize places that don't.

But this too easy. The unhappiness of religiously minded colleagues at the University of XYZ suggests that they oppose a legal pillar on which public universities are constructed: for secular public universities are compelled by their charters to ensure that students' or professors' faith convictions do not distract from educational work. That is why there are no prayer meetings before physics classes at McGill.

And since there is no faith test in the public universities, all imaginable points of view and lines of research and argument are alive and well (or should be) in a university worth the name. If abortion comes up in a mathematics class at Ryerson University, it is likely the question would be discussed in the hallway, since it has no mathematical interest. But this does not mean that an *anti-abortion ideology prevails* in that mathematics class. By the same token, the fact that pro-life advocates at public universities openly discuss their views in public meetings does not mean that the university's policy of pluralism is about to be abandoned.

A crucial further point: some universities working in a faith tradition have demonstrated a strong commitment to academic freedom. Federated theological schools and universities in most of the larger Canadian public universities are explicitly committed to academic freedom. The Université St-Paul in Ottawa, a Pontifical Catholic institution, has negotiated a strong academic freedom clause with its faculty union (see Appendix IV for the text of that clause). St Thomas More (University of Saskatchewan) and St. Francis Xavier are protected by academic freedom clauses in their respective collective agreements.

These last cases put in doubt the claim that secular universities have no room for religious conviction or "exclude" the possibility of religious faith. At the public universities I have listed, people of faith work comfortably as teachers and researchers.

3. *It is a reasonable limitation of professors' academic freedom to say they must act responsibly and in line with the institutional mission. They must not forget the "good" of the larger sponsoring religious communities.*

Putting aside the question who decides what passes for "responsible" and what counts as "good," a counter-argument to three would start by asking what "academic" and "freedom" mean. One might propose an alternate reading: A responsible academic under conditions of academic freedom, will act so as to pursue well-evidenced truth. It is contrary to academic freedom to set aside the pursuit of truth in order to meet a religious goal or to suit the demands of a particular religious community.

On the other side of this question, religiously committed university people may say something like this: we want to make a community whose ethical standards rely on transcendent religious principles, whose attitudes of care and consideration extend to everyone in the community at the University of XYZ — and beyond to the whole world.

The proponents of confessional higher education mentioned in Appendix III do indeed say this. Alas! They rarely mention the arbitrary and compulsory administrative policy and practice that go hand-in-hand with the "transcendent" religious doctrines in private confessional universities.

Religious conviction and authoritarianism are worrisome twins.

4. *Our American neighbours have broadened and reinterpreted the 1940 and 1970 versions of the academic freedom statement of the AAUP [American Association of University Professors] to allow most of us confessional universities to do pretty much what we have always done. Why can't the Canadians do likewise?*

A comment by the President of the AAUP, Cary Nelson, is helpful:

> *The AAUP has an exceptions clause for religious institutions in its statement on academic freedom and tenure . . . [for] a significant number of religiously affiliated schools still want to be seen as being in the mainstream of American higher education . . . It is in our interest to draw them into the mainstream.*[29]

The American idea is if confessional universities warn candidates for appointment in advance of areas of work where academic freedom will be limited and make the warning in writing, then a signature on that document protects the confessional university but gives the AAUP and other liberally minded organizations a way of working toward deeper reform over the long term.

Nelson agrees that some antediluvian colleges will never agree to the requirements of academic freedom; in those cases, no such document should ever be signed. Public and political pressure should be brought to bear to persuade such universities of the error of their ways. But Nelson, and with him the AAUP, hold out the hope that other confessional, religiously minded institutions might of their own accord — in some distant future — accept the value and necessity of academic freedom.

There is no "exceptions clause" in Canada. Canadian academics in their majority choose not to dilute their academic freedom. Instead, the limits of academic freedom in Canada have to do with ordinary civil and criminal law (academic freedom does not protect professors from libel charges, for instance), and contract law (academic freedom does not license academics to cease teaching and research, nor does it prevent the university from evaluating the quality of that teaching and research).

5. *The Association of Universities and Colleges of Canada [AUCC] is broadening its ideas of academic freedom. It has watered down the second central feature of academic freedom (the right to criticize the university's policy and practices). It represents the administrations of universities in Canada. Doesn't it know best?*

It is unsurprising that an organization of administrators should wish to reduce public and academic criticism of its members. Yet the AUCC is deeply divided on the matter of academic freedom. The President of the University of Toronto, David Naylor, publicly and noisily refused to accept the language of the new AUCC policy. He and several other presidents are convinced that it is best for universities if internal and external criticism of them continues to be possible, and if it continues to be vigorous.

It is at least possible that President Naylor takes the view that in the absence of debate and criticism of administrative policy and practice, the university would become a community of yes-women and yes-men. Canadian academics say a good deal about the dead hand of bureaucracy and about the dangers of ideological homogeneity in the society. They say the same of the university.

Any policy that discourages pluralism, difference, and debate in the university — and about the university — encourages a deadening homogeneity. In that sense, the recent AUCC statement on academic freedom is a step backward.

6. *We in faith-based universities think secular public universities in Canada teach an ideology, a liberal and materialist ideology, and that all public university instruction has an indoctrinatory aspect.*

Now proponents of academic freedom say they would stop (if they had the power) indoctrinatory teaching, whether it be about concepts, or principles, or factual evidence. In order to keep doctrine and dogma at bay, the purveyors of academic freedom claim to rely on peer review, department and faculty scrutiny of curricula and pedagogy, and administrative transparency to the public. Accountability requires these things in any case. But also, if one wants to do everything possible to discourage indoctrination, these things (peer review, public scrutiny, and so on) are simply essential.

It would be idle and silly to say that public universities are free of doctrine and dogma. All one can do is work endlessly to discourage narrowly conceived, ideologically tendentious, or doctrinally based teaching and research. That is the job of professors and administrators alike.

If one takes academic freedom seriously, one might consider an idea from Bertrand Russell. Russell in 1928 suggested the wisdom of a moderated, rational skepticism everywhere in life and learning:

> I am prepared to admit any well-established result of science, not as certainly true, but as sufficiently probable to afford a basis for rational action. The skepticism I advocate amounts only to this: (i) that when the experts are agreed, the opposite opinion

> cannot be held to be certain; (ii) that when they are not agreed, no opinion can be regarded as certain by a non-expert; and (iii) that when they all hold that no sufficient grounds for a positive opinion exist, the ordinary man would do well to suspend his judgment . . . Education should fit us for truth . . . the habit of forming our opinions on the evidence, and holding them with that degree of conviction which the evidence warrants.[30]

An open-minded and humane skepticism does not offend academic freedom. For one thing, this kind of skepticism can and should be turned on itself. Every belief is to be tested to see if its logic is possible and how it makes its sense, and then to see what evidence for it there may be. That goes for skepticism itself.

Under some circumstances, even a moderate skepticism can endanger academic freedom. For instance, in times of budget cuts, when provincial governments may want to impose a narrow vocationalism on the university, a skeptical university may look weak and undecided. When decisive action is required to preserve university autonomy, it is risky for the university to spend precious time and energy on alternative theories and policies for X or Y. In Alberta, during the worst of Premier Ralph Klein's cuts, the provincial universities were persistent in their defence of humane and liberal curricula; to journalists of the period, it seemed that university people were fiddling as Rome burned. Even so, and despite its political cost, broad skepticism is less dangerous to the university than the indoctrination promised in such places as Briercrest Bible College.

7. *What gives you the right to criticize us? You have no official role in evaluating our programs or governance or policy.*

Critics of confessional higher education in daily press and in the academy have indeed been sharply critical. The Canadian Association of University Teachers is by no means alone in taking a stand on private and confessional higher education in Canada. The recent announcements of the Canadian Council of Law Deans have added another voice, in connection with the proposed foundation of a law school at Trinity Western University.

The question from the "confessionals" was, "What right have you?" The answer is, of course, that these organizations and individuals — the deans, the CAUT, the nation's university presidents, and Christian Higher Education Canada — have no more or less right to say their say than the Burnaby Knitting Club or the Ottawa Lawn Bowling Association or Mr. Brown down the street.

***

The claims and arguments presented by supporters of private and confessional higher education in Canada have a noticeably political tone. One should not be surprised. For among the objectives of a confessional university — putting aside for the moment its strictly religious vocation — are (i) independence from the state and (ii) successful resistance to unfriendly intellectual and social movements. For religiously minded supporters of confessional higher education, one great fear is that the increasing popularity of "liberalism," understood in whatever sense, will unsettle or even destroy the religious communities from which supporters come and on which they rely. There is a natural anxiety that dependency on the state, however understated, justified by various forms of and appeals to liberal "critical" thinking, may undermine private religious belief.

The main claims and questions in debates of the past half-decade are thus as much political as they are theological.

## ENVOI

Leslie Armour writes that:

> Without inferences we would all be prisoners of our immediate associations of ideas, creatures of whim or slaves to our instincts, biological drives, conditioned reflexes and habitual pattern of thoughts . . . When

> we claim to be free, we are claiming that we, not our passions or habits, make our choices.[31]

Armour thinks freedom must rely on unhindered access to facts and evidence, unlimited choice among inferences we draw from them, unrestricted discussions of ethics and values, and an open mind about where facts and logic may lead us in daily life.

It is entirely possible for people with religious convictions to agree to all of this. Indeed Canadian academics in public universities do have lively religious convictions, and yet maintain their support for academic freedom. As Catherine Gidney wrote in the conclusion to her study of Protestant religious practice and activism in Canadian universities:

> I am not contending that religion in any of its manifestations simply disappeared . . . For significant numbers of the university community, personal faith was and remains an animating force in their lives and their work.[32]

Religious belief, it should be said straightaway, is treated as is any belief (about science, politics, the world, and so on).

In confessional institutions, by contrast, there typically is official policy that limits reason, debate, unrestricted research, and open-minded teaching — for the sake of an ultimate "truth," a divine truth. The confessionally minded will say that relativism is the last refuge of the secular mind. Secularism must be resisted and, if possible, thwarted.

Meanwhile the public universities continue to work out the meaning and practice of academic freedom for themselves. To judge by the number of cases where public universities have failed to live up to the high standard of full academic freedom, there is a considerable distance to go.

We have, then, two quite different ways of seeing university teaching, research, service, administration, and outreach. An overarching value, the value of academic freedom, could and should contain them both. In at least some parts of the Canadian academy, there is some distance to go before that value is sustained in practice and in theory.

The essentials remain: dogma and doctrine, religious or disciplinary or intellectual orthodoxy, must not drive academic or administrative policy in the university. Academics must be free to criticize the administrative practice of the university and the practices of government and society in the world around and to criticize fearlessly.

Confessional universities, and in particular private confessional universities and colleges, could and should take on board the principles and practice of academic freedom. They worry that their sponsors and owners will be unhappy if they do. Oddly enough, the same could be said of non-confessional universities and colleges. In the end, the public interest and the needs of students and professors alike are paramount: that interest and those needs cannot be met without a full measure of academic freedom.

## APPENDIX I: MORE ON THE HISTORICAL BACKGROUND TO RELIGIOUS CONVICTION AND RELIGIOUS PRACTICE IN CANADIAN HIGHER EDUCATION

If one considered only the past hundred years or so of Canadian history, the idea that universities and colleges would impose a faith test might seem strange and outlandish. But seen in historical perspective, it is not so. Some Canadian academics have, until fairly recent times, thought it appropriate and even fair that a university, privately funded and owned, should impose standards of behaviour justified by an appeal to dogma. It was and remains legal to organize and run such a university in Canada.

Until the First World War, most universities imposed arbitrary behavioural and doctrinal standards on their faculty, staff, and students. There was an explicit faith test in Quebec's Catholic universities and colleges from the mid-seventeenth century.[33] They needed a revolution, the *révolution tranquille* of the 1960s, to end that practice.

To this history of religious and doctrinal oppression, one should add the peculiar facts of Canada's constitutional history. Our constitutional arrangements have permitted a patchwork of university policy and practice to continue, in some cases allowing private universities to adopt policies explicitly denying academic freedom to professors.

The difficulty is that the Canadian constitutions of 1867 and 1982 allow, although they do not necessarily legitimate, private religious colleges and universities. These constitutions guarantee freedom of choice in religious expression with due regard to the human and civil rights of others. Religious choice and expression are limited by the usual and universal provisions of the common law (property, defamation law, contract, and so on) and of the criminal law, but not otherwise.

But in universities, the free speech protections of the common law did not and do not assure academic freedom. By academic freedom, I mean especially (i) the right to hold religious views essentially different from those of the university leadership and (ii) the right to criticize administrative policy and practice.

The first tests of academic freedom in post-Confederation Canada showed the weakness of the law in protecting professors' academic freedom, but coincidentally exposed the weakness of the arguments used by religionists to maintain conformity. At McGill and Toronto, the first courageous proponents of the higher criticism of biblical scripture were given a hard time by university administrators and journalists alike. But by now there were whole schools of moral and logical theory that could (and did) provide powerful arguments to show that there were many possible ways of construing the biological past and the social-ethical future of the human race. The idealists and neo-Kantians, the first followers of J.S. Mill in Canada, the earliest proponents of what would later be called social democracy (including the future Prime Minister Mackenzie King) were teachers or pupils in philosophy and literature departments.[34] And they were well-armed to offer entirely new arguments for the basis of knowledge, revolution, and evolutionary notions of social morality and alternative political economies.

In short the old edifices of political ideology and religious belief began to disintegrate. As the Great War was followed by economic depression in the 1930s, then another world war, Canadians were less and less willing to see the old links between religious conviction and social stability as helpful or durable.

As late as 1940 non-sectarian and public colleges and universities still did not entirely keep their distance from Christianity. University presidents of public non-denominational universities have been Protestant clergymen (for example, Robert Falconer at Toronto 1907—32) or sympathizers (Norman Mackenzie at UBC 1944—62).[35] And until various dates in the early twentieth century, Queen's University (Presbyterian), University of King's College in Halifax (Anglican — requiring adherence to the "Thirty-nine Articles" of the Anglican church), imposed faith tests. Even in the legislation introduced at the House of Commons to secularize Queen's, Parliament agreed that Queen's University

> would "continue distinctively Christian" and . . . the trustees should "satisfy themselves of the Christian character of those appointed to the teaching staff."[36]

But after 1912 there was no requirement at Queen's to declare one was a practising Presbyterian or Christian.[37] But if there were no explicit faith test there or (say) at McGill, life for non-believers and Jewish people could be difficult.[38]

As late as 1949, Prime Minister Louis St. Laurent defended the new Massey Royal Commission on the Arts, Letters, and Sciences in explicitly religious terms:

> There is another side to human life that is quite as important as the dollars and cents resulting from trade. Upon that side of the normal activities of civilized, Christian human beings, sufficient attention has not been focused nationwide.[39]

The end of the cozy relations between universities and organized religion came quickly after 1945. It was an amicable but final divorce.

For one thing, Canadians had enjoyed remarkable educational and scientific advances from the beginning of the century to 1945.[40] Most of those advances were connected in one way or other to the rising tide of teaching and research in Canadian universities. Canadians thought they had a good thing in hand, and they wanted more of it.

## APPENDIX II: CHRISTIAN HIGHER EDUCATION CANADA

Christian Higher Education Canada [CHEC] is an association of private Christian universities and colleges. It has thirty-two members made up of twenty-nine full and three associate members . The information presented here is taken directly from the readily accessible CHEC website:

www.checanada.ca/Default.aspx?pageId=110189
[accessed 15 April 2013]

| | |
|---|---|
| **Member Campuses** | 32 |
| **Full Members** | 29 |
| **Associate Members** | 3 |
| **Enrolment range** | 50 to 2600 |
| **Graduate and Seminaries** | 5 and 11 |
| **Bible and Christian Colleges** | 19 |
| **Universities** | 9 |
| **Total student enrolment** | 17,000 |

**Ambrose University College**,
Calgary, AB T3H 0L5
**Booth University College**,
Winnipeg, MB R3B 2P2
**Canadian Mennonite University**,
Winnipeg, MB R3P 2N2
**Carey Theological College**,
Vancouver, BC V6T 1J6
**Columbia Bible College**,
Abbotsford, BC V2T 2Z8
**Bethany College**,
Hepburn, SK S0K 1Z0
**Briercrest College & Seminary**,
Caronport, SK S0H 0S0
**Canadian Southern Baptist Seminary and College**, Cochrane, AB T4C 2G1
**Christ for the Nations Bible College**, Surrey, BC V4N 3G6
**Crandall University**,
Moncton, NB E1C 9L7

**Emmanuel Bible College**, Kitchener, ON N2A 2H2
**Heritage College / Heritage Theological Seminary**, Cambridge, ON N3C 3T2
**Master's College and Seminary, The**, Peterborough, ON K9H 5T2
**McMaster Divinity College**, Hamilton, ON L8S 4K1
**Peace River Bible Institute**, Sexsmith, AB T0H 3C0
**Providence College and Seminary**, Terburne, MB R0A 1G0
**Steinbach Bible College**, Steinbach, MB R5G 1T4
**Summit Pacific College**, Abbotsford, BC V2S 7E7
**Tyndale University College & Seminary**, Toronto, ON M2M 4B3
**Eston College**, Eston, SK S0L 1A0
**Horizon College and Seminary**, Saskatoon, SK S7H 2M9
**The King's University College**, Edmonton, AB T6B 2H3
**Kingswood University**, Sussex, NB E4E 1E6
**Pacific Life Bible College**, Surrey, BC V3S 2A6
**Prairie Bible Institute**, Three Hills, AB T0M 2N0
**Redeemer University College**, Ancaster, ON L9K 1J4
**Rocky Mountain College**, Calgary, AB T2L 1L1
**St. Stephen's University**, St. Stephen, NB E3L 3E2
**Trinity Western University and ACTS Seminaries**, Langley, BC V2Y 1Y1
**Vanguard College**, Edmonton, AB T5G 2J9

## APPENDIX III: SELECTED ARTICLES AND PAPERS PUBLISHED 2009–12 IN THE INTERNET

Publications listed below were mostly written in response to CAUT reports under CAUT *Procedures in Academic Freedom Cases Involving Allegations of Requirement of an Ideological or Faith Test as a Condition of Employment* — or as rejoinders or rebuttals. All URLs were functioning as of April 15, 2013. The list below appears in date order of original publication. Journalistic articles on this question are numerous and continue to appear. A full list is beyond the scope of this essay.

The list emphasizes the case of Trinity Western University and the investigation of it by the Canadian Association of University Teachers, but there are similar bodies of criticism and response in regard to all of Canada's confessional, private post-secondary universities and colleges.

John G. Stackhouse, "CAUT versus Trinity Western," *University Affairs/Affaires Universitaires,* 2010 January 11. www.universityaffairs.ca/caut-versus-trinity-western.aspx

Erin Millar and Ben Coli, "Academic freedom at Trinity Western?" *Maclean's Magazine*, 2010 January 21. http://oncampus.macleans.ca/education/2010/01/21/academic-freedom-at-christian-universities/

Wintery Knight [pseud.—blog], "The Secular Left Takes Aims at Canadian Christian Universities," 2010 January 24. http://winteryknight.wordpress.com/2010/01/24/the-secular-left-takes-aim-at-canadian-christian-universities/

Adrian Macnair, "Clamping Down on Canadian Christians," *National Post*, 2010 January 25. http://network.nationalpost.com/np/blogs/fullcomment/archive/2010/01/25/adrian-macnair-clamping-down-on-canadian-christians.aspx

Al Hiebert, *Faith Today*, 2010 January-February, 32-8. www.evangelicalfellowship.ca/NetCommunity/Page.aspx?pid=7106

Todd Pettigrew, "The End of the Religious University," *Maclean's Magazine*, 2010 January 25. http://oncampus.macleans.ca/education/2010/01/25/the-end-of-the-religious-university/

Craig Carter, "The Dictatorship of Relativism," [blog—general title "The Politics of the Cross Resurrected"], 2010 January 26. http://politicsofthecrossresurrected.blogspot.ca/2010/01/dictatorship-of-relativism.html

Kathleen Gilbert, "Canadian Professors' Union Blacklists Christian University over Academic Freedom," *Lifesite News*, 2010 February 10. www.lifesitenews.com/ldn/2010/feb/10020308.html

[anon.: blog], "Professor Stupid Bigot," *Two Wrongs*, 2010 February 03. http://heyitsjustablogman.blogspot.com/2010/02/professor-stupid.html

Charles Lewis, "Petition Backs Universities in Academic Freedom Dispute," National Post, 2011 February 07. http://life.nationalpost.com/2011/02/07/academics-back-christian-universities-in-academic-freedom-dispute/

Charles Lewis, "Christian University Says It Won't Cooperate with Investigation from Teachers Federation," *National Post*, 2011 February 09. http://life.nationalpost.com/2011/02/09/christian-university-says-it-wont-co-operate-with-investigation-from-teachers-federation/

# APPENDIX IV: ACADEMIC FREEDOM PROVISION IN THE COLLECTIVE AGREEMENT IN FORCE AT THE UNIVERSITÉ ST-PAUL D'OTTAWA (FRENCH ORIGINAL TEXT AND ENGLISH TRANSLATION)

## LIBERTE UNIVERSLTAIRE

L'Université oeuvre pour le bien commun de l'Eglise et de la société en contribuant à la quête et à la diffusion du savoir, de la vérité et des idées, et en encourageant la pensée autonome et son expression parmi son personnel universitaire et ses etudiants. Or, ces objectifs ne peuvent être atteints sans la liberté universitaire.Tous les Membres ont le droit de jouir de la liberté universitaire.

La liberté universitaire comprend le droit à la liberté d'enseignement et de débat; la liberté de mener des recherches et d'en diffuser et d'en publier les résultats; la liberte de produire et d'exécuter des ouvrages de creation; la liberté de s'engager au service de l'Université, de l'Eglise et de la collectivité; la liberté d'exprimer librement son opinion au sujet de l'Université, de son administration ou du système au sein duquel la personne travaille; la liberté de ne pas être assujetti à la censure institutionnelle; la liberte d'acquérir, de préserver et de rendre accessibles des materiaux documentaires de toutes sortes; et la liberté de participer aux activités d'organismes universitaires représentatifs.

La liberté universitaire n'exige pas la neutralité de la part du personnel universitaire. La liberté universitaire comporte le droit de se servir de cette liberté d'une façon qui soit conforme à l'obligation du savant de fonder ses recherches, son enseignement et sa science sur une quête honnête du savoir. La liberté universitaire ne confère pas l'immunité légale, non plus qu'elle ne vient tempérer l'obligation qui incombe aux Membres de satisfaire à leurs responsabilités envers I'Université.

## ACADEMIC FREEDOM

The university works for the common good of the church and of society by searching for and by disseminating knowledge, truth, and ideas, and encouraging independent thought and its expression among staff and students. These objectives cannot be reached in the absence of academic freedom. All members have the right to academic freedom.

Academic freedom includes the right to free teaching and debate; the freedom to conduct research and to disseminate and publish its results; the freedom to produce and to complete creative works; the freedom to engage in the service of the university, of the church, and of the collectivity; the freedom to express freely one's opinion on the subject of the university, its administration or the system in which one works; freedom from subjection to institutional censure; freedom to acquire, preserve, and make accessible documentary materials of all kinds; and the freedom to participate in the activities of representative university organizations.

Academic freedom does not require neutrality of a university teacher. Academic freedom brings with it the right to use that freedom taking into account the scholar's duty to base his or her research, teaching, and science on an honest search for understanding. Academic freedom does not confer legal immunity, nor does it temper members' duty to fulfill their responsibilities to the university.

# 8

# ACADEMIC FREEDOM FROM A CHRISTIAN UNIVERSITY PERSPECTIVE: A PERSONAL REFLECTION

*Gerald Gerbrandt*

It is a privilege to participate in this conversation on academic freedom. My approach to academic freedom arises out of an interaction between research and theoretical thinking on one side, and my personal experience on the other. For the past thirty years I have been involved with university administration, first as academic dean and then as president. As most university administrators, however, I entered post-secondary education as a junior professor, and currently look forward to returning to the classroom.

It is also important to note that the setting in which I worked was a Christian institution, the kind of place frequently considered to be opposed to academic freedom. My academic and administrative home for my first twenty-five years was a small college in Winnipeg known as Canadian Mennonite Bible College (CMBC). In 2000 it merged with two other small colleges to form Canadian Mennonite University (CMU). Although my primary home was a small church-related institution, since 1964 it had been an Approved Teaching Centre of the University of Manitoba. As academic dean of CMBC I became actively involved in negotiating understandings around academic freedom with faculty and academic administration at a public university. In other words, I approach the topic as someone who has worked both on the academic side and administration, as someone whose primary context has been a Christian institution, but also has worked with the public university. My reflections below are strictly personal, and should not be taken to represent CMU, or for that matter, other Christian institutions.

A final preliminary observation: I acknowledge that over the past forty years my understanding on academic freedom has evolved. I do see it differently today than I did earlier in my career, and project that as I continue to reflect, read and have conversation with fellow travellers my position will continue to evolve. That is what makes life in a university setting so exciting.

I begin with an affirmation. I understand myself to support strongly academic freedom as fundamental to the mission of a university. In fact, I was surprised to see the theme for the recent Harry Crowe Foundation conference on academic freedom to be "The Limits of Academic Freedom." It is not that I think academic freedom is absolute or limitless — clearly it cannot be that. But I find myself less drawn to conversation about the limits of academic freedom than to how we might foster greater academic freedom for creative imaginative thinkers in our universities.

I understand academic freedom as a mutually agreed upon compact between universities and society, a convention which benefits and serves both. The case for academic freedom is based directly in the mission or task of the university. Universities exist to serve the common good. That cannot be expressed too often. That common good is represented most significantly by the more local or particular community with which that university works, but includes larger humanity as well. In this respect good universities are good global citizens. Ultimately it is the common good of all humanity that the university must keep in mind, but its particular context and relationships influence and largely determine how that is worked out in practice.

That holds true both for provincial universities as well as independent ones like CMU. Each has a responsibility to serve the larger common good, even as it relates in a more concerted manner to a particular region or people. In the case of Christian schools, the particular people to which they relate tends to be a more concrete body of loyal stakeholders, or constituency, with a strong sense of identity and commitment to the institution and its mission. These stakeholders may be a Christian denomination, a combination of denominations, or an association of individuals who have chosen to support that institution.

Having a strong constituency base can be a significant strength for such schools, even as it also complicates some dynamics. On more than one occasion, I have had to defend and promote a vision for a genuine university among friends of the school, some of whom at least tended to see the role of the institution largely limited to inculcating a particular tradition into the next generation. Such debates can be stimulating as well as frustrating. Having this concrete constituency thus can impact the dynamics of an independent Christian university, but it does not really change the larger understanding of the mission of a university.

Within that framework, universities are places where generations together think as clearly and systematically as possible about any and all aspects of our world, never simply satisfied with the answers of the past or the consensus of the day. They are places where tradition or previously generated knowledge is passed on from one generation to another as well as where that tradition is interrogated, to be affirmed, reformulated, or even rejected. A recent Canadian university president regularly summarized the task of a university as preserving, teaching and creating knowledge.

The balance or tension between questioning and affirming tradition may vary from discipline to discipline as well as from context to context. When I recently shared my definition of a university with a biologist, I noticed that he immediately became somewhat uncomfortable with how little weight this language gave to accumulated knowledge painstakingly arrived at by previous generations of scientists. He was anxious that the phrase "never simply satisfied with the answers of the past or the consensus of the day" might give too much credence to those who question evolution and other hard-won victories of science. Researchers in the humanities might be more comfortable with this approach.

Academic freedom then is the principle developed to protect faculty from undue pressure in this process of thinking clearly and systematically, as they serve the larger good through the pursuit of truth and technique for a better life. Academic freedom has the goal of ensuring that the answers of the past, the consensus of the day, or the political pressures of the moment do not unduly limit or prejudge the directions that investigation might take. As tradition is questioned, and new solutions tested, it is inevitable that researchers will head down many dead-end streets or wrong turns. It has been suggested that one reason the Silicon Valley is so successful is that people have come to terms with the fact that the majority of business ventures will fail. Similarly, creative thinking about important matters is a high-risk adventure, with missteps a necessary element of the process. I have often used the phrase "faculty have a right to be wrong" in defending academic freedom. In fact, if they have never been wrong, they probably have not been doing cutting-edge thinking. Academic freedom protects this potential to be wrong.

I thus affirm the Canadian Association of University Teachers (CAUT) when it speaks of academic freedom as: "free of orthodoxy or threat of reprisal and discrimination." It is striking that in speaking of academic freedom, CAUT borrows language from the Christian tradition, and appropriately so. Literally, orthodoxy means correct or right thinking, but, practically, both in the church and in general society, it has come to refer to the answers provided by tradition. Within the church this has meant the creeds or confessions; within society it has come to refer to the consensus within a field of knowledge.

My commitment to the Christian church has only intensified my convictions around academic freedom. The church today is in the midst of major change and transition. Phyllis Tickle, founding editor of the Religion Department of *Publishers* Weekly, has suggested that the church is moving into a period of change comparable to that of the sixteenth-century Reformation.[2] Such major transition and transformation is inevitably accompanied by heated, vigorous debate. The Christian church, not atypical of long-standing institutions, has a natural tendency to be conservative, to allow inertia to limit the constant need to change and rethink the historic Christian faith or orthodoxy in relationship to a new time and context. In this time of foment it is critical for the future of the church and its mission that its scholars are able to think about God and the world and the people of God empowered through academic freedom.

And yet, despite my commitment to academic freedom, I consider it appropriate and justifiable for Christian universities like CMU to expect its faculty members to be practising Christians. Let me add immediately, I say this without making use of the argument that religious freedom gives such institutions a kind of exemption to override academic freedom. Rather, I believe the practice is defensible in of itself, serving the Canadian common good, and consistent with a commitment to academic freedom. In other words, I do not consider this one of "the limits of academic freedom."

Religious freedom is important for me, and I believe for Canada. You have to remember I am a Mennonite, part of a people who fled from central Europe to Prussia, from there to the Ukraine, and from there to Canada and the US, in each case attempting to escape religious persecution, or searching for greater religious freedom. It is important that Canadian society retain a commitment to religious freedom, a freedom which only means something when there is disagreement over an issue, or when a religious group is at odds with general societal practices or assumptions. There may be times when Christian universities may need to invoke the religious freedom principle, but that is not what I am arguing here.

Academic freedom — freedom of religion — freedom of the press — freedom of speech — all are important in civil society. They remain important even if obviously each cannot be absolute. With this recognition it becomes inevitable that these freedoms may on occasion bump heads with each other. Such potential conflict cannot be avoided by placing them in a hierarchy, or by attempting to judge ahead of time which is more significant. Further, Christian universities may at times appeal to freedom of religion to protect some aspect of their enterprise. Should that happen, careful assessment is needed by society to determine whether it is justifiable.

I also recognize that although I maintain that a university expecting its faculty members to be Christian is not in tension with a commitment to academic freedom, there is as long history of tension between Christianity and careful, systematic thinking which has led to intense battles, battles in which the Christian community doggedly defended its orthodoxy in the face of careful reflection. The seventeenth-century battle over the nature of the universe, and the twentieth-century struggle over evolution are just two such examples. I also accept that Christian institutions have at times (often?) understood their role as less than that of a university, largely as institutions preserving and carrying on their tradition rather than critically interacting with it, with no consideration for academic integrity or freedom. Institutions like that may have had their place, but the church of today, as well as society, needs universities which move beyond that.

As an aside, I was twelve years old when the Harry Crowe case[3] blew up in Winnipeg. I was raised in a small, rural Manitoba town where my father was a Mennonite pastor. I remember seeing the headlines in the *Tribune*, and hearing my father reflect on how the university was mistreating him. Not that many years earlier, Crowe had been a student at a Mennonite Bible college where a professor had been released, supposedly for theological reasons. He lamented the actions of that college since the professor released had been his most influential professor. My sense is, however, that we have learned from the Harry Crowe case. The United Church of today is not the United Church of 1958 when it operated United College (now University of Winnipeg) from which Crowe was released, nor are other denominations the same.

Policies which require that faculty hired be Christian are defensible both on internal and external grounds. First, a consideration of internal realities: in order for such a practice to be consistent with a commitment to academic freedom requires distinguishing between the expectation that a faculty member espouse a particular theological position or creed, and the expectation that the faculty member work at his or her discipline within a larger tradition and community. That tradition provides questions and issues which must be considered, but does not provide the answers to them. In this it is not foundationally different from what happens in any established discipline. The Christian faith for a faculty member cannot serve as a shortcut to knowledge or truth. Careful, systematic thinking about the world, regardless of the disciplinary method employed, inevitably involves painstaking, rigorous work. The Christian researcher, whether in a Christian university or not, works with the conviction that the results of this systematic interrogation of data will not contradict his or her Christian faith, even if it may lead to a revision or refinement of how that faith intersects with or understands life.

When it comes to the teaching side, additional dynamics must be noted. Most professors in Christian institutions have received their own training at large public universities. They have been influenced by their professors, frequently continuing in relationship with them, occasionally continuing to collaborate in research. Continuity between their own graduate programs and what they now do in the classroom is high. Further, when these professors teach, they are always mindful that their goal is not only helping students to excel in their classrooms, but also preparing these students for success in graduate programs in other universities. This latter requires that the students receive solid training in the basic elements of the discipline in a manner recognizable by, congruent with what they will experience in grad school.

The impact of the above is that faculty in Christian universities teach in a manner similar to the norm at public universities. What is taught in political studies or biology or mathematics or psychology in a Christian university is not essentially different from what is taught at a public university. In the early years of CMBC's Approved Teaching Centre arrangement with the University of Manitoba, CMBC students were required to take the same exams given to students on the main campus. Appropriately, each faculty member will give the subject her or his own colouring, but academic freedom allows for that in both settings. In both settings, the canons of critical inquiry, or the scientific method employed by all, would be essentially identical. Historically students from Christian institutions have tended to make the transition into public university graduate programs very well, performing successfully in those programs.

But education is about more than gaining empirical knowledge and vocational skills. It is also about more than learning truth, despite what Christianity has sometimes unfortunately overly emphasized. Education with soul includes character formation, it includes helping students become better persons, adults who individually and together with others contribute to the common good, to the reduction of pain and discord. In a Christian university, the Christian faith becomes a lens through which the academic community, faculty, and students together search for wisdom and meaning, encouraging compassion and hope and commitment and service. It provides a perspective from which the methodology and assumptions of the discipline are questioned, always keeping in mind a larger commitment to the common good, and what those students might contribute to it.

The difference of a Christian university is more in this additional expectation. Here the professors together with the students are expected to participate in conversation and reflection around meaning and wisdom and God in relation to the results of their empirical investigation. Harvey Cox recently wrote a book called *The Future of Faith* in which he acknowledges, much to his surprise, and in conflict with his projections in his 1965 *The Secular City*, that religion has not faded from the landscape, but according to him is, in fact, making a resurgence.[4] This resurgence he associates with a transition from what he calls an age of belief to an age of the spirit. In the age of belief, assenting to orthodoxy or correct doctrine was the defining characteristic of Christianity. The age of the spirit, he suggests, is characterized by less emphasis on dogma, more emphasis on spirituality, with faith becoming Christianity's defining quality. In a Christian university, each faculty member is expected to participate with students in the enterprise of exploring faith, without institutional parameters dictating exactly how this is done. This they can only do with passion and integrity if they are participants in that tradition, with a personal sense of compassion and commitment to service. With this approach, I do not consider Christian faith as needing to be a formal limiting factor on academic freedom within a Christian university.

And yet I am not claiming there is absolute academic freedom at Christian universities. That simply is not the case. The primary pressures undermining it, however, are more informal than formal. The combination of peer pressure and the larger mood of the times, either in society in general or the Christian community in particular, are more of a factor than the expectations of administration or owners. In this Christian universities are little different from public universities where similarly the factors interfering with thinking about life as clearly and systematically as possible come more from informal forces such as the disciplinary guild, research grant expectations, a desire for approval, than from formal institutional limitations. Religious affiliation and limitations can and have limited academic freedom in Christian institutions in the past, but today the prevalent culture of political correctness is a more significant factor infringing upon academic freedom.

I might even suggest that practically, the range of academic freedom at a Christian institution is as great as that at a public university, even if perhaps not identical in territory. It is for this reason that I find discussion of academic freedom focused entirely on the freedom of an individual faculty member, or more specifically, the potential abuse of that freedom, an inadequate defence of this valuable aspect of university life.

Historically tenure has been considered the key mechanism for protecting academic freedom. CAUT appropriately notes, "Tenure constitutes the primary procedural safeguard of academic freedom, and is essential for the maintenance of intellectual liberty and high standards in postsecondary education and in scholarship."[5] This I affirm, but it is not enough. In the past few decades, in the face of financial pressures, the portion of student credit hours (remember that often sessionals teach the large classes) taught by fully tenured professors has decreased substantially. How can the academic freedom of sessionals and those on the way to tenure more helpfully be enhanced?

Rather than being primarily defensive, perhaps institutions might take to offence, to asking what might be done to foster academic freedom. A strong case can be made that a significant responsibility of university administrators, both larger institutional administrators and academic leaders, is to smooth the way for the academics as they teach and do research at the edge of old knowledge, in the process of exploring new knowledge. This is needed both on a general level as well as in relationship to particular issues. Given the natural inertia of communities and organizations, academic freedom should not be only a passive right — we affirm and individual's right to it — but also one proactively promoted.

This may require asking explicitly where informal pressures and dynamics are so strong that researchers have difficulty investigating as freely as they might, without being unduly influenced by past answers, current consensus, or I might add, political divisions. Every age, every setting, every community tends to have issues which become so controversial, or so politicized, that despite all general rhetoric about academic freedom, it is largely overwhelmed in the heat of the debate. Communism was one of those issues in the 1950s — the Middle East, gender, race, and sexuality each have the potential to become so polarized or subject to political correctness that genuine debate is inhibited. Perhaps every institution should explicitly name those issues that have become so political and divisive that "affirmative action" is required to ensure that careful, systematic thinking is possible around them.

Affirmative action might also be a helpful way to balance the natural tendency for Christian universities, as well as departments which develop a particular ideological bent, to develop a group think approach to the world. In both there is a tendency to hire those who think similarly to those already there. A proactive approach could include intentionally bringing in visiting scholars and resources which reflect a divergent perspective.

An experience at CMU over the past decade has encouraged me to call for this intentional diversity in settings which, for whatever reason, has become somewhat uniform. For the past decade or so CMU has been involved in regular dialogue with a group of Muslim clerics from a university in Iran. At first this was limited to formal conversations between faculty from CMU and a few other Mennonite institutions with scholars from Iran. It then progressed to having students from Iran study at CMU, and there is discussion about having students from CMU going to Iran for a course.

These conversations have been extremely stimulating, highlighting the value of thinking about important matters with people who see the world very differently from what we are used to seeing. They highlight the value of not requiring the conversation partner to think like we do, including on the issue of academic freedom. They also lead me to me ask whether Canada would not be a better place if there were a greater diversity of institutions, not only public and Christian, but also possibly Muslim and Jewish and Hindu and so on.

This last observation raises the question of external dynamics or the larger Canadian context. I began by noting that universities have as their mission the service of the common good. Unlike in the USA where the small liberal arts college, often church-related, remains a significant part of the post-secondary scene, in Canada that scene is dominated by large, public universities. Despite the emphasis on individual academic freedom in the public university, and despite the twentieth and twenty-first century calls for diversity in the Western world, Canadian universities are becoming increasingly similar to each other. The drive for efficiency and competition, and the appropriate practice of learning from each other, all contribute toward a kind of homogenization of post-secondary education.

It is always difficult for those in the majority or the dominant position to appreciate fully how powerful and overwhelming they are to those of a divergent position. It might be argued that the greatest threat today to academic freedom and out-of-the-box thinking on matters important to the human race is the increasing dominance of a single approach to reality. The larger good of Canadian society may be best served by proactively affirming genuine diversity in post-secondary institutions rather than only the same diversity within each institution.

Christian universities have the potential to contribute to this diversity by providing a valuable alternative and supplement to the larger public universities. I do not argue that they should ever be the norm for a country like Canada. As a Mennonite, I come from a tradition which is always nervous about enforced uniformity, whether instituted by state, church, or in some other manner. Admittedly all too often faculty at Christian universities have functioned largely in their own world, with insufficient consideration of and conversation with their counterparts in the public university. Both, I believe, could benefit from increased interaction, with frank and open conversation about any and all matters.

When I was installed as president of CMU, I spoke of the university as a place where faculty together with students are expected to ask critical questions about any and all aspects of life, including the consensus of the day, the dogmas of our faith, and the traditional ways of the university. All are open to critical examination, with the outcome not predetermined by answers of the past. Within the Canadian context, Christian universities committed to academic freedom symbolize and represent one way of asking critical questions about the "ways of the university," and, in so doing, serve the common good of society.

# IV. ACADEMIC FREEDOM AND EQUITY

# 9

# DEMONSTRATIONS ON CAMPUS AND THE CASE OF ISRAELI APARTHEID WEEK

*Richard Moon*

## INTRODUCTION

In the public sphere, expression is subject to relatively few legal restrictions. Canadian law includes "content" restrictions on obscenity, hate speech, defamation, and false advertising.[1] There are also some legal restrictions on the manner or character of expression, including limits on speech that is intimidating or threatening. Finally there are laws that regulate the time or location at which expression may occur and are concerned with co-ordinating expression with other activities in the public sphere.

The issue I want to consider in this chapter is whether the limits on expression should be stricter in the university environment — whether the university has particular or stronger reasons to limit some forms of speech, even when it occurs in the open or public spaces of the campus. Since the university is not (as a general matter) a government actor, subject to the *Canadian Charter of Rights and Freedoms*, this is significantly a political or institutional question about the kinds of speech that advance the university's educational mission or are consistent with its operation.[2] Speech may be subject to significant limits in the classroom or meeting room, concerning who speaks and when, and the manner and subject of the speech; however, in the public spaces of the campus the scope of protected speech (in the form of demonstrations, leaflets, posters) should be very broad, similar to that in the general public sphere. Yet a case can be made that racist and other forms of bigoted speech, even when it is not so extreme that it breaches general hate speech laws, should be prohibited on campus. A commitment to academic freedom supports the free and open exchange of ideas and information but also certain standards of communicative engagement — most notably the treatment of others in the academic community as interlocutors, as conversation partners who should be addressed and listened to. Racial (and other) stereotypes and insults are inconsistent with the educational mission of the school and the idea of membership in an educational community. More generally, the injury of racist speech may be more acute in the closer environment and tighter community of the campus. However, the exclusion of a broad category of racist speech from university campuses raises a variety of issues. First, the scope of a ban on hate speech (that is broader than the ban in the *Criminal Code*) may be difficult to define and contain. Second, the university administration may be inclined to define a ban very broadly, so that it encompasses not just racist speech, but also any speech that is seen as offensive or provocative and likely to disturb campus peace or upset alumni and donors. Third, the growing use of new communicative technologies by students, both on campus (even in the classroom) and outside, and by instructors as part of the educational process, has made the boundaries of the campus and the scope of university speech less clear.

In addressing the question of the appropriate limits (or forms of regulation) of speech on campus, and campus demonstrations in particular, I will consider the case of Israeli Apartheid Week [IAW], an event that takes place each year on several Canadian campuses. More particularly I will consider whether IAW (and its claim that Israel is an apartheid state) is anti-Semitic and appropriately banned from campuses. The Canadian Parliamentary Coalition to Combat Anti-Semitism in its recent report has suggested that IAW is anti-Semitic, at least in practice; however, the report is reluctant to say that the event should be prohibited on campus and instead calls for measures to ensure that other views are heard.[3]

## FREEDOM OF EXPRESSION IN THE PUBLIC SPHERE

Freedom of expression protects the individual's freedom to communicate with others. The right of the individual is to participate in an activity that is deeply social in character and that involves socially created languages and the use of community resources. Freedom of expression is valuable because human agency and identity emerge in discourse.[4] We become individuals capable of thought and judgment, and we develop as rational and feeling persons when we join in conversation with others. When an individual expresses something not only does she/he formulate it (in a socially created language) but she/he places it in a public space and joins with others in a common act of focusing on a particular matter.[5] The creation of meaning is a shared process, something that takes place between speaker and listener. The speaker understands her/his articulated ideas and feelings in light of the reactions and responses of others. The listener locates and evaluates the speaker's words within the framework of her/his knowledge and experience.[6] The social emergence of human thought, feeling, and identity can be expressed in the language of truth or individual autonomy or democratic self-government. Each of the traditional accounts of the value of freedom of expression (democratic-, truth-, and self-realization-based accounts) represents a particular perspective on, or dimension of, the constitution of human agency in communicative interaction. At the same time, the variety of these accounts reflects the different roles that expression plays in the life of individual and community — that different relationships and different forms of communication contribute to the realization of human agency and the formation of individual identity.

Recognition that individual agency and identity emerge in communicative interaction is crucial to understanding not only the value of expression but also its potential for harm. Our dependence on expression means that words can sometimes be hurtful. Our identity is shaped by what we say and by what others say to us and about us. Expression can cause fear, it can harass, it can mislead, and it can undermine self-esteem. Because expression is a relationship between speaker and listener, it can be compromised by manipulation and deceit, and by incivility and ridicule. However, standards of civility — of respectful discourse — are conventional and difficult to establish in a complex society. Different cultural groups within the larger community will have very different views about the requirements, and even the importance, of civility or respect. Free expression must protect speech that challenges social norms — including, perhaps, norms of social respect and interaction.[7] Moreover, individuals are sometimes quite emotional when they speak about issues that matter to them and the emotional force of their speech may be an important part of their message. They may be angry or frustrated about a particular action or policy. They may use strong words to gain the attention of others or to shake the audience from its complacency.

A commitment to freedom of expression means that the speaker must be free to express his/her views on a range of issues and the audience must be free to hear what others say and to make their own judgment about the merits of what is said. If the speaker is wrong then his/her speech should be answered, not censored.[8] An important corollary of this is that the speaker should not be held responsible for the (harmful) actions his/her audience may take in response to her/his speech — either because audience members are persuaded by her/his message, or opposed to it. This broad protection of expression rests on two assumptions: that humans are substantially rational beings capable of evaluating different claims, and that public discourse is open to a wide range of views or that all individuals have a meaningful opportunity to participate in public discourse.[9]

Freedom of expression doctrine, though, recognizes that these assumptions do not always hold and permits the restriction of "manipulative" expression in exceptional circumstances. Expression is viewed as manipulative (or as incitement) when it takes a form and/or occurs in circumstances that limit the audience's ability to rationally assess the claims made and the consequences of acting on those claims. For example, in *On Liberty* J.S. Mill argued that the authorities would be justified in preventing a fiery speech given near the home of a corn merchant to a crowd of farmers angry about crop prices.[10] A heated speech delivered to a "mob" appeals to passion and prejudice, and might lead to impulsive and harmful actions. In American free speech jurisprudence the classic example of a failure in the conditions of ordinary rational discourse comes from a judgment of Justice Holmes, who asserted that: "The most stringent protection of free speech would not protect a man in falsely shouting fire in a theatre and causing a panic."[11] The false yell of fire represents an identifiable and discrete deviation from the conditions of ordinary discourse. The theatre audience in such a case would not have the time to stop and think carefully before acting on the communicated message. The panic that would follow the yell of fire in these circumstances would likely result in injury.

The state then may restrict appeals to passion and prejudice in exceptional circumstances — when the time and space for independent judgment are compressed and emotions are running so high that individuals are less likely to stop and reflect on the claims made and more likely to respond impulsively.[12] The Canadian courts, though, have gone further than this and upheld restrictions on speech that are harmful or carry a risk of harm, in the sense that they might lead or persuade the audience to take harmful action. Notably, the Canadian courts have upheld restrictions on (extreme) hate speech because they believe that the risk of serious harm from such speech is significant.

## HATE SPEECH REGULATION

Hate speech in Canada is currently restricted by both federal and provincial laws. The *Criminal Code* of Canada prohibits the advocacy or promotion of genocide, the incitement of hatred against an identifiable group, and the wilful promotion of hatred against such a group.[13] Hate speech is also restricted by human rights laws. For example, section 13 of the *Canada Human Rights Act,* which prohibited Internet communication that is likely to expose the members of an identifiable group to hatred or contempt, was repealed in 2013. However, similar provisions remain part of the human rights codes of British Columbia, Alberta, Saskatchewan, and the Northwest Territories.[14]

There are two kinds of hate speech — or perhaps more accurately two kinds of harm caused by hate speech.[15] Hate speech may cause harm directly to the members of a racial, or other, target group (the group that is both the subject and audience of the hate speech). The direct harms of hate speech include fear, intimidation, insult, and emotional trauma. The other kind of harm associated with hate speech is the spread of hateful views in the community or, in less general terms, the instilling of hateful attitudes about the members of a minority group in the minds of members of the larger community, who may then act in a violent or discriminatory way toward these group members. The type of harm caused by a particular instance of hate speech will depend significantly on the audience to which the speech is directed. The same speech act, of course, may contribute to both kinds of harm.

The challenge to freedom of expression is different depending on the type of harm the law seeks to prevent. The restriction of speech that threatens others is easily reconciled with a commitment to freedom of expression. The limited free speech value of these acts must be weighed against the intended and significant injury to others. The meaning and force of a racist threat depends significantly on the larger background of racist expression and action. A burning cross, planted in front of the home of the first black family to move into a previously all-white neighbourhood, is experienced as threatening because it evokes the history of Klan violence against blacks.[16] Similarly, a march with swastikas and SS uniforms in a Jewish neighbourhood is experienced as threatening because it evokes the history of Nazi persecution of Jews.[17] Even if these threats do not seem realistic or immediate to an outside observer, they must be viewed from the perspective of a target group member who experiences them as part of a continuing practice of violence against his or her group. The history and context of violence gives rise to genuine and understandable fear and insecurity. Even if the members of the target group know that the threat cannot be carried out (although it is not clear why they would feel confident about this), it is so closely linked to a larger practice of violent oppression that it is bound to cause significant anxiety and upset. The broader context of racist violence provides a basis for distinguishing unacceptable threats from "the rough and tumble of public debate," which is sometimes unpleasant and impolite. The context of racist violence and discrimination may also provide a basis for treating racist insults differently from other insults. Racist insults are different not only because they are often a prelude to violent behaviour, but also because the context of violence, discrimination, and oppression adds significantly to their emotional impact. As well, a racist insult is not an isolated occurrence. The frequent expression of such insults (coming from different sources) means that they cannot easily be avoided by individual target group members. Each insult is experienced as part of a practice of harassment that gives rise to a general injury of emotional upset, humiliation, and fear. Racist insults have been restricted — as constituting harassment or discrimination — in closed contexts such as the workplace.

A more significant challenge to freedom of expression is raised when hate speech laws address the more general harm of the spread of hateful views in the larger community. Hate speech claims that the members of a racial or other identity group share a dangerous or undesirable trait — that they are by nature violent or dishonest and should be feared or despised. The object of a ban on such speech is not to prevent hurt feelings or offence but rather to limit the spread of dangerous falsehoods — that may encourage violent or discriminatory actions against the members of the targeted group. However, under most accounts of freedom of expression, the state is not justified in restricting expression because it "causes" harm by persuading its audience. The audience must be free to hear different views and to make its own judgment on the merit of those views. The listener and not the speaker is responsible for the judgments she/he makes and the actions she/he takes. Yet despite our commitment to freedom of expression and our formal faith in public reason, we know that in some times and places reason does not always operate. Racist claims often play to fears and frustrations (of moral decay or unemployment) in a context in which the space for critical reflection is reduced. These claims draw on the social background of bigotry and racial stereotyping and give shape to popular but inchoate assumptions and attitudes. Moreover, hate speech often occurs in a form and context that limits the possibility of response. It is noteworthy that the Internet has become the primary vehicle for the communication of hate speech. Because the Internet audience is highly fragmented, it is easy for a particular website to operate at the margins. While most websites are public in the sense that they are generally accessible, the audience for a particular site is often self-selecting and sympathetic, and sometimes quite small. Thus these sites can be an effective means for individuals and groups who hold hateful views to encourage others to adopt more extreme views or to take violent action. "More speech" is a hollow response, if the individuals who visit these marginal sites are uninterested in exposing themselves to other views. When directed at an insular audience, extreme speech may reinforce and extend bigoted views without being exposed to public criticism. Individuals, already weighed down by prejudice or susceptible to manipulation or already part of an extremist subculture, will see in these claims a plausible account of their social and economic marginalization and a justification for radical action. And so the failure to ban the extreme or radical edge of prejudiced speech (that which even implicitly calls for or justifies violence) may carry too many risks, particularly when it circulates within the racist subculture that subsists on the Internet.

## PUBLIC FORUMS AND DEMONSTRATIONS

The courts have held that the *Canadian Charter of Rights* protects the individual's right to communicate on a state-owned property, if that property is open to the public and its ordinary operation or function will not be significantly impaired by communicative activity.[18] Parks and streets are the standard examples of "public forums" — the common or shared spaces in which individuals are free to exchange ideas and information. Historically these properties have served as communicative forums or platforms for individual who do not have easy access to the broadcast or print media. Moreover, the parks and streets are places where individuals can congregate in large numbers to express together — demonstrate — their position on an issue. However, the privatization of important gathering places and the growth of new communication technologies have reduced the significance of parks and streets as locations for communication. Public meeting places, the places where individuals gather and interact, are increasingly owned by private corporations. Individuals congregate in shopping malls and office buildings, but have no right to communicate on these properties. More significantly, the scale of political community has grown to such an extent that meaningful public discourse is no longer conducted face-to-face, by speaking at community meetings or handing out leaflets on street corners. Public discourse is instead mediated. It takes place in the pages of privately owned newspapers or in the programs of privately (and publicly) owned television and radio stations and more recently on the Internet. Members of the community have come to rely on these media to provide them with information and ideas, and are inclined to regard the ideas expressed in leaflets or from "soap boxes" on street corners as eccentric.

The Internet may have reduced the role of parks and street as forums for communication; yet demonstrations, the public gathering of many in support of a common cause, continue to occur. There are, I suspect, a number of reasons for the continuing significance of demonstrations. The participants in a demonstration experience a sense of solidarity, strength, action, and even performance. Because a demonstration takes place in a public or common space, it may be witnessed by bystanders, and if it gains media attention, it may reach an even larger and more diverse audience; although, the media generally pay attention only if the demonstration is disruptive and tend to focus on the disruption rather than the message.[19] While the Internet enables individuals to communicate with both small and large groups of like-minded individuals (indeed the Internet is often used in the organization of demonstrations), Internet communication lacks the physical immediacy of a demonstration and seldom reaches a diverse audience.

While parks and street corners sometimes serve as forums for speech, they also serve other functions, such as recreation and transit. The coordination of different uses of public property was the central issue in several recent cases concerning the Occupy movement. In each of these cases a municipality sought an injunction requiring the dismantling of tent camps in public parks. The courts in these cases accepted that the Occupy camps were a form of expression.[20] Yet, at the same time, they decided that the restriction of this expression — the closing down of the camps — was justified. According to the courts, the participants did not have the right to maintain indefinitely structures that interfered with other legitimate or ordinary uses of the properties.[21] The protestors could not be permitted to "hog" the park and "intimidate" other users.[22] According to the courts, the message of the residents of the camps had been communicated for some time, and the same, or at least a similar, message could be communicated in other ways that would not interfere to the same degree with other uses of the parks. The courts, though, may have been too willing to discount the significance of the Occupy message or too quick to see a conflict between that message and other uses of the property. Most public speech is commercial in content and mediated in form. Commercial ads are everywhere, and so we take them for granted. Indeed, their ubiquity is vital to their impact.[23] The Occupy message was exceptional because it challenged the basic assumptions of the commercial culture, and because it was unmediated.[24] When speech — and political speech in particular — occurs in this direct way it is more likely to be experienced as invasive or disruptive.[25] Indeed, it is not clear whether the Occupy protests "interfered" with the "ordinary" use of the parks (picnicking, dog walking, etc.) because they displaced these uses or simply because a group of strangers brought (unorthodox) politics into a space that most people thought should be reserved for recreation.

Political demonstrations on campus may be seen differently because the university has an educational mission. Campus demonstrations often address university issues — and may be an effective way to reach the narrower university audience. Even when the issue being addressed is of more general significance, and is not simply a university concern, a campus demonstration may be seen differently because university students are expected to think about such issues, and because they lack significant resources and hence alternative venues.[26]

## FREEDOM OF EXPRESSION ON CAMPUS

Expression may be subject to stricter limits when it occurs in a particular institutional context. While the expression of racial and other stereotypes or insults may not breach general laws against hate speech (which catch only a narrow category of extreme speech), when it occurs in the workplace or in the schools it may be treated as harassment or discrimination and punished. Employees in a workplace are a captive audience, and so cannot easily avoid insults from co-workers.[27] Different standards of civility and respect apply because the workplace is both closed and hierarchical, and because it has a particular function that may be undermined by these forms of speech. The workplace is not a democratic forum, a place of free and open discourse, even if employees retain expression rights that are compatible with its function.

A university campus is a workplace and a place of learning. To what extent should the free speech rules then be different on campus? Should there be enforceable standards of civility and respect similar to other work places — or should campus speech be treated in the same way as speech in the larger public sphere? Certainly stricter standards should be applied in the classroom. Exchanges in the classroom must be respectful, and personal attacks ought to be avoided. The rules of speech are different, are stricter, because the classroom is a place of learning based on thoughtful discussion, because the members of the class are in an ongoing relationship, because they are part of a captive audience, and because there is a hierarchy in the classroom based on the teacher's authority.[28] The rules of speech may also be stricter in a university residence or dormitory. Individuals should be free of discriminatory speech in their living environment. But what about speech outside the classroom or residence — that is part of a political event in a "public space" or a space designated for extracurricular events? Should speech that occurs on campus in contexts other than the classroom be subject to rules of civility or respect enforced by the university that are stricter than those applied to general public discourse?

A university is not like other workplaces. The advancement of its educational purpose or mission requires free inquiry and open debate. The members of the university community (students and faculty) should be free to express views on political and other matters that are controversial, unorthodox, and perhaps even distasteful to others.

The right of a student or staff member to express him/herself in the common spaces of the university should be similar to the individual's right to communicate in public spaces such as the parks. However, while the university's educational mission may require the protection of free expression, it may also justify the imposition of certain limits on the scope of that protection. The members of the university community have ongoing relationships. They work, and sometimes even live, together. The university's educational purpose is realized through dialogue and engagement. The objection to sexist or racist speech on campus is not, or not simply, that it is irrational and sometimes vitriolic and so unlikely to contribute to thoughtful discourse; it is more significantly that hate speech seeks to undermine the standing of some community members. Students and faculty are members of an academic community, and membership carries with it the right to be addressed and heard.

The university environment is closer and membership is narrower than in the general community. The university's function or purpose may support the expression of a wide range of views, but like any institution there are limits to this. And so even if in the larger public sphere all values and assumptions are open to debate, in an educational community speech that questions the membership of some on the basis of their race or gender should be limited.[29] Racist, sexist, and homophobic speech, even when it is not so extreme that it breaches the *Criminal Code* or human rights codes, is appropriately restricted by the university.[30]

However, a general ban on racist (sexist etc.) speech on campus is not without difficulties. The first is the difficulty in defining the scope of such a ban. Because less extreme forms of discriminatory expression, such as stereotypes and insults, are so commonplace (and reflect widely held assumptions), it is difficult to establish clear and effective rules for their identification and exclusion. Stereotyping, in subtle forms, is everywhere. The regulation of discriminatory speech on campus then will require the administration to draw difficult distinctions based on its assessment of the meaning and potential harm of different speech acts. Because the lines are so unclear, the university's response to discriminatory speech (including the use of stereotypes) on campus should be educative and non-punitive.

Secondly, university administrators may be tempted to define the scope of unprotected speech quite broadly to avoid visible strife on campus or to appease alumni and donors. Campus demonstrations raise many of the same issues that arise with demonstrations in the larger public sphere, even if these issues have a slightly different shape in the campus context. The principal issue is the compatibility of the demonstration with other activities on campus. The university's educational role is advanced by free expression, which may take the form of a protest or demonstration. However, the particular time or location of a demonstration may have a negative effect on other parts of the education process. The university then may regulate the time and place of demonstrations to protect other activities. For example, it may restrict noise that disrupts classroom instruction or private study. While the university has a responsibility to prevent breaches of the peace or interferences with classroom learning, it must not use this as an excuse to ban speech that is controversial or provocative. The desire to maintain the institution's public image or the good will of alumni or the appearance of calmness and collegiality among students may lead administrators to improperly shut down (or try to shut down) expression that falls within the ambit of academic freedom or freedom of expression. The university may try to do this directly through a ban on a particular event or speech, or indirectly through the imposition of security costs on demonstrators or the sponsors of an event — so that the threat of disruption by those opposed to a particular view results in its effective exclusion.

University administrators have struggled with the issue of counter-demonstrations, which seem to occur on campuses with increasing frequency and force. Such demonstrations often occur when an individual, who has been invited to speak usually by a campus group, is thought by others on campus (the counter-demonstrators) to represent views that are offensive or bigoted. There are several reasons why counter-demonstrations may be more common and more heated on campus. The members of the university community often feel they have a stake in what happens on campus.[31] To protest the presence of a speaker on campus is not necessarily to advocate her/his censorship. Universities are not open to all speakers. Some individuals are invited and others are not. Members of the university community are within their rights to argue that someone should not have been invited because their views are foolish or offensive. However, there have been a number of occasions when protestors on Canadian campuses have sought to prevent an invited speaker from addressing an audience (of individuals who have chosen to attend the talk). If the speaker's expression does not cross the line into racist or sexist speech, then a counter-protest, while permitted, must not interfere with the event. While the university may be concerned about the reaction spinning out of control and leading to violence, it must not respond by suppressing the primary speech (or the counter-speech) — except in extraordinary circumstances, when no other response is practically available to prevent violence.[32]

If the scope of the restriction on discriminatory speech is broad and its boundaries unclear and open to contest, the members of the university community, who are accustomed to significant autonomy in speech and action, will sometimes seek to enforce their own views about when speech is or is not acceptable. Importantly, though, this is an issue that cannot be decided by individuals or groups on campus but must be resolved according to standards and practices established by the institution.[33]

## ISRAELI APARTHEID WEEK

Israeli Apartheid Week [IAW], a campaign that occurs annually on several university campuses, has generated significant controversy and even calls for it to be banned. The focus of IAW is the occupation by the state of Israel of the West Bank and the exclusion or marginalization of the Palestinian residents of these territories as well as the discriminatory treatment of Arabs residing in Israel. It involves a series of protests, lectures, and workshops. Its aim is "to educate people about the nature of Israel as an apartheid state and to build Boycott, Divestment and Sanctions (BDS) campaigns . . ."[34]

If we understand the speech that occurs as part of the IAW campaign to be political (i.e., criticism of the policies of the government of Israel or the state of Israel) then no matter how emotional the speech, and no matter how unfair or partial it may seem to some, it ought not to be silenced by the university. Some have argued, however, that criticism of Israel (or the criticism that occurs in the context of IAW) is not simply political speech that is unreasonable or erroneous. It is, they argue, anti-Semitic in character and so properly excluded from university campuses.[35] The claim that IAW is anti-Semitic was made in the report of the Canadian Parliamentary Coalition to Combat Anti-Semitism (CPCCA) — which was released in July 2011.[36]

In its report the coalition relied on the following definition of anti-Semitism:

> Anti-Semitism is a certain perception of Jews, which may be expressed as hatred toward Jews. Rhetorical and physical manifestations of anti-Semitism are directed toward Jewish or non-Jewish individuals and/or their property, toward Jewish community institutions and religious facilities.[37]

Anti-Semitism frequently charges Jews with conspiring to harm humanity, and it is often used to blame Jews for why things go wrong. It is expressed in speech, writing, visual forms, and action, and employs sinister stereotypes and negative character traits.[38]

According to the coalition, anti-Semitism increasingly takes the form of "anti-Israel discourse" that questions the right of "the Jewish people . . . to self-determination"[39], compares the policies and actions of the state of Israel with those of Nazi Germany, and regards Jews as "collectively responsible for actions of the state of Israel."[40] In the coalition's view, "such discourse crosses the line from legitimate criticism of Israel into anti-Semitism."[41]

The coalition report described IAW as a "well-organized, aggressive campaign designed to make the Jewish state and its supporters pariahs."[42] The object of IAW, according to the coalition, is "to demonize Israel as a Jewish homeland" to a captive audience.[43] To use the term "apartheid" is to deny to "the Jewish people their right to self-determination . . . by claiming that the existence of a State of Israel is a racist endeavour."[44] The coalition also pointed to the use during IAW of the "symbols and images associated with classic anti-Semitism" (and more particularly the "blood libel") such as the 2009 poster that "featured an Israeli helicopter bombing a helpless Palestinian child clutching a teddy bear, inside a concentration camp."[45]

The coalition noted that a number of Jewish students gave evidence that they are "afraid to be visibly Jewish on campus because they are wary of being harassed" and claimed that the supporters of IAW have "hijack[ed] any open and honest dialogue regarding the Middle East" and "fostered . . . a hostile, and sometimes unsafe environment . . . for identifiable Jews and advocates for Israel."[46] The coalition was told that "Jewish students, particularly those who are forthrightly supportive of Israel, have faced harassment from other students, hostility from professors, smears on their ancestral homeland and libelous attacks on their personal integrity for supporting that homeland."[47] This, the coalition observed, is "antithetical to academic debate and devoid of the integrity and nuance that should govern the Canadian university system."[48] The coalition, however, stopped short of calling for a ban on IAW:

> Because of our commitment to free speech, and to the maintenance of open discourse on university campuses, the Inquiry Panel does not think, despite the vulgarity of Israeli Apartheid Week, that it would be appropriate for university administrators to refuse to allow the event to take place.[49]

Yet, if the coalition is right that IAW is anti-Semitic, then a ban might be justified.[50]

How might criticism of the state of Israel, and more particularly that which occurs during IAW, amount to a racist attack on the Jewish people? According to the calition's report, "IAW is also occasionally associated with the use of 'symbols and images associated with classic anti-Semitism.'"[51] While little or no evidence is given to support this claim, anti-Semitism remains a significant problem, and so it is certainly possible that familiar forms of anti-Semitic speech sometimes surface at IAW events — including representations of Jews as dishonest or conspiratorial or displays of anti-Semitic symbols such as the swastika. If these forms of anti-Semitic speech are heard with enough frequency during Israeli Apartheid Week, it might be argued that the entire event is tainted and ought to be banned. But there seems to be no evidence that these standard forms of anti-Semitic speech occur during IAW except rarely and marginally. In any event, a prophylactic response to racist speech (in this case shutting down IAW entirely) would do great harm to free speech interests and ought to be avoided except in the most extreme situations. To shut down a demonstration or event because some participants might act wrongfully is to make everyone bear the costs of the wrongs of a few. Any restriction should focus on the actual instance(s) of anti-Semitic speech and not on the entire event.

The coalition's report, though, might be making a different argument — that criticism of Israel, even that which is not discriminatory or anti-Semitic, ought to be limited or avoided because of the risk it may encourage or feed bigoted attitudes in the general community. But even if it were sometimes true that criticism of Israel reinforced the anti-Semitic views of some audience members — and this would be difficult to demonstrate — a commitment to free speech means that the speaker should not be held responsible for how some in the audience understand or use her/his speech — most obviously when this understanding is at odds with the speaker's intent. We may ask the speaker to be careful in her/his choice of words and to be conscious of the potential impact of her/his speech, but we cannot justify censoring her/him because others may misconstrue or misuse her/his words.

The report, though, suggests two other, less direct, ways in which IAW may be anti-Semitic. The coalition objects to what it sees as IAW's holding of all Jews accountable for the actions of Israel and singling out Israel for condemnation. Concerning the first claim — that IAW holds Jews collectively responsible for the wrongs of the state of Israel

— there is no evidence of this and indeed the only specific claim made in the report is that Jewish students who were forthright in their support of Israel were subjected to criticism. But it is perhaps not surprising that the coalition would attribute such a position to the supporters of IAW, since the coalition sees a strong link between the Jewish community as a whole and the state of Israel. The coalition sees Israel as the Jewish homeland and regards criticism of Israel (an "attack" on Israel) as an attack on all Jews. It is easy then for the coalition to project onto the supporters of IAW, and other critics of Israeli policy, the view that all Jews are responsible for the actions of Israel — even though many of these supporters reject the idea that there is a necessary link between Israel and the Jewish community.[52] Indeed, it may be that what the coalition really objects to is the IAW's questioning of the need for, or morality of, an exclusively Jewish state — a Jewish homeland.

The coalition also takes exception to what it sees as IAW's practice of "[s]ingling Israel out for selective condemnation."[53] According to the report: "criticism of Israel similar to that levelled against any other country cannot be regarded as anti-Semitic . . . [b]ut singling out Israel for selective condemnation and opprobrium" is discriminatory.[54] The claim seems to be that a different standard of behaviour is imposed on Israel because it is a Jewish state. The coalition observes that IAW focuses on the (perceived) wrongs of Israel and ignores the greater wrongs of other countries, such as Syria, and thinks that the explanation for this must be anti-Semitism. But the supporters of IAW may have a number of reasons, other than anti-Semitism, for taking political action in relation to Israel. These may include Israel's formal establishment as an ethnic/religious political community, its claim to be a Western-style democracy (and the perception that, despite its location, Israel is of the West rather than the Middle East — in contrast to the general perception of Syria as a pariah state), and the substantial political and economic support it receives from the United States and Canada — and hence the ability of these countries to influence Israeli policy.

For those who oppose IAW, the link between criticism of Israel and anti-Semitism may not be contingent — may not depend on the occurrence of explicit anti-Semitic statements or the likely impact of the criticism on the audience, or the singling out of Israel for criticism. The coalition and other opponents of IAW do not regard all criticism of Israel as anti-Semitic and unacceptable — or at least they make this formal claim. What is anti-Semitic and unacceptable, according to the coalition, is criticism "that brings into question the viability of Israel as a Jewish state."[55] Because the state of Israel has come to play such an important role in Jewish identity (a role that cuts across religious and cultural divisions), an attack on Israel — on its viability as a Jewish state — is experienced as an attack on Jews. The flourishing, and even the survival, of the Jewish people are understood to depend on the existence of Israel. The coalition regards the advocacy of any action that might undermine the viability of Israel as a Jewish state as anti-Semitic — as a call for the destruction not just of the state Israel but of the Jewish people. To deny Israel's "right to exist" is to threaten to leave the Jews without a "homeland" and in the words of the coalition report is "discriminatory and hateful . . ."[56] It follows from such a view that the call for a "one-state solution" and the end of Israel as an exclusively Jewish state is anti-Semitic.[57]

Here is where the distinction between political speech and anti-Semitism becomes the subject of contest. We must define the scope of legitimate public/political debate broadly. There is room for debate about what is or is not necessary to the viability of Israel as a Jewish state. Indeed, there might also be room for debate about whether the existence of a Jewish state is critical to the existence of the Jewish people — and more specifically about the appropriateness of a two or one state solution. (Just as there may be debate about how to address the needs and interests of Palestinians.) I may believe that certain positions are naïve, foolish, insensitive. But the scope of legitimate public debate cannot be restricted on such grounds. If we understand the speech that occurs as part of Israeli Apartheid Week to be political (the criticism of the policies of the government or state of Israel and even the criticism of Israel an ethnic-religious state), then no matter how emotional the speech, how unfair or unbalanced the speech may seem to some in the community, it ought not to be silenced by the university. University administrators have generally understood this.

## CONCLUSION

There is a case to be made that racist and other forms of bigoted speech, even when it is not so extreme that it breaches general hate speech laws, should be prohibited on campus. Most obviously, stricter standards of speech are applicable in the classroom, which is a place of learning and a closed environment with a captive audience. But stricter standards may also be appropriate outside the classroom, in the university's "public" spaces or spaces designated for extracurricular events. A commitment to academic freedom supports the free and open exchange of ideas and information but also certain standards of communicative engagement — most notably a requirement that others in the academic community be treated as interlocutors. Racial (and other) stereotypes and insults are inconsistent with the educational mission of the school and the idea of membership in an educational community. More generally, the injury of racist speech may be more acute in the closer environment and tighter community of the campus.

In a recent report, the Canadian Parliamentary Coalition to Combat Anti-Semitism (CPCCA) argued that Israeli Apartheid Week (IAW) is anti-Semitic. If the CPCCA is right about this, then IAW ought to be banned from campus. However, the CPCCA claim that IAW is anti-Semitic appears to rest on the politically contestable view that the existence of Israel as a Jewish state is vital to the continued existence of the Jewish people and that any criticism of actions taken by Israel to ensure its viability or any questioning of Israel's religious/ethnic identity constitutes an attack on the Jewish people as a whole. But these are politically contestable claims — about the link between nation and state, the treatment of religious-ethnic minorities, and the actions necessary to ensure the viability of the state, etc. The challenge to these claims must be treated as a legitimate part of political debate and cannot be excluded from campus.

# 10
# BALANCING ACADEMIC FREEDOM AND FREEDOM FROM DISCRIMINATION IN CONTESTED SPACES

*Anver Saloojee*

In the coming years, academics; their organizations, principally the Canadian Association of University Teachers (CAUT); and post-secondary institutions will face uncomfortable challenges related to the relationship between academic freedom and in particular freedom from discrimination. Academic freedom has many roots — one of which is in nineteenth-century liberalism. It is a freedom the academy rightly both advances and guards fiercely. The evolution and development of academic freedom however, is intimately linked to the prevailing socio-economic and political conditions; it has never been a static concept yet the academy accords it a position of privilege.

Over the past few decades, other rights and freedoms have also been articulated and advanced inside and outside the academy. Most notable is freedom from discrimination. These two freedoms exist in an uneasy alliance often not coming into direct conflict with each other. The uncomfortable questions are: how do we as academics respond, and what do we do when academic freedom and freedom from discrimination collide?

## THE ARGUMENT IN BRIEF

Discrimination, harassment, and a poisonous work environment all have a deleterious effect on the academic freedom of the person or persons on the receiving end of discrimination. And this is all the more so if the person does not have tenure. Discrimination erodes and deteriorates academic freedom. Those who discriminate should not be afforded the opportunity to hide behind the cloak of academic freedom.

This is about redefining academic freedom in light of the incredible growth of knowledge as a result of the diversification of the academy to include feminist, anti-racist, Aboriginal, and LGBTT2SIQQ[2] academics.

Academic freedom is about the expansion and inclusion of new knowledge; it is not about resistance to the new knowledge by the use of academic freedom as a weapon of exclusion. Rethinking, reimagining academic freedom in the light of competing freedoms require that we think carefully about what constitutes the common or public good and the context in which to advance the public good by not causing harm. Academic freedom after all serves socio-political and cultural purposes.

Another part of the argument is that it is incumbent on us to untether academic freedom from its self-appointed gatekeepers, but not from its guardians like the Canadian Association of University Teachers.

## ACADEMIC FREEDOM AND FREEDOM FROM DISCRIMINATION

In the context of a historically homogeneous academy that is now becoming more representative, how is academic freedom reconciled with the various challenges of diversity? As long as the historically homogenous academy reproduced itself this question did not arise. But, as the academy has become more diverse, conflicting interpretations of academic freedom about the neutrality of the scholar, and questions about the appropriate balance between two equally legitimate freedoms, academic freedom and freedom from discrimination, arise and will persist.[3]

For Michiel Horn, academic freedom in Canada is rooted in three traditions — nineteenth-century German tradition concerned with freedom to teach and publish; the nineteenth-century British tradition with its emphasis on freedom to express opinions on public issues; and the nineteenth-century growth of research universities in the United States.[4]

In the period of early liberalism both inside and outside the academy, academic freedom was a significant issue; however, other freedoms were not even on the table — notably freedom from discrimination, freedom to enter the academy if one were a person of colour or a woman or an Aboriginal First Nations person. This is far from surprising, for as Horn notes, "Overall, the history of the Canadian university has been the history of exclusion."[5]

In that era, there was no concept of harm — which it can be argued is intimately linked to the broader common good so central to guarding academic freedom. Today we consciously ask about the relationship between protecting academic freedom and undermining the public good by doing harm. In the nineteenth or even early tweneieth century, this question would not even have been posed.

We take for granted that the philosophers and scholars in ancient Greece advanced early notions of academic freedom. For Richard Hofstadter, "Academic Freedom is a modern term for an ancient idea. Although the struggle for freedom in teaching can be traced at least as far back as Socrates' eloquent defense of himself against the charge of corrupting the youth of Athens, its continuous history is concurrent with the history of universities since the Twelfth Century."[6] It behooves one to remember the ancient Greeks rationalized slavery and the concomitant ethnocentrism of the Greek city states.

The academics of the early slave and colonial era were more concerned with protecting academic freedom from Church and State, and the repressive arms of the state, than they were with challenging the socio-economic basis of slavery and the concomitant racism. Many of them became the ideologues justifying European colonialism — with respect to Western understandings of the Middle East, Said rightly and roundly criticizes this as "Orientalism" which describes the "subtle and persistent Eurocentric prejudice against Arabo-Islamic peoples and their culture."[7]

It was not until the great social movements of the twentieth century began that other notions of freedom including freedom from — colonial subjugation, from racial oppression, from sexism and heterosexism — entered the public domain, including in the exclusive academy.

Sections of the academy only very latterly became concerned with a conception of public good that was fundamentally anti-colonial, anti-racist, anti-sexist, anti-homophobic, etc.

Ironically, it was post-war twentieth-century capitalism, with its focus on the marketplace, and individual rights and innovation (with commercial application), that also funded the opening up of universities. So it is no surprise that the post-war opening up also opened spaces for contestation.

Prior to the twentieth century, the primary threats to academic freedom came from the church, the military establishment, feudal despotic leaders, and of course prevailing dominant classes in society. Through the twentieth century, the threats to academic freedom multiplied and now they include (but are not limited to): underfunding, contingency, authoritarian administration, the national security agenda, political intolerance, neo-liberal assaults on academic disciplines, the conscious and unconscious secretion of the marketplace and the ideology of the marketplace into the academy, challenges with collegial governance, the impact of globalization, and opposition to human rights, and the reduction of the public good to a narrow conception of what is good for tax payers.[8]

But the opening up of universities in Canada has simultaneously opened space for academics to rethink and re-imagine academic freedom, which is historically contested and is socially constructed. Academic freedom exists in relation to law, power, differential access to power, and social location of the academic in the discursive spaces of the academy and the more it is contested, the greater is the realization that it is up to academics to take up this vital challenge.

There is another important question related to the set of arguments advanced in this chapter: how can one contest the notion of academic freedom embedded in the "marketplace of ideas" conception? In such a conception, a faculty member who is a so-called scientific racist is accorded academic freedom — he or she can do his or her research, speak about it on university campuses, even teach in his or her classes — and those who are offended and demeaned by it are told they must contest the ideas and not stop the faculty member from speaking. More speech, liberals say, is what is required.

The defence of their academic freedom is rooted in a marketplace of ideas conception of academic freedom where all ideas, no matter how odious, should be aired. The most cogent defence of this conception was offered by John Stuart Mill, who says, "The peculiar evil of silencing the expression of an opinion is, that it is robbing the human race; posterity as well as the existing generation; those who dissent from the opinion, still more than those who hold it. If the opinion is right, they are deprived of the opportunity of exchanging error for truth: if wrong, they lose, what is almost as great a benefit, the clearer perception and livelier impression of truth, produced by its collision with error . . . We can never be sure that the opinion we are endeavouring to stifle is a false opinion; and if we were sure, stifling it would be an evil still."[9]

Are we really in a marketplace of ideas where all ideas have a right to circulate and the consumers of ideas can cherry pick which ideas they like and which they do not? These ideas are certainly not devoid of power, power differentials.

In such a conception, one is free not to attend the lecture or hear the remarks or even read the article. Further one has the right to engage in peer review and critique. Interesting that engaging in the latter, particularly the academic, no matter how critical, legitimates the racist and legitimates his or her ideas and in so doing they reify both what C.B. MacPherson calls possessive individualism and the uncontested notion of academic freedom rooted in nineteenth-century liberalism.

Interestingly no academic would accord academic freedom to an academic who is an ardent proponent of a flat earth or one who denies the Holocaust occurred. There may well be a spirited argument about freedom of expression and even hate speech, but one would be would be hard pressed to make an academic freedom case (Moon makes an interesting argument about the "social character" of freedom of expression and the constitutional challenges to freedom of expression).[10] Yet when it comes to a Rushton who puts forward so-called evidence of racial superiority and inferiority (despite a huge body of literature, which debunks the biological concept of "race" and which speaks to race as a social construct), the academy, including the guardians and protectors of academic freedom, rush to defend his academic freedom.

When he accepted his Nobel Prize in 2001, Joseph Stiglitz addressed the relationship between social responsibility and academic freedom:

> We have the good fortune of living in democracies, in which individuals can fight for their perception of what a better world might be like. We as academics have the good fortune to be further protected by our academic freedom. With freedom comes responsibility: the responsibility to use that freedom to do what we can to ensure that the world of the future be one in which there is not only greater economic prosperity but also more social justice.[11]

This is very much in keeping with the CAUT policy statement on academic freedom, which reads, in part, "Post-secondary educational institutions serve the common good of society through searching for, and disseminating, knowledge and understanding and through fostering independent thinking and expression in academic staff and students. Robust democracies require no less. These ends cannot be achieved without academic freedom."[12]

In keeping with the CAUT policy statement, it can be argued that the fight against racism, sexism and discrimination in the academy, research on discrimination, research on human rights abuses all contribute to greater social justice. This may not be dispassionate so-called neutral research, but it is research that ultimately advances the public good. And again it is in keeping with the CAUT Policy statement on academic freedom, which says, "Academic Freedom does not require neutrality on the part of the individual."[13]

## THE CORE ARGUMENTS

- Discrimination in the academy diminishes academic freedom of all and in particular diminishes the academic freedom of the victim of that discrimination. Conversely the perpetrator should not be allowed hide behind a hard-won freedom.

- For historically marginalized groups getting into the academy was extremely difficult (and because they were not in, they had no academic freedom to exercise, and academic freedom was infinitely poorer for this because the range of perspectives they could have offered were not available).

- Now that they are entering the academy in greater numbers, they challenge the exclusionary practices embedded in hiring, tenure, and promotion. They call into question departmental priorities. They engage in critical enquiry. And they call into question the status quo in departments, faculties, and the universities.

- Self-appointed gatekeepers of academic freedom should not be allowed to get away with the argument that academic freedom is threatened by scholars from historically disadvantaged groups who contest contemporary discourses and who raise issues related to the exclusionary academy. These self-appointed gatekeepers want to preserve their academic freedom and restrict the academic freedom of marginalized faculty members by arguing that so-called political correctness poses a threat to academic freedom. In reality it is the practice of discrimination that poses a grave threat to academic freedom.

An academic environment that does not value the knowledge creation of academics from diverse backgrounds significantly hinders the academic freedom of scholars who engage in counter-hegemonic knowledge creation and dissemination. The fifth argument also is related to the CAUT policy statement on academic freedom, which states: "The Canadian Association of University Teachers is dedicated to the promotion and protection of academic freedom. The common good of society depends upon the search for knowledge and truth and its free expression. Academic freedom is essential for these purposes. Academic freedom does not require neutrality on the part of the individual. Rather academic freedom makes commitment possible."[14]

Discrimination, undervaluing (for the purposes of hiring, tenure, and promotion) the research of academics of colour, for example, not only seriously diminishes their academic freedom (and reproduces the exclusive university and academy), but it also has a negative impact on the common good. It legitimates only some forms of knowledge creation while diminishing other forms of knowledge creation and dissemination. The common good is never served by discrimination and by diminishing the academic freedom of others.

In the name of academic freedom, some academics have written volumes about the colonized in ways that depict them as inferior, uncultured, and uncivilized. People of colour around the world were subjected to colonialism and racism. The impact of centuries of slavery, indentured labour, colonialism, colonial oppression and subjugation, and apartheid produced an ideology that justified racism and sexism. Today, as scholars questions these discourses, they are being accused of being "politically correct" and are seen as a threat to academic freedom. What we have here is precisely a fundamentally European discourse — academic freedom — rooted in the history of one part of the world being used to deny others the right to critical engagement. There is thus no winning here.

Today, when the organic intellectuals of the Third World diaspora question racism and colonialism, they are accused of threatening the academic freedom discourse (one they had no part in fashioning but one they are now subject to). The new knowledge they create, that is counter hegemonic, is discarded and delegitimized in the name of preserving academic freedom. Anti-racist, anti-colonial, counter-hegemonic knowledge is not subversive to academic freedom and ought not to be seen as such: it elevates and nourishes academic freedom.

The CAUT policy statement on academic freedom says academic freedom is essential for society and does not exist as an end in itself. It is to advance the public good; the autonomy of the university; encourage scholarly enquiry; and the timely dissemination of research and knowledge.

The policy statement continues: "Academic staff, like all other groups and individuals, are entitled to enjoy recognized civil, political, social and cultural rights. Therefore, all academic staff must enjoy freedom of thought, conscience, religion, expression, assembly and association as well as the right to liberty and security of the person and liberty of movement. They must not be hindered or impeded in exercising their civil rights as citizens, including the right to contribute to social change through freely expressing their opinion of state policies and of policies affecting higher education. They must not suffer any penalties simply because of the exercise of such rights."[15]

The CAUT definition is equally compelling: "Academic staff are entitled to the exercise of academic freedom. Academic freedom includes the right, without constriction by prescribed doctrine, to freedom of teaching and discussion, freedom in carrying out research and disseminating and publishing the results thereof, freedom in producing and performing creative works, freedom to engage in service to the institution and the community, freedom to express freely their opinion about the institution, its administration, or the system in which they work, freedom from institutional censorship and freedom to participate in professional or representative academic bodies."[16]

For CAUT, tenure is indispensable to the exercise of academic freedom. But here lies one of the central arguments of this chapter — if tenure is indispensible to the exercise of academic freedom, then two issues arise:

- those who historically were excluded from the academy did not have academic freedom to exercise.
- Those who do not have tenure will exercise academic freedom very guardedly — and this extends with equal force to contingent academic staff.

Simply put, how can a faculty member of colour exercise his or her academic freedom when he or she cannot get through the academic door? And secondly, if he or she does get in, how can he or she exercise their academic freedom if his or her research is not valued and he or she does not get tenure?

## THE DIFFICULT CHALLENGES WE CONFRONT

First, now that the academy is becoming more representative, how is academic freedom reconciled with the various challenges of diversity? Second, how do faculty associations and unions deal with the subtle discrimination in the hiring process, the tenure review process (discrimination, which, for example, could stem from the undervaluing of new forms of knowledge production from racialized minority faculty), and the promotion process?

The CAUT policy statement provides us with glimpses into potential trouble spots. Academic staff must not be "forced to teach against their own best knowledge and conscience or be forced to use curricula and methods contrary to national and international human rights standards."[17] It assigns to academic staff the predominant role in determining the curriculum and assessment standards. And it notes that academic staff must be able to perform (and exercise their academic freedom) without discrimination of any kind and without fear of repression by the state or any other source.

Implicit in the above is recognition that academic staff can be subject to discrimination and that discrimination has a detrimental effect on their exercise of academic freedom. A more contextual reading suggests that discrimination creates an inhospitable work environment in which those who are discriminated against cannot perform to the best of their abilities.

The concept of academic freedom is in need of repair and reshaping. In undertaking such a reshaping, we in the academy (not arbitrators or the courts) need to recognize the complex interplay between freedom from discrimination and academic freedom as reconcilable freedoms, which coexist in an uneasy juxtaposition.

Academic freedom does not give a faculty member the right to discriminate against another on any of the grounds enumerated in the human rights legislation. It does not confer on a faculty member the right to engage in sexual or racial harassment, intimidation, or the creation of a poisoned work environment. And it does no confer on a faculty member the freedom to interfere in the academic freedom of others. Those who have power in the academy should not use it to discriminate against others on the grounds of race, gender, disability, etc. Nor should they hide behind the cloak of a hard-won freedom — academic freedom. Horn argues that the "Near exclusion of non-Caucasians [from the academy] raises the same issues as the treatment of Jews. To discriminate against people on the grounds of ethnicity or religion, sex, matters not central to the academic enterprise, is as objectionable as discriminating against them for their opinions. Because members of these groups offer a wide range of perspectives, their exclusion artificially diminishes the quality and extent of discussion and debate, weakening academic freedom."[18]

In this conception academic freedom must be located in the context of social relations in the academy; it is not aloof from inequality of status and power differentials, and in this sense the university (despite a deep veneer of collegiality) is like any other workplace that is hierarchically structured. There is a need to strengthen faculty association collective agreements on both fronts — strengthen academic freedom clauses and anti-discrimination clauses. Faculty associations must encourage and promote throughout the university community respect for diverse forms of knowledge production and disseminations; respect for diversity in research.

As the first step in a meaningful conversation about rethinking academic freedom and its relationship to the public good, there needs to be recognition, acknowledgement, an open conversation about the deleterious effects of discrimination, exclusion and gatekeeping on the academic freedom of vulnerable academics in specific and concrete instances where the effects of racism and sexism are corrosive.

This is not about creating hierarchies of freedom where one freedom is privileged over another. This is about academics and their representative institutions taking charge and thinking anew about freedoms. This is about the politics of academic freedom — a politics that is messy and contested but a politics that is the academy's to sort out.

At the 2013 Harry Crowe Foundation conference "The Limits of

Academic Freedom," Jon Thompson quoted Frank Underhill as saying: "The best way to protect academic freedom is to exercise it." For academics the best way to protect academic freedom is to exercise it to promote the public good. Further, they shoud not use power differentials to undermine or restrict the academic freedom of others.

## CONCLUSION: A PERSONAL REFLECTION

Do calls for inclusivity, freedom from discrimination, and respect for fundamental human rights erode traditional university values such as academic freedom, university autonomy, freedom of inquiry, and the right to disseminate knowledge? For me the answer is "no" because these values need to be historically situated and deconstructed. They need to be weighed against competing freedoms, notably freedom from discrimination and a nuanced understanding of the public good. Academic freedom and freedom from discrimination do not stand in opposition; they exist in a creative tension.

The arguments advanced in this chapter lead me to two points which form a line in the sand for me as a public intellectual. One relates to pedagogy and the other is political.

The one related to pedagogy is really a growing discomfort — I am arriving at a point where I no longer find it a useful pedagogical tool to cite racist, homophobic, Islamophobic, or sexist quotes and texts so as to deconstruct them in class. I increasingly think about and reflect on the impact those texts have on students. For some, it may reinforce stereotypes while for others it causes hurt and harm. So I do question whether I am self-limiting my own academic freedom. Frederick Schauer suggests that universities are spaces where academics can be social critics:

> In the United States, we believe that academic institutions ought to be havens for heresy, ought to be the kind of place where things can be said or thought or written that would otherwise be unthinkable. That may or may not be a good idea, but it is no mere matter of style: when it is most controversial, it turns

> out to be a matter of substance. And when it is most controversial, it makes the classroom a less equal, less comfortable, and less inclusive place. For example, a discussion of the heritability of intelligence will make some students in class uncomfortable and therefore less able to participate in that learning environment.[19]

The second point is intensely political. In the past, the CAUT defended the academic freedom of Philippe Rushton. Were I on the executive at that time or if CAUT were to take a similar stand in defence of a proponent of so-called scientific racism today, I would resign my position in CAUT. Would I be denying a Rushton or someone like him his or her academic freedom? Quite possibly. But I would have to argue no as pseudo-scientific racism is unjustifiable in the academy. It is worse than flat earth theory because, as pseudo-science, it does not promote the public good; it harms the public good. The defence of racist theory is not a defence of academic freedom. It makes a travesty of academic freedom. Academic freedom is a too hard won a freedom to be used in this fashion, and the cost of protecting it absolutely is a social cost that needs to be measured against an inclusive notion of promoting and protecting the public good.

# 11
# ACADEMIC FREEDOM AND THE FEDERAL IDEA

*David Schneiderman*

The openness of institutions of higher learning to everyone without discrimination has given rise to significant challenges to the traditional ways of academic life. Unexamined practices regarding the hiring and promotion of faculty or the endorsement of certain scholarly voices over others are being appropriately contested.[1] It is with the worthwhile objective of attending to such challenges that post-secondary institutions have adopted respectful workplace policies — rules that ensure that no one is required to feel unwelcome in educational environments of higher learning. These codes regulate not only serious misconduct, such as those that may give rise to actionable complaints under statutory human rights codes, but also institute vague prohibitions which are difficult to apprehend in advance. These hard-to-pin-down policies are in serious tension with the practices we associate with academic freedom, simply put, the freedom to teach and to write as one pleases. Some say the conflict is irresoluble.[2]

This may be so. Rather than resolving the conflict, I propose another way of framing it. I offer up a version of federalism that recognizes pluralism and autonomy as a means of facilitating diversity.[3] Non-territorial versions of federalism, prevalent in the English-speaking world in the early twentieth century, promoted self-government within the multiple places in which persons lived their political and social lives. Universities, according to this account, are self-governing associations of persons in the pursuit of practices of thinking.[4] President Robert Falconer of the University of Toronto drew on this frame in a noteworthy 1922 address. "Universities," he declared, "are not pontifical colleges for the propaganda of authoritative doctrines, but self-governing Dominions inheriting assured truths which they test anew . . ."[5] This is an approach to group rights that accommodates — indeed, encourages — change within associations as a consequence of robust and rational debate.[6] This is the reflexive ideal that the academy precisely aspires to; an ideal that questions all and takes little for granted (but which the academy, too often, fails to live up to).[7] It is an approach that has the benefit of both addressing the challenge of change while building on a political form familiar to many around the world. It may generate a viable, if imperfect, way out of this impasse.

## ACADEMIC FREEDOM'S DEEP PLURALISM

Academic freedom typically is understood as entailing the freedom to teach, research, and write within parameters laid down by one's peers.[8] It also entails an ability to continually renew and reshape knowledge and the standards by which professional knowledge is assessed. Academic freedom enables scholars to be free of outside constraints or considerations other than those expected from those working within the community of scholars.[9] It is, in other words, an associational or co-operative activity that insists upon self-regulation.

The origins of an insistence upon freedom and autonomy usually are traceable back to the medieval German university,[10] but one can see obvious linkages to ideas of federalism, particularly those propounded by British political pluralists of the early twentieth century.[11] British political pluralism was inaugurated by Frederick Maitland's introduction and translation of a fragment of Otto Gierke's work on the German corporation in 1900 (what he described as "a twentieth part" of the great work).[12] Maitland there ridiculed the English legal system's failed attempts at reconciling the "manyness of the members" with the "oneness of the body."[13] "[I]njustice will continue to be done," he wrote, "unless corporateness is treated as a matter of fact."[14] Political theorists in the early part of the twentieth century (John Neville Figgis,

G.D.H. Cole, and Harold Laski, among them)[15] deepened the pluralist account that society was made up of so many groups, of which the state was but one.[16] The fact was, they maintained, that group life was being experienced in many places outside the apex of the Crown-in-Parliament: on the workshop floor, for instance, in local government, and in the university.[17] A "federalist feeling is curiously widespread," observed Ernest Barker.[18] Behind it "lies a feeling that the single unitary state, with its single sovereignty, is a dubious conception, which is hardly true to the facts of life."[19] The pluralists maintained that society was federal and what merely was required was that British laws simply recognize the fact of federalism.

This idea of federalism runs deep in the norms associated with academic freedom: it runs from claims to institutional autonomy made by university administration to individual scholars' claims to academic freedom.[20] It is the idea, premised on the notion of *universitas*, that persons are associated for "some common purpose, in the pursuit of some . . . specified enduring interest."[21] Whether likened to federalism, divided sovereignty, associative democracy,[22] the freedom of the guild,[23] institutional autonomy,[24] or group life,[25] there is a deep pluralism undergirding this conception of academic freedom.

For this reason, academic freedom should be distinguished from freedom of expression and to liberty claims more generally. It is important to recognize the distinction between, on the one hand, an ability to communicate all "expressions of the heart and mind" encompassed by constitutionally protected freedom of expression[26] and, on the other hand, a freedom that is applied within the institutional confines of the academy in accordance with the conventions and methods of the academic disciplines. Academic freedom is not a liberty right to do whatever one wishes. Academic speech, for this reason, is subject to certain "quality controls — professional self-regulating ones — for which there are no equivalent constraints in public discourse."[27]

It also makes little sense to distinguish too sharply between "institutional" academic freedom and "individual" academic freedom.[28] The CAUT's policy statement[29] goes so far as to exclude institutional autonomy from the scope of academic freedom. From a federalism angle, this is pretty indefensible. Much is lost by cutting the university off, as an institution, from sharing in the collective enterprise that is the pursuit of academic freedom.[30] Relatedly, there is not much clarity gained by characterizing academic freedom as comprising "individual" rights. To be sure, individuals will make claims to academic freedom. It is a strange individual right, however, that is difficult to evaluate without reference to practices and standards established by self-regulating professional disciplines. We might instead characterize academic freedom as a "special"[31] right rather than a general right or part of the "common rights of citizenship."[32]

Jon Thompson traces this individualistic approach to Bora Laskin's pioneering work on behalf of CAUT.[33] In his report for York University, "Freedom and Responsibility in the University,"[34] Laskin associates academic freedom with ideas like "toleration" and "liberty" that resonate in the language of individual autonomy. These are the same terms University of Toronto President Robert Falconer used to describe academic freedom in the 1922 address, already mentioned.[35] Falconer, we are told, was prompted to address this question in response to calls by financier Reuben Wells Leonard to dismiss the sociologist Robert MacIver.[36] Academic freedom, for Falconer, was another "chapter in the history of Toleration," and is best understood as a "phase of the general course of people's development in liberty of thought."[37] The problem is that toleration appears to provide a less secure foundation for academic freedom than the federal account I am offering here. Toleration usually is associated with the idea of "putting up" with views one finds "wrong mistaken or undesirable."[38] Academic freedom, for this reason, is best not treated as equivalent to mere toleration.[39] There may be good reason for public opinion not to tolerate — even to find objectionable — certain forms of academic expression.

Nor, lastly, does it make sense to liken academic work to that done by judges, "particularly in the rendering of its decisions," an analogy drawn both by both President Falconer and more recently by Justice Frank Iacobucci in his report on academic freedom at York University.[40] Judges, who have the capacity to deprive people of their liberty, have an obligation to be "civil," Jon Thompson reminds us.[41] Academics are as likely to be "uncivil," indeed, they might be likened to ancient truth tellers (*parreshiasts*) described by Foucault: one who "throws the truth in the face of the person with whom he is in dialogue."[42] There is also much more to be expected of judges. They are "pillars of the entire justice system," according to the Supreme Court of Canada, and embody the "ideals of justice and truth on which the rule of law and the foundation of democracy are built."[43] Academicians seek no such heavy responsibility.[44] Instead, they seek to impart their wisdom (constituting partial views of the world, to be sure) to students enrolled in their classes and to those who read their published work.

## RESPECTFUL WORKPLACE POLICIES

I turn now to the task of describing the friction between respectful workplace policies and the idea of academic freedom described above. I should acknowledge, at the outset, that I view as unfounded complaints about the decay of society and ruination of the university resulting from the prevalence of so-called "political correctness."[45] It is appropriate always to treat fellow human beings with respect and decency, and to call out racism, sexism, and ethnocentrism wherever it rears its head, especially in academic circles. It is an entirely different thing, however, to punish scholars based on vague and unmanageable standards having to do with promoting "respectful" workplaces. I take one such workplace policy as a representative sample, the Ontario College of Art and Design University's [OCADU] "Respectful Work and Learning Environment" policy.[46] I don't mean to pick on OCADU. Its policy statement resembles many others in place at institutions of higher learning, but it stands out due to its impressive level of detail.

There is some pretty egregious conduct targeted by the policy statement, to be sure, but there is also much that is less than serious — one might say unclearly serious — and which provides little or no guidance as a code of conduct. It is declared, for instance, that members of the university community are expected to "conduct themselves in an appropriate manner, treating others fairly with dignity and respect," and to maintain "a respectful environment by demonstrating respect for others."[47] OCADU, the statement declares, is committed to "inclusive and respectful working and learning environment[s], free from harassment, discrimination, and bullying."[48] Bullying is defined to include "calling into question [a student's] commitments"[49] or "aggressive behavior such as finger pointing." Harassment is defined to include "unwelcome comments" which, among other things, "diminish the dignity of recipients and serve no legitimate work or academic related purpose,"[50] or that apply "stereotypes or generalizations based on . . . prohibited grounds." These grounds include not only the expected ones, like race and ethnicity, but also "political belief" and "political association."[51] Also prohibited is any "unwanted conduct" that "affects an individual's dignity."[52]

Harassment, it is declared, does not include "legitimate and constructive and fair criticism of a student's performance,"[53] nor is the policy intended to abridge academic freedom. Yet this is no mere aspirational sentiment; it is actionable policy — subject to informal and formal enforcement mechanisms, appointments of "Fact Finders" and appeal "Adjudicators" — which can attract a variety of sanctions, including even dismissal.

As mentioned, a variety of offending conduct is assimilated under the rubric of "harassment, discrimination, and bullying." The most serious of these will be actionable, one would think, under statutory human rights codes (in the case of discriminatory conduct and sexual harassment in Ontario there must be a "course of vexatious" behaviour) and the *Criminal Code* of Canada (in the case of non-consensual touching). As for everything else, what I have called the "unclearly serious," they include a wide variety of behaviour not typically proscribed via statute. It is not the case, then, that these sorts of policies merely "reflect existing human rights obligations," providing "students with an alternative means of lodging a complaint about a professor's classroom conduct."[54]

Instead, the workplace policy significantly overreaches. It does not distinguish, Finkin and Post remind us, between "respect for persons" and "respect for ideas."[55] All ideas do not typically receive equal respect in a classroom. In the large classes that I teach in constitutional law, dealing with contentious subjects over which reasonable people disagree such as hate speech and abortion, it seems inevitable that I will offend someone's "political beliefs" or "political association." Bernice Schrank puts it this way: "Disturbing students in the classroom situation is often a preliminary to making them think. It is not a bad thing."[56]

Moreover, there is little consensus about the sort of behaviour that diminishes individual "dignity." The Supreme Court of Canada recently concluded that the concept is unworkable, after having made it a central part of its equality analysis for about a ten-year period, and so has declared that it will not be employing human dignity as a referent in its equality jurisprudence any longer.[57] There is even not a lot of consensus, I would maintain, about what constitutes the promotion of "hatred" under Canada's *Criminal Code*. We know that it covers full-time neo-Nazis and Holocaust revisionists, but there is agreement on little else.[58]

Perhaps the most problematic feature of the policy is that the relationship between the impugned behaviour and "academic related purposes" is to be determined not by a community of scholarly peers but by "fact finders" and "adjudicators" who might have little or no knowledge of the subject matter giving rise to the controversy.[59] These are regimes, in other words, not of academic self-regulation but of discipline by centralized university administrations. To be sure, there should be a healthy dose of deference to university-wide policies that are expressions of the university's institutional autonomy. But in cases where the institutional claim conflicts with the principle of self-regulation, such expressions are deserving of less deference. This amounts not to an expression of scholarly judgment but the application of vague "community standards" of tolerance.[60]

## THE CORRESPONDING STUDENT SPHERE

A robust conception of academic freedom, not susceptible to discipline under respectful workplace policies, suggests a corresponding sphere of freedom that is available to others, including students, in the pursuit of their associational lives. Returning to Foucault's deployment of the ancient practice of *parrhesia*, truth tellers run the risk of having to "pay a price" for their truthfulness.[61] In ancient Rome, this could even include death. Good pedagogy, we happily can report, avoids these sorts of consequences. But there are lesser consequences, I maintain, that flow from an ability to enjoy academic freedom.

What I am thinking of is independent of the question of whether students enjoy academic freedom.[62] Even if students accrue the benefits of academic freedom, they may also feel unfairly done by it. In which case, we should accept, even encourage, student speech about academics and their subjects. Students should be entitled, for instance, to critique, even treat with contempt, views professed in the classroom. However much we might feel the need to put a lid on such criticisms in the classroom context in the service of furthering teaching objectives, there will be no such justification outside of the classroom. It was appropriate, then, that Western University students made known, within the bounds of legality and classroom decorum, their objection to tenured psychology professor Philippe Rushton's racist theories linking IQ to cranium sizes.[63]

We should be troubled, however, by post-secondary institutions, like the University of Calgary, that have sought to discipline students for ridiculing their professors outside of the classroom. This is irrespective of whether the *Charter*'s 2(b) guarantee of freedom of expression applies to universities. Academic institutions, in the pursuit of their mission of research and teaching, should not deliberately stifle academic criticism by students.[64]

The Pridgen case stands out for this reason. The University of Calgary disciplined the Pridgen brothers for having participated, even if only "tacitly," in criticizing their law and society professor on a student's Facebook page.[65] The law and society course had not gone well for its sessional instructor, Aruna Mitra.[66] The Facebook wall attracted numerous vitriolic comments — the Pridgen brothers' comments mostly were innocuous by comparison — resulting in disciplinary action being taken by the university against several students at the request of Professor Mitra.[67] To be sure, Professor Mitra is no Phillipe Rushton — she did not deserve any of the opprobrium more appropriately showered upon the tenured Rushton. Indeed, many of the online complaints concerned her grading policy — a predictable complaint in competitive university settings. Nonetheless, Professor Mitra and her university employer sought to stifle student assessments of her classroom performance rather than recognize that the price of academic freedom is to turn a blind eye to these sorts of things. According to the dean (as summarized by the Alberta Court of Appeal), a finding of non-academic misconduct was warranted because the Facebook page "called into question Professor Mitra's qualifications and alleged a lack of due diligence in the University's hiring processes."[68] This was an unfortunate determination that worked to no one's benefit.[69] Despite the eager vindication of the professor's reputation by her employer, testimony in the case reveals that the University of Calgary did not rehire Professor Mitra.[70]

Of some legal significance was the fact that Alberta Court of Queens Bench Justice Strekaf and Alberta Court of Appeal Justice Paperny applied the *Charter of Rights and Freedoms* to the University of Calgary, finding that the students' *Charter* right to freedom of expression had been unreasonably limited.[71] Two of the three justices on appeal would have found for the Pridgens without going so far as applying the *Charter*, instead, relying on more limited findings regarding the university's failure to apply the rules laid down.[72] The *Charter* application question was controversial — indeed, CAUT opposed *Charter* application in this case — because the Supreme Court of Canada had earlier concluded in McKinney that universities were not government actors for the purposes of *Charter* application.[73] When it came to the hiring, firing, and mandatory retirement of university staff, the *Charter*, the Court declared in McKinney, did not apply.[74] Justices Strekaf and Paperny found otherwise by virtue of Alberta legislation that delegated, in very general terms, to universities the ability to fine, suspend, and expel students.[75] *Charter* application doctrine has been moving generally in this direction — and in cases of specific delegated governmental authority, the *Charter* will have application[76] — which portends greater scope for *Charter* application on university campuses.

There is a disconcerting language, however, in Justice Paperny's

Court of Appeal ruling. In the course of emphasizing the academy's "public" functions, she declared the university was established "for the benefit of the public generally" and "not just for some narrow and arguably outdated conception of a community of scholars."[77] "One can no longer maintain a pastoral view of university campuses as a community of scholars removed from the rest of society," she announced.[78] Justice Paperny failed to see the critical linkage between academic freedom and self-government and the ability of allowing students to talk freely about goings-on at their university, including the quality of the teaching and scholarship of their professors. She also raised worries about new battles that will have to be fought over old-fashioned ideas like academic freedom.

## CONCLUSION

Having recourse to ideas about federalism helps to mediate, though not permanently resolve, recurring tensions between academic freedom and diversity. Can it be said with confidence, however, that federal sub-units handle diversity well? If federalism accommodates diversity across various sub-units there is no necessary resulting diversity within each of those sub-units. Without some overarching steering authority — absent in this account — minority voices are vulnerable to silencing and stigmatization. The disciplines often have jealously guarded their ramparts, after all, on grounds having to do with difference (such as class, race, and gender).[79]

The ways and means of academic freedom suggest otherwise. It is a central part of the academic mission to continuously reevaluate methods and conclusions, to engage in the reflexive practice of critical self-evaluation.[80] To be sure, accommodating change remains a challenging task within many disciplinary communities and university organizations. But change is part of academic DNA — remaining static means ossification. From this angle, we can think of the academy's disciplinary communities as does Joan Scott, as "provisional entities called into being to organize relations of difference." In which case, its "standards and rules become heuristic practices around which argument is expected and change anticipated."[81]

It is contradictory of the academic mission to foreclose routes away from its staid routines. From this angle, academic freedom is not under threat by the fact of diversity within university settings. Rather, proponents of academic freedom should welcome the challenge of living up to its promise of openness and re-examination of its modes of inquiry. Even if academic freedom coexists uneasily with respectful workplace codes of conduct, its nerve centres are capable of adjustment precisely for the purpose of absorbing the lessons learned from increasing diversity within the academy.

# V. ACADEMIC FREEDOM AND THE GROWTH OF UNIVERSITY-INDUSTRY COLLABORATIONS

# 12

# ACADEMIC FREEDOM, CONFLICTS OF INTEREST, AND THE GROWTH OF UNIVERSITY-INDUSTRY COLLABORATIONS

*Sheldon Krimsky*

## INTRODUCTION

I was once asked by a student activist, "How do you preserve your values when you leave the university?" My reply was that you should choose your place of employment carefully to insure that it possesses values that are compatible to yours. To survive at an institution whose core human values are compromised by finance, greed, or power will require that you adapt in order to survive and then you will need to rationalize the adaptation. The consequence of a bad choice could result in a lifetime of cognitive dissonance between your true values and those you have to play by.

University students spend four years at institutions of higher learning which purport to operate on high principles of academic and moral integrity. Virtues such as honesty, respect for other opinions, truth must pre-empt power and authority, and an environment where freedom of expression and thought are savoured. The virtues students experience at the university are the building blocks for calibrating their value choices in post-university life.

Universities play multiple roles. In addition to their mission in educational training for the student's profession of choice, universities also are places where students undergo "value socialization." They learn early on that plagiarism is wrong and that selecting evidence that only supports your bias will not get you to the truth.

The world-class universities, beginning in the Middle Ages, were designed as non-profit institutions whether publicly funded or privately endowed. This structure insured that they would not become handmaidens to corporations or politics — both of which depended on the knowledge of educated men and women the universities produced.

In 1919, one of America's leading sociologists, Thorstein Veblen, wrote a monograph titled *Higher Learning in America*. In his book he spoke about the dangers of having the universities governed by businessmen. Veblen understood the tendencies to model the management of higher education on what were at the time modern business practices, such as efficiency, quality control, labour productivity, and Taylorism. He wrote: "If these business principles were quite free to work out their logical consequences . . . the outcome should be to put the pursuit of knowledge in abeyance with the university and to substitute for that objective something for which the language hitherto lacks a designation."[1] Veblen understood that if the university were run by businessmen in a command-control fashion the scholars would be constrained from "following any inquiry to its logical conclusion" because some conclusions might conflict with the trustees or managers of the institution.[2]

Seventy-five years later Nobel Laureate Philip Sharpe, who shared the 1993 Nobel Prize in physiology or medicine with Richard J. Roberts for "the discovery that genes in eukaryotes are not contiguous strings but contain introns, and that the splicing of messenger RNA to delete those introns can occur in different ways, yielding different proteins from the same DNA sequence," wrote: As universities become more identified with commercial wealth, they also lose their uniqueness in society. They are no longer viewed as ivory towers of intellectual pursuits and truthful thoughts, but rather as enterprises driven by arrogant individuals out to capture as much money and influence as possible.[3]

Notwithstanding the often-used term "ivory tower" to describe institutions of higher learning, universities were never completely insulated from the commercial world. The university's board of trustees is often filled with men and women who made their success in the business world — a compromise to Veblen's fear of business management. Their perspective is often shaped by their experience in business management, markets, and efficiency. Universities also cultivate wealthy benefactors for gifts that include buildings, endowed professorships, research programs, and student scholarships.

In his book *Science-Mart: Privatizing American Science*, Philip Mirowski found that while commercial concerns had always been part of academic science, something changed in academia from 1980 to the present. The passage of Bayh-Dole, as well as other events, resulted in a qualitatively different form of knowledge production. He referred to it as a "globalized privatization regime," involving scientific labour, intellectual property agreements, and a new generation of university-industry partnerships.

In order to capitalize on the economic value of discoveries made on campus, universities develop intellectual property offices. The modern research university invests heavily in acquiring patents and licensing agreements for the discoveries of its faculty. Some universities go a step further and become equity partners in companies started by one of its faculty.

This chapter explores the arena within which university and commercial partnerships take place and suggests that some of these relationships can unduly compromise the mission, core values, autonomy, or public trust in the integrity of the institution. Once these institutional values have been compromised, academic freedom is an inevitable casualty.

## COMMERCIALIZATION OF THE UNIVERSITY: CROSSING THE BOUNDARY

I shall begin with a premise. There are some university-industry relationships that threaten the university's role as an independent, non-profit, publicly accountable institution. Of course the boundary of acceptable versus unacceptable activity might be broad. We cannot assume that a laser-fine line separates the dark from the bright side of academic commercialization.

Let me begin with a few examples. Suppose a university accepts a contract from a for-profit company that pre-empts traditional academic values such as research autonomy, open communication in science, research integrity or the right of publication. Contracts have been accepted by universities that give the corporate sponsor the right over the data including the right not to publish.

How might a university rationalize this practice? The administrators might say that the contract is a collaboration between the professor and the commercial scientist and therefore both should have veto power over publication. One of the problems with this rationalization is that there can be no genuine collaboration between an academic and an industry scientist. The professor, who engages in research, is not accountable to the university administration or board of trustees for the published work. The same cannot be said about an industry scientist. Internal research results that threaten the bottom line of the company may be viewed as unpublishable. The norms of academic freedom that lie at the bedrock of the university simply do not play a similar role at a corporate institution. With this in mind, university contracts that allow the sponsor to determine whether the results are publishable should never be accepted.

Another case in point is one that actually occurred. A non-profit arm of a corporation signs a contract with a public university that describes the conditions laid out by the sponsor for funding a new economics curriculum. The purpose of the funding is to establish a new program at the university "to advance the understanding and practice of those free voluntary processes and principles that promote social progress, human well-being, individual freedom, opportunities and prosperity, based on the rule of law, constitutional government, private property and the laws, regulations, organizations, institutions and social norms upon which they apply."[4] The purpose of the funding was to expand research and teaching related to economic institutions and political economy. The Charles Koch Foundation is an example of private philanthropy with an ideology. Its billionaire founder, Charles Koch, is an advocate of minimalist government (a vestige of a nineteenth-century-style free-market economic system), personal responsibility in lieu of social safety nets, privately financed education, and an end to the government-run social-security system. Koch and his brother David have been among the leading funders of the libertarian Tea Party and support its organizations and political candidates.

The university agreed to give the foundation the authority to decide the selection criteria used to fill the economics faculty positions that it paid for, and the right to veto candidates of whom it did not approve. This agreement is a marked departure from the well-established separation between private academic philanthropy and faculty hiring decisions. Florida State University (FSU) insisted that it was aware of the threat to its independence, and was prepared to pull out of the agreement if it felt that its integrity was being undermined by outside influence.

According to the agreement, performance objectives for the program would be reviewed by a three-member advisory board, chosen by the Koch foundation, which will monitor the performance of faculty members and check whether they remain true to the program's mission. The agreement also states that "Individuals holding the sponsored professorship positions will be treated similarly to all other FSU faculty of similar rank." It is unimaginable that the faculty handbook of FSU or any other state or private university uses "advancement of the practice" of a political ideology to measure academic success. This would be like evaluating the professor of Spanish anarchism by his or her success in practising anarchism. The agreement also stipulates that an "Undergraduate Political Economy Committee" should be set up in the FSU Economics Department, with one outside member chosen by the foundation. The purpose of this committee is to shape the undergraduate curriculum to ensure that it meets the goals of the agreement. I would argue that these conditions are unacceptable at any high-rank university. The contract asks the university to forego its autonomy in evaluating professors on their work and gives an external ideological organization power over the university's faculty and curriculum.

In response to this contract I wrote in *Nature,* "Let there be no mistake: the controversy over the FSU–Koch agreement is not about the diversity of views on economics at America's universities. It is not even, as the university likes to portray, about whether it hired the [faculty] it wanted to. It is about the wider threat to the independence and autonomy of academic appointments, and the proper boundaries between philanthropy and a university's choices about faculty and curriculum. Compromising these values, even under conditions of financial exigency, will turn a university against itself and corrupt its integral value to society."[5]

## INSTITUTIONAL CONFLICT OF INTEREST

The previous case is an example of "institutional conflict of interest." Institutional conflict of interest (ICOI) is characterized as a situation in which the financial investments or holdings of the university or the personal financial interests or holdings of institutional leaders might affect or reasonably appear to affect institutional processes for the design, conduct, reporting, review, or oversight of research, education, or management practices. Gordan DuVal notes, "to the extent that an institution, or an institutional official, has a financial interest in the outcome or findings of research, their interests are substantially aligned with those of the industry sponsor, and those interests are sometimes incongruent with the relevant primary obligation."[6]

A second case involves the president of the MD Anderson Cancer Center at the University of Texas. Ronald DePhino became the new President of MD Anderson in June 2011. In his disclosure documents he listed all the companies that he and his wife had received compensation from prior to his appointment.[7] His financial conflicts of interest are as large as they get even for a person of his stature. In his letter to the executive vice-chancellor he wrote: "In addition to past compensation and/or ownership interests my wife and I may at some point receive future compensation from Aglos Pharm, Aveo Phar, Karyopharm Therapeutics, Eden Therapeutics, Epizyme, Metamark Genetics, Merck, Sanofi Aventis, Sidney Kimmel Foundation, and/or Dana Farber that may further trigger the application of Institutional Policy."[8] A number of these companies were actively involved in research at MD Anderson. President DePhino requested and received a waiver of MD Anderson's conflict of interest policy with respect to three pharmaceutical companies with which he continued to possess financial ties that have active clinical human subjects research at MD Anderson. Under the waiver, the president of MD Anderson will be allowed to retain his equity and financial ties to companies that are engaged in research at the institution as long as he has a management plan in place.

The rationale behind the waiver is that the president will be asked to recuse himself from any decisions that pertain to the active programs at MD Anderson involving drug companies with which he has an affiliation. However, faculty researchers and university administrators are well aware of the president's affiliation. Institutional values from the top echelon have a way of insinuating themselves in other decision makers at the university. "Researchers themselves who are amassing and analyzing data could be influenced by an awareness that their own institution's financial health [or that of higher level administrators] may be affected by the results of their research if their institution [or high level administrators] holds a significant stake in the drug or device being tested."[9] This is precisely why government agencies require senior officials to sell off stocks or set up blind trusts.

After a period of negative publicity about the waivers and MD Anderson faculty expressing concerns about persistent conflicts held by its president, DePhino stepped down from two corporate boards whose service required a waiver from MD Anderson's COI policy. In a story run in the *Houston Chronicle,* DePhino was called a "quintessential multivested scientist administrator."[10] The MD Anderson case raises the question on whether the president of a university who gets contracts from certain corporations should be allowed to hold investments in those corporations. Can such cases be managed or should there be zero tolerance for such institutional FCOIs?

## ZERO TOLERANCE FOR TOBACCO FUNDS

A number of universities or their subdivisions, i.e., schools of public health, have banned tobacco sponsorship on their campuses. They based their decisions on growing evidence that the tobacco industry had been unethical in manufacturing uncertainty over tobacco-related illnesses resulting in many preventable deaths. Among their ruses was to set up rogue institutions that looked like independent research centres to act like scientifically informed bodies. Tobacco companies financed a large number of studies intended to discredit the findings of the International Agency for Research on Cancer (IARC). A report of the World Health Organization stated that "the tobacco companies planned an ambitious series of studies, literature reviews and scientific conferences to be conducted largely by front organizations or consultants, to demonstrate the weaknesses of the IARC study and of epidemiology to challenge [environmental tobacco smoke] toxicity and to offer alternatives to smoking restrictions."

Organizations like the American Association of University Professors (AAUP) were opposed to selective bans on sponsored research. They argued that even a destructive industry like tobacco can sometimes fund useful research. And more to the point, faculty members should be free to choose their research agendas and to accept the funding from a sponsor to conduct the research. Anything else would be a constraint on academic freedom.

Some medical schools and schools of public health have argued that their goals and those of the tobacco industry are in irreconcilable conflict, citing the industry's suppression of internal research linking tobacco to cancer and the industry's efforts to buy their science to stave off regulation. Five University of California (UC)campuses voted to refuse tobacco funds in 2007. The UC regents require each campus chancellor to review and decide whether or not to approve new tobacco funding. Schools of public health at Arizona, Columbia, Harvard, Iowa, Johns Hopkins, and South Carolina, as well as schools of medicine at Emory, Harvard, and Johns Hopkins, do not accept tobacco funding.

As institutions, universities are neither purely libertarian nor purely communitarian. Faculty have more autonomy than employees at most other institutions. But despite their independence, they must operate under principles and norms of governance that apply uniformly to each individual. Some universities have banned research that is classified or prohibit weapons research or research contracts funded by faculty-owned companies.

I have argued elsewhere that there are two normative levels for deciding on a zero-tolerance rule for research, which I refer to as the meta-level and the ground level norms. The normative conditions for the meta-level norms should be invariant for all institutions of higher learning. The norms at the meta-level require investigators of a study to be fully responsible for the data, the contents of the published work, and the timing and place of publication. Finally, a faculty member must not, by contract or volition, give up his/her autonomy over his/her research. As stated in the journal *Environmental Health Perspectives*, "all authors are required to certify that their freedom to design, conduct, interpret, and publish research is not compromised by any controlling sponsor as a condition or review of publication."[11]

The ground level norms for acceptable sponsored research are contextualized for that institution. Not all constraints on sponsored research need meet auniversal invariant standard. Some research restrictions arise from the unique goals and values held by different academic institutions. A university committed to sustainability may wish to restrict funding from a coal-oriented corporation. This norm must be chosen according to the appropriate procedures of faculty governance and not dictated by a single individual. This idea may be inconsistent with AAUP standards, which are more libertarian in giving the researcher the right to accept legal funding from any corporation.

## THE GROWING AWARENESS OF INSTITUTIONAL COIs

The idea that academic institutions can have conflicts of interest grew slowly from the national response to the FCOIs of academic scientists. The National Academy of Sciences wrote, "Because institutional conflicts of interest have not received as much attention as individual conflicts of interest, there is less evidence about their characteristics or impacts."[12] In 2001 the Association of American Universities issued a report titled "Individual and Institutional Financial Conflict of Interest."[13]

The report made a reasonable effort to define institutional conflicts of interest.

> An institutional financial conflict of interest may occur when the institution, any of its senior management or trustees, or a department, school, or other sub-unit, or an affiliated foundation or organization, has an external relationship or financial interest in a company that itself has a financial interest in a faculty research project. Senior managers or trustees may also have conflicts when they serve on the boards of (or otherwise have an official relationship with) organizations that have significant commercial transactions with the university. The existence (or appearance) of such conflicts can lead to actual bias, or suspicion about possible bias, in the review or conduct of research at the university. If they are not evaluated or managed, they may result in choices or actions that are incongruent with the missions, obligations, or the values of the university.

The AAU lists three ways to address the ICOI: always disclose; manage the conflicts in most cases; prohibit the activity when necessary to protect the public interest or the interest of the university. Most universities have decided to operate within the overlapping space of academia and commerce but to disclose and manage the transactions within that space. In managing that space, recusal and sequestration are two of the primary tools. A high official with a COI should be kept out of the decision-making process. This was the initial management strategy for President DePhino of MD Anderson.

The AAU does not offer any meta-norms for universities to adopt. Their report is largely process-oriented. They recommend that universities adopt ICOI guidelines and, through a series of questions, apply their guidelines to cases that arise in the transaction space of commerce and academia. For example, they ask universities to consider:

> Are there rules governing whether companies in which the university has an equity stake — acquired

> through the university's technology transfer activities — can sponsor research at the university? Are there rules if the equity stake is acquired through investments from the university's endowment? If the company can sponsor research, can the principal investigator have an equity stake in the company? Can that individual be an officer of the company? Are there any rules governing a group of faculty, such as those in a private practice plan, using their resources to purchase large equity positions in companies that directly relate to their area of research or clinical practice?[14]

Are the cases of each institution so idiosyncratic that universal norms cannot be set? How can any institutional management plan be evaluated? Do we base the evaluation on whether the ICOI is properly neutralized so that public trust is not diminished? Do we base it on whether the ICOI is not associated with an actual or perceived risk of bias? Do we base it on whether the ICOI compromises one of the core values of the university? The challenge for any ICOI policy is to define the space of proscribed behaviour.

There has been considerable pushback by federal agencies and professional associations to set meta-level universal norms for institutional conflicts of interest. For example, in 2004, the U.S. Department of Health and Human Services (DHHS) issued a guidance document pertaining to financial conflicts of interest in clinical trials.[15] It proposed a set of recommendations to manage ICOIs that included reducing or eliminating the interest, disclosing the interest to prospective human subjects, separating financial from research decisions (sequestration), using an independent monitor without any financial ties to oversee the research, and otherwise modifying the roles of research scientists. Each institution is given discretion for how it will address both the individual or institutional FCOIs for clinical research. However, institutions at every level of administration have a financial incentive for managing rather than proscribing ICOIs.

In the most recent DHHS guidelines (proposed rule) issued in 2010 for addressing researcher FCOIs, there is a short reference to ICOIs. The document states that ICOIs are not addressed in the current regulations. DHHS stated that "further careful consideration is necessary before PHS regulations could be formulated that would address the subject of institutional conflict of interest in the same comprehensive manner as the proposed regulations regarding Investigator FCOI."[16] The document welcomes comments "on whether the regulations should be further revised to require Institutions, at a minimum, to adopt some type of policy on institutional conflict of interest."[17]

## THE HIERARCHY OF ADMINISTRATIVE ICOI ACCOUNTABILITY

When do university administrators take responsibility for ICOIs? No one doubts that the president, board of trustees, and the provost are sufficiently high enough in the chain of command to fall under ICOI guidelines. What about deans and department chairs? Do their individual commercial affiliations fall under the ICOI framework? In the Institute of Medicine's report on institutional conflicts of interest it wrote: "a department chair or dean who has a major equity holding in a medical device company could make decisions about faculty appointments and promotions or assignment of office or laboratory space in ways that favor the interests of the company but compromise the overall research, educational, or clinical mission of the institution."[18]

To assess the state of ICOI policies and practices in US medical schools, Ehringhaus et al. completed a national survey of deans at 125 allopathic medical schools between February 2006 and December 2006.[19] They received responses from eighty-six of the survey sample. Only thirty respondents had adopted ICOI policies applicable to financial interests held by the institution, while a much larger number had ICOI policies for officials — fifty-five for senior officials, fifty-five for mid-level officials, and fifty-one for board members. Most of the reporting institutions which have adopted ICOI policies covering senior and mid-level officials believed that the significant financial interest of an institutional research official in a commercial sponsor of research at their institution is a potential ICOI. In a concluding remark, authors of the study noted, "Despite strong national recommendations from two prominent higher education organizations, adoption of ICOI policies by U.S. Medical Schools is far from complete on both dimensions [ICOI held by institutions and by institutional officials]."[20]

Another national study surveyed departmental chairs in 125 US accredited allopathic medical schools from February 2006 to October 2006. Of the 688 eligible departments, 459 (67 per cent) completed the survey.[21] Their findings showed that 80 per cent of the clinical departments and 43 per cent of non-clinical departments had at least one form of relationship with industry. Among the most telling findings of the chairs was the following: "When asked about the impact of chairs' personal relationships on a department's ability to pursue independent, unbiased research, the majority of chairs (72%) considered a chair having a substantial role in a start-up to have a negative effect on a department's ability to pursue independent research."[22]

This illustrates that ICOIs held through middle- and high-ranking administrators at universities can introduce risks to the core mission of the institution. What criteria can be used to address ICOIs through academic administrators? In a commentary in *The Journal of the American Medical Association* Johns, Barnes, and Florencio proposed a test for exceeding a zero-tolerance standard for ICOIs.[23] They proposed a rebuttable presumption of zero tolerance for ICOIs. "One means of restoring balance to industry-academia relationships that would reduce both the appearance of bias and the potential for actual bias, but would not eliminate the financial incentives that genuinely promote innovation in research, would be to require individual and corporate possessors of significant industry-related financial interests and relationships to have a legitimate justification for such interests and relationships."[24] The authors argue that possessing ICOIs would be a privilege and responsibility rather than a right. "Absent a legitimate justification, divestiture of significant industry-related financial interests and relationships or recusal from research oversight responsibilities would be expected."[25] The burden must be placed on those with the ICOIs to legitimate their relationships. Other than personal benefit, it is unlikely that President DePhino of MD Anderson could pass the justification test. Of course the authors allow both divestiture and "recusal from research oversight" as solutions. But they are very different responses. The latter does not eliminate the known fact that the president has interests in companies that are actively sponsoring work on the campus. That known fact can influence the outcome of the research carried out by scientists who are ultimately accountable to the president.

## CLINICAL TRIALS AND FCOIs

The Jesse Gelsinger case was a game changer in the in the national conversation about financial conflicts of interest in clinical trials. Mr. Gelsinger was an eighteen-year-old who struggled his entire life with an X-linked genetic disease called ornithine transcarbamylase deficiency (OTCD). Missing a particular enzyme, Mr. Gelsinger lacked the ability to break down ammonia, a by-product of protein metabolites. His disease was not known to have been inherited but probably resulted from a spontaneous genetic mutation after conception. His form of the disease was not as severe as the inherited form because some of his cells had the correct form of the gene, and as a result Mr. Gelsinger was able to survive on a restricted diet and medications.[26]

Mr. Gelsinger enrolled himself in a clinical trial that planned to use gene therapy to treat the disease. Phase One of the trial was designed to test the safety of an adenoviral vector carrying a corrective gene for the enzyme missing in OTCD patients. On September 13, 1999, Mr. Gelsinger received an infusion of trillions of particles of the adenoviral vector. Four days later, on September 17, Mr. Gelsinger died from a systemic inflammatory response affecting multiple organs — believed to be a direct result of the adenoviral vectors. He was the first person to have died in a human gene therapy trial.

Years before the trial had begun, the Conflict of Interest Standing Committee of the University of Pennsylvania Medical Center reviewed the FCOIs of James W. Wilson, Director of the Institute of Human Gene Therapy and Chief Clinical Investigator of the trial. Wilson was founder of Genovo, Inc., which held the rights to market his gene transfer techniques in humans and his patents, including the adenoviral vectors. At the time of the trial Genovo was funding Wilson's institute for more than $4 million per year. Wilson and his family held a 30 per cent non-voting equity interest in Genovo; the University of Pennsylvania had a 3.2 per cent equity interest in the company.

In 1995 the Standing Committee reported in its minutes: "Since Dr. Wilson's research efforts will be directed towards the solution of a problem in which he has a financial interest in the outcome, how can Dr. Wilson assure the University that he will not be conflicted when making decisions that could have an impact on either Genovo, Biogen [another biotechnology company that had invested in Genovo] or the further development of his intellectual property?"[27]

The Standing Committee recommended management of the FCOIs of Wilson but had nothing to say about the ICOI of the University of Pennsylvania except to note the liability of the university if someone died in the trial.

After Gelsinger's death, questions arose about the financial conflicts of interest of the clinical investigator and the university. Should those FCOIs have been permitted? If permitted, how should they have been managed? What is the role of the Institutional Review Boards in overseeing the ethics of the trial? It resulted in a national conversation about the role of FCOIs in clinical trials.

The University of Pennsylvania was at the epicentre of the conversation. It had paid an undisclosed amount of money to the Gelsinger family and was issued an enforcement action by the Department of Justice that included punitive fines amounting to more than half a million dollars for violations of protocols.[28] In 2003 the University of Pennsylvania revised its FCOI policies for faculty participating in clinical trials. The new policy prohibited FCOIs of "significant financial interests," including an equity interest in a product or patent exceeding $10,000 for faculty participating in clinical trials. It was hardly a zero-tolerance policy since it included waivers when there are "compelling circumstances." In Steinbrook's account he notes that some experts believe that "a presumption that financial conflicts of interest should be eliminated, not managed, [was] too draconian because it will impede vital research. Others argue that less radical approaches are doomed to fail."[29]

Liang and Mackey note that "the Gelsinger case epitomizes the inherent risks to patient safety associated with institutional conflicts of interest."[30] The University of Pennsylvania issued a new conflict of interest policy, effective as of 2012, in a document titled "Guidelines on Institutional Conflicts of Interest: For the Leadership and Senior Administrators, University of Pennsylvania Health System." The guidelines focus exclusively on managing the ICOIs and do not propose a zero-tolerance standard.[31] If the University of Pennsylvania had not learned a lesson of zero tolerance for some ICOIs, with the publicity and financial liability it faced in the Gelsinger case, it would seem doubtful that other universities have an incentive to set a higher standard. Ironically, a year after Gelsinger's death Genovo was sold to Targeted Genetics Corporation. Wilson reportedly earned $13.5 million and the University of Pennsylvania earned $1.4 million in the sale, proving that even failed ICOIs can be financially profitable.[32]

## THE AAUP AND ICOIs

Under the AAUP's newly released "Recommended Principles and Practices to Guide Academy Industry Relationships," the organization has comes as close as it ever has to a zero-tolerance standard for FCOIs or ICOIs in clinical trials. Following a tradition of regulatory burden of proof, the AAUP has introduced a "rebuttable presumption" standard.

> "A rebuttable presumption against permitting the [clinical trial] research should govern decisions about whether conflicted researchers or conflicted institutions should be allowed to pursue a particular human research protocol or project, unless a compelling case can be made to justify an exception. To maximize patient safety and preserve public trust in the integrity of the research enterprise, there should always be a strong presumption against permitting financial COI related to experimental studies involving human subjects."[33]

The AAUP derives its "rebuttable presumption" standard from the Institute of Medicine (IOM) and a joint report of the American Association of Medical Colleges (AAMC) and the American Association of Universities (AAU), both of which proposed a similar standard. The IOM describes the standard as follows: "The 'rebuttable presumption' concept is taken from the law and refers to assumptions that are taken to be true unless they are explicitly and successfully challenged in a particular case . . . A compelling circumstance would exist, for example, if a researcher with a conflict of interest has unique expertise or skill with implanting and adjusting a complex new medical device and this expertise is needed to carry out an early-stage clinical trial safely and competently. Generally, some kind of management plan would then be devised."[34]

If the "rebuttable presumption" is close to a zero-tolerance plan, then its integrity rests on the conditions for and frequency of a waiver — what counts as a "rebuttable argument." According to the AAUP, "in some exceptional cases it may be necessary to allow a university investigator, who has a financial conflicts of interest, to participate in human subject research, if the testing and development of a potential new drug, therapy, or procedure would be unable to proceed without that faculty member's participation (as in the case of a surgeon, who may be the only skilled expert capable of testing a new medical technique)."[35] Returning to the Gelsinger case, it is easily imaginable that James Wilson would have met the criterion for an exception because of his unique involvement with and expertise in the development of the adenoviral vector.

In the view of the AAUP, such waivers from possessing an FCOI while participating in a clinical trial should be granted rarely, and once granted should be made public. AAUP cites the IOM panel report: "In most cases of a conflict of interest [related to human subject research], no compelling argument that the investigator's participation is essential can be made. Even if the investigator's participation is essential, the elimination of the conflict of interest (e.g., through the sale of stock) is the preferred step."[36] In other words, "zero tolerance" is the preferred choice.

## MONITORING ICOIs

If institutional conflicts of interest (ICOIs) are triggered when academic administrators possess FCOIs, who monitors them and the institution? As previously noted, the federal government has issued no regulations on ICOIs. In 2004, the U.S. Department of Health and Human Services (DHHS) issued a guidance document on the identification and management of institutional and individual FCOIs in research with human subjects. The guidance offered questions and suggested procedures, including the use of institutional review boards (IRBs) to monitor FCOIs in clinical trials. This brought into national conversation the expansion of IRB responsibility to include evaluating and managing FCOIs at the institution. The IRBs at universities are made up of volunteers who have a significant responsibility in protecting the safety and informed consent procedures for human subjects. Moreover, the members of the IRBs themselves would have to be vetted by some other entity for any FCOIs that they might have. Campbell et al. surveyed 2,989 faculty members from 121 US medical schools. Of those who served on IRBs within the previous three years, 47 per cent were paid consultants to industry.[37] Because "institutional pressures may lead Institutional Review Boards to approve research activities in which the institution has a financial stake or may be insufficiently rigorous in their review of such protocols"[38] some have recommended that an institution with an ICOI should use the IRB of another institution to review a clinical trial. But that does not eliminate potential FCOIs.

Also "IRBs are already overburdened, do not necessarily have the technical expertise to evaluate and recommend corrective actions to remedy institutional conflicts of interest, and may not be perceived as sufficiently independent from the institution." [39]

Without a set of meta-norms or rebuttable zero-tolerance criteria, universities will address the issue through a management process that will allow them to benefit from the industry-university collaboration while giving the appearance of attention to ethical concerns. The guiding principles of the 2008 AAMC-AAU report made a strong case for "zero tolerance" most of the time. "Decisions about whether or not to pursue a particular human research [project] in the presence of an institutional conflict of interest should be governed by a 'rebuttable presumption' against doing the research at or under the auspices of the conflicted institution."[40]

It is easy to understand how "most of the time" can slide back to "some of the time."

## CONCLUSION

Biomedical research is now heavily financed by industry, which funds 70 per cent of all clinical trials in the United States.[41] As a consequence, there has been "a reduction in the free flow of research information . . . and . . . a shift toward a more entrepreneurial ethos in academic research."[42] Academic freedom cannot be fully realized at a university that has structural constraints, which inhibit the free flow of information, or that infuse research with financial goals that create incongruent interests. Managing active ICOIs in clinical trials does not solve the problem, but rather shifts it to another segment of the university. The sensitivity of human subjects research speaks for a meta-norm of zero tolerance that leaves little wiggle room and offers nothing less than a firewall between those individuals and committees responsible for the protection of human subjects and those who have a personal or institutional financial interest in the outcome.

# 13

# UNIVERSITY-INDUSTRY RELATIONS IN THE UNITED STATES: SERVING PRIVATE INTERESTS

*Risa L. Lieberwitz*

## INTRODUCTION

University-industry relationships in the United States have a long history reaching back to the early growth of industrial capitalism in the nineteenth century. Corporate funders expected that this financial support would build university-industry relationships in which academic research and teaching would benefit industrial needs. The United States Congress strengthened this relationship through legislation promoting universities as engines of industrial growth. The *Morrill Act* of 1862 created land grant colleges to provide education and training for students who would enter the growing industries, including manufacturing and commercial agricultural ventures. The land grant colleges also provided applied research for industry and agriculture performed by faculty in new departments, such as agriculture, mechanical arts, commerce, and business administration. In the first part of the twentieth century, though, corporate expectations were interrupted by the successful collective faculty demand for academic freedom and autonomy as essential to fulfilling the public mission of the university.

This chapter will explore the tension between the societal role of the university as an independent institution and its ongoing relationship with industry. The discussion will provide an historical overview that shows the factors that have favoured progressively close university-corporate relationships since industrialization in the late nineteenth century. This has not been, however, simply a linear process of one type of funding arrangement or relationship replacing another. Rather, it is more a layering process, where new arrangements and relationships are added over time to shape and respond to social, political, and economic conditions. Depending on the nature of such conditions, certain types of relationships between business and universities will be possible. At some moments, universities will assert independence from corporations. At others, direct exchanges between them will be openly cultivated. Further, at any moment there may be multiple types of relationships at work across the academic and business spheres.

This chapter will analyze the consequences — both actual and potential — flowing from the continual additions of layers of university-industrial relations. Closer ties between universities and business have serious implications for faculty academic freedom, university institutional independence, and ultimately for the public interest.

## HISTORICAL FACTORS RELATED TO ACADEMIC FREEDOM: GAINS AND LOSSES

The post-Civil War era marked the beginning of the modern American research university, as the acceptance of the scientific method of inquiry in the natural sciences provided a vehicle for a major break from the antebellum model of the religious college. By the late 1800s, higher education had evolved from a religious undertaking to a secular system.[1] The development of the modern university in the late 1880s created favourable conditions to develop faculty autonomy, particularly in the natural sciences, where faculty could argue persuasively that their competence could not be evaluated by ecclesiastical or secular boards of trustees and college officials.[2] Instead, faculty called for autonomy to rely on peer evaluations, which was made possible by the formation of professional organizations of scholars in specialized fields of the natural sciences. Gaining autonomy was more difficult for faculty in the social sciences, which were rapidly growing in the late nineteenth and early twentieth centuries.[3] As in the natural sciences, the demand for academic freedom in the social sciences rested on the need for peer review by experts in specialized fields. Unlike the natural sciences, however, social science faculty came into conflict with the growing power of business interests. As industrialization expanded so did corporate donations to universities, shifting from thousands to millions of dollars.[4]

Between the Civil War and World War I, the federal government did not fund university research due to concerns by politicians and faculty of government interference with faculty autonomy.[5] Yet corporate funding continued to grow, along with industrialists' expectations that universities would serve corporate interests. During this period, corporations funded contracts for academic research in fields of science, engineering, business, and labour.[6] Faculty raised critiques of the influence of industries' commercial interests on universities, including Thorstein Veblen's *The Higher Learning in America* (1918). Further, within the expanding social science disciplines were faculty who critiqued the social and labour practices of corporate funders. In the resulting clash, university administrators yielded to pressure from industrialists to curb academics, including the forced resignation of economist E.A. Ross from Stanford University and the dismissal of economist Edward W. Bemis from the University of Chicago because of their public political positions, such as advocacy of public ownership of utilities.[7]

In 1915, in response to university administrators' repressive conduct, faculty engaged in collective action by forming the American Association of University Professors (AAUP). The new organization's "Declaration of Principles" claimed faculty rights of academic freedom as essential to fulfilling the fundamental role of the university as an institution with a public mission, which requires disinterested and nonpartisan teaching and research. To achieve these goals universities and faculty must be independent from third parties, whether from legislatures, corporate funders, or other organizations. The declaration described academic freedom as providing individual and collective rights. Faculty members' individual rights encompass academic freedom and autonomy in teaching, research, and extramural speech.

To ensure the protection of academic freedom, the declaration calls for the lifetime job security of tenure, with due process rights prior to discipline or dismissal of a faculty member. The declaration also makes the case for collective rights of academic freedom through faculty self-governance, including peer review to evaluate faculty competence and qualifications for hiring and promotion to a tenured status.[8]

The AAUP's "Declaration of Principles" was an extraordinary achievement. Its basic tenets were restated in the AAUP's "1940 Statement of Principles on Academic Freedom and Tenure," which was endorsed by the Association of American Colleges and over subsequent decades by over 170 academic professional organizations and universities.[9] The AAUP academic freedom principles have been internalized by the academic profession and public and private universities, as reflected in institutional policies and practices. Faculty members exercise rights of academic freedom in their research, in teaching a wide range of courses across the curriculum, in criticizing university policies, and in speaking out on local, national, and international issues. Faculty self-governance includes collective autonomy through the peer review process for tenure and through the deliberations of faculty senates over academic policy.

The institutional acceptance of norms of academic freedom and self-governance has been central to developing an academic research culture based on the university's public mission. It is worth remembering the strength of the 1915 declaration's call for a wall of separation of corporate donors and other third parties and faculty. Academic freedom is required to ensure that professors, who are "trained for, and dedicated to, the quest for truth," state their own conclusions and "not the echoes of the opinions of the lay public, or of the individuals who endow or manage universities." The declaration places its faith in the scientific method, applied in both the natural sciences and the social sciences, as it requires "disinterestedness and impartiality" free from the influence of either "vested [private] interests" or legislators.[10]

The AAUP's achievement in creating professional norms of academic freedom and tenure rights is all the more remarkable when placed in the context of the US legal norm of employment insecurity, which has governed most employment relationships in the US since at least the nineteenth century. The common law doctrine of "employment at will" emphasizes employers' unilateral power to decide whether to initially employ or continue to employ an individual.[11]

As important as academic freedom has been for protecting faculty rights of expression, due process, and collective governance, it has always had significant flaws and omissions. In its early formative period, the AAUP explicitly rejected the goal, advocated by a syndicalist faction of the AAUP, of restructuring higher education into a public system with faculty control over appointments of administrators and university officers. Instead, the AAUP chose a more limited strategy of carving out a position of faculty autonomy within the existing institutional structure of a largely private system of higher education run by powerful administrators.[12] Professor Ellen Schrecker has criticized the resulting peer review structures as being "self-policing," rather than self-governing, as faculty will avoid interference in their decisions only by making judgments that are acceptable to the administration and trustees.[13] This leaves tenure-track faculty subject to highly subjective evaluations by their colleagues in reviews for promotion to tenure.

## CORPORATIZATION TRENDS

### POST-WORLD WAR II FUNDING FROM GOVERNMENT AND CORPORATIONS

During World War I, university scientists engaged in research for the government after they were inducted into the armed forces.[14] But it was not until World War II that the federal government directly funded universities to engage in academic research as part of the war effort.[15] High levels of federal funding for research continued in the post-war period, particularly in the science and engineering disciplines.[16] Since 1960, federal funding has consistently constituted 60 to 70 per cent of university research support.[17] The question of whether such funding has always been used to promote the public interest has often been controversial, including academic researchers' roles during the war in developing nuclear weapons. Post-World War II, the federal government has continued to fund academic research useful to military and intelligence agencies, leading to critiques and protests against universities and faculty engaged in research that support the military-industrial complex.[18] As part of the campus protests of the 1960s, student and faculty activists demanded that universities be held accountable for the political, social, and economic consequences of their research programs.[19]

The campus protests revealed the problems with academic research that directly supports a political agenda. Where academic research contributes to government programs such as the Vietnam War, the separation between the academy and the government funder is obliterated. This use of public funds fuelled protests against research conducted on university campuses to support an unethical war. As a result of public engagement on these issues, students and faculty successfully pressured universities to refuse to accept government research contracts that required secrecy in conducting classified research.[20]

Even in less controversial and politically charged circumstances, though, it may be difficult to maintain faculty independence in research programs that depend on external financial sources. Any funder will influence academic research in some way. Public funding appropriations will be shaped by government priorities for certain areas of research. The decision-making process, though, has a transparency that enables public debate about whether the government should fund certain types of research and whether universities and faculty should engage in such research.[21] Further, federal agencies such as the National Institutes of Health (NIH) and the National Science Foundation (NSF) follow protocols for public calls for research proposals and peer review committees to evaluate and recommend proposals for funding awards. This process adds to the transparency and legitimacy of the decisions on the merits of the research proposals being evaluated. Corporate funding for academic research, by contrast, is a less transparent process. Negotiations between universities and corporations can be done privately or even secretly. While there may be debate over whether private funding promotes the university's public mission, objections could not be based on the inherently public nature of the use of taxpayer money.

## INCREASED UNIVERSITY PATENTING AND LICENSING SINCE THE 1980S

As federal funding to academic research dropped during the economic downturn of the mid-1970s, corporate research funding grew. This development combined with other political changes to insert corporations more directly into decisions about academic research. Since the late 1970s, the industry role in funding and influencing academic research has changed dramatically. The prevalence and scope of industry and business considerations are due to a convergence of developments in three areas: science, politics, and law.

The discovery of recombinant DNA (rDNA) technology in the mid-1970s has been described as "the single pivotal event in the transformation of the 'basic' science of molecular biology into an industry."[22] In the new age of biotechnology, the line between basic and applied research has been increasingly blurred, as the potential commercial value of basic research becomes clearer at an earlier stage and as the time period between basic research and its application is shortened.[23] During this period, university research created further innovations in computer science and technology, launching the era of the "knowledge-driven economy."[24]

These changes in science and technology research coincided with the political shifts in the US toward privatization of governmental functions. One expression of this policy shift was the 1980 *Bayh-Dole Act,* which authorized and encouraged federal fund recipients, including universities, to apply for patents on results of federally funded research. Congress justified the *Bayh-Dole Act* as a means of increasing US global competitiveness by expanding commercialization of publicly funded research results, particularly through collaboration between universities and industry.[25] Prior to the *Bayh-Dole Act,* federal law had granted the government title to inventions developed with federal funds, a policy that favoured placing these inventions in the public domain. The government agency could choose to dedicate the invention to the public domain by publishing the results without obtaining a patent or by providing non-exclusive licences to private parties seeking to use a government-owned patent.[26] In the 1960s and 1970s, universities could patent and license federally funded academic research in cases where the funding agencies, most notably the Department of Defense and to a lesser extent the National Science Foundation and the Department of Health, Education, and Welfare, transferred title in the research to the universities.[27]

Developments in the courts further strengthened the commercial potential of academic research. In 1980, the United States Supreme Court held, in *Diamond v. Chakrabarty*, that life forms can be patented, in this case a genetically engineered bacterium that degraded crude oil. In 1982, Congress created the Federal Circuit Court of Appeals with exclusive jurisdiction of patent appeals. The Federal Circuit is known for its pro-patent philosophy. This judicial philosophy, combined with the Supreme Court's 1980 Chakrabarty decision, resulted in expansion of patents in the biotechnology field, including patents on basic research.[28]

The interaction of these developments in the three spheres of science and technology research, legislation, and the courts created a fertile ground for university policies and practices favouring commercialization of university research. There has been an explosion of university technology transfer offices to facilitate the growth of patents and licences in universities. In 1979, before the *Bayh-Dole Act,* US universities obtained 264 patents, compared with 1997, when US universities obtained ten times that number, at 2,436 patents.[29] From 1980 to 1990, patent applications on NIH-funded inventions increased by almost 300 per cent.[30] From 1991 to 2000, the patents granted to US universities increased by 131 per cent and licences granted by the universities increased by 158 per cent.[31] Between 1988 and 2003, US patents awarded to academic institutions quadrupled, from about 800 to more than 3,200 per year.[32] Biomedical patents constitute close to fifty per cent of university patent activity.[33] Private biotechnology companies and universities have sought patents on basic research tools, including gene sequences.[34]

## GROWTH OF UNIVERSITY-INDUSTRY RELATIONSHIPS SINCE THE LATE 1970S

Since the late 1970s, universities and faculty have entered increasingly close relationships with industry. Individual faculty consulting for business has increased. Faculty often enter into consulting arrangements with businesses while continuing their university teaching and research, with an estimate that about half of life sciences faculty act as consultants for industry.[35] Since the mid-1980s, 21 to 28 per cent of life sciences faculty have consistently received research support from industry.[36] Faculty have also taken on dual identities as academics and owners of businesses that are spinoffs from their academic research. About seven to eight per cent of faculty report that they hold equity in a company related to their research.[37] During the 1980s and 1990s, faculty participated in founding twenty-four Fortune 500 companies and over 600 non-Fortune 500 companies in the life sciences.[38]

Faculty interactions with corporations go beyond the life sciences to relationships in fields such as information technology and financial services industries.[39] As an AAUP report on academy-industry relationships observes, the active role of economics and business faculty in private financial institutions is an understudied phenomenon. Although faculty relationships in financial firms range from consultants to senior officers much of this has not been disclosed to the public.[40]

The university-industry relationship goes in both directions. Not only are faculty becoming involved in business, but industry has also become more directly involved in the university. Although federal funding remains the largest external source of academic research overall, at 60 percent compared to 6 per cent from private sources, industry funding has increased dramatically.[41] Industry funding of university research programs increased by 93 per cent between 1980 and 1984.[42] In the 1970 to2000 period, industry funding of academic research tripled, amounting to a tenfold increase.[43] Some universities depend heavily on industry funding, from 12 per cent to as much half of their research and development budgets.[44]

Industry funding is targeted to particular faculty and academic programs in fields with the greatest commercial potential — medicine, biology, chemistry, engineering, economics, business, and agriculture.[45] As noted in the AAUP report on academy-industry relations, while the extent of industry funding to biomedicine has been widely reported, greater study and public information is needed concerning the level of industry funding in other academic disciplines.[46] In 1994, 90 per cent of life sciences companies had a relationship with an academic institution, including a significant increase in industry funding of life science academic research, estimated at $1.5 billion (11.7 per cent) of the $12.8 billion of all extramural support of life science academic research.[47] These relationships can provide further financial gains to universities through university income from licensing of patents. The AAUP report cites to a 2006 survey of department chairs at medical schools and large teaching hospitals that revealed that 67 per cent had relationships with industry, with 27 per cent of non-clinical departments and 16 per cent of clinical departments receiving income from commercial licensing of university-owned patents.[48]

University-industry agreements provide for the terms of the exchange, including corporate licensing rights to university-owned patents and corporate involvement in university research functions. As corporate funding becomes more significant, the likelihood increases that the corporation will negotiate for exclusive licensing rights and a significant presence in the university.[49] At the largest scale of industry funding are strategic corporate alliances (SCAs), which increased in the 1980s and 1990s.[50] Under an SCA, a single corporation provides tens of millions of dollars to finance an entire academic department or research program in exchange for exclusive licenses, influence over research agendas, and access to the university facilities, faculty, and graduate students.[51] For example, the 1994 MIT-Amgen agreement provided for $30 million of corporate funding to the Department of Biology and the Department of Brain and Cognitive Sciences over a ten-year period in exchange for resulting patents to be owned jointly by MIT and the pharmaceutical firm Amgen.[52] The head of Amgen, Gordon Binder, described the agreement "as a 'model for industry-academic partnerships.'" [MIT President] Vest called the agreement 'an essential element in the kind of future I see for MIT: a synergy of basic research efforts at universities and long-term commitments by industry.'"[53] SCA terms make the corporation an active participant in the university's use of the corporate funds. As an article in *Science* described Binder's approach: "Binder defends the [MIT-Amgen] agreement as a wise investment, but he adds that such deals can fail unless the research — and the expectations — are carefully managed: "'What doesn't work is to give a university a ton of money' and then sit back to wait for useful returns."[54]

Under the controversial and much-publicized 1998 agreement between Swiss pharmaceutical corporation Novartis/Syngenta and University of California at Berkeley (UC Berkeley), Novartis/Syngenta agreed to provide $25 million over five years to Berkeley's Department of Plant and Microbial Biology, in exchange for exclusive corporate licensing rights to about a third of the department's discoveries.[55] The negotiations for this SCA were conducted in secret.[56] As part of the deal, UC Berkeley gave Novartis/Syngenta two of five seats on the department's research funding committee, the right to review all proposed publications and presentations by participating faculty and their graduate students, and the right to ask for a ninety-day publication delay to provide time for patent applications.[57]

The SCA, with its large-scale and long-term dimensions, may be on the wane. This may be, in part, due the wide criticism of the UC Berkeley-Novartis/Syngenta SCA. UC Berkeley commissioned an external evaluation of the SCA, which concluded that universities should avoid such agreements due to the conflict of interests created within the university.[58] Corporations have reportedly concluded that SCAs are not as lucrative as originally envisioned, particularly in the lack of "short-term payback of such deals — especially in a weak economy . . ."[59] Instead, Roger Beachy, President of the Donald Danforth Plant Science Center in St. Louis, predicted, "'There will be . . . more emphasis on individual linkages rather than institutional ones.'"[60] The Donald Danforth Plant Science Center is heavily subsidized by Monsanto. Glenn Hicks, former research Director for the San Francisco biotech company Exelixis, has expressed the view that industry agreements for university research will be "more targeted."[61]

With changes in short-term economic conditions, market responses, and industry profitability, there will be an ebb and flow of different kinds and levels of university-industry agreements. For the moment, SCAs may be on the wane as corporations return to more targeted funding of academic research. Industry funding of biomedical faculty was reduced in the 1995 to 2006 period, from 28 to 20 per cent.[62] Regardless of these short-term variations, though, universities and industry have cemented close relationships based on their perception of common interests. As Lita Nelson, MIT's technology licensing Office Director, observed, even after the MIT-Amgen SCA ended, the benefits are the relationships developed. As she stated, "You don't do this kind of deal for patents but to get to know the leaders in a field."[63] In building these relationships, universities see industry as partners. Through SCAs and more targeted funding, corporations have inserted themselves into the core research functions of the university by deciding what sorts of academic research they wish to fund, having access to academic researchers, and contracting for rights of pre-publication review and licensing rights.

As market actors, universities create contract relationships with industry partners and other corporations for exclusive or non-exclusive licensing of university-owned patents. Universities join with corporate co-owners of patents to assert their ownership rights in patent infringement suits against other corporations and even against faculty members. Increased patenting and licensing activities have contributed to the privatization of academic research and the shift of university identity to a market actor. Consistent with this identity, universities have taken action to protect their ownership interests. In an important decision in 2013, though, the US Supreme Court placed some limits on patenting that will restrict university market activities to some extent. In *Ass'n for Molecular Pathology et al. v. USPTO* (*Myriad*), the University of Utah Research Foundation owned the patents on the isolated human genes, BRCA1 and BRCA2, which correlate with increased risk of breast and ovarian cancer.[64] The discoveries of these breast cancer genes were based, in part, on academic research funded by the NIH.[65] The University of Utah Research Foundation exclusively licensed the patent to Myriad Genetics, Inc., which defended its patent by seeking to block academic medical institutions from testing patients for mutations in the BRACA1/2 genes.[66] The Supreme Court granted review to decide whether the isolated genes may be patented as "human-made inventions" or whether they are "products of nature" that may not be patented.[67] Throughout the litigation of this case, the University of Utah Research Foundation acted jointly with Myriad.[68] In a unanimous decision, the Court held that the isolated BRACA1/2 genes are not patentable because they are "'[l]aws of nature, natural phenomena, and abstract ideas.'"[69] Such "'basic tools of scientific and technological work' . . . lie beyond the domain of patent protection" and belong to the public domain for further use in research and innovation.[70] The Court held, however, that synthetically created BRCA cDNA is not a "product of nature" and is patent eligible.[71]

The Myriad decision is a positive development in restricting universities and others from patenting naturally occurring genetic material. The resulting expansion of the public domain will provide access to basic research tools and may well lower the cost of genetic testing for the BRCA genes. The limits of the decision, though, should also be recognized. As the Court notes, it was not faced with patentability claims concerning new methods of manipulating genes on new applications of knowledge about the BRCA genes or on scientific alteration of the genetic code.[72] Such claims would be patent eligible. Moreover, these legal issues are independent from the ethical questions of whether the university's patent and licensing activities are incompatible with its public mission.

## NEGATIVE IMPACT ON ACADEMIC FREEDOM

The current state of university-industry relations is far from the traditional vision of university and faculty independence from third party funders. The emphasis on commercializing academic research through university-industry partnerships and university market activities ignores the underlying principles that support the need for independent academic institutions. The AAUP's "1915 Declaration of Principles on Academic Freedom and Academic Tenure" and its "1940 Statement of Principles on Academic Freedom and Tenure" defined academic freedom and autonomy as central to the university's ability to fulfill its public mission. Without independence from corporate funders, faculty would be caught in the inherent conflict between their funders' private interests and the public interests of the academy. These public interests are promoted by the culture and ethics of communalism, disinterestedness, and independence in academic research, which support the quality, legitimacy, and integrity of research. Communal values are in conflict with the self-interested goals of research and development in industry.[73]

Guarding against research that is compromised by conflicting goals is a structural issue; that is, structures must be put into place to guard against both conscious and unconscious influences on faculty from third-party interests. One structural protection is placing academic research results in the public domain, where they are freely available for use by other researchers, government, corporations, and other private parties. When the *Bayh-Dole Act* compromised this structural protection for federally funded research, the wall of separation between universities and industry was transformed into a porous membrane. Bayh-Dole encouraged commercialization of academic research as part of a national political agenda of privatization. Universities embraced this agenda and the opportunity to become market actors licensing university-owned patents and developing new forms of university-industry partnerships.

Legislative and institutional policies and practices promoting privatization and commercialization of academic research define the interests of universities and industry as compatible. Given the historical and current evidence of the conflict of interests between the university's public mission and industry's private interests, achieving compatibility between these two spheres means that one or both of them must change. In the context of national and global privatization, this has entailed a change in the culture of the academic institution to be compatible with industry. The commercialization of university research has compromised the traditional values of communalism, disinterestedness, and independence of science. University scientists report changes in their relationships with colleagues engaged in research financed by private corporations. Those colleagues are unwilling to discuss their research methods or results, either because of corporate funding contracts that restrict the researcher from sharing information or that give the corporation the right to see this information first, or because of the researcher's interest in protecting information for future patents.[74] Universities typically agree to delays of publication for periods ranging from three to six months, or even longer, to provide time for a corporate funder to review research results and for a patent application to be filed prior to disclosure through scholarly publication.[75] There have been incidents of corporate pressure to change research reports to eliminate negative results in relation to a corporate product or to suppress disclosure of the report.[76] Studies have reported that corporately financed researchers are significantly more likely to reach favourable results concerning a corporation's product, including pharmaceutical products.[77]

The altered university culture is captured by the new lexicon of the entrepreneurship that is pervasive in university officials' speech, new university administrative titles, and university programs. Faculty are lauded for their entrepreneurial activities in working with university technology transfer offices to file for patents on their academic research results, in launching spinoff corporations growing out of academic research, and in developing close relationships with industry partners. In this context, disclosure of financial interests is the primary structural device used to guard against conflicts of interests. Universities and federal grant applications require faculty to complete conflict of interest disclosure reports.[78] The scientific journals *Nature, New England Journal of Medicine, Journal of the American Medical Association,* and *Lancet* now require that authors of articles accepted for publication submit funding sources, employment records, and financial investment histories. In January 2012, the American Economic Association adopted new standards for disclosure of authors' financial conflicts of interest in the AEA's journals.[79] The theory behind disclosure requirements is that the public can take financial interests into account when evaluating the academic researcher's findings. Disclosures do not, however, address the underlying substantive issue of whether conflicting interests should be avoided to protect the quality and integrity of the research.[80]

## MERGING UNIVERSITY AND INDUSTRY MISSIONS, RESEARCH, AND TEACHING IN THE 21ST CENTURY

### CORNELL NYC TECH: AN ENTREPRENEURIAL CAMPUS

So close have university and industry interests become that the only way they could get any closer is for them to become identical. That is, in fact, the next step that some universities have taken; they have merged university interests with those of industry. One example is the launch in January 2013 of the Cornell University New York City Technology program, known as Cornell NYC Tech, in which the "close relationship [between the university and industry] is not merely the desired outcome; it is the founding premise."[81] The mission of this graduate program is to create an applied science and engineering campus focused on commercialization of academic research. Cornell NYC Tech describes its "vision" of a program to "immerse [students] in an entrepreneurial culture with deep ties to the local business community, and spur the creation of new companies and new industries in New York City and around the globe."[82] At the heart of the program, "[c]ore interdisciplinary academic and research activities will generate and attract substantial commercial and entrepreneurial activity, applied and basic research, deep and multi-faceted relationships with companies, student internships, and company projects."[83] The Cornell NYC Tech website has links to news coverage about the program, including a *New York Times* article, "New Cornell Technology School Tightly Bound to Business," which explains that the program's exclusive focus on graduate students in applied sciences "allows it to bypass the broad educational needs of undergraduate students to focus instead on one distinct, but shared goal: 'cultivating entrepreneurial technologists' in the words of Gregg Pass, the former Twitter executive who is Cornell NYC Tech's chief entrepreneurial officer."[84]

The main Cornell University campus is in the city of Ithaca, which is in a rural area in central New York. The Cornell NYC Tech campus will be constructed in New York City to make it possible for full integration of the academic program with industry. The creation of Cornell NYC Tech was triggered by New York City Mayor Bloomberg's plan to develop the information technology industry in New York.[85] Bloomberg's vision is part of current political efforts to exploit the economic potential of universities to create jobs in the knowledge economy.[86] Bloomberg opened a competition to universities to apply for an award of $100 million in funds and $300 million worth of real estate from NYC to build an applied science and engineering campus. The hope is that faculty and students will become entrepreneurs through spinoff corporations that "will create tens of thousands of new jobs."[87] Stanford University was one of the competitors, but pulled out prior to the decision to award the grant to Cornell.[88]

The NYC Tech program is similar in some ways to Stanford University's "porous interaction" with neighbouring Silicon Valley in California.[89] Many of the high-tech firms in Silicon Valley were launched as spinoff corporations by Stanford engineering faculty, and there is an ongoing close relationship between Stanford faculty and students and the high-tech firms. Stanford and Silicon Valley have a "symbiotic relationship" and "a borderless community."[90] Cornell NYC Tech, though, takes the Silicon Valley model a step further by eliminating any separation between the infrastructure of the university and corporations and the interaction of faculty, students, and industry representatives. As the *New York Times* described the Cornell NYC Tech model: "[T]he most striking departure of all may be the relationship it sets forth between university and industry, one in which commerce and education are not just compatible, they are also all but indistinguishable. In this new framework, Cornell NY Tech is not just a school, it is an 'educational start-up,' students are 'deliverables' and companies seeking access to those students or their professors can choose from a 'suite of products' by which to get it."[91] Although the Cornell NYC Tech's first class, which started in January 2013, consists of only seven students, the program envisions having two-thousand full-time students and several hundred faculty when it is fully operational in 2037.[92]

To enhance NYC Tech's ability to commercialize academic research Cornell brought in a partner, the Technion-Israel Institute of Technology, which is known for its history of commercializing new technology and creating start-up companies in Israel. Irwin Jacobs, the founding chairman of mobile technology giant Qualcomm has donated $133 million to fund the Joan and Irwin Jacobs Technion-Cornell Innovation Institute, which will be located on the Cornell NYC Tech campus.[93] In addition to Cornell graduate degrees in fields such as information science, engineering, and business, the program will offer a dual Cornell/Technion Master of Science.[94] Jacobs, Bloomberg, and Google Executive Chairman Eric Schmidt will make up a steering committee "to provide advice to tech campus leadership on the educational, research, economic development and community engagement functions of the campus, helping to promote new national and international models connecting academia and industry."[95] Google has donated twenty thousand square feet of space of its NYC headquarters for the Cornell NYC Tech to use while the campus is under construction.[96]

All structural and academic aspects of the NYC Tech program are designed to promote entrepreneurship, commercialization, and the integration of faculty, students, and industry. The physical layout will include corporate offices on campus or nearby. The curriculum and graduate student committees integrate corporate representatives. Each Friday is reserved for students to interact with corporate employees. Instead of a master's thesis, students may complete a "master's project" by working with a business. Conversely, a company's employees may work in the program on projects with faculty and students. Professors will be encouraged to work with for-profit companies or non-profit organizations. NYC Tech will create contracts with companies to ease technology transfer.[97] Cornell and the U.S. Department of Commerce have entered a "partnership . . . to speed commercialization of ideas generated at Cornell Tech."[98] A Department of Commerce representative will have an office on the NYC Tech campus in the " . . . first time a U.S. government agency has joined forces with a university to give students and researchers direct access to resources to bring ideas — and the companies and jobs they create — to market."[99]

## CHANGING – OR LOSING – THE UNIVERSITY'S IDENTITY

As Lita Nelson observed about SCAs, their greatest significance is in strengthening relationships between business and the university.[100] Such university-industry funding "partnerships" have brought academic and corporate interests closer together by inserting corporations into the academic research process and linking corporate funding to intellectual property rights. Similarly, Cornell administrators emphasize that Cornell NYC Tech is about building relationships, rather than seeking corporate funding. Cornell NYC Tech Dean Huttenlocher explains that "companies that can pay the most money don't necessarily make the best partners."[101] Rather, "to the degree to which interaction with a company can help us attract better faculty or generate better research, that's incredibly valuable."[102] By fully integrating the campus and industry, the NYC Tech model goes further than SCAs or Silicon Valley to build relationships through merged university and corporate interests. The steering committee is made up of major corporate executives who are financially involved in the program and who will actively guide its curriculum and commercialization activities. The physical and functional proximity of the faculty, students, and corporate employees is designed to create a seamless relationship to promote commercialization and entrepreneurship. The NYC Tech campus infrastructure will accommodate corporate offices. Corporate representatives sit on graduate committees and graduate students work on corporate research projects, including the possibility of substituting such projects for a traditional master's thesis. Students can sign non-disclosure agreements concerning their work on industry projects. Faculty are encouraged to spend time working for corporations. The Department of Commerce office on campus seeks to enhance the flow of technology transfer, avoiding the contractual negotiating difficulties experienced in other university-industry partnerships.

In defining its entrepreneurial mission, Cornell NYC Tech has adopted an institutional identity based on for-profit corporate values rather than the values of universities serving the public good. As in other university ventures into technology transfer and partnerships with industry, NYC Tech claims that the program will serve the public interest by creating new companies and "increas[ing] the talent pool in New York City," which will "positively influence the New York

City economy."[103] As in other university market activities, though, these claims ignore the conflict of interests between for-profit corporations and institutions with a public mission. Cornell University President David Skorton and NYC Tech Dean Daniel Huttenlocher have expressed concerns about the conflicts of interests that may result from the close relationship between NYC Tech and industry. As Skorton states, "How are we going to deal with some very obvious conflicts of interest the closer we get to industry? It's a huge concern."[104] Similarly, Huttenlocher states, "I think there are lots of risks in trying to bring what are fundamentally different cultures and sets of goals together. Companies need to make a profit. Universities have different motives — partly societal good, partly education — and that leads to different value systems."[105] Skorton gives an example of a conflict of interest arising from faculty entrepreneurial work: "Is there a teacher being motivated by the all mighty buck or motivated by things that are educational?"[106] When students work for corporations, Skorton explains, "If you don't protect that interaction crisply and clearly, you could be concerned about the student basically working in an unpaid capacity for industry."[107] Although students may sign non-disclosure agreements with the companies, Huttenlocher states that any work "done for academic purposes may not be kept confidential."[108] Robert Buhrman, Cornell's Senior Vice -rovost for Research and Vice-President for Technology Transfer, is "confident" that conflicts of interests can be handled "with full reporting by our faculty and with proper management."[109] Similar to other university-industry relationships, though, disclosures do not address the substance of the issues underlying the conflict of interests.[110] In an institution created to fully integrate the university and industry activities, disclosure becomes an empty exercise.

The creation of Cornell NYC Tech has already had a negative impact on the "shared governance" model of collegial decision making, which is part of collective rights of academic freedom. Cornell University's process of creating its proposal for the NYC competition was marked by secrecy, including the decision to bring in the Technion as a partner.[111] This secret process resonates with a corporate top-down model of decision-making. It eliminated the public debate and deliberation by faculty that are hallmarks of meaningful shared governance over university policies and programs affecting academic matters.

In merging its interests and functions with industry, the NYC Tech program may undermine the essence of what it means to be a university. Columbia University's then-Executive Vice-Provost of technology transfer operations Michael Crow, in an interview with author Jennifer Washburn, explained, "[O]ne of the things I've tried to do here [at Columbia] is to stay true to the academic mission, which is to let these faculty members do what their noses tell them to do. Don't interfere with them."[112] Crow criticized the University of Mississippi's plan to "to put a company in the [university] lab . . . *on the university's campus.*"[113] In Crow's view, this approach to technology transfer is "stupid"; it would "wreck the university."[114] Most striking about this critique is the fact that it came from a successful administrator in university technology transfer. Although Crow made his comments in regard to plans by "second-, third-, and fourth-tier schools,"[115] his observations are relevant more broadly. His analysis raises the fundamental difference between doing research aimed strictly at its commercial value and the academic mission of research done for its own sake, where faculty "follow their noses." Ultimately, putting the two systems together will likely impede the quality and integrity of the research.

## A COLLECTIVE FACULTY RESPONSE FOR THE 21ST CENTURY?

The history of university-industry relations shows the long-term tension between the values and goals of the university's public mission and those of for-profit business. The layering of the types of relationships that bring universities and corporations closer together will make it extremely difficult to restore university and faculty independence. Yet it is essential to build opposition to the expansion of commercialization of academic research, whether it takes the form of university patents and exclusive licensing of academic research, faculty financial interests in their academic research, or the integration of academic programs and corporations on the university campus.

Organized opposition to commercialization of the university will require faculty to reconnect with their role in building the institutional identity of the university that promotes the public interest. Faculty will also need to return to the communal values of the academic profession, based on individual and collective rights of academic freedom, openness of research methods and results, and independence of faculty from conflicting interests. Given the extensive nature of faculty-industry relationships, many faculty may not join efforts to reduce their own commercial activities or those of the university. Even so, there may be a critical mass of faculty who find that the merging of university and industry interests has gone too far, as in programs that integrate corporations into the core elements of academic programs.

It is possible that university administrations may have engaged in overreaching that could motivate faculty opposition. One instance may be found in the US Supreme Court's 2011 decision in *Stanford v. Roche*, in which universities argued that the *Bayh-Dole Act* automatically vests ownership in the university of federally funded faculty research. The Court rejected this argument and held that the act had not disturbed the basic principle that ownership rights to an invention rest with the inventor. Thus, under the *Bayh-Dole Act*, universities could not patent the research unless faculty assign their ownership rights to the university.[116] While such assignment of rights is routinely done in universities,[117] faculty could engage in collective resistance against being compelled to assign their rights. For example, faculty governance bodies could draft intellectual property rights policies that maintain ownership control in faculty rather than having compulsory assignments of ownership rights to the university.[118] To effectively address the underlying issues, though, such collective action will be meaningful only if it is aimed at pushing back against the university's patenting and exclusive licensing activities. Faculty control over their research could build a movement toward returning academic research to the public domain. Such faculty collective actions would reinvigorate fundamental principles of the public mission of university and faculty academic freedom.

# 14

# PROTECTING THE INTERGRITY OF ACADEMIC WORK IN CORPORATE COLLABORATIONS

*James L. Turk*

As universities turned themselves into big businesses in the twentieth century, they increasingly developed closer working relationships with the corporate sector and modelled themselves on the private-sector corporation. Governments, university boards, and administrations have been promoting the transformation of the core of university work — educating students and expanding knowledge through research and scholarship — to be more consistent with market priorities and corporate practices.[1]

This has meant defining educational worth in terms of vocational relevance and determining research priorities by their potential commercial significance. "Innovation"[2] has become a watchword, and collaborations with industry *de rigueur*.[3]

Formal research and program collaborations between universities and corporations and other third parties have blossomed. While such collaborations can be mutually productive, and, in some fields, necessary to do specific kinds of scientific work, they can compromise academic inquiry and undermine the university's unique and vital role in society. As research priorities, values, and standards are shaped by the nature of the institutions undertaking the scientific inquiry, the differences between corporate interests and academic interests must be acknowledged and dealt with. Private-sector corporations exist to make a profit for their shareholders; universities exist to extend and deepen human understanding through research, scholarship, and teaching.

The differences in priorities have manifested themselves historically in numerous ways that suggest collaborations should be approached cautiously and with built-in protections for academics and their universities.

The most clear-cut example of different priorities has been the persistent effort of corporate-funded research to undermine scientific findings adverse to corporate interests. No instance is clearer than the tobacco industry's efforts over more than seven decades to call into question the link between smoking and lung cancer and to undermine the scientific research showing that second-hand smoke is equally lethal.[4] But tobacco is by no means unique. Similar attempts by corporate science and corporate scientists to undermine the scientific findings adverse to their interests have been documented for the asbestos industry[5], the lead industry (in paint, in gasoline, etc.)[6], the beryllium industry[7], the chemical industry[8], and the pharmaceutical industry,[9] among others.

Beyond this history of corporate science attempting to discredit academic science, there is now a substantial body of work that shows that corporate funding of academic research results in a greater likelihood of pro-industry conclusions — a phenomenon now dubbed "the funding effect."[10]

A pioneering study by Stelfox and colleagues in the 1990s found that conclusions from research into whether calcium channel blockers (used to treat hypertension) increased the risk of heart attacks were shaped by whether the researchers had financial ties to the drug manufacturers. Ninety-six per cent of those favourable to the use of calcium channel blockers had financial ties to drug manufacturers, compared to 60 per cent who were neutral, and 37 per cent who were critical.[11] Subsequently, a number of others have documented the funding effect in regard to other research.[12]

Academic scientists whose work has raised questions about the safety, efficacy, or utility of corporate products have sometimes suffered serious consequences for their careers. Not uncommonly, they were unable to get appropriate support and assistance from their own universities or academic research centres as they defended their scientific work.[13]

Even some critics of university-corporate collaborations have faced difficulties as a result. Perhaps the best-known case is that of Ignacio Chapela at the University of California at Berkeley (UCB). It was the site of one of the largest collaborations in the 1990s between UCB and the Swiss pharmaceutical manufacturer Novartis. In 1998, Novartis entered into a five-year collaboration with the UCB College of Natural Resources' Department of Plant and Microbial Biology. For its part, Novartis gave $25 million, along with access to trade secrets principally in genetics. In return, Novartis was given a voice in what research academics did and privileged access to potentially lucrative discoveries. The research committee, which reviewed and approved proposals, consisted of three named by UCB and two named by Novartis.

Chapela, a young, untenured professor in the College of Natural Resources (CNR) had been named Chair of the CNR's executive committee shortly before the proposed collaboration was brought forward publicly. A rising star with an impressive scholarly record, Chapela was a vocal critic of the collaboration, both as chair of the executive committee and as a concerned faculty member. When he came up for tenure in 2003, he was denied by the university. The denial was hard to explain except as a reaction to his vigorous opposition to the Novartis-UCB deal as he had overwhelming support from his department, his chair, his dean, and an unprecedented number of external reviewers. The chronology is as follows:

- Spring 2002: department votes 31-1 (three abstentions) in favour of tenure (twelve external evaluators recommended tenure).

- Summer 2002: chair supports recommendation and forwards to dean.

- Summer 2002: dean supports recommendation and forwards to

Campus Ad Hoc Tenure Committee.

- October 2002: Campus Ad Hoc Tenure Committee unanimously recommends tenure;
- vice-provost asks committee chair to re-evaluate with additional external evaluators.
- Three additional external letters sought:— two recommend tenure, one does not.
- Departmental chair reaffirms his recommendation for tenure.
- Referred to Senate Budget Committee (SBC), the university-wide committee that deals with tenure.
- Dean objected to the one biologist on SBC claiming he had a conflict of interest.
- Chancellor says there is no conflict of interest.
- Dean reaffirms his recommendation of tenure.
- Two more external letters requested: one declines to provide a letter, one recommends.
- June 2003: SBC preliminary decision: denial of tenure.
- Two more external letters requested. Both recommend tenure.
- Chair and dean reaffirm their recommendations.
- November 2003: SBC final decision: tenure denied.
- November 2003: chancellor denies tenure.

Chapela was denied tenure despite a department vote of 31-1-3 in favour of tenure; the Campus Ad Hoc Tenure Committee voting unanimously in favour of tenure; the support of his departmental chair and the dean and seventeen of eighteen external reviewers recommending tenure. There was considerable outrage over the decision.

A year-and-a-half later, Berkeley's newly appointed Chancellor Robert Birgeneau agreed to establish a review committee whose recommendation late that spring resulted in Chapela being granted tenure.[14]

An independent, third-party review of the Novartis-UCB collaboration was undertaken by a team of scholars at Michigan State University — a term of the agreement between Novartis and UCB that was added in the face of the initial opposition to the planned collaboration. The lengthy review ends with a caution:

> We would do well to remember both parts of Eisenhower's warning quoted in the epigraph to this volume: He warned us about the need to avoid both the domination of university faculty by money and the capture of public policy by a scientific-technological elite. We now face the possibility of a scientific elite dominated by money and in charge of public policy. That does not bode well for the critical inquiry necessary to sustain democracy.[15]

Concerns about protecting the integrity of academic science and academic freedom in corporate collaborations prompted the Center for American Progress to undertake a review of ten major American university collaborations with the energy industry.[16] The collaborative agreements studied were:

- Arizona State University and BP PLC [$5.2 million]
- University of California at Berkeley and BP PLC [$500 million]
- University of California at Davis and Chevron Corp. [$25 million]

- Colorado School of Mines and Chevron Corp. [$2.5 million]

- University of Colorado, Boulder; Colorado State University, Colorado School of Mines and twenty-seven firms, including ADM, Chevron, ConocoPhillips, Dow, DuPont, GMC, Shell, Suncor, Weyerhaeuser, and W.R. Grace. [$6 million]

- Georgia Institute of Technology and Chevron Corp. [$12 million]

- Iowa State University and ConocoPhillips Co. [$22.5 million]

- Stanford and ExxonMobil, GE, Toyota, and Schlumberger [$225 million]

- Texas A&Mand Chevron Corp. [$5.2 million]

- University of Texas, Austin; Rice University and Baker Hughes, BP, Conoco Phillips, Haliburton, Marathon Oil, Occidental Oil and Gas, Petroleo Brasileiro, Schlumberger, Shell, Total [$30 million][17]

The study's findings were chilling as most commonly the universities had ceded fundamental aspects that protected the integrity of academic research to the participating companies:

- In nine of the ten agreements, the university partners failed to retain majority academic control over the central governing body charged with directing the university-industry alliance. Four of the ten alliances actually give the industry sponsors full governance control.

- Eight of the ten agreements permit the corporate sponsor or sponsors to fully control both the evaluation and selection of faculty research proposals in each new grant cycle.

- *None* of the ten agreements requires faculty research proposals to be evaluated and awarded funding based on independent expert peer review.

- Eight of the ten agreements fail to specify transparently, in advance, how faculty may apply for alliance funding, and what the specific evaluation and selection criteria will be.

- Nine of the ten agreements call for no specific management of financial conflicts of interest related to the alliance and its research functions. None of these agreements, for example, specifies that committee members charged with evaluating and selecting faculty research proposals must be impartial, and may not award corporate funding to themselves.

- In seven of the ten contracts, industry sponsors are granted broad, upfront, exclusive commercial rights to alliance research — even, in some cases, when certain "background knowledge" was developed prior to the creation of the alliance and not funded by the sponsor.

- None of the ten agreements abide by the NIH recommended maximum sixty-day academic research publication delay; most far exceed it.[18]

Concerned by the findings of this major study of American university collaborations, the Canadian Association of University Teachers examined Canadian university collaborations to assess the extent to which they had provisions to protect academic freedom and the integrity of academic research, unlike many of the American counterparts.[19] The CAUT report[20] examined twelve collaborations. Seven were research collaborations and five were academic program collaborations. [See Table 1]

| Table 1: Canadian University Collaborations | | |
|---|---|---|
| Collaboration | Universities | Collaborating Partners |
| Research Collaborations | | |
| Alberta Ingenuity Centre for In-Situ Energy (AICISE) | University of Calgary | Government of Alberta; Shell; ConocoPhillips; Nexen; Total E&P; Repsol YPF |
| Centre for Oil Sands Innovation (COSI) | University of Alberta | Imperial Oil<br>Alberta Innovates – Energy Environmental Solutions |
| Consortium for Heavy Oil Research By University Scientists (CHORUS) | University of Calgary | Core Sponsors: Nexen; ConocoPhillips; Petrovera Resources; Husky Energy |
| Consortium for Research and Innovation in Aerospace in Quebec (CRIAQ) | Concordia University; École de Technologie Supérieur; École Polytechnique de Montréal;<br>McGill University; Université de Sherbrooke; Université du Québec à Chicoutimi; Université du Quebec à Trois-Rivières;<br>Université du Quebec à Montréal; Université du Quebec à Rimouski;<br>Université Laval;<br>Université de Montréal;<br>University of Ottawa; HEC Montréal; Institut national de la recherche scientifique | Fifty-two companies[21]<br>Nine research centres[22] |
| Enbridge Centre for Corporate Sustainability | University of Calgary | Enbridge Inc. |

| | | |
|---|---|---|
| Mineral Deposit Research Unit (MDRU) | University of British Columbia | Canadian mining industry[23] |
| Vancouver Prostate Centre | University of British Columbia | Pfizer Inc.<br>British Columbia Cancer Agency |
| Program Collaborations | | |
| Balsillie School of International Affairs | University of Waterloo<br>Wilfrid Laurier University | The Centre for International Governance Innovation (CIGI)[24] |
| Munk School of Global Affairs | University of Toronto | The Peter and Melanie Munk Charitable Foundation[25] |
| University of Ontario Institute of Technology/ Durham College/Ontario Power Generation Partnership | University of Ontario Institute of Technology<br>Durham College | Ontario Power Generation |
| University of Toronto/Pierre Lassonde-Goldcorp Inc. Partnership | University of Toronto | Pierre Lassonde-Goldcorp Inc. |
| Western University/Cassels Brock & Blackwell LLP Partnership | Western University | Cassels Brock & Blackwell LLP |

The findings from CAUT's study of Canadian university collaborations also raise serious concerns about universities willingness to sacrifice protections for the integrity of the academy[26]:

- Ten of the twelve agreements were secret at the time of approval — making public transparency impossible.

- Seven of the twelve agreements provide no specific protection for academic freedom.

- In only half of the collaboration agreements did the universities ensure that they retained control of all academic matters affecting their students and faculty.

- Only one of the collaborative agreements requires disclosure of institutional or individual conflicts of interest that may arise in relation to the collaboration.

- Of the ten agreements in which it is possible to have a financial interest in the collaborating partner, only one has a provision forbidding such a financial interest.

- Five of the agreements provide for unrestricted publication rights for participating academics; five do not, and two do not provide enough detail to be able to determine if there could be restrictions on academics right to publish the results of their research.

- Half of the twelve agreements have no provision to ensure that recruitment and evaluation of faculty members and post-docs are not influenced by their potential involvement in the collaboration.

- None of the collaborative agreements provides for regular, publicly accessible assessments of the collaborative project.

- Only one of the twelve agreements includes a provision for an independent post-agreement evaluation of the collaborative project.

- Only one of the seven research collaborations provides that decisions about funding for research done through the collaboration will be made using peer review.

- Only three of the seven research collaborations provides details about how faculty can apply for funding and what the criteria will be.

- In only two of the seven research collaborations are the researchers specifically ensured access to all the data collected in relation to their projects.

Both the American and Canadian studies of university collaborations show a similar pattern of universities' willingness to sacrifice core values in pursuit of money and corporate collaborators. As universities become commercialized and pressured to apply the discipline of the market to their teaching, scholarship, and research, they are in jeopardy of losing that which makes them distinct and important to society. That is the ability to advance knowledge by raising deeply disturbing questions and provocative challenges to conventional wisdom, taken-for-granted practices and ideas, and to explore new directions and approaches based on their professional experience and judgment, not whether there is any practical or commercial outcome in view. The academic freedom to undertake such discovery-driven inquiry is unique to the university and under threat.

The principal organizations representing academics in the United States and Canada have developed guidelines to protect academic freedom and academic integrity when collaborative relationships are necessary or desirable.[27] Faculty at individual institutions have organized successfully to change offensive collaborative arrangements[28], and, where change has not been possible, have rejected them.[29]

The siren call of corporate money and resources is attractive but must be responded to with caution. As Canada's most prominent Nobel laureate, John Polanyi, has noted, when governments or industry try to direct scientific inquiry, rather than allowing the scientific community to do so through its rigorous peer-review system that protects the integrity of the work, our scientific horizons shrink and our future is diminished.[30] In a speech to the Perimeter Institute in 2003, Mike Lazarides, founder of Research in Motion, speaking of academic research, said, "What we need are those creative people to be left to do creative things just for the hell of it. This is the game changer that forms the raw material for industry to capitalize."[31] The university is the only institution that affords researchers the academic freedom to pursue knowledge unrestrained by orthodoxy, third-party interest, government priority, or administrative preference, and from that the value to the public through the advancement of knowledge is made possible.

The guidelines put forward by CAUT and AAUP provide the basis for ensuring academic freedom and integrity, but this can happen only if academic staff insist on it and mobilize to ensure that their insistence is acted upon.

# VI. ACADEMIC FREEDOM AND FREEDOM OF EXPRESSION

# 15

# GIVING AND TAKING OFFENCE: CIVILITY, RESPECT, AND ACADEMIC FREEDOM

*Jamie Cameron*

## INCIVILITY'S RISE

Few choose to be offended, and it is little surprise that the instincts react quickly and protectively, demanding that transgressors be stopped or punished and shared values restored. The law in Canada addresses high-level offensive expression by prohibiting hate speech under the *Criminal Code* and regulating discrimination through human rights provisions. Measures that restrict expressive freedom in the name of equality mean that tolerance for offensiveness can be low where comments target visible minorities or disadvantaged groups that are protected by the law. By way of example, a recent human rights decision concerned an open mike comedy show at a restaurant one evening, which assumed an ugly tone when the host called out and insulted lesbian customers. In proceedings arising from the incident he argued, to no avail, that unscripted comedy shows are notoriously tasteless, and often trade on stereotype for humour. Any suggestion that the audience or targets of his remarks would or should not take the material at face value was quickly dismissed.[1]

Hate speech and human rights provisions place well-established, though controversial, limits on expressive freedom. A more recent phenomenon is the civility juggernaut, a movement that has gained momentum in response to the perception that uncivil conduct has reached epidemic proportions.[2] There is now a healthy literature, both popular and academic, on the phenomenon and on what steps must be taken to reverse the so-called "culture of incivility." [3] If it hardly counts as a new discovery, the meteoric rise and escalation of incivility is much ballyhooed just the same. Whatever can or cannot be proved, it is widely assumed and believed that incivility endemically infects current government, business, media. and social media processes.[4] It is all around and must be curbed.

Corrections are becoming increasingly commonplace across the spectrum. Early in 2013, behaviour in the House of Commons became so dysfunctional that Nathan Cullen decided to launch an initiative he termed the "Civility Project."[5] Partisan exchanges in the House may be uncivil by definition, and it is unclear in any case how serious Cullen was about implementing the proposal. Under his plan, incivility in Parliament would be monitored by empowering the Speaker to suspend offenders without pay and withhold their privileges in Question Period. After being discussed and even ridiculed for a time, Cullen's Civility Project fell away and has not been heard from in months.[6]

Otherwise, civility standards are taken seriously in the legal profession, where law societies have the power to discipline lawyers for breaches of ethical and professional standards, including incivility. To date the decision-maker's authority to decide which words, gestures, and actions are polite enough to satisfy a lawyerly standard of courtesy has not been especially controversial.[7] One critic who questions civility enforcement in the legal profession points out that a focus on manners, and vocabulary, in particular, is misplaced because it can deflect attention from the serious ethical issues at stake.[8]

Meanwhile, the status of expressive freedom at universities is a perennial debating point, with some taking the view that there should be freer rein on campus, and others claiming that restrictions are necessary to support a safe environment for learning and the pursuit of knowledge. If the principle of academic freedom points up what is distinctively at stake when speech activities on campus are restricted, hate speech laws, human rights codes, and other limits on expression, such as the law of defamation, apply here, as elsewhere. Despite academic freedom, there is much to suggest that tolerance for language and remarks perceived to be offensive may be just as low at universities.[9]

Far from being insulated from it, universities are in the vanguard of the current civility movement, and institutions of higher learning have eagerly taken up the cause. By now, any variety of well-intentioned policies aimed at bringing civility to, or restoring it on, campus have been introduced. Though they place significant limits on expressive freedom and engage the principle of academic freedom at its core, the implications of these policies have not been fully explored. This short paper fills that gap by explaining how policies that institutionalize a standard of civility — or courtesy — threaten the freedoms that anchor the university mission. In doing so, the discussion draws insights from the traditions of academic and expressive freedom to show why it is imperative that expressive freedom be protected to its maximum in university settings. In particular, the analysis leverages the *Charter of Rights and Freedoms* and its guarantee of expressive freedom to reinforce academic freedom and broaden the scope of protection for freedom on campus.[10] It concludes that civility is an aspiration that is better served by collaborative, rather than regulatory, measures, and maintains that restrictions on speech activities must be limited to instances of more transgressive conduct, such as harassment and bullying.

## CIVILITY, RESPECT AND THE UNIVERSITY

Restrictions on free inquiry and debate at universities have taken many forms over the years. It was not so long ago that controversy swirled around the "campus codes" which took aim at racist, sexist, and other discriminatory messages that target identifiable communities.[11] As ongoing debates about these and other forms of hate speech show, restrictions are problematic in any setting because the line between what is merely offensive and what is harmful enough to prohibit and punish is hard to draw. Definitions are a particular concern because vague and overbroad regulations place expressive freedom in danger and create a risk of censorship. In the university context, there is a further dynamic at work, and that is the principle of academic freedom. Though it also has a broader and more inclusive meaning, it is accepted by most academics that academic freedom is, in more specific terms, a professional entitlement of faculty, and not a right that belongs to other or all members of the community, such as students.[12] On that view, academic freedom has a distinctive function and cannot be tasked with defending free speech in the myriad ways it is challenged on campus.[13] Though academic and expressive freedom serve and protect different purposes, the two overlap and share an interest in civility standards and their negative consequences for freedom on campus.

In recent years, universities have begun to supplement existing regulations on highly offensive speech with policies on civility and a respectful workplace. As any number of online resources attest, institutions of higher learning across North America have embraced the civility cause in earnest. One example is the University of Missouri's Show Me Respect project, which serves as an umbrella for a concept of civility, broadly understood, and includes materials on bullying as well as a "civility toolbox."[14] Another is the University of Wisconsin Oshkosh, which in 2011 hosted a well-publicized forum titled Civility in Everyday Life.[15] The temper of the times is reflected in the forum's stated premise that "we demonstrate civility when we show respect for others, especially those with beliefs, lifestyles and political beliefs that are different from our own," and aspiration of engaging campuses in "critical civility conversations and best practices that will serve as catalysts for campus climate change."[16]

If initiatives that rest on a conception of incivility as "the quality of being uncivil" lack content and parameters, the movement has not been deterred by that and has proceeded to set, promote, and enforce campus standards of courtesy. Some incorporate, and overlap with, pre-existing and separate policies on discrimination, harassment, and bullying, though more generally their purpose is to monitor the content, manner, and tone of relationships and engagement on campus. It is critical to understand that, unlike regulations that focus on more extreme expressive activity and attempt to set well-defined limits on speech, civility and respectful workplace standards extend the concept of what is offensive in significant ways. These standards speak not only to the content but also to the manner of discourse, debate, and exchange. Whatever can or might offend is potentially within the purview of these policies.

Though it is a white paper, not university policy, the University of Maryland's 2013 report, "The Civility Discourse," provides colour on the direction and tone of today's civility projects.[17] Having accepted that "[d]espite scholars' attempts to offer a simple comprehensive definition, civility is an expansive term open to subjective interpretation,"[18] the report notes that civility has been defined as "'civilized conduct; especially: courtesy, politeness', or simply 'a polite act or expression,'" and then adopts "niceness to others" as its working definition. As explained, this definition was chosen because niceness "may easily be understood by all parties affected."[19] The report describes it as nebulous, and endorses a definition of incivility as "'low intensity deviant behavior with ambiguous intent to harm the target, in violation of university norms for mutual respect.'"[20] Under these definitions, it is not surprising that uncivil encounters can occur between students and faculty, faculty and staff, and staff and students. That said, the white paper declares that because the behaviour trickles from the top down, "it is important to stamp out uncivil behavior within the highest ranks while training those in subordinate roles how to handle incivility from leaders."[21] According to the report, there is good support on campus for "a zero-tolerance approach to incivility," with every individual, including campus leaders, being held accountable and a system in place to provide a remedy to aggrieved parties and a means of enforcement for administration.[22]

With less fanfare, Canadian universities have responded with their own protocols, which run the spectrum from conduct that is directly harmful or threatening, to expressive activity that may insult, marginalize or upset another person. Two examples are the University of Toronto's "Human Resources Guideline on Civil Conduct"[23] and Ryerson University's "Guide to Civility" and "Workplace Civility and Respect Policy."[24] Because they juxtapose civility and incivility, and establish an institutional standard of courtesy, both can be considered fairly representative.[25]

The Toronto guideline describes civil conduct, variously, as "treating others with dignity, courtesy, respect, politeness, and consideration," "speaking in tones of voice that are appropriate for the circumstances," and "managing conflict with others in a respectful way rather than a confrontational way."[26] Meanwhile, Ryerson's "Workplace Civility and Respect Policy" less expansively states simply that "[c]ivility involves treating others with dignity and respect and acting with regard to other's feelings," and requires that "even the most critical feedback be delivered respectfully, privately and courteously."[27]

As for its opposite, the Toronto guideline defines uncivil conduct, among other things, as "humiliating, degrading, demeaning, belittling, insulting, frightening or intimidating another person," "distributing comments about an individual that are unjustified and likely to have a negative impact on the individual," and "telling inappropriate jokes."[28] Ryerson's checklist is more extensive, and includes "unprofessional behaviour; rudeness; shouting or swearing; intimidation or bullying; threatening comments or behaviours/actions; [and] unsolicited and unwelcome comment . . . gestures, actions or contact that cause offence, humiliation or physical or emotional harm."[29] In more detail, Ryerson's policy also states that uncivil behaviour includes comments or conduct a person knows or ought to know is "unwelcome, offensive, embarrassing or hurtful," and cautions that "behaviour that is considered perfectly acceptable by some people, and in some cultures, may be considered inappropriate and rude by others."[30] Uncivil behaviour is not excused, under the policy, because it is subjective or unintentional. Because it is the experience of incivility that is important, its genesis — including who the speaker is and what the context was — seems to matter little, if at all.[31]

The purpose of these policies is to prevent and address behaviour that is perceived as offensive because the content, tone, or manner of delivery may be rude, insensitive, forceful, or thoughtless. It is accepted without hesitation that civility and respect are the hallmarks of effective and rational debate, and their value in human discourse, whether academic or non-academic, is not open to question. After all, who does not prefer civility to barbarism?[32] From that perspective, it may seem quite reasonable to establish and then enforce standards for discourse. The problem is that regulations of this kind cannot be institutionalized without compromising academic and expressive freedom.

Definitions are a central concern. The forum on Civility in Everyday Life frankly admits that "what constitutes civility (or incivility, for that matter) is neither well understood nor readily apparent," but suggests, optimistically, that this is due to the lack of "shared opportunity to reach agreement on what constitutes civil behaviour."[33] More alarming is the white paper's standard of "niceness to others" which, on its face, is without limits on what civility can encompass. The utter subjectivity of these standards is also evident in muzzy concepts like "camouflaged aggression."[34] Ryerson's policy acknowledges that subjectivity, though not in a way that cautions against an overextension of the standard, but for the opposite reason of emphasizing that it is the experience of incivility — however subjective the response may be — that matters. When and in what circumstances another person might take offence at things said a certain way is unpredictable and highly situational. Civility policies necessarily lend themselves to selective enforcement: though most will not, some offenders will be singled out for institutional attention; by definition and in practice, even-handed application of the standard is impossible. Short of a pattern of behaviour that satisfies definitions of harassment and bullying, mere rudeness and a lack of courtesy is just too pervasive and constant to be sensibly regulated.

A second definitional issue concerns the relationship between civility and respect standards and more serious transgressions, such as harassment, bullying, and discrimination.[35] Specifically, conduct that is often or usually addressed in separate regulations may also be included in civility policies. This creates a synergy that is problematic, in the first instance, because associating incivility with more serious forms of harm upgrades conduct that otherwise would be notable only as a breach of courtesy.

At the same time, the scope of those more serious behaviours is also expanded when conduct that is no more than discourteous or disrespectful is drawn into the zones of harassment and bullying.

At OCADU, for instance, bullying includes "discrediting a person, spreading rumours [or] calling into question his or her convictions"; "preventing a person from expressing himself or herself"; "no longer talking to an individual or ignoring their presence"; "destabilizing a person"; and "finger pointing." [36] It is unclear how persistent any of those behaviours must be or what impact they must have to cross the threshold from bad behaviour to bullying. Another example is Memorial University's "Respectful Workplace" policy, which states that "[h]arassment in any form is unacceptable," and then defines harassment as "any comment or conduct towards another person which is abusive, offensive or demeaning."[37] Porous definitions that do not establish a threshold of harm or set boundaries between levels of harm aggravate the interference with academic and expressive freedom.

The further risk under these policies is that a focus on incivility will deflect attention from content and sideline messages that might be critically important.[38] Moreover the pall or chill these policies may place on debate, discourse, and exchange is costly. In that regard, it must be remembered what academic and expressive freedom protects. These entitlements are not an apology for bad behaviour, and, although they defend the free speech of individuals, the more important point is that freedom is the condition that inspires human potential. To stifle or silence those who reject convention or refuse to conform to norms of civility is to risk losing that potential, including what the uncivil outliers among us have to offer. As Justice Jackson of the US Supreme Court so famously and dramatically observed, "compulsory uniformity of opinion achieves only the unanimity of the graveyard."[39] If a statement made during wartime and debate about the constitutionality of compulsory flag salute is more freighted with significance than solicitude for those who choose to be rude, the point is that coercion of thought — and in this context, manner can be added — is a dead end for freedom.

Taking account of these concerns, it is open to question whether incivility, defined in the policies and proposals discussed here, is harmful enough to justify the interference with freedom and the commitment of resources that are needed to enforce standards of courtesy.

On any view, policies that purport to set a standard of civility cut deeply into choices not only about what can be said but also how a message must be presented. Imposing norms of civility and respect put a bounty on the kind of open discourse that defines the university mission. Just as policies that hold faculty to a standard of courtesy and manners violate the principle of academic freedom, policies that muffle the raw energy of students' activities violate their expressive freedom.

The point is not to legitimize or excuse rudeness, incivility, or offensiveness. Yet it is well-known that these lapses of civility are pervasive in public spaces, including and perhaps especially the Internet. Few of us can avoid offence for any sustained period, as modern life exposes us to giving or taking it in much of what we do. The answer is not to compel compliance with a standard of courtesy, not even for good reason, because the cost to freedom is too high. This is especially true at universities, which must promote a fearless spirit of inquiry, not tame it.

It is disappointing that, if they address it at all, civility and respectful workplace policies seem to assume that those it binds — faculty, students, and employees — have forfeited their rights of expressive freedom. Though most universities declare unflinching commitment to the principle, academic freedom also plays a curious role, at best, in these policies. Some do not mention it at all, and appear to have forged ahead with civility as though consideration of academic freedom is irrelevant.[40] Others make hortatory gestures to academic freedom before declaring that mandatory standards of civility and respect do nothing to subtract from or interfere with this principle.[41] Finally, some also suggest that the two can be harmonized as, for instance, by stating the "simple truth" that "incivility threatens academic freedom while civility enhances, nurtures and supports it."[42]

More detailed consideration of these policies, together with a deeper analysis of the relationship between academic and expressive freedom, must be left to another day. For now, this much can be said. Academic freedom is at the core of the university mission, but it cannot be fully exercised or enjoyed in the absence of expressive freedom.[43] At the same time, though it is not a student entitlement, students inhabit and contribute dynamic force to an environment which accepts and commits to the principle of academic freedom. It follows that whether and how students exercise expressive freedom in that environment must be inflected by that principle.

With the foregoing framework in place, the law can now be brought into the analysis. The *Charter of Rights and Freedoms* and its guarantee of expressive freedom under s.2(b)[44] should figure prominently in any analysis of expressive freedom at universities.[45] The discussion which follows shows that the *Charter* jurisprudence can refresh, reinforce, and even expand protection for academic freedom — understood both in broad terms as a descriptor of an entitlement belonging to the university community at large, and in its conventional sense as a vocational or professional entitlement of faculty. Two assumptions ground the analysis which follows. First, it is difficult to imagine expressive freedom having less status at universities than in other settings; it should have at least as much protection on campus as it does elsewhere and not less. Second, and equally vital, the university context and principle of academic freedom inflect the *Charter*'s concept of expressive freedom because the university plays distinctive social, public, and intellectual roles. The gravitational pull of academic freedom as the foundation of intellectual growth, discovery, and creativity should mean fewer restrictions on free speech at universities. What emerges from these considerations is a model for freedom on campus that can be constructed by joining the two entitlements and allowing them to complement each other.

## EXPRESSIVE FREEDOM AND THE UNIVERSITY

Recognizing that academic freedom and expressive freedom overlap, but do not serve identical purposes, is the starting point and it is important, as a result, to be clear about their interface in this paper. If academic freedom does not directly or explicitly protect expressive freedom, at the least its function and status explain why free speech must be at its apex in a university setting. At the same time, university policies draw the *Charter* into the discussion and show in this instance why civility and respectful workplace policies — with their open-ended definitions and restrictions on the content and manner of expression — infringe academic freedom as well as expressive freedom.

An initial, technical question about the *Charter* is whether it applies to or binds universities. It is clear that the *Charter* prohibits governments from violating the rights and freedoms of Canadians, but less certain which actors and institutions are bound by it because they represent government or serve a government function. Canadian universities are for the most part public, rather than private, institutions. They may be constituted or incorporated by statute and are substantially funded, as well as regulated to some degree, by government. Those connections may indicate that the *Charter* should apply, though the Supreme Court found to the contrary early in its history when it wrote a landmark decision holding that mandatory retirement policies were not subject to the *Charter*.[46] That was some time ago, and the Court's view could shift in light of subsequent developments, including a recent decision in which university students raised s.2(b) of the *Charter* when the university brought discipline proceedings against them for a Facebook posting.[47] That said, the universities are not immune from the *Charter*, and its formal application is one way, but not the only way, for the s.2(b)'s guarantee to support free speech on campus.[48]

Whether or not the *Charter* applies is less critical because of a parallel branch of Supreme Court jurisprudence which addresses the broader role of *Charter* values in Canada's legal and political culture. Under this branch of doctrine, *Charter* values influence the evolution of the law and fetter the discretion of those who exercise decision-making authority. A prime example is defamation — a field of private law not subject to the *Charter* — which has been modernized through the direct incorporation of *Charter* values into common law doctrine.[49] In addition, the Supreme Court has responded on a second front by requiring that decisions affecting constitutionally protected rights and freedoms comply with *Charter* values.

*Doré v. Barreau du Québec* is instructive on that question because it pitted expressive freedom against civility in the context of discipline proceedings that reprimanded a lawyer for sending an offensive letter to a judge.[50] In the circumstances, the Supreme Court upheld the Barreau's twenty-one-day suspension of the lawyer but also stated that the free speech rights of lawyers must receive strong protection. As Abella J. indicated, the importance of civility in the legal profession must be measured against the severity of the conduct and the "public benefit in ensuring the right of lawyers to express themselves about the justice system in general and judges in particular."[51] Specifically, she stated that "proper respect" for expressive freedom requires discipline bodies to tolerate a certain amount of "discordant criticism."[52] In particular, she held that the decision maker had to demonstrate that expressive freedom received due regard, and noted in particular "an individual lawyer's right to expression and the public's interest in open discussion."[53]

In these ways the *Charter* exerts influence through the concept of *Charter* values. What that influence is and how it should be measured raise questions that will depend on the context. To illustrate, *Charter* values play an important role in the law of defamation because the rules of libel have serious consequences for expressive freedom. By the same token, Doré is an illustration of the way *Charter* values are incorporated into the structure of administrative decision making. By analogy, *Charter* values should have significant influence in defining expressive freedom on campus, not only because universities are public institutions — regardless of their status under the *Charter* — but also because the values at stake are at least as compelling, if not more compelling, in a university setting.

Context is a central concept in the Supreme Court's s.2(b) jurisprudence and a fundamental consideration in any discussion of expressive freedom at universities. Briefly, taking account of context means that the scope of free speech on campus cannot be determined without considering academic freedom and the critical role it plays in framing the university mission. In other words, whatever freedom might require under s.2(b) must reference academic freedom and what it requires, not simply to survive, but more importantly to thrive. That, in essence, is the role context plays in *Charter* analysis.

The affinities between s.2(b)'s underlying values and the fundamental purposes of academic freedom are readily apparent.[54] Both recognize and value the freedom to explore, create, and share without constraints or conditions, because the search for truth — understood in relative terms as a process for the enlargement of knowledge and experience, rather than as a pretext for privileging dogma and orthodoxy — can only prosper when that search is open, fearless, and boundless. Expressive freedom is a key element of academic freedom, and faculty cannot fully exercise and enjoy their professional entitlement when the content or manner of their debates, exchanges, and discourse are unjustifiably limited. In addition, students who cannot claim academic freedom in their own right are nonetheless its beneficiaries, and have their own rights of expressive freedom which must be interpreted by reference to the university setting and its commitment to learning. For these reasons, expressive freedom has a distinctive texture and urgency at universities which must be reflected in the way *Charter* values apply to this context. All this to say that expressive freedom applies at full force, and then some, at universities. What s.2(b) and the *Charter* add are concrete principles — the way to make the argument — that will maximize expressive freedom on campus for student members of the community as well as for faculty. These concrete principles, which are identified below, explain why civility and respectful workplace policies place academic freedom and expressive freedom so much at risk.

Over the last thirty years s.2(b) of the *Charter* has attracted considerable attention and generated a rich body of jurisprudence at the Supreme Court of Canada. The Court has issued strong pronouncements about s.2(b) but also upheld a variety of restrictions on offensive expression, including restrictions on hate speech under the *Criminal Code* and in human rights legislation.[55] Overall, the jurisprudence is disappointing because the Court has too readily and consistently endorsed limits on expression without proof that it causes harm, and done so on the basis that "low value" expression should receive less protection under the *Charter*. This approach, which assumes that constitutional protection should turn on subjective perceptions of an idea's value, unfortunately shows how unwilling or unable the Court has been to recognize what censorship is and to adopt principles that will prevent it from happening.[56]

Although the Supreme Court's methodology is flawed, that should not obscure the fact that restrictions on offensive expression in the era of the *Charter* are narrow in scope and exceptional in nature. The Court confirmed that view in its 2013 decision in *Saskatchewan (Human Rights Commission) v. Whatcott*, which upheld a hate speech provision in human rights legislation but in doing so placed significant restrictions on its scope.[57] In discussing civility and respectful workplace policies, it is critically important to recognize that Whatcott relied heavily on a distinction between hate speech and offensive expression. Specifically, the Court compared hate speech to expression that is repugnant, offensive, humiliating, or belittling, and concluded that hate speech causes harm and can be regulated for that reason, but that the others do not and are protected by the *Charter*.[58]

More detail demonstrates just how crucial the distinction was to members of the Court. Rothstein J.'s majority opinion explained that hate speech is concerned with extreme and egregious expression, not that which is "merely offensive or hurtful."[59] Accordingly, he maintained that hate speech does not target ideas and is not aimed at discouraging "repugnant or offensive ideas," because "[a] blanket prohibition on the communication of repugnant ideas would offend the core of freedom of expression."[60] In other words, hate speech can be prohibited because of its particular and distinctively harmful effects, but other offensive expression — including the highly offensive — is not harmful enough to override s.2(b)'s guarantee of freedom. It is striking that the Court made the point forcefully in Whatcott, and repeated it several times.

In carving out a narrow area for the regulation of hate speech and granting protection to other forms of offensive expression, Whatcott reinforced first principles in the s.2(b) jurisprudence.[61] Foremost is the principle of content neutrality, which was adopted early in the s.2(b)'s history, and states that the *Charter* protects all expressive activities indiscriminately, and without regard to content, "so as to ensure that everyone can manifest their thoughts, opinions, beliefs, indeed all expressions of the heart and mind, however unpopular, distasteful or contrary to the mainstream."[62] Content neutrality is the indispensable condition of expressive freedom, and is based on an assumption of equal status between ideas. Under this concept of freedom, expression cannot be censored, targeted, or discriminated against because of the message. As such, it embeds an equality principle for speech that is based on a presumption against censorship and content discrimination.

Section 2(b)'s core values are another vital component of the jurisprudence. Values which include truth seeking, democratic governance, and self-realization are deeply entrenched in the jurisprudence. They are of primary importance because they confirm that expressive freedom must be valued in the abstract, at large, and without reference to its content. A commitment to those values recognizes that the guarantee's core is freedom — and not the content of any particular message, whether noble or ignoble. Section 2(b) must be understood at this level of abstraction for freedom to be meaningfully protected in the particular. Otherwise, the instinct to censor and suppress messages because of their offensive content or manner of delivery will easily prevail.

A third key element is the concept of proportionality, which governs the question of reasonable limits on rights and freedoms that are permitted under s.1 of the *Charter*. Again, an aside on the technicalities of the *Charter* must be added. In textual terms, the *Charter*'s structure separates the protected rights and freedoms from the concept of reasonable limits, which allows *Charter* violations to be "saved" if the government can demonstrate that they are justified.[63] Here, as well, the Supreme Court's jurisprudence is disappointing because it has softened the burden of justification the government must satisfy and allowed too many limits to be upheld. As noted above, it has misused s.2(b)'s abstract values against expressive freedom, to support restrictions on speech when the content is deemed to be of low value.[64] Nonetheless, what matters more is the guiding principle, emphasized and reinforced by Whatcott, that narrow regulation is required where expressive freedom is at stake.

Context, content neutrality, the underlying values, and proportionality are the leading s.2(b) principles. Without applying them in a mandatory, structured way, they influence the concept of *Charter* values and what compliance with those values will require in any given circumstances. It is clear, under these principles, that civility and respectful workplace policies place restrictions on freedom that undermine the *Charter*'s commitment to free speech. Restricting expressive activities because their content or manner of delivery is offensive violates the principle of content neutrality. Rules that impose conventions of civility also undermine the underlying values of academic and expressive freedom, and compromise the integrity of the freedom those values are meant to protect.

Typically, these policies contemplate more pervasive and intrusive limits on expressive freedom than regulations that address hate speech, harassment, bullying, and discrimination. The problem is that defining uncivil conduct in broad and overreaching terms unavoidably offends the *Charter*'s concept of proportionality. For these reasons, expressive activities that are subject to institutional regulation because they disclose a lack of courtesy or respect fall well outside the boundaries of regulation carefully mapped by Whatcott.

To this a word about enforcement can be added. The subjectivity and selectivity of what is enforced, and against whom, is unavoidable under civility and respectful workplace policies. And although enforcement under these models can take many forms, most create a system or process for making and hearing complaints. Whether or not, and to what extent they are enforced, it should not be forgotten that, even without enforcement, these policies undermine freedom because they inhibit and chill frank discussion and candid exchange. When enforced, they pose an even greater danger to the mission of the university.

The requirements of freedom are compelling because free inquiry in the ongoing aspiration of enhancing knowledge and experience is the *raison d'etre* of the university. To put constraints on the content, tone, and manner of discourse, exchange, and communication in the name of courtesy is to place the university and its central purposes in harm's way. Short of more transgressive behaviours which cause direct harm, such as a pattern of harassment or bullying, expressive activity should not be regulated simply because it violates a standard of courtesy and is offensive for that reason.

## CIVILITY AND FREEDOM

Rudeness in most instances is counter-productive and should not be excused. The values that civility and respectful workplace policies seek to enforce are important and should be supported. Yet it is a different question whether standards of behaviour should be enforced by institutional regulation.

Freedom is fragile because those who seek its protection are often or invariably the ones who are least sympathetic. Their expressive activities invite attention and oversight because they are offensive, confrontational, and even abusive: they reject the standards the rest of us observe, and that offends our sensibilities. As much as we may disapprove of the content or manner of their expression, that is not reason enough to silence or punish their interventions. Unless and until they cross a threshold of harm that justifies a regulatory response, transgressions that are merely offensive must be tolerated and addressed by other means.

Defining that threshold is a challenge that cannot be taken up in the late stages of this paper. Suffice to say that the threshold will be reached when there is a pattern of behaviour that is persistent and targeted enough to pose a risk of harm that outweighs the interest in protecting academic and expressive freedom. Whether characterized as harassment, bullying, fighting words, or hate speech, conduct that is regulated under these headings must also be defined narrowly and with care to avoid unnecessary interference with these freedoms.

Freedom is primordial at universities. This paper has shown that civility and respectful workplace policies take the authority to set standards of courtesy for granted, and appear to do so despite serious consequences for academic and expressive freedom. It has drawn on the *Charter* to demonstrate that expression cannot be regulated simply because it is taken or experienced as offensive. It has explained that the university context and its principle of academic freedom call for particular vigilance where institutional policies seek to deter or punish expressive activity simply because its content or manner is considered uncivil or disrespectful.

The analysis leads to the conclusion that, in the absence of more careful definitions, civility and respectful workplace policies violate academic and expressive freedom. Policies that include enforcement mechanisms should be abandoned in favour of alternative approaches that are collaborative rather than coercive in nature.

# CONTRIBUTORS

**JOHN BAKER** was educated and taught at Oxford until moving to the Philosophy Department at the University of Calgary. His recent publications have been on restorative justice, on rights, and on the nature of moral reasoning.

**WILLIAM BRUNEAU** is Emeritus Professor at the University of British Columbia. He has specialized in the field of university politics and history. His publications have been concerned mainly with European universities, and more recently Canadian post-secondary education. He has served as editor of the *Canadian Jiournal of Education* and the *Revue d'histoire de l'éducation*. He is co-editor of Volume 18 of the *Collected Papers of Bertrand Russell*. He is a former Presdent of the Canadian Association of University Teachers, and, from 2003 to 2009, served on the CAUT's Academic Freedom and Tenure Committee.

**JAMIE CAMERON** is Professor of Law at Osgoode Hall Law School, York University. She holds law degrees from McGill University and Columbia University, clerked at the Supreme Court of Canada for the Hon. Justice Brian Dickson, and was on the faculty at Cornell Law School before joining Osgoode. She is one of Canada's senior constitutional scholars who has written extensively on the *Charter of Rights and Freedoms*, freedom of expression and the press, the Supreme Court of Canada, criminal law, American constitutional law, and judicial biography. She has been the editor and co-editor of a dozen book collections, including the annual *Constitutional Cases* volumes, *The Charter's Impact on the Criminal Justice System, Reflections on the Legacy of Justice Bertha Wilson*, and *The Charter and Criminal Justice: Twenty-Five Years Later*. She has been a Director and Vice-President of the Canadian Civil Liberties Association for twenty years, and for ten years served on the Board of Directors for the BC Civil Liberties Association, and has represented the CCLA in cases at the Supreme Court of Canada. She served six years as a member of the CAUT Academic Freedom and Tenure Committee.

**LEN FINDLAY** is Professor of English, Director of the Humanities Research Unit, Distinguished Chair and founding member of the Indigenous Humanities Group at the University of Saskatchewan, and President of Academy One (Arts and Humanities) of the Royal Society of Canada. His recent publications relating to academic freedom include "Can the Institution Speak? The University as Testimony in Canada Today" (*Humanities Review*), "Extraordinary Renditions: Translating the Humanities Now" (in *Retooling the Humanities*), "Citizenship and the University: Beyond the Ugly Canadian and the Semiotic Stockade" (*Journal of the Humanities Institute*), "Academic and Artistic Freedom and the Israel-Palestine Conflict: Towards a Pedagogy of the Suppressed" (*Cultural and Pedagogical Inquiry*), and a major CAUT report on the Ramesh Thakur affair. With Paul Bidwell he co-edited *Pursuing Academic Freedom: "Free and Fearless"?* (2001). He is Chair of the CAUT Academic Freedom and Tenure Committee.

**MATTHEW W. FINKIN** is the Albert J. Harno and Edward W. Cleary Chair in Law at the University of Illinois. He is the author or editor, singly or in collaboration, of nine books, including *For the Common Good: Principles of American Academic Freedom* (with Robert Post), *The Case for Tenure, Privacy in Employment Law,* and the last five editions of *Labor Law* (with the late Archibald Cox, Derek Bok, and Robert Gorman). His awards include the Alexander von Humboldt Foundation's Research Prize for "internationally acknowledge achievements in labor law" and honorary doctorates from the University of Trier and the University of Athens. He is the joint editor of the *Comparative Labor Law & Policy Journal* and also serves on the editorial boards of the Bureau of National Affairs book series, International Labor and Employment Laws, and periodicals, the *Canadian Labour and Employment Law Journal,* the *European Labour Law Journal,* and the *Zeitschrift für ausländisches und internationales Arbeits- und Sozialrecht.* For over four decades, he has been active in the American Association of University Professors, including service as general counsel, hair of its Committee A on Academic Freedom and Tenure, and on numerous committees.

**MARK A. GABBERT** is Associate Professor and past head of the Department of History at the University of Manitoba. He earned his PhD. at the University of California at Santa Barbara and specializes in twentieth-century world history and the history of socialism. He is a past-president of the University of Manitoba Faculty Association and is currently in his second term as a member of the CAUT Academic Freedom and Tenure Committee. With John Baker, he is the co-author of the "Report of the CAUT Ad Hoc Investigative Committee into Academic Freedom at Canadian Mennonite University."

**GERALD GERBRANDT** is President Emeritus and Professor Emeritus of Bible at the Canadian Mennonite University. Gerald has spent most of his working life at Canadian Mennonite Bible College/Canadian Mennonite University. He has a Bachelor of Christian Education, CMBC; a BA from Bethel College, North Newton, Kansas; a Master of Divinity, Mennonite Biblical Seminary, Elkhart, Indiana; and a Doctor of Philosophy from Union Theological Seminary, Richmond, Virginia. He has been a Fellow at Tyndale House in Cambridge, England; a Fellow at the Institute for Ecumenical and Cultural Research, Collegeville, Minnesota; and a Visiting Scholar at Acadia Divinity College in Wolfville, Nova Scotia.

**SHELDON KRIMSKY** is the Lenore Stern Professor of Humanities and Social Sciences in the Department of Urban & Environmental Policy & Planning in the School of Arts & Sciences and Adjunct Professor in Public Health and Family Medicine in the School of Medicine at Tufts University; and is the Carol Zicklin Visiting Professor of Philosophy at Brooklyn College. His research has focused on the linkages between science/technology, ethics/values, and public policy. He is the author of 12 books and over 180 papers. Recently he has co-authored *Genetic Justice: DNA Databanking, Criminal Investigations and Civil Liberties;* co-edited *Race and the Genetic Revolution co-edited Genetic Explanations: Sense and Nonsense.* He has been elected Fellow of the American Association for the Advancement of Science for "seminal scholarship exploring the normative dimensions and moral implications of science in its social context."

**RISA L. LIEBERWITZ** is a Professor of Labor and Employment Law in the Cornell University School of Industrial and Labor Relations (ILR). Professor Lieberwitz's research addresses a broad range of issues in labour and employment law, including academic freedom, employment discrimination, and constitutional issues in the workplace. Much of her work has focused on the "corporatization" of the university and the implications of these developments on academic freedom and the role of higher education in a democratic society. Her current research includes a comparative study of issues of "research assessment" and academic freedom in the US and UK. Her publications on academic freedom include "Faculty in the Corporate University: Professional Identity, Law, and Collective Action,"16 *Cornell Journal of Law and Public Policy* 263 (2007); and "Confronting the Privatization and Commercialization of Academic Research: An Analysis of Social Implications at the Local, National, and Global Levels,"12 *Indiana*

*Journal of Global Legal Studies* 109 (2005). She received a J.D. degree from University of Florida Law School, where she was Senior Executive Editor of the *University of Florida Law Review* and subsequently was an attorney for the National Labor Relations Board in the regional office in Atlanta, Georgia. She is a member of the American Association of University Professors Committee A on Academic Freedom and Tenure.

**RICHARD MOON** is a Professor in the Faculty of Law, University of Windsor. He is the author of *The Constitutional Protection of Freedom of Expression* (2000) and *Freedom of Conscience and Religion* (2014), editor *of Law and Religious Pluralism in Canada* (2008) and a contributing editor to *Canadian Constitutional Law* (4th ed) (2010). His current research deals with freedom of religion and is funded by a grant from the Social Sciences and Humanities Research Council of Canada. He was the President of the Canadian Law and Society Association from 2003—05. He has been the recipient of both the law school and university-wide teaching awards at the University of Windsor.

**DAVID M. RABBAN** is Dahr Jamail, Randall Hage Jamail, and Robert Lee Jamail Regents Chair in Law at the University of Texas School of Law and is a member of the University's Academy of Distinguished Teachers. After graduating from Stanford Law School in 1974, he practised union-side labour law in New York City. He joined the legal staff of the American Association of University Professors (AAUP) as associate counsel in 1976 and became counsel in 1980. Since 1983, he has taught at the University of Texas School of Law. His publications have focused on labour law, the law of academic freedom, the history of free speech, and intellectual legal history. His book, *Free Speech in Its Forgotten Years* was the co-winner of the Morris D. Forkosch Prize presented by the *Journal of the History of Ideas* for "the best book in intellectual history published in 1997" and the Eli M. Oboler Award of the American Library Association Intellectual Freedom Round Table for "the most significant work on intellectual freedom published in 1996 and 1997." His most recent publication is *Law's History: American Legal Thought and the Transatlantic Turn to History*. He served as general counsel of the AAUP from 1998 to 2006 and as Chair of the AAUP's Committee A on Academic Freedom and Tenure from 2006 to 2012.

**ANVER SALOOJEE** is a member of the Department of Politics and Public Administration at Ryerson University. He is a former Special Advisor to the Presidency, Government of South Africa. He is President of the Ryerson Faculty Association. He is the recipient of the inaugural CAUT Equity Award.

**JOAN W. SCOTT** is Harold F. Linder Professor in the School of Social Science at the Institute for Advanced Study. She is the author most recently of *The Fantasy of Feminist History*. She was a member of the American Association of University Professors' Committee A on Academic Freedom and Tenure from 1993 to 2006, serving as Chair of the Committee from 1999 to 2005; she rejoined the committee in 2013. She is the author of several articles on academic freedom, "Academic Freedom as an Ethical Practice" in *The Future of Academic Freedom,*" edited by Louis Menand, and "Knowledge, Power, and Academic Freedom" in *Social Research* (Summer 2009).

**DAVID SCHNEIDERMAN** is Professor of Law and Political Science at the University of Toronto where he teaches Canadian and US constitutional law and international investment law. He has written numerous articles and edited several books on Canadian and comparative constitutional law and on constitutionalism and globalization. He has co-authored *The Last Word: Media Coverage of the Supreme Court of Canada* and written *Constitutionalizing Economic Globalization: Investment Rules and Democracy's Promise* and *Resisting Economic Globalization: Critical Theory and International Investment Law*. He has been Visiting Professor of Law at Georgetown University Law Center and at the Faculty of Law, Hebrew University in Jerusalem, and Fulbright Visiting Scholar at the New School for Social Research and the School of Law, Columbia University.

**JON THOMPSON** is a Professor Emeritus in the Department of Mathematics and Statistics, University of New Brunswick. He is a former Chair of the department and a former President of the faculty union at UNB. He chaired the Academic Freedom and Tenure Committee of the Canadian Association of University Teachers from 1985—88. He was a co-author or author of three reports on academic controversies: "Integrity in Scholarship" (with Harry Arthurs and Roger Blais, Montreal: Concordia University, 1994); *The Olivieri Report* (with Patricia Baird and Jocelyn Downie, Toronto: Lorimer, 2001); and *No Debate: The Israel Lobby and Free Speech at Canadian Universities* (Toronto: Lorimer, 2011).

**JAMES L. TURK** is the Executive Director of the Canadian Association of University Teachers. He has written extensively on education, academic freedom, civil liberties, commercialization, and related public policy issues. His has edited a number of books, including *Universities at Risk, Free Speech in Fearful Times* (with Allan Manson), *Disciplining Dissent: the Curbing of Free Expression in Academia and the Media* (with William Bruneau), and *The Corporate Campus*. Jim is Adjunct Research Professor at the Institute of Political Economy at Carleton University and a member of the Executive and of the Board of Directors of the Canadian Centre for Policy Alternatives.

# NOTES

## PREFACE

1 Harry W. Arthurs, "Academic Freedom: When and Where?" (notes for a panel discussion at the Annual Conference of AUCC, Halifax, Nova Scotia, October 5, 1995). Arthurs is a former President of the Canadian Civil Liberties Association and a former President of York University.

2 "Statement on Academic Freedom," Association of Universities and Colleges of Canada (AUCC), accessed January 12, 2013, www.aucc.ca/media-room/news-and-commentary/canadas-universities-adopt-new-statement-on-academic-freedom.

3 Thomas L. Haskell, "Justifying the Rights of Academic Freedom in the Era of 'Power/Knowledge,'" in *The Future of Academic Freedom*, ed. Louis Menand (Chicago: University of Chicago Press, 1996), 47.

4 Frank H. Underhill, "Academic Freedom in Canada," *CAUT Bulletin* 8, no. 2 (1959): 6-16.

## INTRODUCTION

1 "Policy Statement on Academic Freedom," *Canadian Association of University Teachers*, accessed August 26, 2013, www.caut.ca/about-us/caut-policy/lists/general-caut-policies/policy-statement-on-academic-freedom.

2 Matthew W. Finken and Robert C. Post, *For the Common Good: Principles of American Academic Freedom* (New York: Yale University Press, 2009), 39.

3 Ibid., 11-27.

4 American Association of University Professors, "1915 Declaration of Principles on Academic Freedom and Academic Tenure," *Policy Documents and Reports*, tenth edition (2006): 291-301, accessed August 23, 2013, www.aaup.org/report/1915-declaration-principles-academic-freedom-and-academic-tenure.

5 Thomas L. Haskell, "Justifying the Right of Academic Freedom in the Era of 'Power/Knowledge,'" in *The Future of Academic Freedom*, ed. Louis Menand, (Chicago: University of Chicago Press, 1996), 48-53; Finkin and Post, *For the Common Good*, 30-31; Laurence Veysey, *The Emergence of the American University*, (Chicago: Chicago University Press, 1965), 397-404.

6 American Association of University Professors, "1915 Declaration of Principles on Academic Freedom and Academic Tenure: Prefatory Note," accessed August 23, 2013, www.aaup.org/report/1915-declaration-principles-academic-freedom-and-academic-tenure.

7 Kenneth McNaught, *Conscience and History: A Memoir* (Toronto: University of Toronto Press, 1999), 101-132; Michiel Horn, *Academic Freedom in Canada: A History* (Toronto: University of Toronto Press, 1999), 220-245.

8 V.C. Fowke and Bora Laskin, "Report of the Investigation by the Committee of the Canadian Association of University Teachers into the Dismissal of Professor

H.S. Crowe by United College, Winnipeg, Manitoba," November 21, 1958, www.caut.ca/docs/default-source/af-ad-hoc-investigatory-committees/report-of-the-investigation-into-the-dismissal-of-professor-h-s-crowe-by-united-college-(1958).pdf.

9 For one of the most lucid discussions of these four aspects of academic freedom, see Finkin and Post, *For the Common Good,* 53-148.

10 In 2008, the Charles G. Koch Foundation offered sizable donations to universities to establish academic centres with a mission to study capitalism and free enterprise, with the stipulation that the Foundation would have a voice in who was hired. Florida State and Utah State universities both accepted the money on these conditions. See Dan Berrett, "Not Just Florida State," *Inside Higher Ed,* accessed August 26, 2013, www.insidehighered.com/news/2011/06/28/koch_foundation_gifts_to_colleges_and_universities_draw_scrutiny#ixzz2dCVc43UM.

11 On March 21, 2013, the U. S. Congress approved a measure that prohibits the National Science Foundation from funding political science research unless a project is certified as "promoting national security or the economic interests of the United States." See Mollie Reilly, "Tom Coburn Amendment Limiting National Science Foundation Research Funding Passes Senate," Huffington Post, accessed August 26, 2013, www.huffingtonpost.com/2013/03/21/tom-coburn-national-science-foundation_n_2921081.html.

12 The Association of Universities and Colleges of Canada issued its new statement on academic freedom in October 2011 that specifically excluded any reference to intramural academic freedom (the right to criticize the university). It also excluded any reference to extramural academic freedom (the right to exercise one's rights as a citizen without sanction by the university). "Canada's Universities Adopt New Statement on Academic Freedom," *AUCC,* accessed August 26, 2013, www.aucc.ca/media-room/news-and-commentary/canadas-universities-adopt-new-statement-on-academic-freedom.

13 "Donors Threaten Academic Freedom," *CAUT Bulletin,* December 2002, accessed August 26, 2013, ww.cautbulletin.ca/en_article.asp?ArticleID=1448.

14 Kemal Gürüz, "University Autonomy and Academic Freedom: A Historical Perspective," *International Higher Education 63* (2011): 13.

15 Conrad Russell, *Academic Freedom* (London: Routledge, 1993),4.

16 "Recommendation concerning the Status of Higher Education Teaching Personnel," *United Nations Educational, Scientific and Cultural Organization,* November 11, 1997, para 17, accessed August 24, 2013, http://portal.unesco.org/en/ev.php-URL_ID=13144&URL_DO=DO_TOPIC&URL_SECTION=201.html.

17 See page 23 in this volume.

18 See page 49 in this volume.

19 See page 65 in this volume.

20 See page 89 in this volume.

21 See page 111 in this volume.

22 American Association of University Professors, "1940 Statement of Principles on Academic Freedom and Tenure," *Policy Documents and Reports*, tenth edition (2006), 3-5, accessed August 23, 2013, www.aaup.org/report/1940-statement-principles-academic-freedom-and-tenure.

23 American Association of University Professors, "1970 Interpretative Comments," *Policy Documents and Reports*, tenth edition (2006), 5-7, accessed August 23, 2013, www.aaup.org/report/1940-statement-principles-academic-freedom-and-tenure.

24 See "CAUT Procedures in Academic Freedom Cases Involving Allegations of Requirement of an Ideological or Faith Test as a Condition of Employment," *Canadian Association of University Teachers*, accessed August 24, 2013, http://bit.ly/14w0Nw7.

25 For the list of universities and copies of the investigatory reports, see "Universities that impose a faith or ideological test," *Canadian Association of University Teachers*, accessed August 24, 2013, www.caut.ca/issues-and-campaigns/academic-freedom/faith-ideological-test. Several of these universities are members of the Association of Universities and Colleges of Canada despite AUCC requiring the institution's commitment to academic freedom as a condition of membership.

26 See, for example, the reply of Trinity Western University to the CAUT investigatory report on its requirement of a faith test www.caut.ca/docs/reports/response-of-trinity-western-university.pdf?sfvrsn=0 (accessed August 24, 2013).

27 See page 129 in this volume.

28 See page 147 in this volume.

29 See page 175 in this volume.

30 See page 207 in this volume.

31 Starting in the 1980s, Rushton published a number of articles and books based on his controversial research that found racial differences in terms of brain size, intelligence, sexual restraint, and rates of maturation. His research was criticized by many in the academic community, defended by some, and created a public outcry which resulted in the Ontario Premier demanding that he be fired. The university defended his academic freedom while distancing itself from his position. The Council of Ontario Universities (COU)issued a statement that included the following:

2. Concerning the validity of Professor Rushton's published and orally communicated research findings and theories. COU considers it no dereliction of responsibility to leave this evaluation to the judgment of those individuals-colleagues at Western, peers in other universities. similarly qualified independent researchers, who are competent to provide contmentary and, if appropriate, criticism. This process has begun. It is a slow process, one easily overshadowed by other developments, and not perfect; it is likely to be more sure and just than the alternatives,

3. COU also wishes to offer comment on a third matter, this involves the beliefs and values that we cherish in Canadian society. and the threats and potential

threats that can be leveled against them. Prominent among them is our respect for the human dignity of all members of our community regardless of race, creed. gender or other factors. Council applauds the senate of the University of Western Ontario for its concurrent statement on racism. While defending Professor Rushton's academic freedom and encouraging his peers to subject his work, to the rigorous scrutiny' due all research, the Council of Ontario Universities deplores the. Insensitivity and absence of social responsibility that has accompanied Professor Rushton's public statements and informed his vocabulary.

Quoted in *York University v. York University Faculty Association*, CanLII 50108 (ON L.A. 2007), p. 13, *dms.corp.caut.ca/docushare/dsweb/Get/Document-39780/York%20 University%20vs.%20YUFA%20re%20Noble%20Grievance%20(2007-09-26). PDF.* See also: John Allemang, "Philippe Rushton, professor who pushed limits with race studies, dead at 68," *Globe and Mail*, accessed August 23, 2013, www.theglobeandmail.com/news/national/philippe-rushton-professor-who-pushed-limits-with-race-studies-dead-at-68/article4901806/?page=all#dashboard/follows/; John Miner, "Controversial prof Philippe Rushton dead," *lfpress.com*, accessed August 23, 2013, wwwwresslcom/20w12/10/04/controversial-prof-philippe-rushton -dead.

32 See page 187 in this volume.

33 See page 221 in this volume.

34 See page 233 in this volume.

35 See page 253 in this volume.

36 See page 275 in this volume.

37 See page 289 in this volume.

## CHAPTER 1

1 "AAUP Declaration of Principles" (1915), reprinted in *Academic Freedom and Tenure*, ed. Louis Joughin (Madison: University of Wisconsin Press, 1969), 157-76.

2 *Sweezy v. New Hampshire*, 354 U.S. 234, 250 (1957).

3 *Id.* at 261-62.

4 *Id.* at 263.

5 *Keyishian v. Board of Regents*, 385 U.S. 589, 592 (1967).

6 *Id.* at 603.

7 *Regents of the University of California v. Bakke*, 438 U.S. 265, 312 (1978).

8 *Grutter v. Bollinger*, 539 U.S. 306, 329 (2003).

9 *Id.* at 362.

10 *Id.* at 364.

11 *Widmar v. Vincent*, 454 U.S. 263, 278 1981).

12 *Id.* at 280.

13 *Regents of University of Michigan v. Ewing,* 474 U.S. 214, 226 (1985).

14 *Board of Regents of University of Wisconsin System v. Southworth,* 529 U.S. 217, 238 (2000).

15 *Regents of University of Michigan v. Ewing,* 474 U.S. 214, 226 n.12 (1985).

16 *Cooper v. Ross, 472 F. Supp. 802, 813* ( E.D. Ark. 1979).

17 *Id.* at 814.

18 *Piarowski v. Illinois Community College District 515,* 759 F.2d 625, 629 (7th Cir. 1985).

19 *Id.* at 627-28.

20 *Id.* at 630.

21 *Urofsky v. Gilmore,* 216 F.3d 401, 404 (4th Cir. 2000).

22 *Id.* at 409 n.9.

23 *Id.* at 409-10.

24 *Id.* at 415.

25 *Id.* at 415 n.17.

26 *Id.* at 438-39.

27 *Id.* at 426.

28 *Id.* at 434.

29 *Id.* at 428.

30 *Id.* at 432-33.

31 J. Peter Byrne, *Academic Freedom: A "Special Concern of the First Amendment,"* 99 Yale L.J. 251, 255 (1989).

32 *Id.* at 306.

33 *Id.* at 308 and n.223.

34 *Id.* at 308.

35 *Id.* at 338.

36 J. Peter Byrne, "Constitutional Academic Freedom in Scholarship and in Court," *The Chronicle of Higher Education,* Jan. 5, 2001, at B13.

37 Frederick Schauer, *Is There a Right to Academic Freedom?* 77 U. Colo. L. Rev. 907, 919 (2006).

38 Paul Horwitz, *First Amendment Institutions* 114 (Harvard University Press, 2013).

39 *Id.* at 117.

40 *Id.* at 318 n.37.

41 *Id.* at 118-19.

42 Matthew W. Finkin, *On "Institutional" Academic Freedom,* 61 Texas L. Rev. 817, 818 (1983).

43 *Id.* at 839-40.

44 *Id.* at 850.

45 *Id.* at 854.

46 David M. Rabban, *A Functional Analysis of "Individual" and "Institutional" Academic Freedom Under the First Amendment,* 53 Law and Contemp. Problems 227, 284 (1990).

47 *Id.* at 287-90.

48 *Id.* at 289.

49 *Id.* at 290.

50 *Id.* at 285-86

51 *Id.* at 284.

52 Judith Areen, *Government as Educator: A New Understanding of First Amendment Protection of Academic Freedom and Governance,* 97 Georgetown L.J. 945, 994-95 (2009).

53 Robert C. Post, *Democracy, Expertise, Academic Freedom: A First Amendment Jurisprudence for the Modern State* (New Haven: Yale University Press, 2012), 61, 79, 90.

54 Ibid, 89.

55 Ibid, 80.

56 *Garcetti v. Ceballos,* 547 U.S. 410, 421 (2006).

57 *Id.* at 438.

58 *Id.* at 425.

59 *Hardy v. Jefferson Community College,* 260 F.3d 671, 674-75 (6th Cir. 2001).

60 *Id.* at 679.

61 *Piggee v. Carl Sandburg College,* 464 F.3d 667, 671 (7th Cir. 2006).

62 *North Central Texas College v. Ledbetter,* 566 F. Supp. 2d 547 (5th Cir. 2006).

63 *Hammond v. Board of Trustees of Southern Illinois University,* 1988 WL 95923 (S.D. Ill. 1988).

64 *Schrier v. University of Colorado,* 427 F.3d 1253 (10th Cir. 2005).

65 *Hetrick v. Martin,* 480 F.2d 705 (6th Cir. 1973).

66 *Mayberry v. Dees,* 663 F.2d 502 (4th Cir. 1981).

67 *Johnson-Kurek v. Abu-Absi,* 423 F.3d 590 (6th Cir. 2005).

68 *Wirsing v. Board of Regents of the University of Colorado,* 739 F. Supp. 551 (D. Colo. 1990).

69 See, e.g., *Brown v. Armenti,* 247 F.3d 69 (3d Cir. 2001); *Parate v. Isibor,* 868 F.2d 821 (6th Cir. 1989); *Lovelace v. Southeastern Massachusetts University,* 793 F.2d 419 (1st Cir. 1986); *Hillis v. Stephen F. Austin State University,* 665 F.2d 547 (5th Cir.

1982); *Stronach v. Virginia State University*, 577 F. Supp. 2d 788 (E.D. Va. 2008).

70 *Hetrick v. Martin*, 480 F.2d 705, 707 (6th Cir. 1973).

71 *Id.* at 706.

72 *Parate v. Isibor*, 868 F.2d 821, 828-30 (6th Cir. 1989).

73 *Rabban, "Individual" and "Institutional" Academic Freedom*, 295.

74 *Areen, Government as Educator*, 948, 987, 994.

75 *Kerr v. Hurd*, 694 F. Supp. 2d 817, 843-44 (W.D. Ohio 2010).

76 *Id.* at 844 n.11.

77 *Id.* at 844.

78 *Adams v. Trustees of the University of North Carolina-Wilmington*, 640 F.3d 550, 561 (4th Cir. 2011).

79 *Id* at 564.

80 *Savage v. Gee*, 716 F. Supp. 2d 709, 718 (S.D. Ohio 2010).

81 *Gorum v. Sessoms*, 561 F.3d 179 (3d Cir. 2009).

82 *Id.*

83 *Huang v. Rector and Visitors of University of Virginia*, 896 F. Supp. 2d 524 (W.D. Va. 2012).

84 *Hong v. Grant*, 516 F. Supp. 1158, 1166 (C.D. Cal. 2007).

85 *Turkish Coalition of America, Inc. v. Bruininks*, 804 F. Supp. 2d 959, 966 (D. Minn. 2011).

86 *Ony, Inc. v. Cornerstone Therapeutics*, 2012 WL 1835671 (W.D.N.Y. 2012).

87 *Wagner v. Jones*, 664 F. 3d 259 (8th Cir. 2011).

## CHAPTER 2

1 Robert Hassan, *The Chronoscopic Society: Globalization, Time and Knowledge in the Network Economy* (New York: Peter Lang, 2003), 138.

2 Kevin Page, former Canadian Parliamentary Budget Officer, quoted in Bill Curry, "Former budget officer to shadow PBO," *The Globe and Mail*, July 27, 2013.

3 Findlay, Len M. and Paul Bidwell eds. *Pursuing Academic Freedom: 'Free and Fearless'?* (Saskatoon: Purich Press, 2001).

4 Eric Barendt, *Academic Freedom and the Law: A Comparative Study*, (Oxford: Hart Publishing, 2010), 8, 165ff.

5 Robert C. Dickeson, *Prioritizing Academic Programs and Services: Reallocating Resources to Achieve Strategic Balance*, revised and updated (San Francisco: John Wiley, 2010). This book was promoted by Glen Murray in Ontario and is the sole authority behind the massive downsizing underway at the University of Saskatchewan.

6 George Steiner, *Antigones*, (New Haven: Yale University Press, 1996), 248.

7 Ernst Hartwig Kantorowicz, *The King's Two Bodies: A Study in Mediaeval Political Theology* (Princeton: Princeton University Press, 1957).

8 Kantorowicz's work was seen at the time as a "homage" to Carl Schmitt whose work is discussed below. Only later would it be seen as pro-democratic. Kantorowicz changed his politics when he exchanged Hitler's Germany for McCarthy's America. See Michael Heffernan, "Mapping Schmitt," in *Spatiality, Sovereignty, and Carl Schmitt*, ed. Stephen Legg (Abingdon: Routledge, 2011), 235-38.

9 Edmund Burke, *Reflections on the Revolution in France*, ed. William B. Todd (New York: Holt, Rinehart, and Winston Inc., 1959), 95. Burke goes on, in the role of reactionary prophet, to anticipate for education, the emergent hope of the multitude, a fate so repugnant it mobilized underclasses across Europe: "Along with its natural protectors and guardians, learning will be cast into the mire, and trodden under the hoofs of a swinish multitude." It can't come quickly enough for me.

10 John Borrows, "Landed Citizenship: An Indigenous Declaration of interdependence," in *Recovering Canada: The Resurgence of Indigenous Law*, ed. John Borrows (Toronto: University of Toronto Press, 2002), 138-158.

11 Ferdinand de Saussure, *Course in General Linguistics*, eds. Charles Bally and Albert Sechehaye, trans. Roy Harris (La Salle, Illinois: Open Court), 1983.

12 Karl Marx, "Contribution to the Critique of Hegel's Philosophy of Law," in *Karl Marx and Frederick Engels: Collected Works. Vol. 3* (London: Lawrence & Wishart, 1975), 4-187.

13 Plato, *The Republic*, Vol. 2, ed. and trans. Christopher Emlyn-Jones and William Preddy (Cambridge: Harvard University Press, 2013).

14 L. M. Findlay, ed. *Introduction to Rethinking the Humanities. A special issue of English Studies in Canada 26*, no. 1 (2012): 1-168.

15 George Schwab, "Introduction," in *Political Theology: Four Chapters on the Concept of Sovereignty*, trans. Schwab (Cambridge: MIT Press, 1985), 7.

16 Ibid., 13.

17 Tobi Cohen, "Not time to 'commit sociology': Harper," *The Saskatoon Star-Phoenix*, April 26, 2013.

18 Schwab, "Introduction," xvi.

19 Alan E. Steinweis, *Art, Ideology, and Economics in Nazi Germany: the Reich Chambers of Music, Theatre, and the Visual Arts*, (Chapel Hill: University of North Carolina Press, 1993).

20 Chantal Mouffe, ed., *The Challenge of Carl Schmitt* (London: Verso, 1999).

21 Schwab, "Introduction," xxi.

22 Paul Davidson, "Universities as economic asset," *The Saskatoon Star-Phoenix*, May 22, 2013.

23 "Annual Symposium: Social Justice in the 21st Century," The Royal Society of Canada, Rsc-src.ca.en/annual-symposium-social-justice-in-21st-century.

24 For such rebuttal in British and international perspective see parts IV and V of *The Assault on Universities: A Manifesto for Resistance*, ed. Michael Bailey and Des Freedman (London: Pluto Press, 2011).

25 Carl Schmitt, *The Nomos of the Earth in the International Law of the Jus Publicum Europaeum* (New York: Telos Press, 2003), 104.

26 Rinaldo Walcott, "Afterword: Sentiment or Action," in *Transnationalism, Activism, Art*, ed. Kit Dobson and Ainé McGlynn (Toronto: University of Toronto Press, 2013), 229.

## CHAPTER 3

1 Judith Butler, "Academic Norms, Contemporary Challenges: A Reply to Robert Post on Academic Freedom," *Academic Freedom After September 11*, ed. Beshara Doumani (New York: Zone Books, 2006), 107.

2 Robert Post, "The Structure of Academic Freedom," in *Academic Freedom After September 11*, ed. *Beshara Doumani* (New York: Zone Books, 2006), 61.

3 And a prolegomenon to a longer excursion. Matthew F. Finkin and Robert C. Post, *For the Common Good: Principles of American Academic Freedom* (New Haven: Yale University Press, 2009).

4 Butler, "Academic Norms," 127. (Italics in original.)

5 Butler, "Academic Norms."

6 Butler, "Academic Norms."

7 Butler, "Academic Norms," 112-113.

8 Ibid., 114.

9 Ibid.

10 Ibid., 115.

11 Ibid.

12 Ibid., 116.

13 Ibid., 117.

14 Robert Post, *The Structure of Academic Freedom*, 77:

> *[T]he application of professional norms involves judgment and interpretation and is therefore always contestable. It can be quite controversial whether, in any given case, professional norms ought to be interpreted in a manner that tolerates variant forms of scholarly practice. In exceptional cases we can even conceptualize such controversies as testing the very boundaries of professional standards themselves. It might be said, then, that in extreme circumstances protecting independence of thought and inquiry requires striking some balance between enforcing and suspending professional standards.*

15 Butler, "Academic Norms," 117:

> *The model of applying a preestablished set of terms is one that assumes a fundamentally technical model of judgment, one in which the terms by which we judge — the standards according to which we judge — are fixed in advance, and the case before us appears as an instance to be classified or not under the general model of "complying with professional norms" that we have on hand.*

16 Ibid., 120.

17 *Butler*, "Academic Norms," 127.

18 Judith Jarvis Thomson, "Ideology and Faculty Selection," in *Freedom and Tenure in the Academy*, ed. William Van Alstyne (Durham: Duke University Press, 1993).

19 In the fourteenth century the medical faculty of the University of Bologna was required by the university's statutes to house a chair in astrology. Hastings Rashdall, *The Universities of Europe in the Middle Ages*, eds. F. M. Powicke and A. B. Emden (1997), 242-243. The discipline drew on ancient roots, much respected in the Renaissance, and had the benefit of intense empirical and mathematical rigor. Although astrology's predictive value was often wanting, it could explain those failures in the inadequacy of the data. As Anthony Grafton has pointed out, the role astrology had performed in the medieval university is taken up in the modern university by economics. Anthony Grafton, *Cardano's Cosmos: The World and Works of a Renaissance Astrologer* (1999), 10.

20 James Brudney and Lawrence Baum, "Oasis or Mirage: The Supreme Court's Thirst for Dictionaries in the Rhenquist Robert Eras" (working paper, Fordham U. Law School, January, 2013).

21 *Thomson*, "Ideology and Faculty Selection," 160.

22 *Id.* at 156.

23 In 1557, Felix Platter secured a doctorate in medicine from the University of Basel in a step toward his appointment to the faculty. His obligatory academic *disputatio* concerned the subject of natural heat. The Basel medical faculty was much taken with the theories of Arab medicine, but Platter had been educated at Montpellier where Galenism held sway. According to Emmanuel Le Roy Ladurie, Platter "crushed" his opponent in the dispute with a science that distinguished plants, which are cold, from animals, which stand closer to heat and fire. "Bread, meat, wine, pepper, mustard, blood, sperm, spirit, heart, liver, and spleen can be classed with the hot," he pointed out, "the brain is cold and moist." Emmanuel Le Roy Ladurie, *The Beggar and the Professor*, trans. Arthur Goldhammer (Chicago: University of Chicago Press, 1997), 332. Today, we would consider this to be, at best, proto-science. It is no longer professed as medical truth; but Platter was surely correct to confound the conventional with what was then the latest in the discipline. How else should he have been judged as fitting for professorial appointment?

24 *See generally*, Bernard Barber, "Resistance by Scientists to Scientific Discovery," *Science 134*, no. 3479 (1961): 596; *see also* Moti Nissani, "The Plight of the Obscure Innovator in Science: A Few Reflections in Companario's Note," *Social Studies of Science 25* (1995): 165.

25 "Cold Fusion," for example, which has gained little or no support among physicists, still seems to captivate some chemists. Stephen Ritter, *Reviving Cold Fusion, Chemical & Engineering News 90*, (May 14, 2012): 42.

26 Jennifer Schessler, "In History Departments, it's Up With Capitalism," *New York Times*, April 7, 2013. ("'After decades of history from below', focusing on women, minorities and other marginalized people seizing their destiny, a new generation of scholars is increasingly turning to what, strangely, risked becoming the most marginalized group of all: the bosses, bankers, and brokers who run the economy.")

27 For legimation in that very regard he might point to Kepler College in Shoreline, Washington (www.kepler.edu/home, accessed January 23, 2013). It was authorized by the Washington State Higher Education Coordinating Board to give degrees in *Eastern and Western Traditions: the History of Philosophy and Transmission of Astrology* through March of 2012.

28 Butler, "Academic Norms," 129.

29 Robert Wuthnow, *Communities of Discourse: Ideology and Social Structure in the Reformation, the Enlightenment, and European Socialism* (Cambridge: Harvard University Press, 1989), 5.

30 David Hollinger, *Cosmopolitanism and Solidarity: Studies in Ethnoracial, Religious, and Professional Affiliation in the United States* (Madison: University of Wisconsin Press, 2006), 79.

31 *Churchill v. The University of Colorado*, 285 P. 3d 986, 991-92 (Colo. 2012). Actually, the targets of Professor Churchill's "Eichmann" remarks were more narrowly defined. See *infra* n. 38.

32 *Id.* at 994.

33 *Id.* at 996.

34 *Id.* at 1008.

35 Marjorie Heins, "Academe's Still-Precarious Freedom," *The Chronicle of Higher Education Review*, Feb. 8, 2013.

36 *Butler*, "Academic Norms," 124-125.

37 "Committee A Statement on Extramural Utterances," *AAUP Policy Documents and Reports 32* (10th ed. 2006). ("The controlling principle is that a faculty member's expression of opinion as a citizen cannot constitute grounds for dismissal unless it clearly demonstrates the faculty member's unfitness to serve.").

38 Professor Churchill wrote a "stream-of-consciousness interpretive reaction" to what he termed the "September 11 counterattack," on a website. "'Some People Push Back': On the Justice of Roosting Chickens," *kersplebedeb*, accessed May 3, 2013, www.kersplebedeb.com/mystuff/s11/churchill.html. In it, he addressed the attackers as combatants in a war of the United States' initiation and treats the "counterattack" as just. As to the claim that the attackers had targeted " 'innocent civilians,' " he termed targets in the World Trade Center a "technocratic corps at the heart of America's global financial empire," a "relatively well-educated elite" "braying . . . self-importantly, into their cell-phones, arranging lunches

and stock transactions." As he later described it, his remarks were addressed to "the investment bankers, stock brokers, and other finance technicians killed" in the attack. Churchill, *Struggle for the Land,* 141. He did not address the status of the many low -age minority and immigrant service workers also killed in the attack; for example, to characterize them as being similarly culpable for American aggression or to justify their killing as regrettable but unavoidable collateral damage. In fact, he does not mention them at all. It would seem fair to inquire of whether such extraordinary selectivity or willful blindness to the facts in a cry of outrage in the name of the oppressed might similarly characterize aspects of his professional work as well, professional work that had been called into question previously in its selective treatment of sources.

39 A useful summary of the subtlety of the concept and a bibliography on it is supplied by Richard Wright in "Causation in the Law," *in Routledge Encyclopedia of Philosophy,* ed. E. Craig, accessed April 21, 2013, http://www.rep.routledge.com/article/T062SECT2.

40 *Cf. Williams v. Boorstin,* 633 F. 2d 109 (D.C. Cir. 1980). Discharge of employee whose background investigation, triggered by engagement in protected activity, revealed misrepresentation of his credentials was not wrongful.

41 Ward Churchill, *Struggle for the Land* (1993), n. 5 at 27 ("for further analysis"); n. 19 at 66-67; n. 47 at 71; n. 50 at 71; n. 3 at 309; n. 44 at 448.

42 Id. n. 8 at 28 ("for a very good survey"); nn. 65 & 66 at 74; n. 39 at 447 ("for an outstanding survey").

43 Id. n. 64 at 72; n. 66 at 74; n. 47 at 448.

44 University of Colorado Faculty Senate Committee on Privilege and Tenure, Panel Report Regarding Dismissal for Cause of Ward Churchill (April 11, 2007).

45 Ward Churchill, "The Myth of Academic Freedom: Experiencing the Application of Liberal Principle in a Neoconservative Era," Works and Days 26/27, (2008-09): 139.

46 Two witnesses in the field of American Indian Studies testified to this proposition and their testimony was summarized by the hearing committee, Panel Report at 17-18. They were Prof. Robert A. Williams, Jr., Professor of Law and of American Indian Studies at the University of Arizona, and Professor Eric Cheyfitz, Professor of American Studies and Director of the American Indian Program at Cornell University. Professor Cheyfitz was to write separately in defence of Ward Churchill. Eric Cheyfitz, "Framing Ward Churchill: The Political Construction of Research Misconduct," Works and Days 26/27 (2008-09): 231. The hearing committee set out Professor Cheyfitz's defence of Professor Churchill in the Panel Report at 63-64.

47 Freud, ever the slayer of humour, managed to kill an old Jewish joke by recounting it:

A. borrowed a copper kettle from B. and after he had returned it was sued by B. because the kettle now had a big hold in it which made it unusable. His defense was: "First, I never borrowed the kettle from B. at all; secondly, the kettle had a hold in it already when I got it from him; and thirdly, I have him back the kettle undamaged."

*Sigmund Freud, Jokes and their Relation to the Unconscious,* trans. James Strachey (New York: Norton, 1960), 72. I am indebted to Dr. Jordan Finkin for bringing this reference to my attention.

48 I am indebted to my colleague, Andrew Leipold, who clerked for Justice Powell on the United States Supreme Court, for capturing the function this way.

49 Lawrence Principe, *The Secrets of Alchemy* (Chicago: University of Chicago Press, 2013), 63.

50 Three of those who had agreed to have the work appear under their names were identified as having university affiliations.

51 University of Colorado, Panel Report, 64. And, one might add, the omission of the work on the person's bibliography would give ground for inquiry.

52 Quoted in University of Colorado, Panel Report, 63.

53 Churchill, "The Myth," 361, quoting Eric Cheyfitz.

54 Churchill, "The Myth," 362, quoting Robert Williams.

55 Id., citing Homi K. Bhabha, *The Location of Culture* (New York: Routledge, 1994), Ch 11.

56 This might be one of the themes sketched in the essay cited by Professor Churchill's witness. Homi Bhabha, "How Newness Enters the World," in *The Location of Culture*, 223 (emphasis in original):

As the autotelic specularity of the class category witnesses the historic loss of its own ontological priority, there emerges the possibility of a politics of social difference that makes no autotelic claims — "capable of interpellating itself"; — but is genuinely articulatory in its understanding that to be discursively represented and socially representative — to assume an effective political identitiy or image — the limits and conditions of specularity have to be exceeded and erased by the inscription of otherness.

In fact, there is a rich history and critical depth on the use of pseudonymous publication in literature. See generally, Robert Griffin, ed., *The Faces Of Anonymity: Anonymous And Pseudonymous Publication From The Sixteenth Century To The Twentieth Century* (New York: Macmillan Palgrave, 2003).

57 And at least one such coo-perative has long existed. See Maurice Mashaal, *Bourbaki: A Secret Society of Mathematicians* (Providence: American Mathematical Society, 2006).

58 This is not to argue that such would be Professor Butler's conclusion were she to have sat on the hearing committee. It is to argue that her critique lends itself readily to this line of reasoning.

## CHAPTER 4

1 Carl Becker, "The Cornell Tradition: Freedom and Responsibility," *Bulletin of the American Association of University Professors* 26, no. 4 (October,1940): 509, accessed January 5, 2013, www.jstor.org/stable/40219223.

2 See Walter LaFeber, "Fred Harvey Harrington," *Diplomatic History* 9, no. 4 (October, 1985): 313, accessed August 7, 2013, http://onlinelibrary.wiley.com.proxy2.lib.umanitoba.ca/doi/ 10.1111/j.1467-7709.1985.tb00540.x/pdf (emphasis mine).

3 CAUT Policy Statement on Academic Freedom, *Canadian Association of University Teachers*, November, 2011, accessed August 2, 2013, /www.caut.ca/about-us/caut-policy/lists/ general-caut-policies/policy-statement-on-academic-freedom.

4 Cary Nelson, *No University is an Island: Saving Academic Freedom* (New York: New York University Press, 2010), 7.

5 Edwin R. A. Seligman, et al., "General Report of the Committee on Academic Freedom and Academic Tenure: General Statement of Principles," *Bulletin of the American Association of University Professors* 1, no. 1 (December, 1915): 33, accessed July 29, 2013, www.jstor.org/stable/40216731. The passage reads as follows: "The liberty of the scholar within the university to set forth his conclusions, be they what they may, is conditioned by their being conclusions gained by a scholar's method and held in a scholar's spirit; that is to say, they must be the fruits of competent and patient and sincere inquiry, and they should be set forth with dignity, courtesy, and temperateness of language."

6 See Matthew W. Finkin and Robert C. Post, *For the Common Good: Principles of American Academic Freedom* (New Haven: Yale University Press, 2009), 83-86 for a discussion of the difference between the place of "dogmatic knowledge" in Mathematics as opposed to English literature and Economics.

7 Thomas L. Haskell, "Justifying the Rights of Academic Freedom in the Era of 'Power/Knowledge,'" in *The Future of Academic Freedom*, ed. Louis Menand (Chicago: University of Chicago Press, 1996), 44, 53.

8 In addition to *For the Common Good* see Post's earlier "The Structure of Academic Freedom," in *Academic Freedom after September 11*, ed. Beshara Doumani (New York: Zone Books, 2006), 61-106.

9 Finkin and Post, *For the Common Good*, 7-8, 35-41.

10 Finkin and Post, *For the Common Good*, 38-9; 56-60; Post, *Democracy, Expertise, Academic Freedom*, 8-10, 25.

11 See Finkin and Post, *For the Common Good*, chapters 3 and 4.

12 Ibid., 116, 123-5

13 Ibid., 139-40, 148.

14 Ibid., 73-77.

15 Ibid., 54-60; Post, "The Structure of Academic Freedom," 71-2.

16 Finkin and Post, *For the Common Good*, 59-60.

17 Ibid., 61.

18 Ibid., 60.

19 Joan Scott, "Academic Freedom as an Ethical Practice," in *The Future of Academic Freedom*, ed. Louis Menand (Chicago: University of Chicago Press, 1998),

163,175, quoted in Finkin and Post, *For the Common Good,* p. 56.

20 Judith Butler, "Academic Norms, Contemporary Challenges: A Reply to Robert Post on Academic Freedom," in *Academic Freedom after September 11,* ed. Beshara Doumani (New York: Zone Books, 2006), 107-142. The Post intervention in question was his "The Structure of Academic Freedom", which appeared at pp. 61-106 of the same collection.

21 Ibid, 121-2.

22 Ibid., 122.

23 Nelson, *No University is an Island,* 105.

24 Thomson Reuters, "Thomson Reuters Partners with Leading North American Universities to Evaluate and Promote Research Output," press release (August 30, 2012). This release was downloaded on December 16, 2012. as it turned out, only seven of the fifteen so-called U15 institutions had, in fact, subscribed, with the University of Manitoba among those not participating. Minutes of the University of Manitoba Senate, October 3, 2013, p. 5, accessed December 19, 2013, http://umanitoba.ca/admin/governance/media/2012_10_03_Senate_Minutes_%282%29.pdf.

25 "Calibrate Your Strategic Research Vision," *Thomson Reuters,* slide 7, accessed August 11, 2013, www.slideshare.net/ThomsonReuters/incites-calibrate-your-strategic-research-vision-4160072.

26 Alex Usher, "Left Behind Again," Higher Education Strategy Associates, One Thought to Start your Day (blog), January 8, 2013, accessed August 3, 2013, http://higheredstrategy.com/left-behind-again.

27 Vivek Chibber, *Postcolonial Theory and the Specter of Capital* (London: Verso, 2013), 293-6.

28 "Canada's Universities Adopt New Statement on Academic Freedom, October 25, 2011," *Association of Universities and Colleges of Canada,* accessed August 6, 2013, www.aucc.ca/media-room/news-and-commentary/canadas-universities-adopt-new-statement-on-academic-freedom.

29 Wayne D. Peters and James L. Turk, on behalf of the Canadian Association of University Teachers, letter to Stephen Toope and Paul Davidson or the Association of Universities and Colleges of Canada, "Open Letter of the CAUT to the Association of Universities and Colleges of Canada," November 4, 2011, accessed August 14, 2013, www.caut.ca/docs/default-document-library/caut_to_aucc_academic_freedom.pdf?sfvrsn=0.

30 Ellen Schrecker, *The Lost Soul of American Academe: Corporatization, the Assault on Academic Freedom, and the End of the American University* (New York: New Press, 2010), 42.

31 Ellen Schrecker, *No Ivory Tower: McCarthyism and the Universities* (Oxford: Oxford University Press, 1986), 74-5; 97;105-112; 185-6; 225-6.

32 See ibid., 105 for Sydney Hook's promotion of this view, and 13-14 for a more general comment.

33 Schrecker, *Lost Soul*, 17.

34 For a fuller account of the Churchill case upon which this narrative is based, see Schrecker, *Lost Soul*, 123-41. See also Sheila Slaughter, "Academic Freedom, Professional autonomy and the State," in *The American Academic Profession: Transformation in American Higher Education*, ed. Joseph C. Hermanowicz (Baltimore: The John's Hopkins University Press, 2011), 241-273. For Churchill's own account, see Ward Churchill, "The Myth of Academic Freedom: Experiencing the Application of Liberal Principle in a Neo-conservative Era," in *Academic Freedom in the Post 9/11 Era*, eds. Edward J. Carvalho and David B. Downing (New York: Palgrave MacMillan, 2010), 65-113. There is also the university's time line at www.cusys.edu/regents/communique/churchill-timeline.html (accessed August 7, 2013). This site provides links to some of the relevant committee reports, but the links are apparently dead and lead only to blank pages except for a link to one statement registering a correction in the report of the Investigation Committee. See Ward Churchill Case — Statement from Marianne Wesson, Chair of the Investigative Committee dated August 14, 2007, accessed August 7, 2013, www.cusys.edu/regents/communique/churchill-wesson-stmt.html.

35 Schrecker, *Lost Soul*, 123-6; 128-9.

36 Schrecker, *Lost Soul*, 130-2.

37 See Schrecker, *Lost Soul*, 133-138 for details of the charges and investigation. The report of the Investigative Committee (Marianne Wesson, Robert N. Clinton, et al., *Report of the Investigative Committee of the Standing Committee on Research Misconduct at the University of Colorado at Boulder concerning Allegations of Academic Misconduct against Professor Ward Churchill* (May 9, 2006) was originally at http://www.colorado.edu/news/reports/churchill/ churchillreport051606.html but has since been removed.

38 Schrecker, *Lost Soul*, 139. Don Eron, Suzanne Hudson, Myron Hulen, "Colorado Conference of the American Association of University Professors: Report on the Termination of Ward Churchill," *AAUP Journal of Academic Freedom* 3 (2012): 38, accessed August 11, 2013, www.academicfreedomjournal.org/VolumeThree/ConferenceReport.pdf.

39 Schrecker, *Lost Soul*, 137.

40 Nelson, *No University is an Island*, 248.

41 Eric Cheyfitz, "Framing Ward Churchill: The Political Construction of Research Misconduct," *Works and Days* 26/27, (2008-09): 240-41, accessed August 14, 2013, www.worksanddays.net/2008-9/File10.Cheyfitz_011309_FINAL.pdf.

42 Cheyfitz, "Framing Ward Churchill," 241-2.

43 Eron, et al., "Colorado Conference."

44 Eron, et al., "Colorado Conference," 60.

45 As Cheyfitz, "Framing Ward Churchill," 235, points out, the Investigative Committee itself registered this (see Wesson, et al., *Report*, 3-5). For more on the university's policy, see Churchill, "The Myth of Academic Freedom," 65-6. Schrecker, *Lost Soul*, 140, is very clear about the political nature of the firing.

46 Slaughter, "Academic Freedom," 262.

47 Cheyfitz, "Framing Ward Churchill," 233-35; Nelson, *No University is an Island,* 249.

48 Vijay Gupta, et al., "A Filing of Research Misconduct Charges Against the Churchill Investigating Committee," May 10, 2007, accessed August 14, 2013, http://archived.wardchurchill.net/41-c_may_10_2007_rm_complaint.pdf.

49 Nelson, *No University is an Island,* 236.

50 Schrecker, *Lost Soul,* 140.

51 *Churchill v. University of Colorado at Boulder,* 54 CO (2012), accessed August 14, 2013, www.courts.state.co.us/userfiles/file/Court_Probation/Supreme_Court/Opinions/2011/11SC25.pdf. The judgment contains the court's review of the entire mater from the initial events through the various court cases.

52 Quoted in Scott Jaschik, "Supreme Court rejects appeal from Ward Churchill," *Inside Higher Ed,* April 2, 2013, accessed August 10, 2013, www.insidehighered.com/news/2013/04/02/ supreme-court-rejects-appeal-ward-churchill. For an account of the Sweezy case, see Robert C. Post, *Democracy, Expertise, Academic Freedom: A First Amendment Jurisprudence for the Modern State* (New Haven: Yale University Press, 2012), 69-72, 74.

53 *Urofsky v. Gilmore,* 216 F.3d 401-Court of Appeals, (4th Cir. 2000), 2, 4-8, accessed August 10, 2013, http://scholar.google.ca/scholar_case?case=2904778273227067629&q=urofsky+v.+ gilmore&hl=en&as_sdt=2,5&as_vis=1. For an analysis of the case, see Slaughter, "Academic Freedom," 255-9.

54 Slaughter, "Academic Freedom," 258-9.

55 Slaughter, "Academic Freedom," 259. Robert Post has strongly criticized the *Urofsky* decision on the grounds that the *First Amendment* must be seen to protect not just the democratic legitimacy of free speech in the realm of public discourse but also the production of expert knowledge since such knowledge makes a crucial contribution to what he defines as "democratic competence" (see his *Democracy, Expertise, Academic Freedom: A First Amendment Jurisprudence for the Modern State,* 80-81 for comments on *Urofsky*). In Post's view, the *Urofsky* decision fails to register the Supreme Court's commitment to "the constitutional value of democratic competence, which is straightforwardly implicated by the need of individual professors to pursue professional research free from government interference . . . "(81) For a full account of the increasing prominence of "institutional" academic freedom in American constitutional law, see the chapter in this volume by David Rabban, "Professors Beware: The Evolving Threat of 'Institutional' Academic Freedom."

56 Butler, "Academic Norms, Contemporary Challenges," 121-2.

57 Joan Wallach Scott, "The Campaign Against Political Correctness: What's Really at Stake," *Radical History Review* 54, (Fall 1992): 76, accessed August 15, 2013, http://rhr.dukejournals. org.proxy2.lib.umanitoba.ca/content/1992/54/59.full.pdf+html.

58 Kai Bird, *The Color of Truth: McGeorge Bundy and William Bundy, Brothers in Arms*

(New York: Simon and Schuster, 1998), 136. The quotation is from an interview with McGeorge Bundy.

59 This account of Dworkin's views is based on his "We Need a New Interpretation of Academic Freedom," in *The Future of Academic Freedom*, ed. Menand, 183-191.

60 Dworkin, "We Need a New Interpretation," 186.

61 Ibid., 191.

62 Ibid., 186.

63 Ibid., 191.

64 See Joan Delfattore, *Knowledge in the Making: Academic Freedom and Free Speech in America's Schools and Universities* (New Haven: Yale University Press, 2010), 178 for her view of Dworkin's position as limiting the rights of colleagues to "gate keeping."

65 Dworkin, "We Need a New Interpretation," 189.

66 Ibid., 189-90.

## CHAPTER 5

1 Different and earlier versions of this paper were published as "Knowledge, Power, and Academic Freedom," *Social Research 76*, no. 2 (summer, 2009): 451-480; and as "Academic Freedom as an Ethical Practice," in *The Future of Academic Freedom*, ed. Louis Menand (Chicago: University of Chicago Press, 1996).

2 Matthew F. Finkin and Robert C. Post, *For the Common Good: Principles of American Academic Freedom* (New Haven: Yale University Press, 2009), 44.

3 Ibid., p. 45.

4 John Dewey, "Academic Freedom," in *John Dewey: the Middle Works, 1899-1942*, ed. Jo Ann Boydston (Carbondale and Edwardsville: Southern Illinois University Press, 1976), 9-66.

5 Arthur O. Lovejoy, "Academic Freedom," in the *Encyclopedia of the Social Sciences*, ed. E. R. A. Seligman (New York: Macmillan, 1937), 384.

6 Glenn Morrow, "Academic Freedom," *International Encyclopedia of the Social Sciences, Vol I*, ed. David L. Sills (New York: Macmillan and the Free Press, 1968), 5-6.

7 Norman Hampson, "The Big Store," *London Review of Books* (January 21- February 3, 1982): 18; Lawrence Stone, "Only Women," *New York Review of Books*, April 11, 1985, 21-27; Joan W. Scott, "Academic Freedom as an Ethical Practice," in *The Future of Academic Freedom*, ed. Louis Menand (Chicago: University of Chicago Press, 1996).

8 John Searle, "Rationality and Realism: What is at Stake?" *Daedalus 122* (Fall 1992): 72.

9 American Association of University Professors, "Response to an Inquiry by Professor Paul Brest," in "Report of Committee A for 1985-86," *Academe 72* (September 1986): 13a, 19a. Cited again in *Academe 74* (September/October 1988): 55.

10 Marjorie Heins, *Priests of Our Democracy: The Supreme Court, Academic Freedom, and the Anti-Communist Purge* (New York: NYU Press, 2013), 246-248.

11 Ibid., p. 247.

12 Ibid., p. 248.

13 American Association of University Professors, "General Report of the Committee on Academic Freedom and Academic Tenure," *Bulletin of the AAUP 1*, part 1 (December 1915): 20-43.

14 American Association of University Professors, "1940 Statement of Principles on Academic Freedom and Tenure," *Policy Documents and Reports*, tenth edition (2006), 3-10, /www.aaup.org/report/1940-statement-principles-academic-freedom-and-tenure.

15 American Association of University Professors, "Academic Freedom and Tenure: the University of Illinois," *AAUP Bulletin* (Spring 1963), 26.

16 Ibid., 27.

17 Ibid., 28.

18 Ibid., 34.

19 Ibid., 37.

20 Ibid., 40.

21 Ibid., 41.

22 Ibid., 42.

23 Ibid., 43.

24 Ibid., 43.

25 Ellen Schrecker, *No Ivory Tower: McCarthyism and the Universities* (New York: Oxford University Press, 1986).

26 Christopher Lasch, *The Agony of the American Left* (New York: Knopf, 1969).

27 American Association of University Professors, "Reports on Academic Freedom and Tenure: The University of California at Los Angeles," *AAUP Bulletin* (Autumn 1971), 398.

28 Ibid., 391.

29 This all took place before Davis was indicted in the jailbreak attempt of George Jackson.

30 Ibid., 417.

31 Eric Cheyfitz, "Framing Ward Churchill: The Political Construction of Research Misconduct," *Works and Days 51/52, 53/54, Vols. 26 & 27* (2008-09), www.worksanddays.net/2008-9/File10.Cheyfitz_011309_FINAL.pdf; Ellen Schrecker, "Ward Churchill at the Dalton Trumbo Fountain: Academic Freedom in the Aftermath of 9/11," *AAUP Journal of Academic Freedom, Vol. I* (2010), www.academicfreedomjournal.org/Previous/VolumeOne/Schrecker.pdf

32 Dewey, "Academic Freedom," 58.

33 See also Frank Donoghue, *The Last Professors: The Corporate University and the Fate of the Humanities* (New York: Fordham University Press, 2008).

34 Michel de Certeau, "History: Science and Fiction," in *Heterologies: Discourse on the Other*, trans. Brian Massumi (Minneapolis: University of Minnesota Press, 1986).

## CHAPTER 6

1 See my Section nine below where I argue that people can have academic freedom rights only if there are institutions in which these rights are held.

2 There are a variety of interesting and important histories of the development of the idea of academic freedom including most recently chapters 1 and 2 of the excellent Matthew W. Finkin and Robert C. Post, *For the Common Good: Principles of American Academic Freedom* ( New Haven: Yale University Press, 2009). Chapter 8 of Jon Thomson's *No Debate: The Israel lobby and free speech and Canadian Universities* (Toronto: James Lorimer & Company, 2011), especially pages 202ff., gives a useful short review of the development of academic freedom in Canada.

3 Section 1 of the *Canadian Charter of Rights and Freedoms*, of course, begins by stating that the rights and freedoms set out in the *Charter* are " . . . guarantees the rights and freedoms set out in it subject only to such reasonable limits prescribed by law as can be demonstrably justified in a free and democratic society." See further the important Supreme Court of Canada examination of some of the issues in the famous "kirpan" case: *Multani v. Commission Scolaire Margarite-Boureoys*, SCC 6 (2006).

4 An important question which I will not address in this paper is the question of whether there are principled arguments for singling out *religion* for more stringent protections than those to be accorded to other freedoms, that is, protections granted because religion has the nature it has. In his 2013 book *Why Tolerate Religion* (Princeton: Princeton University Press) Brian Leiter provides original and interesting arguments for saying not.

5 The paper is printed in *Recognizing Religion in a Secular Society: Essays in Pluralism, Religion and Public Policy* (Quebec City: McGill-Queens University Press, 2004), 12-34.

6 *Edwards v. Attorney General* of *Canada* [1930] A.C. 124.

7 Cambridge University Press.

8 In 2011 the Association of Universities and Colleges of Canada adopted a radically new definition of academic freedom, effectively omitting reference to the right of academics to express intra and extramural opinions on the governance of their own universities.

9 It is important that my outline specifies only what I count as the core ideas. It is clear that definition of academic freedom that would do justice to all of the complexities of the notion would need to be much longer and much more complex. See for example the CAUT policy statement on academic freedom at www.caut.ca/about-us/caut-policy/lists/general-caut-policies/policy-statement-on-academic-freedom.

10 Newman argued in his 1852 lectures (later published as *The Idea of a University*)

that a university should strive to be a community of thinkers devoted to teaching its students "to think and to reason and to compare and to discriminate and to analyse." However, despite arguing that universities should be entirely free of outside religious interference, he also argued that "religious truth is not only a portion, but a condition of general knowledge. To blot it out is nothing short . . . of unravelling the web of university teaching."

11 D. Hume, *Of Suicide* (New York: Penguin Books, [1783] 2005).

12 It was because he accepted what nowadays is called the social recognition thesis that Jeremy Bentham said that *natural* rights are "nonsense on stilts." He was of course not saying that talk of rights generally as nonsense on stilts: it was only the suggestion that rights exist independently of existing social structures that was, he thought, nonsense. For a useful and recent discussion of some of the issues here and for a useful bibliography, see the recent paper by Rex Martin, "Human Rights and the Social Recognition Thesis", *The Journal of Social Philosophy* 44, no. 1, (Spring 2013): 1–21.

13 Amusingly, the governing body in later years modified this rule to a form Sidgwick was able to sign. As he said, "Last time I swore that I would drive away strange doctrine; this time I only pledged myself to restore any College property that might be in my possession when I ceased to be a Fellow". See *Henry Sidgwick, A Memoir*, eds. E. M. Sidgwick and A. Sidgwick (London: Macmillan, 2006), 400. This quotation is taken from Barton Schultz's 2004 (revised 2012) article "Henry Sidgwick" in the *Stanford University Online Encyclopedia*, http://plato.stanford.edu/entries/sidgwick.

14 The 1997 *UNESCO Recommendation Concerning the Status of Higher Education Teaching Personnel* (despite saying in section 18 that institutional autonomy "is the institutional form of academic freedom", a most regrettable comment) gets most of the above points right: Institutional autonomy is needed if universities are to fulfill their needed roles, but institutional autonomy can only be well exercised if guided and controlled by academic staff, but academic staff can only give wise guidance and control if they are granted the academic freedom to exercise their good judgment in the light of the academic realities that only they are adequately qualified to assess, and academic freedom here of course includes the freedom to criticise the actions of the university.

15 As Wayne Peters (currently President on the CAUT) and James Turk (currently CAUT Executive Director) pointed out in an open letter to Professor Stephen Toope (then Chair of the Association of Universities and Colleges of Canada) on the occasion of the publication of the AUCC's "Statement on Academic Freedom":

> Equally of concern is your statement's conflation of academic freedom with institutional autonomy. It is absolutely true that academic institutions must not restrict the freedom of academic staff because of outside pressure—be it political, special interest group, religious—and institutions need to be autonomous in that sense. But to pretend that building a moat around the university protects academic freedom is disingenuous and ignores the reality of internal threats to academic freedom. The 1915 AAUP statement

arose partially in recognition of internal threats—from boards, administration, colleagues and students. As the CAUT policy statement on academic freedom says, "Academic freedom must not be confused with institutional autonomy. Post-secondary institutions are autonomous to the extent that they can set policies independent of outside influence. That very autonomy can protect academic freedom from a hostile external environment, but it can also facilitate an internal assault on academic freedom. To undermine or suppress academic freedom is a serious abuse of institutional autonomy."

16 At the time of writing the CAUT website lists five Canadian universities or university colleges as " . . . require[ing] academic staff to commit to a particular ideology or statement of faith as a condition of employment," namely, Canadian Mennonite University, Crandall University, Providence University College, Redeemer University College, and Trinity Western University. See "Universities that impose a faith or ideological test," Canadian Association of University Teachers, accessed August 7, 2013, www.caut.ca/issues-and-campaigns/academic-freedon/faith-ideological-test for the list and for links to the reports which led to CAUT listing these institutions.

17 It is worth pointing out that Brian Leiter in chapter II of his *Why Tolerate Religion* addresses the question of what features mark a system of beliefs and values as a religion as opposed to some other kind of such system and he concludes clearly implausibly that one of the features of a religion will inevitably be that some of its fundamental claims are claims grounded only in faith. He thus ignores a whole tradition in religious thought, the tradition usually called "natural theology" and I am calling the "scientific-theology" view.

18 See the philosopher of law Timothy Macklem's *Independence of Mind*, (Oxford: Oxford University Press, 2007), 133, and his "Faith as a Secular Value," *McGill Law Journal 45* (2000): 1-63. Macklem's views are cited and discussed in chapter II of Brian Leiter's *Why Tolerate Religion*.

19 As should be obvious to the aficionados of this literature, what I am referring to as "scientific-theology" is a close relative of what is more traditionally called 'natural theology' and what I am referring to as 'faith-theology' is a close relative of what its more traditionally called "revealed-theology."

20 Thus, for example, at Canadian Mennonite University amongst the governing documents of the university is a statement to the following effect:

> If an employee's outlook changes to the point where that individual is no longer able to embrace and advance the mission of the institution, or impedes effective performance, it is appropriate for the individual and the employer to review whether continued employment is appropriate. Should there be disagreement as to whether continued employment is appropriate, the CMU policy on Grievance and Conflict Resolution may be invoked.

> For a full discussion of Canadian Mennonite University's policies on this kind of issue, see section 2.1.1 of the October 2010 *Report CAUT Investigatory Committee on Academic Freedom at Canadian Mennonite University* — the above quotation is cited in that section of the Report.

21 The phenomenon referred to as "moral distress" was much studied in the 1990s

in in relation to the nursing profession. See for example, J. M. Wilkinson, "Moral Distress in Nursing Practice: Experience and Effect," *Nursing Forum 23*, no. 1 (1987): 16-29.

22 In relation to the resort by nurses to subversion in the face of imposed rules that the nurse believes are counterproductive see S.A. Hutchinson, "Responsible Subversion: A Study of Rule-Bending Among Nurses," *Scholarly Inquiry for Nursing Practice: An International Journal* 4, no. 1 (1990): 3-17.

## CHAPTER 7

1 Lawrence K. Shook, *Etienne Gilson* (Toronto: Pontifical Institute for Mediaeval Studies, 1984), 192-309.

2 This quotation is from my notes of the event, as I was in the audience.

3 The *Oxford English Dictionary* gives for "confessional" several meanings of which I adopt two: "Of or pertaining to Confessions of Faith, or systems of formulated Theology" and "Denominational; holding or according with a certain system of dogmas or beliefs." These meanings apply interchangeably, or at the same time, to the private, religiously-oriented institutions of higher education with which I am concerned. I use interchangeably the phrases "confessional university" and "faith-based university" in this essay, as a matter of convenience and for the sake of verbal economy, but intend the definition given in the OED.

4 Francis Fukuyama, *The End of History and the Last Man* (New York: Free Press, 1992).

5 Canadians are accustomed to the idea of public funding for religious elementary and secondary schools in consequence of s.93 of the *British North America Act* (1867) [BNA]. British Columbia was a special case. It joined the Canadian confederation only in 1871 and interpreted the BNA to mean that it need not offer public financial support to Catholic schools. Catholic schools were treated until 1977 as private, independent entities. After 1977, under the *Independent Schools Support Act* (1977) the provincial state gave reliable annual funding to those and other independent schools. On the British Columbia treatment of Catholic and other religious schools, see V. Cunningham, *Justice Achieved: The Political Struggles of Independent Schools in British Columbia* (Vancouver: Federation of Independent Schools Associations, 2002).

Post-secondary religious institutions in Canada have far greater difficulty acquiring public funding. Their usual solution has been in most cases to "go public," leaving higher education to the public sector. A second solution was to arrange a federation with a public university, agreeing to various administrative conditions (including academic freedom in one form or another) in return for limited and indirect financial assistance. For an historical study of the consequences of federalism in one important case, see Alexander Reford, "St. Michael's College at the University of Toronto, 1958-1978: The Frustrations of Federation," *CCHA, Historical Studies 61* (1995): 171-194. More generally, see Laurence K. Shook, *Catholic Post-Secondary Education in English-Speaking Canada: A History* (Toronto: University of Toronto Press, 1972), 188.

6 On the general question of Canadian governments' involvement in and tolerance

of religious practice, see Richard Moon, "Government Support for Religious Practice," in *Law and Religious Pluralism in Canada*, ed. R. Moon (Vancouver: UBC Press, 2008), 217-238. On the other hand, note that a constitutional amendment (sec. 93A, *Constitution Act*) in 1997 released the Government of Quebec from its constitutional obligation to provide public funding for Catholic or Protestant schools in Quebec (see: http://laws.justice.gc.ca/eng/Const/page-4.html#docCont).

7 For Christian Higher Education Canada, accessed February 28, 2013, www.checanada.ca.

8 A university in Canada must be chartered by a provincial legislature, usually after a majority vote in favour of a private member's bill. In Canada, an institution may not call itself a Canadian university without a provincial charter.

Observers of Canadian post-secondary education occasionally say that membership in the Association of Universities and Colleges of Canada [AUCC], a longstanding organization of university presidents, signals that a university or college has a reasonably high standard of quality in programming, governance, and policy.

The confessional universities and colleges under study in this paper were chartered by the relevant provincial governments. Three have become members of the AUCC: Canadian Mennonite University, Redeemer University College, and Trinity Western University. See the current AUCC membership list: "Member universities," Association of Universities and Colleges of Canada, accessed February 28, 2013, http://aucc.ca.

Meanwhile, religiously-oriented or confessional institutions officially connected to or federated with public universities and colleges are represented by the Canadian Association of University Teachers. For the membership list as of 2013 Feburary 28, see: http://www.caut.ca.

9 A. G. Bedford, *The University of Winnipeg: A History of the Founding Colleges* (Toronto: University of Toronto Press, 1976); W. A. Bruneau, Review of Bedford, *Canadian Journal of Education* 4, no. 1 (1976): 90-94.

10 Michiel Horn, *Academic Freedom in Canada: A History* (Toronto: University of Toronto Press, 1999), Ch. 9, "The Crowe Caws," pp. 220-245; and from the point of view of a person directly involved in the Crowe case, Kenneth McNaught, *Conscience and History: A Memoir* (Toronto: University of Toronto Press, 1999), pp. 73-150.

11 V. Fowke and B. Laskin, "Report of the Investigation by the Committee of the Canadian Association of University Teachers into the Dismissal of Professor H.S. Crowe by United College, Winnipeg, Manitoba," November 1958, Canadian Association of University Teachers, www.caut.ca/uploads/CroweReport.pdf.

12 Bertrand Russell, "Has Religion Made Useful Contributions to Civilization?" *The Debunker and the American Parade*, Girard, Kansas 10, no. 1 (1929): 3-16 reproduced in *Russell on Religion*, eds. L. Greenspan and S. Andersson (London: Routledge, 1999), 169-185. This quotation from p. 173 in Greenspan and Andersson.

13 Canadian Association of University Teachers, Report of an Inquiry Regarding Trinity Western University (Ottawa: CAUT, 2009), Appendix D, "Responsibilities of Membership."

14 Jonathan Raymond, interview, CBC Radio 1, January 21, 2013, accessed January 28, 2013, www.cbc.ca/player/Radio/Local+Shows/British+Columbia/The+Early+Edition/ID/2327555595.

15 Douglas Todd, "Proposal for TWU Law School Under Fire," *Vancouver Sun*, January 17, 2013. Accessed January 28, 2013, www2.canada.com/vancouversun/news/story.html?id =f63c4447-5e5a-444e-be6f-c2920f3ddb23.

16 See Douglas Todd, "A spat over spirituality in higher education," *Vancouver Sun*, February 16, 2013. Some critics of the TWU proposal, it should be said, worry that it is premature or impractical. See, for instance, Jena McGill, et al., "Why Trinity Western University Should Not Have a Law School," *National Post*, January 24, 2013.

17 Northrop Frye made this point in memorable fashion in *The Educated Imagination* (Toronto: CBC, 1962), Massey Lectures for 1962, passim. A recent American book, *Andrew Delbanco's College: What It Was, Is, and Should Be* (Princeton, NJ: Princeton University Press, 2012) argues the same case with unusual rigour and force.

18 On Canadian public opinion vis-à-vis the funding and expansion of post-secondary education, see Robin Harris, *A History of Higher Education in Canada, 1663-1960* (Toronto: University of Toronto Press, 1976), 440ff.; A.B. McKillop, *Matters of Mind: The University in Ontario, 1791-1951* (Toronto: University of Toronto Press, 1994).

19 Kenneth McNaught, *The Pelican History of Canada* (Harmondsworth, Mddx.: Penguin Books, 1969), 289-315.

20 See Catherine Gidney, *A Long Eclipse: The Liberal Protestant Establishment and the Canadian University, 1920-1970* (Montreal: McGill-Queen's University Press, 2004), 93-6.

21 Three references help to support this generalization: *Academic Freedom and the Inclusive University*, eds. S.E. Kahn and D. Pavlich (Vancouver: UBC Press, 2000); M. Patricia Marchak, *Racism, Sexism, and the University: the Political Science Affair at the University of British Columbia* (Montreal: McGill-Queen's University Press, 1996); and Wesley Pue, *Pepper in Our Eyes: The APEC Affair* (Vancouver: UBC Press, 2000).

22 David Cameron, *More Than an Academic Question: Universities, Government, and Public Policy in Canada* (Halifax: Institute for Research on Public Policy, 1991), 315-350.

23 V.C. Fowke, "Professional Association: A History of the C.A.U. T.," in *A Place of Liberty: Essays on the Government of Canadian Universities*, ed. G. Whalley (Toronto: Clarke, Irwin, 1964), 195-215. In a fine review of this collective volume, Claude Bissell, then President of the University of Toronto, summarized the book in the title of his review, "A Case for More Academic Control of Colleges," *The Globe Magazine*, May 30, 1964, 13. Bissell said he agreed with the book.

24 Bora Laskin, "Some Cases at Law," in Whalley, *A Place of Liberty*, 193, accessed April 6, 2013, www.caut.ca/uploads/CroweReport.pdf. It is of at least interest that Fowke and Laskin rely on a topos familiar to reader of John Stuart Mill, who in "The Utility of Religion" (in *Three Essays on Religion* [London : Longmans, Green, Reader, and Dyer, 1874], p. 70) says

> An argument for the utility of religion is an appeal to unbelievers, to induce them to practice a well-meant hypocrisy, or to semi-believers to make them avert their eyes from what might possibly shake their unstable belief, or finally to persons in general to abstain from expressing any doubts they may feel, since a fabric of immense importance to mankind is so insecure at its foundations, that men must hold their breath in its neighbourhood for fear of blowing it down. [emphasis added]

25 "Policy Statement on Academic Freedom," Canadian Association of University Teachers, November 2011, accessed January 30, 2013, www.caut.ca/pages.asp?page=247&lang=1.

26 Ottawa: *CAUT*, 2006, accessed January 30, 2013, www.caut.ca/.

27 A complete list of all published CAUT/Academic Freedom and Tenure investigations, with the relevant texts, is available at www.caut.ca/.

28 The relevant university policy documents are listed and excerpted (in some cases presented in extenso) in the CAUT/Academic Freedom and Tenure reports mentioned in n. 14. For a representative list of commentaries and criticism in the religious and secular press between 2009 and 2012, see Appendix III.

29 Cary Nelson and Stephen Watt, *Academic Keywords: A Devil's Dictionary for Higher Education* (New York: Routledge, 1999), 28-9.

30 Bertrand Russell, *Skeptical Essays* (London: Allen and Unwin, 1928), 12-13, 197.

31 L. Armour and R. Feist, *Inference and Persuasion* (Halifax, NS: Fernwood, 2005), 1.

32 Gidney, *Long Eclipse*, 143.

33 Paul Lacoste, "Church and University," in *A Place of Liberty: Essays on the Government of Canadian Universities*, ed. G. Whalley (Toronto: Clarke, Irwin, 1964), 129-141; Roger P. Magnuson, *The Two Worlds of Quebec Education During the Traditional Era, 1760-1940* (London, ON: Althouse Press, 2005), passim.

34 L. Armour and E. Trott, *The Faces of Reason: Philosophy in English Canada, 1850–1950* (Waterloo, ON: Wilfrid Laurier University Press, 1981), passim; S. E. D. Shortt, *The search for an ideal: Six Canadian intellectuals and their convictions in an age of transition, 1890-1930* (Toronto: University of Toronto Press, 1976).

35 Catherine Gidney, *A Long Eclipse: The Liberal Protestant Establishment and the Canadian University, 1920-1970* (Montreal: McGill-Queen's University Press, 2004), 5-25. Gidney shows how the frankly moralistic and authoritarian views of nnineteenth-century Protestant sects were modified after 1918 to take into account the effects of war and revolution. Religion was said to offer Canadian university teachers and students a "responsible and responsive Christianity" in a growing nation and a chaotic world.

orn, *Academic Freedom in Canada: A History* (Toronto: University of ress, 1999), 34.

37 A.B. McKillop, *A Disciplined Intelligence: Critical Inquiry and Canadian Thought in the Victorian Era* (Montreal: McGill-Queen's University Press, 1979) explains the intellectual environment of Canadian universities before the Great War, but more extensively in *Matters of Mind: The University in Ontario, 1791-1951* (Toronto: University of Toronto Press, 1994).

38 Stanley B. Frost, *McGill University: For the Advancement of Learning* (Montreal: McGill-Queen's University Press, 1980-1984).

39 Louis St-Laurent, quoted in C. Gidney, *Long Eclipse*, p. 23.

40 See P. Stortz and E.L. Panayotidis, eds., *Cultures, Communities, and Conflict: Histories of Canadian Universities and War* (Toronto: University of Toronto Press, 2012), esp. D.H. Avery, "Canadian University Scientists and Military Technology: The Challenge of Total War, 1939-1945," 175-201.

## CHAPTER 8

1 One of the challenges is naming the category of schools I am speaking about. Perhaps the most common designation is "faith-based" colleges and universities. But speaking of them as faith-based may suggest that all thinking at these places is forced into a predetermined mold, and on the other hand, that "non-faith-based" institutions have no foundational commitments or assumptions, neither of which is fully valid. One can also speak of them as "church-related," but that implies a formal relationship to a denomination, or denominations, which may be the case but need not be. Speaking of these institutions as Christian universities avoids these connotations, even though the use of "Christian" as an adjective for an institution is awkward at best.

2 Phyllis Tickle, *The Great Emergence: How Christianity is Changing and Why* (Grand Rapids, MI: Baker Books, 2008).

3 See Michiel Horn, *Academic Freedom in Canada: A History* (Toronto: University of Toronto Press, 1999), 220-244; V. C. Fowke and Bora Laskin, "Report of the Investigation by the Committee of the Canadian Association of University Teachers into the Dismissal of Professor H.S. Crowe by United College, Winnipeg, Manitoba," November 1958, *Harry Crowe Foundation*, www.crowefoundation.ca/documents/crowereport.pdf.

4 Harvey Cox, *The Future of Faith* (New York: HarperOne, 2009).

5 "CAUT Policy Statement on Tenure," *Canadian Association of University Teachers*, last modified November, 2008, www.caut.ca/about-us/caut-policy/lists/general-caut-policies/policy-statement-on-tenure.

## CHAPTER 9

1 There are also restrictions on expression based on privacy or proprietary interests – such as limits on the dissemination of confidential information or copyrighted material.

2 See *McKinney v. University of Guelph*, [1990] 3 SCR 229. However, see also *Pridgen v. University of Calgary*, 2012 ABCA 139 which suggests that a *Charter* claim may

be made against a university in some circumstances.

3 Canadian Parliamentary Coalition to Combat Antisemitism (CPCCA), *Report of the Inquiry Panel* (July 7, 2011) (info@cpcca.ca).

4 For a more general discussion see Richard Moon, *The Constitutional Protection of Freedom of Expression* (Toronto, University of Toronto Press, 2000).

5 Charles Taylor, *Human Agency and Language* (Cambridge: Cambridge University Press, 1985), 260.

6 J.B. Thompson, *The Media and Modernity* (Stanford: Stanford University Press, 1995),39.

7 For a thoughtful discussion of this issue — and the tension between respecting the standards that make speech possible and protecting an open — democratic — discourse, in which all standards are subject to challenge, see Robert C. Post, *Constitutional Domains* (Cambridge: Harvard University Press, 1995).

8 The state bans false factual claims by commercial and professional actors and does not rely on the "marketplace" of ideas to correct errors for a variety of reasons including unequal communicative power.

9 I have elsewhere argued that the idea that the speaker should not be held responsible for the actions of his/her audience may also depend on the state's ability to regulate the audience's behaviour.

10 J.S. Mill, *On Liberty* (Harmondsworth: Penguin, [1859] 1982), 119.

11 J. Holmes in *Schenk v. United States*, 249 US 47 (1919) at 52.

12 In the U.S. this exception is made only for speech that amounts to incitement - when unlawful action follows the speech almost immediately. See *Brandenburg v. Ohio*, 395 US 444 (1969).

13 *Criminal Code*, R.S. 1985, c.C-46, s. 318 -319. An identifiable group means any section of the public identified by colour, race, religion, ethnic origin or sexual orientation.

14 *Canadian Human Rights Act*, R.S., 1985, c.H-6 was repealed in 2013. In June 2012, the House of Commons voted to repeal s. 13 of the *CHRA*. At the time I was writing this chapter, the bill to repeal s. 13 was before the Senate. Similar provisions are included in the human rights codes of B.C., Alberta, Saskatchewan, and the N.W.T. In *Saskatchewan (Human Rights* Commission*) v. Whatcott*, 2013 SCC 11 the Supreme Court of Canada ruled that a similar provision (s. 14) in the *Saskatchewan Human Rights Code* did not breach the *Canadian Charter of Rights and Freedoms.*

15 For a more complete discussion see R. Moon, *The Constitutional Protection of Freedom of Expression*, c. 5 and Richard Moon, *Report to the Canadian Human Rights Commission Concerning Section 13 of the CHRA and the Regulation of Hate Speech on the Internet*, October, 2008.

16 *RAV v. City of St. Paul*, 505 US 377 (1992).

17 *Collin v. Smith*, 578 F.2d 1197 (1978).

18 *Montreal (City) v. 2952-1366 Quebec Inc.*, 2005 SCC 62.

19 It is often complained that demonstrations have no clear message and are simply a show of force. Certainly a demonstration does not convey a message in the same way that a text does. It is intended principally to "demonstrate" support for a position rather than to elaborate or defend the position. A demonstration may involve many people, who have different, if related or overlapping, views. As well a demonstration may appear to lack a clear message, because its message runs against the current of media or cultural orthodoxy. Indeed demonstrations often challenge in a fundamental way central aspects of the established order — such as the commercial character of culture or disparities in wealth — and so are dismissed as unorthodox and even obtuse. Many media commentators — when the media finally started to pay attention — complained that the Occupy movement had no clear message. The problem, though, was that the movement raised concerns about the link between money and politics (and the way in which politics serves the economically powerful) — a link that is so established as to seem either natural or unchallengeable. The movement also sought to model other forms of communal living and organization.

20 See for example *Batty v. City of Toronto*, 2011 ONSC 6862 at para. 66.

21 *Batty* at para. 15: "The Charter does not permit the Protestors . . . to exclude the rest of the public from engaging in their traditional use of the space ..."

22 *Batty* at para. 91.

23 See R. Moon, *The Constitutional Protection of Freedom of Expression*, c. 3.

24 Communication between strangers is generally mediated and commercial in its focus — advertising being the principal example. We often don't feel comfortable with face-to-face communication with people we don't already know.

25 Richard Moon, "Keeping the Streets Safe from Free Expression" in *Legislating Safe Streets: The 'New Vagrancy,'* eds. J. Hermer and J. Mosher (Halifax: Fernwood, 2002), 65.

26 Students (sometimes in a patronizing way) are viewed as citizens in training.

27 However, any ban (and certainly a general ban) on racist insults raises a variety of line-drawing issues such as the distinction between a racist insult and a claim or argument about race or the distinction between a derogatory term used against a particular group and the same term used by members of that group to describe themselves — sometimes in order to neutralize its negative impact.

28 University administrators sometimes make the mistake of extending this requirement of respect to communication between students that takes place outside the classroom — particularly on-line criticism of teachers. See *Pridgen v. University of Calgary*.

29 The limits on the display of offensive or disturbing images may also be different in the context of the university — as workplace and place of learning. The right of anti-abortion activists to display images of aborted fetuses has become an issue at several campuses. These activists may feel that their case is most powerfully conveyed through such images. They may seek to confront others with the brutal

reality of an activity to which they are deeply opposed. They may believe that images have a force that words lack. But, at the same time, the visceral force of such images may justify their restriction in a closed environment with a captive audience. When images that are experienced by some members of the university community as upsetting or offensive are displayed in such a way that they cannot easily be avoided by those who do not wish to see them, the institution may be justified not in censoring them but in requiring that they be displayed in a way that minimizes involuntary exposure. I would note, though, that some student groups, and even some student governments, appear to have gone further than this and sought to shut out entirely the anti-abortion message which they regard as anti-woman.

30 I want to be careful, though, not to push too far the idea of the university as a community. Universities have structures of power that support certain privileges and reinforce conventional views. Speech that questions established practices must be given significant protection, even when it is expressed in strong, even confrontational, terms. But this is something very different from speech that questions the standing of some members of the community.

31 For example when someone like Anne Coulter (who is intentionally provocative and has in the past frequently expressed bigoted views about Muslims and other groups) is invited to speak on campus, it is hardly surprising that some will react negatively to the invitation.

32 It is easy to understand the powerful reaction some members of the University of Toronto community had to the invitation of Glen Baab, the South African Ambassador to Canada during the apartheid period, by a group of law students at the university in 1980 (a group headed by then law-student now Federal Cabinet Minister, Tony Clement). Baab was the representative in Canada of a racist regime that was acting contrary to international law. Even if his views were expressed in a serious and temperate manner, he was speaking on behalf of a racist and violent regime and his presence on campus was bound to be viewed (most obviously by the direct victims of the regime) as legitimating that regime. The objection then was not just to what Baab might say (although his defence of the apartheid regime would have to be viewed as racist) but to the fact that he was invited and given a platform on campus to express his views. A more recent situation (September 2002) involved protests at Concordia University that led to the cancellation of a speech by Benjamin Netanyahu, who had been, and later became again, Prime Minister of Israel.

33 There may be an appropriate time and place for non-violent civil disobedience when the institution makes the wrong decision. But that is a matter for individual conscience and so a different issue.

34 *Israeli Apartheid Week*, accessed June 6, 2013, Apartheidweek.org.

35 David Matas, "Banning Israel anti-apartheid week at universities" (remarks prepared for delivery, Faculty of Law, University of Manitoba, Manitoba Association of Rights and Liberties Forum, October 2010), argues that the event should be banned. In his view, "Calling Israel an apartheid state is a form of incitement to hatred against the Jewish people." According to Matas,

"The accusations of criminality against the Jewish state lead to accusations of criminality against the Jewish community world wide as actual or presumed supporters of this allegedly criminal state. If Israel is an apartheid state, then the Jewish community world wide supports apartheid." While certainly not a refutation of Matas's claim, it may be relevant in assessing its merit to recall that many prominent individuals such as Jimmy Carter and Desmond Tutu have used the term "apartheid" to describe the Israeli occupation of the West Bank. As well, many public figures in Israel, including former Prime Minister Ehud Barak, have said that Israel is at risk of becoming an apartheid state.

36 The CPCCA, although composed of members of Parliament, had no official status. It was privately organized and funded. It members included Ken Dryden, Bob Rae, Carolyn Bennett, Irwin Cotler, Jason Kenney, Peter Kent, Hedy Fry, and Pat Martin. For a more general critique of the report, see James Cairns and Susan Ferguson, "Human Rights Revisionism in the Canadian Parliamentary Coalition to Combat Antisemitism," *Canadian Journal of Communication 36* (2011): 415.

37 CPCCA, *Report of the Inquiry Panel*, 4.

38 Ibid., 5.

39 Ibid., 39.

40 Ibid., 39.

41 Ibid., 39.

42 Ibid., 52.

43 Ibid., 52.

44 Ibid., 52

45 Ibid., 52.

46 Ibid., 53. The coalition relied almost exclusively on the reports of Jewish students of their impressions and feelings about IAW. The coalition either did not hear or refused to acknowledge the views of the supporters of IAW.

47 Ibid., 40.

48 Ibid., 53.

49 Ibid., 54 The Report continued, "However, the Inquiry Panel does have a number of recommendations to protect the safety of Jewish and pro-Israeli students, which are listed at the end of this section." "We recognize the complexity surrounding the issues in the Middle East, and the desire of many Canadians, especially on campus, to debate and propose solutions to those issues. We suggest that the best resolutions and recommendations for complex problems can only be developed through serious and rigorous debate, free of intimidation and threats." "We commend the Legislative Assembly of Ontario for passing a motion condemning Israeli Apartheid Week, and recommend that Canadian politicians openly condemn Israeli Apartheid Week on campus and the intimidation that it creates" (p.55).

50 The reluctance of the Coalition to call for such a ban may indicate an ambivalence about their claim that the IAW is anti-Semitic. This ambivalence may

stem in part from the questionable factual findings in the report — in which they say simply that "we were told by some" that these things were occurring.

51 CPCCA, *Report of the Inquiry Panel*, 53.

52 See for example, Judith Butler, "Remarks to Brooklyn College," *The Nation*, Feb 7, 2013, www.thenation.com/article/172752/judith-butlers-remarks-brooklyn-college-bds#axzz2W9UnxQp9.

53 CPCCA, *Report of the Inquiry Panel*, 3. According to the Coalition Report — citing the submission of a Toronto group, "The organizers and supporters of 'IAW' single out Israel from all other nations on earth, set a negative tone on campus, hold one- sided events with little academic merit, exclude Hillel students and staff from events, and typically flout school protocol regarding use of space on campus" (p. 53).

54 Ibid., 3.

55 Ibid..

56 Ibid.,

57 According to the CPCCA, *Report of the Inquiry Panel*, at p. 6, "Denying the Jewish people their right to self-determination eg. by claiming that the existence of a State of Israel is a racist endeavour."

## CHAPTER 10

1 This paper was first presented at the Harry Crowe Foundation Conference on The Limits of Academic Freedom, February 1-3, 2013, Toronto.

2 LGBTT2SIQQ stands for lesbian, gay, bisexual, trans, transsexual, two-spirit, intersex, queer, questioning academics.

3 Jennie Hornotsy, "Academic Freedom in Social Context," in *Academic Freedom and the Inclusive University*, eds. S. E. Khan and D. Pavlich (Vancouver: UBC Press, 2000).

4 Michiel Horn, *Academic Freedom in Canada: A History* (Toronto: University of Toronto Press, 1999), 7.

5 Michiel Horn, "The Exclusive University and Academic Freedom," in Khan and Pavlich, *Academic Freedom*.

6 Richard Hofstadter, "The Age of the College," in *The Development of Academic Freedom in the United States*, eds. R. Hofstadter and W. P. Metzger (New York: Columbia University Press, 1955), 3.

7 Edward Said, *Orientalism* (New Delhi: Penguin, 2001), 283.

8 Horn, "The Exclusive University" ; Conrad Russell, *Academic Freedom* (New York: Routledge, 1993); Richard Moon, *Freedom of Expression* (Toronto: University of Toronto Press, 2000); Howard Woodhouse, "Are Closer Ties with Business Undermining Academic Freedom?" in *Pursuing Academic Freedom: Free and Fearless*, eds. L. M. Findlay and P. M., Bidwell (Saskatoon: Purich Publishing, 2001); Howard Woodhouse, *Academic Freedom and the Corporate Market* (Montreal: McGill-Queen's University Press, 2009).

9 John Stuart Mill, *Three Essays: On Liberty; Representative Government; The Subjection of Women* (Oxford: Oxford University Press, 1975), 24.

10 Moon, *Freedom of Expression.*

11 Joseph Stiglitz, "Prize Lecture: Information and the Change in the Paradigm in Economics," Nobelprize.org, www.nobelprize.org/nobel_prizes/economics/laureates/2001/stiglitz-lecture.html.

12 "Academic Freedom," *Canadian Association of University Teachers,* last modified November, 2011, www.caut.ca/about-us/caut-policy/lists/general-caut-politices/policy-statement-on-academic-freedom#sthash.cbDVefvr.dpuf.

13 Hornotsy.

14 Ibid.

15 Ibid.

16 Ibid.

17 Ibid.

18 Horn, "The Exclusive University," 54.

19 Frank Schauer, "Academic Freedom: Rights as Immunities and Privileges," in Khan and Pavlich, *Academic Freedom,* 18.

## CHAPTER 11

1 Anver Saloojee identifies some of these challenges in "Issue Draws Diversity of Opinions," Review of *Academic Freedom and the Inclusive University,* eds. Sharon E. Kahn and Denis Pavlich, (Vancouver: UBC Press, 2000), *CAUT Bulletin 49,* no. 4 (April 2002), http://www.cautbulletin.ca/ en_article.asp?ArticleID=1571.

2 See Joan W. Scott, "The Limits of Academic Freedom" in this volume.

3 Roderick A. Macdonald, *Metaphors of Multiplicity: Civil Society, Regimes and Legal Pluralism,* 15 Ariz J Int'l & Comp L 69, 81 (1998).

4 Michael Oakeshott, "The Study of Politics in a University," in *Rationalism in Politics and Other Essays,* ed. Michael Oakeshott (London: Methuen, 1962), 313.

5 Sir Robert Falconer, *Academic Freedom* (Toronto: University of Toronto Press, 1922), 11. Falconer preceded this statement with the following: "A university is a centre for the investigation and impartation of truth. Now truth does not belong to any one province or country or race. It reigns in a Commonwealth of which each university is as it were a nation, and the laws of the Commonwealth are valid in every part."

6 On the university as "an agent of social change," see Jürgen Habermas, "Student Protest in the Federal Republic of Germany," in Jürgen Habermas, *Toward a Rational Society,* trans. Jeremy J. Shapiro (London: Heinemann, 1971), 13.

7 See, again, Scott, "The Limits of Academic Freedom," in this volume.

8 See Bora Laskin, *Freedom and Responsibility in the University* (Toronto: Toronto University Press, 1970), 2. This is the way the Presidential Committee at York,

chaired by Bora Laskin put it: it entails the "freedom to teach, freedom to engage in research, freedom to create, freedom to learn, freedom to study, freedom to speak, freedom to associate, freedom to write and to publish."

9 This is the principle argument in Matthew W. Finkin & Robert C. Post, *For the Common Good: Principles of Academic Freedom* (New Haven: Yale University Press, 2009).

10 Ibid.,19-21.

11 See my discussion of the British political pluralists in David Schneiderman, "Harold Laski, Viscount Haldane, and the Law of the Canadian Constitution in the early Twentieth Century," 48 UTLJ 521 (1998); and David Schneiderman, "Haldane Unrevealed" 57 McGill Law Journal 593 (2012).

12 Frederick Maitland, "Introduction," in *Political Theories of the Middle Age*, trans. Frederick Maitland (Cambridge: Cambridge University Press, 1900), viii.

13 Ibid., xxvii.

14 Ibid., xxxviii.

15 See, for example, John Neville Figgis, *Churches in the Modern State* (London: Longmans Green, 1913); G.D.H. Cole, *Social Theory* (New York: Frederick A. Stokes Company, 1920); and Harold J. Laski, *The Foundations of Sovereignty and Other Essays* (New York: Harcourt, Brace and Company, 1921). Representative collections are Paul Q Hirst, ed., *The Pluralist Theory of the State: Selected Writings of G.D.H. Cole, J.N. Figgis and H.J. Laski* (London: Routledge, 1993) and Julia Stapleton, ed., *Group Rights: Perspectives Since 1900* (Bristol: Thoemmes Press, 1995). For a modern assessment, see David Runciman, *Pluralism and the Personality of the State* (Cambridge: Cambridge University Press, 1997). For a description of the pluralism's intellectual milieu see Isaac Kramnick and Barry Sheerman, *Harold Laski: A Life on the Left* (New York: Allen Lane The Penguin Press, 1993).

16 Expressions of group life could be found in professional and trade associations intended to safeguard professional interests: "Each profession and industry," observed Laski, "had questions and standards peculiar to itself, upon which its own determination was the most competent." Harold J Laski, *The Foundations of Sovereignty and Other Essays* (London: George Allen & Unwin Ltd, 1921),74.

17 Ibid.

18 Ernest Barker, *Political Thought in England, 1848-1914*, 2nd ed. (London: Oxford University Press, 1963), 158.

19 Ibid.

20 After this paper was substantially completed, I had the benefit of reading Paul Horwitz's "institutional" account of the US *Bill of Rights First Amendment*. Horwitz calls for political autonomy and judicial deference under the first amendment for self-governing organizations, such as educational institutions. Horwitz also takes some guidance from the British political pluralists, suggesting in a footnote that "the time is ripe for a scholarly re-examination of the British pluralists and their views." See Paul Horwitz, *First Amendment Institutions* (Cambridge:

Harvard University Press, 2013), 343, fn. 18. Also see Paul Horwitz, *Universities as First Amendment Institutions: Some Easy Answers and Hard Questions*, 54 UCLA Law Review 1497 (2007). Frederick Schauer is credited with having initiated this line of inquiry: see his *Principles, Institutions, and the First Amendment*, 112 Harvard Law Review 84 (1998); and *Towards an Institutional First Amendment*, 89 Minnesota Law Review 1256 (2005).

21 Michael Oakeshott, "On the Character of a Modern European State," in *On Human Conduct* (Oxford: Clarendon Press, 1975), 203.

22 Paul Q Hirst, *Associative Democracy: New Forms of Economic and Social Governance* (Amherst: University of Massachusetts Press, 1994).

23 Robert M MacIvor, *Academic Freedom in Our Time* (New York: Columbia University Press, 1955), 9.

24 See Horwitz, *First Amendment Institutions.*

25 Eric Barendt, *Academic Freedom and the Law: A Comparative Study* (Oxford: Hart Publishing, 2010), 64.

26 *Irwin Toy Ltd v Québec (Attorney General)*, [1989] 1 SCR 927, 58 DLR (4th) 577 at para 41.

27 Barendt, *Academic Freedom and the Law*, at 20.

28 Ibid. at 23.

29 "CAUT Policy Statements: Academic Freedom," *Canadian Association of University Teachers (CAUT) Council*, last modified November, 2011, www.caut.ca/about-us/caut-policy/lists/general-caut-policies/policy-statement-on-academic-freedom.

30 Patrick Deane, in his presentation at the conference, also made this point.

31 Leslie Green, *Civil Disobedience and Academic Freedom*, 41 Osgoode Hall LJ 381 (2003).

32 Will Kymlicka, *Multicultural Citizenship: A Liberal Theory of Minority Rights* (Oxford: Clarendon Press, 1995), 114.

33 Jon Thompson, *No Debate: The Israel Lobby and Free Speech at Canadian Universities* (Toronto: Lorimer, 2011).

34 Laskin, *Freedom and Responsibility.*

35 Falconer, *Academic Freedom.*

36 For accounts of this episode Martin L. Friedland, *The University of Toronto: A History* (Toronto: University of Toronto Press, 2002), 320; Michiel Horn, *Academic Freedom in Canada: A History* (Toronto: University of Toronto Press, 1999), 68-79; and Bruce Ziff, *Unforseen Legacies: Reuben Wells Leonard and the Leonard Foundation Trust* (Toronto: University of Toronto Press, 2000), 31-37.

37 Falconer, *Academic Freedom*, 6.

38 Bernard Williams, "Toleration: An Impossible Virtue?" in *Toleration: An Elusive Virtue*, ed. David Heyd (Princeton: Princeton University Press, 1996), 19.

39 The tension between one's own commitments and those that should be tolerated

might prove, at times, to be intolerable!

40 Falconer, *Academic Freedom*; Frank Iacobucci, "The Mapping Conference and Academic Freedom: A Report to Mamdouh Shakri from Justice Frank Iacobucci," *York University Academic Conference Review* (March 2011), 61, hwww.yorku.ca/acreview/ iacobucci_report.pdf. The quote is from Iacobucci, *ibid.*, 61. For further discussion see Thompson, *No Debate*, 293.

41 Thompson, *No Debate*, 293.

42 Michel Foucault, *The Government of Self and Others, Lectures at the Collège de France, 1982-83*, trans. Graham Burchell (Houndmills: Palgrave Macmillan, 2010), 55.

43 *Re Therrien*, 2011 SCC 35, [2001] 2 SCR 3 at para 109.

44 Instead we are associations of teachers, working within particular academic paradigms, deploying academic methods, "each capable of reaching its own characteristic kind of conclusions." Oakeshott, *Rationalism in Politics and Other Essays*, 313.

45 See, e.g., David Horowitz and Jacob Laskin, *One Party Classroom* (New York: Crown Forum, 2009).

46 Ontario College of Art and Design (OCAD), "Respectful Work & Learning Environment" Policy #8001, *OCAD*, accessed June 2012, www.ocadu.ca/assets/pdf_media/ocad/about/ policies/respectful_work_learning_environment_policy.pdf.

47 Ibid., 5.3.

48 Ibid., 5.4.

49 Ibid., 4.1.

50 Ibid., 7.2.1.

51 Ibid., 7.2.2.

52 Ibid.

53 Ibid., 7.2.3.

54 Judith Macfarlane, *Beyond the Right to Offend: Academic Freedom, Rights and Responsibilities in the Canadian University Classroom*, 20 Dal LJ 78 at 101 (1997).

55 Finkin and Post, *For the Common Good*, 105.

56 Bernice Schrank, *Academic Freedom and University Speech Codes*, 44 UNBLJ 67, 72 (1995).

57 *R v Kapp*, 2008 SCC 41, [2008] 2 SCR 483 at paras 21-22.

58 See, for instance, *R.* v. *Ahenekew* [2009] 329 Sask. Reports 140 and the most recent Supreme Court of Canada statement in *Saskatchewan (Human Rights Commission) v Whatcott*, 2013 SCC 11, 55 DLR (4th) 383.

59 Authority may be delegated to "fact finders" "from within or outside the university" (OCAD, "Respectful Work & Learning Environment," 4.1). Adjudicators will be "internal or external . . . as necessary" (OCAD, "Respectful Work & Learning Environment," 6.2).

60 Barendt, *Academic Freedom and the Law*, 40. This is akin to a constituent component of Canada's vague obscenity law. See *R.* v. *Butler* [1992] 1 SCR 452.

61 Foucault, *The Government of Self and Others*, 56.

62 Robert MacIver is of the view that students do enjoy academic freedom. Students should have the opportunity to freely express "doubts" and "ideas." "In the common enterprise of learning," he observed, the student should be considered the "junior partner of the teacher." MacIver, *Academic Freedom in Our Time*, 206. Whether or not students have the benefit of academic freedom is not precisely at issue here, though I am inclined to side with MacIver on this point.

63 With the campus in turmoil, Rushton withdrew for a time from active teaching, buying out his classroom time with research grants provided by the Pioneer Fund, a "pioneer" in race-based funded research that Rushton headed up from 2002 until 2012. See John Allemang, "Philippe Rushton, professor who pushed limits with race studies, dead at 68," *The Globe and Mail*, November 2, 2012. The Pioneer Fund, according to Tucker, "provided the resources for just about every scientist in the second half of the twentieth century who has opposed the rights of Blacks on the basis of genetic inferiority." See William H. Tucker, *A Closer Look at the Pioneer Fund: Response to Rushton*, 66 Albany Law Review 1145, 1159 (2003).

64 This is what, in the United States, is called "intramural expression." See Matthew H. Finkin, *On "Institutional" Academic Freedom*, 61 Texas Law Review 817 (1983).

65 *Pridgen v University of Calgary*, 2012 ABCA 139, 350 DLR (4th) 1 [*Pridgen*] at para 5. There is a helpful discussion of the case in Colin Feasby, "Failing Students by Taking a Pass on the *Charter* in *Pridgen* v. *University of Calgary*," *Constitutional Forum constitutionnel 22*, no. 1 (2013): 19.

66 The Facebook page was entitled "I NO Longer Fear Hell, I Took a Course With Aruna Mitra." See *Pridgen v. University of Calgary* at para. 6.

67 *Pridgen v. University of Calgary* at para. 13

68 Ibid. at para. 18.

69 This amounts to the "political practice of revenge" via speech regulation. See Wendy Brown, *States of Injury: Power and Freedom in Late Modernity* (Princeton: Princeton University Press, 1995), 73.

70 Mitra purportedly was not rehired "due to evaluations done at the University" (*Pridgen v. University of Calgary* at para. 29).

71 Ibid. at paras 36, 128.

72 Ibid. at paras 173, 176.

73 *McKinney v University of Guelph*, [1990] 3 SCR 229, 76 DLR (4th) 545 at para 45.

74 Ibid at paras 35, 47.

75 *Pridgen v. University of Calgary* at para 105.

76 *Eldridge* v. *British Columbia* [1997] 3 SCR 624 heralds the inauguration of this line of cases in Charter application doctrine.

77 Ibid. at para 108.

78 Ibid. at para 122.

79 Joan W. Scott, "Academic Freedom as an Ethical Practice," in *The Future of Academic Freedom*, ed. Louis Menand (Chicago: The University of Chicago Press, 1996), 169.

80 See Jürgen Habermas, "The University in a Democracy – Democratization of the University," in *Toward a Rational Society*, trans. Jeremy J. Shapiro (London: Heinemann, 1971), 9.

81 Scott, "Ethical Practice," 175.

## CHAPTER 12

1 Thorstein Veblen, *The Higher Learning in America*, (New York: B.W. Huebsch, 1919), 170-171.

2 Ibid.

3 Philip A. Sharpe, "The biomedical sciences in context," in *The Fragile Contract University Science and the Federal Government*, eds. D.H. Guston and K. Keniston (Cambridge, MA: The MIT Press, 1994), 148.

4 Koch Foundation Contract to Florida State University

5 Sheldon Krimsky, "Beware of gifts that come at too great a cost," *Nature 474*, no. 129 (June 9, 2011).

6 Gordon DuVal, "Institutional conflicts of interest: Protecting human subjects, scientific integrity, and institutional accountability," *Journal of Law, Medicine & Ethics 32*, no. 4 (2004): 613-625.

7 Ronald DePhino, President MD Anderson Cancer Center, letter to Kennith I. Shine, Executive Vice Chancellor for Health Affairs, University of Texas System, May 1, 2012.

8 Ronald DePhilo, President MD Anderson Cancer Center, letter to Kennith I. Shine, Executive Vice Chancellor for Health Affairs, The University of Texas System, April 20, 2012.

9 M. Barnes and P.S. Florencio, "Financial conflicts of interest in human subjects research: The problem of institutional conflicts," *J. Law, Medicine and Ethics 30*, no. 3 (2002):390-402.

10 Eric Berger and Todd Ackerman, Hospital chief cutting out conflicts, *Houston Chronicle*, February 13, 2013.

11 Sheldon Krimsky, "When sponsored research fails the admissions test: A normative framework," in *Universities at Risk*, ed. James L. Turk (Toronto: James Lorimer & Co., 2008).

12 National Academy of Sciences (NAS), Board on Health Sciences Policy, Consensus Report, *Conflict of Interest in Medical Research, Education and Practice*, NAS (Washington, D.C., April 21, 2009).

13 Association of American Universities (AAU), Task Force on Research Accountability, *Report on Individual and Institutional Financial Conflict of Interest:*

*Report and Recommendations*, (October 2001), 10.

14 AAU Task Force, *Report*, 17.

15 U.S. Department of Health & Human Services, "Financial relationships and interests in research involving human subject: Guidance for human subject protection," *Federal Register 69*, no. 92 (May 12, 2004): 26393, www.hhs.gov/.

16 U.S. Department of Health & Human Services, "Responsibility of applicants for promoting objectivity in research for which public health service funding is sought and responsible prospective contractors; proposed rule," *Federal Register 75*, no. 98 (May 21, 2010): 28700.

17 Ibid.

18 NAS, *Conflict of Interest.*

19 S. H. Ehringhaus, J. S. Weissman, J. L. Sears, et al., "Response of medical schools to institutional conflicts of interest," *JAMA 299* (February 13, 2008): 665-671.

20 Ehringhaus et al., "Response of medical schools," 669.

21 E. G. Campbell, J. S. Weissman, S. Ehringhaus et al., "Institutional academic-industry relationships," *JAMA 298* (October 17, 2007): 1779–1786.

22 Ibid., 1783.

23 M. M. E. Johns, M. Barnes, and P. S. Florencio, "Restoring balance to industry-academia relationships in an era of institutional financial conflicts of interest," *JAMA 289*, no. 6 (February 12, 2003): 741-746.

24 Ibid., p. 743.

25 Ibid.

26 Robert Steinbrook, "The Gelsinger Case," in *The Oxford Textbook of Clinical Research Ethics*, ed. Ezekiel J. Emanuel, http://cirge.stanford.edu/May%209%20-%20Gelsinger%20vs.%20UPenn/Gelsinger%20-%20Oxford%20Textbook.pdf

27 Ibid., p. 111.

28 U.S. Department of Justice, "U.S. settles case of gene therapy study that ended with a teen's death," February 9, 2005, www.upenn.edu/almanac/volumes/v51/n21/gts.html.

29 Steinbrook, The Gelsinger Case," 118.

30 B. A. Liang and T. Mackey, "Addressing institutional conflict of interest to promote patient safety," *Patient Safety and Quality Health Care* (November-December 2010): 37.

31 "Guidelines on Institutional Conflicts of Interest: For the Leadership and Senior Administrators University of the Pennsylvania Health System," *University of Pennsylvania*, accessed July 21, 2013, http://somapps.med.upenn.edu/fapd/documents/pl00023.pdf.

32 DuVal, "Institutional conflicts of interest," 618.

33 American Association of University Professors, *Recommended Principles and Practices to Guide Academy Industry Relationships,* AAUP (Washington, D.C., 2012): 185.

34 Ibid., p. 185.

35 Ibid., p. 186.

36 Ibid.

37 E. G. Campbell, J. S. Weissman, B. Claridge et al., "Characteristics of medical school faculty members serving on institutional review boards: Results of a national study," *Academic Medicine 78,* no. 8 (2003): 831-836.

38 Duval, "Institutional conflicts of interest," 619.

39 Barnes & Florencio, "Financial conflicts," 398.

40 AAMC-AAU Advisory Committee, *Report on Financial Conflicts of Interest in Human Subjects Research,* AAMC-AAU (February 2008): 12

41 Duval, "Institutional conflicts of interest," 613.

42 Ibid.

## CHAPTER 13

1 Richard Hofstadter and Walter P. Metzger, *The Development of Academic Freedom in the United States* (New York: Columbia University Press, 1955), 341-53.

2 Ibid., 350-51.

3 J. Peter Byrne, "Academic Freedom: A 'Special Concern' of the First Amendment," *Yale Law Journal 99*: 251-340, 271.

4 Hofstadter and Metzger, *Development of Academic Freedom,* 413.

5 Jennifer Washburn. *University Inc.: The Corruption of Higher Education* (New York: Basic Books, 2005), 34.

6 Ibid., 33-34.

7 Hofstadter and Metzger, *Development of Academic Freedom,* 439.

8 Louis Joughin, *Academic Freedom and Tenure: A Handbook of the American Association of University Professors* (Madison: University of Wisconsin Press, 1967), 166-167.

9 American Association of University Professors, *Policy Documents and Reports,* 10th ed. (Washington, D.C., 2006), 1.

10 Joughin, *Academic Freedom and Tenure,* 162-67.

11 Deborah A. Ballam, "Exploding the Original Myth Regarding Employment-At-Will: The True Origins of the Doctrine," *Berkeley Journal of Employment & Labor Law 17* (1996): 93-98.

12 Byrne, "Academic Freedom," 278-79; Walter P. Metzger, "Profession and Constitution: Two Definitions of Academic Freedom in America," *Texas Law Review 66* (1988): 1276-78.

13 Ellen Schrecker, "Academic Freedom: The Historical View," in *Regulating the Intellectuals: Perspectives on Academic Freedoms in the 1980s*, eds. Craig Kaplan and Ellen Schrecker (New York: Praeger, 1983), 23-25.

14 Washburn, *University Inc.*, 40.

15 Ibid., 40.

16 Ibid. 41-42.

17 Martin Kenney, *Biotechnology: The University-Industrial Complex* (New Haven: Yale University Press, 1986), 35-36; Eyal Press and Jennifer Washburn, "The Kept University," *The Atlantic Monthly 285*, no. 3 (2000): 39.

18 Washburn, *University Inc.*, 42-43.

19 Ibid., 45-46.

20 Ibid., 46.

21 Ibid., 83-84.

22 Kenney, *Biotechnology*, 13-15, 23, 32-33.

23 Ibid., 106.

24 Washburn, *University Inc.*, 59.

25 Arti K. Rai and Rebecca S. Eisenberg, "Bayh-Dole Reform and the Progress of Biomedicine," *American Scientist 91*, no. 1 (2003): 54; David C. Mowery, Richard R. Nelson, Bhaven N. Sampat, and Arvids A. Ziedonis, *Ivory Tower and Industrial Innovation* (Stanford: Stanford Business Books, 2004), 181.

26 Rebecca S. Eisenberg, "Public Research and Private Development: Patents and Technology Transfer in Government-Sponsored Research," *Virginia Law Review 82* (1996): 1675-76.

27 Ibid., 1683-84, 1691-92.

28 Yvonne Cripps, "The Art and Science of Genetic Modification: Re-Engineering Patent Law and Constitutional Orthodoxies," *Indiana Journal Global Legal Studies 11* (2004): 4-10.

29 Rai and Eisenberg, "Bayh-Dole Reform," 53.

30 Sheldon Krimsky, "The Profit of Scientific Discovery and Its Normative Implications," *Chicago-Kent Law Review 75* (1999): 22.

31 David Blumenthal, "Academic-Industrial Relationships in the Life Sciences," *New England Journal of Medicine 349*, no. 25 (2003): 2454-55.

32 Josephine Johnston, "Health Related Academic Technology Transfer: Rethinking Patenting and Licensing Practices," *International Journal of Biotechnology 9*, no. 2 (2007): 162.

33 Rai and Eisenberg, "Bayh-Dole Reform," 54.

34 Jacob H. Rooksby, "Myriad Choices: University Patents under the Sun," *Journal of Law & Education 42*: 320; Sam S. Han, "Association of Molecular Pathology Meets Therasense: Analyzing the Unenforceability of Isolated-sequence-related

Patents for UPenn, Columbia, NYU, Yale, and Emory," *Journal of Technology Law & Policy 17* (2012): 17-18; Michael A. Heller, and Rebecca S. Eisenberg, "Can Patents Deter Innovation? The Anticommons in Biomedical Research," *Science 280* (1998): 698-701.

35 David Blumenthal, "Biotech in Northeast Ohio Conference: Conflict of Interest in Biomedical Research," *Health Matrix 12* (2002): 379.

36 Ibid., 378.

37 Ibid., 379.

38 Ibid., 385.

39 "Recommended Principles & Practices to Guide Academy-Industry Relationships," American Association of Universities Professors (AAUP), June 2012, 43, www.aaup.org/AAUP/comm/rep/industry.htm.

40 Ibid., 43.

41 Ibid. 41.

42 Rebecca S. Eisenberg, "Proprietary Rights and the Norms of Science in Biotechnology Research," *Yale Law Journal 97* (1987): n. 2.

43 "Recommended Principles," AAUP, 41.

44 Ibid. 42.

45 Ibid. 43.

46 Ibid. 43-4.

47 Blumenthal, "Biotech," 371-72.

48 "Recommended Principles," AAUP, 42-43; E. G. Campbell, J. S. Weissman, S. Ehringhaus, S. R. Rao, B. Moy, S. Feibelmann, and Susan Dorr Goold, "Institutional Academy-Industry Relationships," *Journal of the American Medical Association 298*, no. 15 (2007): 1779–86.

49 Kenneth Sutherlin Dueker, "Biobusiness on Campus: Commercialization of University-Developed Biomedical Technologies," *Food and Drug Law Journal 52* (1997), 498.

50 Risa L. Lieberwitz, "Confronting the Privatization and Commercialization of Academic Research: An Analysis of Social Implications at the Local, National, and Global Levels," *Indiana Journal of Global Legal Studies 12* (2005): 123-24.

51 Kenney, *Biotechnology*, 55-72.

52 Andrew Lawler, "Last of the Big Time Spenders?" *Science 299* (2003): 330.

53 Ibid., 330.

54 Ibid., 331.

55 Press and Washburn, "The Kept University," 41-42.

56 Lawler, "Big Time Spenders," 331.

57 Press and Washburn, "The Kept University," 41-42.

58 Lawrence Busch et al., *External Review of the Collaborative Research Agreement between Novartis Agricultural Discovery Institute, Inc. and the Regents of the University of California* (2004), www.berkeley.edu/news/media/releases/2004/07/ external_novartis_review.pdf; Rex Dalton, "Biotech Funding Deal Judged to be 'a Mistake' for Berkeley," *Nature 430* (2004): 598.

59 Lawler, "Big Time Spenders," 332.

60 Ibid., 332. See also, Donald Danforth Plant Science Center, www.danforthcenter.org/the_center/about_us/history.asp.

61 Ibid., 332.

62 "Recommended Principles," AAUP, 43.

63 Lawler, "Big Time Spenders," 332.

64 Jacob H. Rooksby, "Myriad Choices: University Patents under the Sun," *Journal of Law & Education 42* (2013): 319.

65 Bryn Williams-Jones, "History of a Gene Patent: The Development and Application of BRCA Testing," *Health Law Journal 10* (2002): 132-33.

66 Joanna Sax, "Financial Conflicts of Interest in Science," *Annals of Health Law 21* (2012): 325.

67 Adam Liptak, "Supreme Court to Look at Gene Issue," *New York Times*, November 30, 2012, www.nytimes.com/2012/12/01/us/supreme-court-takes-up-question-of-patents-in-gene-research.html.

68 *Ass'n for Molecular Pathology et al. v. USPTO*. 2013. Initial Brief: Appellant-Petitioner, n. 5.

69 *Ass'n for Molecular Pathology et al. v. USPTO*. 2013. 133 S. Ct. 2107, 21.

70 Ibid., 21.

71 Ibid., 6, 30.

72 Ibid., 32-33.

73 Bernard Barber, *Science and the Social Order* (Glencoe: Free Press, 1952); Robert K. Merton, *The Sociology of Science* (Chicago: University of Chicago Press, 1973); Rebecca S. Eisenberg, "Proprietary Rights," 181-184; Arti Kaur Rai, "Regulating Scientific Research: Intellectual Property Rights and the Norms of Science," *Northwestern University Law Review 94* (1999): 88-94.

74 Blumenthal, "Biotech," 361-66; Krimsky, "The Profit," 29-31; Mowery et al., *Ivory Tower*, 185-186.

75 Eisenberg, "Proprietary Rights," 216-26; Krimsky, "The Profit," 30; Joshua A. Newberg and Richard L. Dunn, "Keeping Secrets in the Campus Lab: Law, Values, and Rules of Engagement for Industry-University R&D Partnerships," *American Business Law Journal 39* (2002): 192-93.

76 Press and Washburn, "The Kept University," 42; Washburn, *University Inc.*, 20-23, 122-27.

77 Press and Washburn, "The Kept University," 42; Mildred K. Cho and Lisa A. Bero,

"The Quality of Drug Studies Published in Symposium Proceedings," *Annals of Internal Medicine 124*, no. 5 (1996): 485; Mark Clayton, "Corporate Cash and Campus Labs," *Christian Science Monitor*, June 19, 2001, www.csmonitor.com/2001/0619/ p11s1.html; Sheldon Krimsky, *Science in the Private Interest* (Lanham: Rowman & Littlefield Publishers, Inc., 2003), 142-149.

78 Sax, "Financial Conflicts," 307-08, 320.

79 Kathleen Huvane, "Researchers Required to Show Money Trail," *World Watch 15*, no.1: (Jan 1, 2002): 7.

80 Sax, "Financial Conflicts," 308-09; Jesse A. Goldner, "Regulating Conflicts of Interest in Research: The Paper Tiger Needs Real Teeth," *St. Louis University Law Journal 53* (2009): 1244-46.

81 Ariel Kaminer, "New Cornell Technology School Tightly Bound to Business," *New York Times*, Jan. 2013, www.nytimes.com/2013/01/22/nyregion/cornell-nyc-tech-will-foster-commerce-amid-education.html?pagewanted=all.

82 "Unfolding the Vision of Cornell NYC Tech," *Cornell University*, 2012, http://blogs.cornell.edu/tech/files/2012/11/CornellTech_PocketGuide_Final-29tamqt.pdf.

83 Ibid.

84 Kaminer, "New Cornell Technology School."

85 Ibid.

86 Goldie Blumenstyk, "Silicon Valley, New York-Style," *The Chronicle of Higher Education*, October 23, 2011, http://chronicle.com/article/Silicon-Valley-New-York-Style/129502/.

87 Kaminer, "New Cornell Technology School."

88 Ken Auletta, "Get Rich U. There are no walls between Stanford and Silicon Valley. Should there be?" The New Yorker, April 30, 2012, www.newyorker.com/reporting/2012/04/30/120430fa_fact_auletta.

89 Blumenstyk, "Silicon Valley, New York-Style."

90 Auletta, "Get Rich U."

91 Kaminer, "New Cornell Technology School."

92 Kaminer, "New Cornell Technology School"; Sam Gustin, "Cornell NYC Tech: Here's Why a Qualcomm Billionaire Gave $133 Million," *TIME*, April 23, 2013, http://business.time.com/2013/04/23/cornell-nyc-tech-hub-heres-why-a-qualcomm-billionaire-gave-133-million/print/.

93 Gustin, "Cornell NYC Tech."

94 Michael Linhorst, "Cornell to Partner with Technion in Tech Campus Proposal," *Cornell Daily Sun*, October 18. 2011.

95 "Mayor Michael R. Bloomberg, Qualcomm Founder Irwin Jacobs and Google Executive Chairman Eric Schmidt to Guide Growth of Cornell NYC Tech," *Cornell Chronicle*, September 19, 2012, http://news.cornell.edu/print/997.

96 Kaminer, "New Cornell Technology School."

97 Ibid.

98 Caroline Shin, "Cornell NYC Tech and the Commerce Department Partner to Spur Job Creation," *Cornell Chronicle Online*, October 4, 2012, www.news.cornell.edu/ stories/Oct12/NYCDOC.html.

99 Ibid.

100 Lawler, "Big Time Spenders," 331.

101 Kaminer, "New Cornell Technology School."

102 Ibid.

103 Ibid.

104 Jeff Stein, "Cornell Defends Plan for Tech Campus' Corporate Ties," *Cornell Daily Sun*, November 26, 2012, www.cornellsun.com/section/news/content/2012/11/26/cornell-defends-plan-tech-campus%E2%80%99-corporate-ties.

105 Kaminer, "New Cornell Technology School."

106 Stein, "Cornell Defends Plan."

107 Kaminer, "New Cornell Technology School."

108 Stein, "Cornell Defends Plan."

109 Ibid.

110 Sax, "Financial Conflicts," 308-09; Goldner, "Regulating Conflicts," 1244-46.

111 Richard Pérez-Pena, "Alliance Formed Secretly to Win Deal for Campus," *New York Times*, December 25, 2011, www.nytimes.com/2011/12/26/education/in-cornell-deal-for-roosevelt-island-campus-an-unlikely-partnership.html?pagewanted=all.

112 Washburn, *University Inc.*, 187.

113 Ibid., (emphasis in original).

114 Ibid., 187.

115 Ibid., 187.

116 *Stanford v. Roche*. 2011. 131 S.Ct. 2188. Kathi Wescott, "Faculty Ownership of Research Affirmed," *Academe 97*, no. 5 (2011), www.aaup.org/AAUP/pubsres/academe/2011/SO/nb/patentlaw.htm.

117 Robert M. Yeh, "The Public Paid for the Invention: Who Owns It?" *Berkeley Technology Law Journal 27* (2012): 453-55.

118 "Recommended Principles,"AAUP, 14-17, 45-47; Cary Nelson, "Whose Intellectual Property?" *Inside Higher Ed*, June 21, 2012, www.insidehighered.com/views/2012/ 06/21/essay-faculty-members-and-intellectual-property-rights.

## CHAPTER 14

1 Sheila Slaughter and Gary Rhoades, *Academic Capitalism and the New Economy:*

*Markets, State, and Higher Education* (Baltimore: The Johns Hopkins University Press, 2004); Jennifer Washburn, University Inc., *The Corporate Corruption of Higher Education* (New York: Basic Books, 2005); Derek Bok, *Universities in the Marketplace: The Commercialization of Higher Education* (Princeton: Princeton University Press, 2003); James L. Turk, ed., *The Corporate Campus: Commercialization and the Dangers to Canada's Colleges and Universities* (Toronto: James Lorimer & Co., 2000); Howard Woodhouse, *Selling Out: Academic Freedom and the Corporate Market* (Montreal: McGill-Queen's University Press, 2009).

2 In this contest, "innovation" does not mean a new idea, the usual dictionary definition, but "the process of bringing new goods and services to market, or the result of that process." The Prime Minister's Advisory Council on Science and Technology, Public Investments in University Research: Reaping the Benefits — Report of the Expert Panel on the Commercialization of University Research, May 4, 1999, accessed August 24, 2013, http://publications.gc.ca/collections/Collection/C2-441-1999E.pdf.

3 For example, in the 2013 Canadian federal budget, all of the new funding announced for the three academic funding agencies was targeted to support "research partnerships with industry."

4 Stanton A. Glantz, John Slade, Lisa A. Bero, Peter Hanauer & Deborah E. Barnes, *The Cigarette Papers* (Berkeley: University of California Press, 1998); Richard Kluger, *Ashes to Ashes: America's Hundred-Year Cigarette War, the Public Health, and the Unabashed Triumph of Philip Morris* (New York: Random House, 1996); Allen M. Brandt, *The Cigarette Century: The Rise, Fall, and Deadly Persistence of the Product that Defined America* (New York: Basic Books, 2007).

5 Paul Brodeur, *Outrageous Conduct: The Asbestos Industry on Trial* (New York: Pantheon, 1985); Geoffrey Tweedale, *Magic Mineral to Killer Dust: Turner & Newall and the Asbestos Hazard* (New York: Oxford University Press, 2000).

6 Gerald Markowitz and David Rosner, *Deceit and Denial: The Deadly Politics of Industrial Pollution* (Berkeley: University of California Press, 2002); Christian Warren, *Brush with Death: A Social History of Lead Poisoning* (Baltimore: Johns Hopkins University Press, 2000).

7 David Michaels, *Doubt is Their Product: How Industry's Assault on Science Threatens Your Health* (Oxford: Oxford University Press, 2008), 124-141.

8 Ibid., 25-28; 70-78.

9 David Healy, *Pharmageddon* (Berkeley: University of California Press, 2012); Marcia Angell, *The Truth About the Drug Companies: How They Deceive Us and What to Do About It* (New York: Random House, 2004); Jerome Kassirer, *On the Take: How Medicine's Complicity with Big Business Can Endanger Your Health* (New York: Oxford University Press; 2004).

10 See e.g., Sheldon Krimsky, "The Funding Effect in Science and Its Implications for the Judiciary," *Journal of Law & Policy* 13, no. 1 (2005): 43-68; Sheldon Krimsky, "Do Financial Conflicts of Interest Bias Research? An Inquiry into the 'Funding Effect' Hypothesis," *Science Technology Human Values* 38 no. 4 (2013), 566-587.

11 Henry Thomas Stelfox, Grace Chua, Keith O'Rourke, and Allan S. Detsky,

"Conflict of Interest in the Debate over Calcium-Channel Antagonists," *New England Journal of Medicine 338* (1998): 101-106.

12 See e.g., J. Yaphe, R. Edman, B. Knishkowy and J. Herman, "The Association between Funding by Commercial Interests and Study Outcome in Randomized Controlled Drug Trials," *Family Practice 18*, no. 6 (2001): 565-8; M. A. Mandelkern, "Manufacturer Support and Outcome," *Journal of Clinical Psychiatry 18*, no. 6 (1999): 122-3; Joel Lexchin, Lisa A. Bero, Benjamin Djulbegovic and Otavio Clark, "Pharmaceutical Industry Sponsorship and Research Outcome and Quality: Systematic Review," *BMJ 326* (2003): 1167-70; J. E. Bekelman , Y Li, C. P. Gross, "Scope and Impact of Financial conflicts of Interest in Biomedical Research: A Systematic Review" *JAMA 289*, no. 4 (2003): 454-65. 13.

13 See e.g., Jon Thompson, Patricia Baird and Jocelyn Downie, *The Olivieri Report* (Toronto: James Lorimer & Co., 2004); Clare Dyer, "Aubrey Blumsohn: Academic who took on industry," *British Medical Journal 340*, no. 7736 (2010): 22-23; David Healy, *Let Them Eat Prozac* (Toronto: James Lorimer & Co., 2003), 317-322 [Also: www.healyprozac.com/AcademicFreedom/default.htm]; the case of David Kern at Brown University – Jennifer Washburn, "Academic Freedom and the Corporate University" *Academe* (January-February, 2011), www.aaup.org/article/academic-freedom-and-corporate-university#.UgrP_o1QFsk.

14 Alan P. Rudy, Dawn Coppin, Jason Konefal, Bradley T. Shaw, Toby Ten Eyck, Craig Harris and Lawrence Busch, *Universities in the Age of Corporate Science: The UC Berkeley-Novartis Controversy* (Philadelphia: Temple University Press, 67-69).

15 Lawrence Busch et al., *External Review of the Collaborative Research Agreement between Novartis Agricultural Discovery Institute, Inc. and The Regents of the University of California. East Lansing: Institute for Food and Agricultural Standards*, Michigan State University, 2004, 151, www.berkeley.edu/news/media/releases/2004/07/external_novartis_review.pdf.

16 Jennifer Washburn, *Big Oil Goes to College: An Analysis of 10 Research Collaboration Contracts Between Leading Energy Companies and Major U.S. Universities*, Washington: Center for American Progress, 2010, www.americanprogress.org/wp-content/uploads/issues/2010/10/pdf/big_oil_lf.pdf.

17 Ibid., 13-14.

18 Ibid., 60-68.

19 Difficulty in getting access.

20 Canadian Association of University Teachers, *Open for Business: On What Terms*. Ottawa: CAUT, 2013. Available at www.caut.ca/docs/default-source/academic-freedom/open-for-business-(nov-2013).pdf?sfvrsn=4.

21 Bell Helicopter Textron; Bombardier Aerospace; CAE Inc.; Pratt and Whitney Canada; 3M Canada; CMC Electronics; GE Aviation; Héroux-Devtek; L-3 MAS; Rolls-Royce Canada Ltd.; Thales Canada; Turbomeca Canada; Aéroports de Montréal; Aerosystems International; Altitude Aerospace; Aluminerie Alouette; ASCO Aerospace; Canada; AV&R Vision & Robotics; Avianor; Avior Integrated Products; BFI Canada; Composites Atlantic; Creaform; CS Communications & Systems Canada; Delastek; Dema Aeronautics; Dorval Technologies; Edmit Industries; Epsilon RTO; Gestion TechnoCap; GlobVision; Groupe

Soltrem-Maltech; Information Technology Group; JB Martin Composites; JMJ Aéronautique; Luxell Technologies; Mannarino Systems & Software; Marinvent Corporation; Marquez Transtech; MDA Space Missions; MDS Coating Technologies; Mechachrome Canada; Meloche Group; Messier-Buggati-Dowty; Nutaq; OPAL-RT Technologies; Roy Aircraft and Avionic Simulation; SADEC; Silkan; Sonaca NMF Canada; Transtronic; TSLab.

22 Centre de recherche informatique de Montréal; INO; Canadian Light Source; Centre de recherche industrielle Québec; National Research Council; Centre technologique en aérospatiale; Centre interuniversitaire de recherche sur le cycle de vie des produits, procédés et services; Composites Development Centre of Quebec; Optech.

23 The MDRU is funded directly by mining companies through membership fees. The membership fees range from $1,500 to $25,000 per year. There is also an individual membership available for $500. The different levels of membership fees grant different privileges. The membership fees are separate from the money that mining companies contribute for specific research projects. The amounts for research support vary widely.

24 CIGI was founded by Jim Balsillie in 2001. Balsillie then was Co-CEO of Research in Motion. Balsillie chairs the CIGI Board.

25 Peter Munk is the founder and Chair of Barrick Gold, the world's largest gold mining corporation.

26 Canadian Association of University Teachers, *Collaborations and Integrity: Challenges for Canadian Universities* (Ottawa: CAUT, 2013).

27 Canadian Association of University Teachers, *Guiding Principles for University Collaborations* (Ottawa: CAUT, 2012), accessed August 18, 2013, www.caut.ca/uploads/GuidingPrinc_UCollaborationv2.pdf; American Association of University Professors, *AAUP Recommended Principles & Practices to Guide Academy-Industry Relationships*, (Washington: AAUP, 2012), www.aaup.org/file/industryall.pdf.

28 Lindsay Purchase, "Wilfrid Laurier and U Waterloo escape CAUT censure over Balsillie School," *Canadian University Press*, November 29, 2012, accessed August 27, 2012, http://cupwire.ca/articles/53871.

39 James Bradshaw, "York abandons plans to accept $30-million from Balsillie's think tank," *Globe and Mail*, April 2, 2012, accessed August 27, 2012 www.theglobeandmail.com/ news/national/york-abandons-plans-to-accept-30-million-from-balsillies-think-tank/article2390167/#dashboard/follows/.

30 John Polanyi, "Why our scientific discoveries need to surprise us," *The Globe and Mail*, October 1, 2011.

31 Quoted in Victor M. Catano, "Open Letter to Paul Martin," *CAUT Bulletin*, December 2003, www.cautbulletin.ca/en_article.asp?articleid=852.

## CHAPTER 15

1 *Ismail v. British Columbia (Human Rights Tribunal)*, 2013 BCSC 1079 (June 19, 2013). For an indignant view, see R. Murphy, "Please don't call it 'human rights'," *National Post*, April 3, 2010, http://fullcomment.nationalpost.com/2010/04/03/rex-murphy-please-dont-call-it-human-rights/.

2 See L. Collins, "Incivility turning more workplaces 'toxic'," *Deseret News*, August 10, 2011, www.deseretnews.com/article/700169737/Incivility-turning-more-workplaces-toxic.html?pg=all; M. Della Cava, "What happened to civility?" *USA Today*, September 15, 2009, http://usatoday30.usatoday.com/life/lifestyle/2009-09-14-civility-cover_N.htm.

3 See, *e.g.*, D. Twale & B. DeLuca, *Faculty Incivility: The Rise of the Academic Bully Culture and What to Do About it* (San Francisco: Jossey-Bass, 2008); R. P. Forni, *Choosing Civility: The Twenty-five Rules of Considerate Conduct* (New York: St. Martin's Press, 2002); R. P. Forni, *The Civility Solution: What to Do When People are Rude* (New York: St. Martin's Press, 2008).

4 See, *e.g.*, "Nastiness, Name-Calling and Negativity," *The Allegheny College Survey of Civility and Compromise in American Politics*, April 2010, http://sites.allegheny.edu/civility/; R. Williams, "The Rise of Incivility and Bullying in America," *Psychology Today*, July 15, 2012, www.psychologytoday.com/blog/wired-success/201207/the-rise-incivility-and-bullying-in-america; and "Civility in America, 2013," *Weber Shandwick* and *Powell Tate*, August 8, 2013, http://bigthink.com/think-tank/why-so-rude-the-incivility-crisis-in-america?utm_source=feedburner&utm_medium=feed&utm_campaign=Feed%3A+bigthink%2Fmain+%28Big+Think+Main%29.

5 N. Cullen, "'Civility Project' Aims to Restore Decorum to Canada's Parliament," *Toronto Star*, February 9, 2013, www.thestar.com/opinion/editorialopinion/2013/02/09/civility_project_aims_to_restore_decorum_to_canadas_parliament.html. According to the proposal, violators would be warned for a first offence but then suspended from Question Period for one day after a second offence, five days after a third offence, and twenty days following a fourth. Nathan Cullen is a Member of Parliament for the New Democrat Party and House Leader for the Official Opposition.

6 As acerbic CBC wit Rex Murphy pronounced: "The Commons cannot be saved. Let us be done with the calls for civility. Let's take it for what it is — a place of bluster, animus and insult and have done with it." "Civility in the House of Commons," *CBC*, February 1, 2013, www.cbc.ca/thenational/indepthanalysis/rexmurphy/story/2013/01/31/thenational-rexmurphy-013113.html. See also K. McParland, "Nya, nya, you can't make us behave," *National Post*, January 30, 2013, http://fullcomment.nationalpost.com/2013/01/30/kelly-mcparland-the-problem-with-nathan-cullens-civility-project-is-that-mps-dont-want-to-behave/.

7 The Supreme Court of Canada addressed this issue recently in *Doré v. Barreau du Québec*, [2012] 1 S.C.R. 395 (considering whether the Quebec law society's decision to reprimand a lawyer for uncivil behaviour violated his expressive freedom). See *infra*.

8 A. Woolley, "Does Civility Matter," in *Legal Ethics & Professional Responsibility (special issue)*, ed. T. Farrow (2008): 46 Osgoode Hall L.J. 175.

9 Professor Mason at Queen's University made this discovery after being reprimanded for using certain language in quoting from legal transcripts (*i.e.*, racist) and making sexist remarks about female TAs, which were said to be in violation of the university's equity policy. See Canadian Association of University Teachers, *CAUT Ad Hoc Investigatory Committee Report*, www.caut.ca/docs/default-

source/af-ad-hoc-investigatory-committees/report-on-the-situation-and-treatment-of-dr-michael-mason-at-queen%27s-university-%282012%29.pdf.

10 Part I of the *Constitution Act, 1982*, being Schedule B to the *Canada Act 1982 (U.K.)*, 1982, c.11 ("the *Charter*"). Section 2(b) states that everyone has the following fundamental freedoms, including: (b) "freedom of thought, belief, opinion and expression, including freedom of the press and other media of communication."

11 See R. Smolla, "Academic Freedom, Hate Speech, and the Idea of a University," 53 Law & Contemp. Probs. 195 (1990); N. Strossen, "Regulating Racist Speech on Campus: A Modest Proposal," 1990 Duke L.J. 484.

12 R. Post, "The Structure of Academic Freedom," in *Academic Freedom After September 11*, ed. B. Doumani (New York: Nurzone Inc., 2006), 61. But see A. Regnier, "Mapping the Freedom to Learn: Making the Case for Student Academic Freedom" (unpublished LL.M. thesis: Osgoode Hall Law School, 2013; copy on file with author).

13 For clarification, two notes should be added. First, the discussion in this article focuses on the question of free speech on campus because civility and respectful workplace policies address activities that are centered on campus. Though it is not at issue here, academic freedom includes freedom of extramural expression. Second, though the *Charter* specifically guarantees freedom of expression, the text also speaks of free speech though "speech" might be thought of as narrower than "expression."

14 "Show Me Respect: Promoting Civility at the University of Missouri," University of Missouri, http://civility.missouri.edu/.

15 "Civility in Everyday Life," University of Maryland, www.uwosh.edu/chancellor/communications/campus-civility/civility-workshop-2011.

16 Ibid.

17 "The Civility Discourse: Where Do We Stand and How Do We Proceed?" *University of Maryland*, www.umaryland.edu/islsi/pi/Symposium/White%20paper%20final.pdf.

18 Ibid., 7 (emphasis added).

19 Ibid., 7 and 8.

20 Ibid., 9.

21 Ibid., 16.

22 Ibid., 16.

23 "Human Resources Guideline on Civil Conduct," the University of Toronto, last modified December 15, 2009, www.hrandequity.utoronto.ca/Assets/HR+Digital+Assets/ Miscellaneous/Human+Resources+Guideline+on+Civil+Conduct.pdf.

24 "Guide to Civility: Creating a culture of respect at Ryerson & Dealing with incivility in the workplace," Ryerson University, last modified June 2013, www.ryerson.ca/content/ dam/hr/worklife/Guide-to-Civility.pdf; and "Workplace

Civility and Respect Policy" Ryerson University, www.ryerson.ca/policies/board/workcivilitypolicy.html..

25 Civility protocols are diverse and various in nature. While some are specific to workplace actors (*i.e.*, faculty and staff), others are directed at or include student behaviour. This article is not concerned with specific policies or provisions, and does not consider whether and how faculty and students are differently situated under these policies. Rather, it focuses on the assumption of these policies that uncivil conduct can and should be regulated, and that regulation can proceed without undermining academic and expressive freedom.

26 "Human Resources Guideline," the University of Toronto.

27 "Workplace Civility and Respect Policy," Ryerson University.

28 "Human Resources Guideline," University of Toronto.

29 "Workplace Civility and Respect Policy, " Ryerson University.

30 Ibid.

31 As the policy indicates, context is only taken into account for the purpose of explaining how subjective incivility is, for it states, "[d]ifferences including, but not limited to, social role, gender, social class, religion and cultural identity may all affect the perception of a given behaviour." Ibid.

32 C.S. Lewis, *The Four Loves* (Geoffrey Bles, 1960).

33 "Civility in Everyday Life," University of Maryland.

34 D. Twale & B. DeLuca, *Faculty Incivility*.

35 Though civility and respect are not synonyms, these policies suggest a symbiotic relationship between the two: while civility is the standard or norm for conduct, respect is the objective or outcome of that norm; by the same token, it follows that respect will be compromised or withheld as long as instances of incivility remain unredressed.

36 "Respectful Work & Learning Environment Policy" OCAD University, last modified March 2010, www.ocadu.ca/assets/pdf_media/ocad/about/policies/respectful_work_learning_ environment_policy.pdf.

37 "Respectful Workplace," *Memorial University*, accessed August 25, 2013, www.mun.ca/policy/site/policy.php?id=167.

38 N. Finkelstein, "Civility and Academic Life" 108:4 South Atlantic Quarterly 723 (2009) (stating, at 734, in the context of extramural expression, that "the accusation of incivility frequently signals a politically motivated excuse to change the subject" as "[t]hose sincerely committed to the pursuit of truth can see past a barb here and there"; and concluding, at 736, that "the question of civility — whether a dissident academic treats his or her critics according to Emily Post's rules of etiquette — is [] a meaningless sideshow or just a transparent pretext for denying a person the right to teach on account of his or her political beliefs").

39 *West Virginia Bd of Education v. Barnette*, 319 U.S. 624 at 641 (1943).

40 The following, among those mentioned in this paper, do not make explicit

reference to academic freedom: Missouri's "Show me Respect" project; Maryland's Civility Discourse White Paper; Ryerson University's civility policies, and Memorial University's Respectful Workplace document.

41 Two that fall into this category include the Toronto "Guideline," *supra* note 23 (stating that the guideline "is not intended to infringe on academic freedom" but rather "to describe conduct expected of all members of the community even when exercising their academic freedom") and OCAD's "Respectful Work & Learning Environment" policy, *supra* note 36 (defining academic freedom in a way that applies to faculty and students in part 3, at 13, and then stating, in 4.2, at 2, that "[n]othing in this policy is to be interpreted, administered or applied in a way that infringes upon academic freedom . . .").

42 "Show Me Respect," University of Missouri.

43 The constitutive elements of academic freedom are: freedom of research and publication; freedom of teaching; and freedom of extramural expression. R. Smolla, "Academic Freedom."

44 "2. Everyone has the following fundamental freedoms: . . . (b) freedom of thought, belief, opinion and expression, including freedom of the press and other media of communication;" *Constitution Act, 1982*, http://laws-lois.justice.gc.ca/eng/const/page-15.html.

45 *Constitution Act, 1982*.

46 The landmark Supreme Court decision is *McKinney v. University of Guelph*, [1990] 3 S.C.R. 229 (rejecting the *Charter*'s application to universities on the question whether mandatory retirement violates the right to equality).

47 *Pridgen v. University of Calgary*, 2012 ABCA 139 (Alberta Court of Appeal). Paperny J.A. rejected the argument that the *Charter* does not apply to universities, applied the *Charter* in this case, and dismissed the university's argument that it should be sheltered from *Charter* review to protect its institutional autonomy and academic freedom. Although the majority opinion did not engage the *Charter*, Paperny J.A.'s strong concurrence upheld the lower court's opinion on this point.

48 The Court has drawn a distinction between community colleges and universities. See *Douglas/Kwantlen Faculty Assn v. Douglas College*, [1990] 3 S.C.R. 570 (concluding that a community college was "government" for purposes of the *Charter* because it was a Crown agency established by the government to implement government policy); and Lavigne v. Ontario Public Service Employee Assn, [1991] 2 S.C.R. 211 (also applying the *Charter* to a community college). See also Eldridge v. British Columbia *(AG)*, [1997] 3 S.C.R. 624 (applying the *Charter* to hospital services and the failure to provide sign language interpreters, and expanding the concept of "government" under the *Charter*).

49 See Grant v. Torstar Corp., [2009] 3 S.C.R. 640 (creating a new defence of "responsible communication"); and WIC Radio Ltd. v. Simpson, [2008] 2 S.C.R. 420 (modernizing the fair comment defence to make it more protective of expressive freedom). The journalist-source privilege has also been revised to take account of *Charter* values and the need to strengthen protection for expressive freedom: *R. v. National Post*, [2010] 1 S.C.R. 477; *Globe & Mail v. Canada (AG)*,

[2010] 2 S.C.R. 592 (applying *Charter* values to enhance protection for the expressive freedom of journalists, albeit with different results).

50 *Doré v. Barreau du Québec.*

51 Ibid. at para. 63.

52 Ibid. at para. 65.

53 Ibid. at para. 66. Although the suspension was upheld because the balancing of values was a "fact dependent and discretionary exercise," what remains is the point of principle that the authority to discipline a lawyer for incivility is subject to the *Charter*'s concept of expressive freedom. Ibid.

54 R. George Wright, "The Emergence of First Amendment Academic Freedom," 85 Neb. L. Rev. 793 (2006-2007) at 809-16 (proposing a focus on the linkages between academic freedom and the free speech values of the pursuit of truth and of collective self-development).

55 *R. v. Keegstra*, [1990], 3 S.C.R. 697 (upholding the *Criminal Code* provision); Canada (Human Rights Commission) v. Taylor, [1990] 3 S.C.R. 892 (upholding the Canadian *Human Rights Code* hate speech provision).

56 I explain this assessment of the s.2(b) jurisprudence in J. Cameron, "A Reflection on Section 2(b)'s Quixotic Journey, 1982-2012," in J. Cameron & S. Lawrence, eds. *2011 Constitutional Cases*, (2012) 58 S.C.L.R.(2d). I should point out that the s.2(b) jurisprudence is compromised by a fundamental contradiction between the Court's endorsement of an anti-censorship principle under s.2(b) and its development of a methodology that rests on an assumption of censorial content distinctions under s.1. This makes it difficult to understand the relationship between concepts. For further explanation, see *infra* note 64.

57 2013 SCC 11

58 Ibid.paras. 50, 51, and 58.

59 Ibid. para. 46.

60 Ibid. paras. 51 and 50

61 Despite pointing to Whatcott's promising implications for expressive freedom, I have been highly critical of the Court's decision. See J. Cameron, "The McLachlin Court and the *Charter* in 2012," in B. Berger, J. Cameron & S. Lawrence, eds., *Constitutional Cases 2012*, (2013), 63 S.C.L.R. (2d); forthcoming, fall 2013).

62 *Irwin Toy Ltd. v. Quebec (AG)*, [1989] 1 S.C.R. 927, at 968.

63 Section 1 states: "The *Canadian Charter of Rights and Freedoms* guarantees the rights and freedoms set out in it subject only to such reasonable limits prescribed by law as can be demonstrably justified in a free and democratic society." *Constitution Act, 1982*.

64 At this point it may be helpful to elaborate on a fundamental contradiction in the jurisprudence. The principle of content neutrality governs almost absolutely under s.2(b), which is the stage at which the scope of the guarantee is defined, but then is abandoned under s.1 of the *Charter*, where the methodology asks whether the expressive activity at stake has high or low value and decides, as a

result, that limits on low value expression can be easily justified. Though the results are bizarre and incoherent, the central point is that it is not the principles that are disingenuous, but the Court's approach to willingness to practice content discrimination under s.1, despite recognizing its dangers in defining the guarantee under s.2(b).

# ACKNOWLEDGEMENTS

Like all books, this one is the result of the work of many people, principally the contributors, to whom I want to express appreciation. The idea for this book and its focus grew out of more than a decade of stimulating discussions with the members of the American Association of University Professors' Committee A on Academic Freedom and Tenure, who have graciously allowed me to be a guest at their meetings for more than a decade. The Harry Crowe Foundation and the Canadian Association of University Teachers made production of the book possible. Jon Thompson merits special recognition for his lifetime of work in advancing academic freedom and has been my friend and mentor. Finally, I cannot adequately acknowledge my debt to my partner, Lynne Browne, for her love, intelligence, and sense of perspective.

JLT

# INDEX